Comparative Welfare State Politics

Welfare state reform occurs in all advanced capitalist democracies, but it does not occur in identical ways, to the same degree, or with similar consequences. In *Comparative Welfare State Politics*, Kees van Kersbergen and Barbara Vis explain the political opportunities and constraints of welfare state reform by asking "big" questions. Why did we need a welfare state in the first place? How did we get it? Why did we get different worlds of welfare and do we still have them? What does the welfare state actually do? Why do we need to reform the welfare state? Why is reform so difficult, but why does it nevertheless happen? Can and will the welfare state survive the Great Recession? This book informs the reader comprehensively about the welfare state, while contributing to the ongoing debate on the politics of welfare state reform.

Kees van Kersbergen is professor of comparative politics in the Department of Political Science and Government at Aarhus University in Denmark.

Barbara Vis is professor of political decision making in the Department of Political Science and Public Administration at VU University Amsterdam in the Netherlands.

Comparative Welfare State Politics

Development, Opportunities, and Reform

KEES VAN **KERSBERGEN**
Aarhus University, Denmark

BARBARA VIS
VU University Amsterdam, The Netherlands

CAMBRIDGE
UNIVERSITY PRESS

32 Avenue of the Americas, New York NY 10013-2473, USA

Cambridge University Press is part of the University of Cambridge.

It furthers the University's mission by disseminating knowledge in the pursuit of education, learning and research at the highest international levels of excellence.

www.cambridge.org
Information on this title: www.cambridge.org/9780521183710

© Kees van Kersbergen and Barbara Vis 2014

First published 2014

A catalogue record for this publication is available from the British Library

Library of Congress Cataloguing in Publication data
Kersbergen, Kees van, 1958–
Comparative welfare state politics : development, opportunities, and reform / Kees van Kersbergen, Barbara Vis.
    pages   cm
Includes bibliographical references and index.
ISBN 978-1-107-00563-1 (hardback) – ISBN 978-0-521-18371-0 (paperback)
1. Welfare state.   2. Comparative government.   I. Vis, Barbara.   II. Title.
JC479.K47   2013
361.6'5–dc23   2013026795

ISBN 978-1-107-00563-1 Hardback
ISBN 978-0-521-18371-0 Paperback

Contents

Tables and Figures

TABLES

FIGURES

Preface and Acknowledgments

Like most books, this one has been quite some time in the making. The idea for writing it was born in 2006, when Gøsta Esping-Andersen asked one of us (Kees) to (co-)teach a course on comparative social policy at Universitat Pompeu Fabra (Barcelona). Many thanks to Gøsta for his suggestion to structure the course around "big" questions, which subsequently shaped the book's composition. The course was adapted as a PhD course on the political opportunities and constraints in welfare state reform, taught at the Oslo Summer School in Comparative Social Science Studies in 2009. We would like to thank the MA students in Barcelona and the PhD students at the Oslo Summer School for their many questions and critical comments.

The field of comparative welfare state studies is rich with books on welfare state reform in specific countries and in specific policy fields, but there was no book that asked, let alone answered, the "big" questions about the politics of welfare state development and reform in a single volume. Why did we need a welfare state in the first place? How did we get it? Why did we get different worlds of welfare and do we still have them? What does the welfare state actually do? Why do we need to reform the welfare state? Why is reform so difficult, but why does it nevertheless happen? Can and will the welfare state survive the Great Recession (which, at the time we began thinking about these questions, was "just" a financial crisis)? We decided that it was time for a book that answered these questions, could be used in teaching, and would be of value to scholars generally interested in the politics of welfare state reform. To this end, we wished to bring together the existing vast, varied, and rich knowledge on welfare state reform, but also to add our own theoretical approach and empirical analyses. The result is a distinctive cross between a textbook and a research monograph.

We have presented drafts of the different chapters at various workshops and conferences: the workshop "Ideas and/on Welfare in Europe," Oxford, the United Kingdom (2010); the Dutch/Flemish Politicologenetmaal, Leuven, Belgium (2010); the International Research Seminar of the Foundation for International Studies on Social Security, Sigtuna, Sweden (2010); the workshop "Politics in Hard Times," Mannheim Centre for European Social Research, Germany (2010); the NIG Workconference, Maastricht, the Netherlands (2010); the Dutch/Flemish Politicologenetmaal, Amsterdam, the Netherlands (2011); the ECPR Joint Sessions of Workshops, St. Gallen, Switzerland (2011); and the workshop "Political Parties and Welfare State Reform," Aarhus University, Denmark (2011). We thank all participants in these events for their helpful comments and suggestions. This book has also benefited greatly from the advice of many colleagues. A (nonexhaustive) list includes Christoph Arndt, Michael Baggensen Klitgaard, Uwe Becker, Martin Carstensen, Verena Dräbing, Christian Elmelund-Præstekær, Patrick Emmenegger, Jørgen Goul-Andersen, Christoffer Green-Pedersen, Steffen Heinrich, Anton Hemerijck, Carsten Jensen, Mikko Kuisma, Lars Thorup Larsen, Gijs Schumacher, Martin Seeleib-Kaiser, Menno Soentken, Matthias Stepan, Sabina Stiller, and Arco Timmermans. Neda Delfani, Eva Entenmann, and Sjoerd van Heck have offered excellent research assistance. Barbara Vis also thanks the Netherlands Organization for Scientific Research for a Veni grant (grant nr. 451–08–012) and a Vidi grant (grant nr. 452–11–005) that supported her research.

Various parts of this book are based on previously published material. Parts of Chapter 8 were published in Barbara Vis (2011), "Under Which Conditions Does Spending on Active Labor Market Policies Increase? A FsQCA Analysis of 53 Governments between 1985 and 2003," *European Political Science Review*, 3(2): 229–52. Parts of Chapter 9 appeared in Barbara Vis and Kees van Kersbergen (2007), "Why and How Do Political Actors Pursue Risky Reforms?" *Journal of Theoretical Politics*, 19(2), 153–72; in Barbara Vis (2011), "Prospect Theory and Political Decision-making," *Political Studies Review*, 9(3): 334–43: and in Barbara Vis (2010), *Politics of Risk-Taking: Welfare State Reform in Advanced Democracies*, Amsterdam: Amsterdam University Press. Segments of Chapter 10 appeared in Barbara Vis, Kees van Kersbergen, and Tom Hylands (2011), "To What Extent Did the Financial Crisis Intensify the Pressure to Reform the Welfare State?" *Social Policy and Administration*, 45(4): 338–53. We thank Tom Hylands for allowing us to make use of this co-authored work here. We first presented our open functional approach to welfare state reform (see Chapters 2 and especially 6) in Barbara Vis and Kees van Kersbergen (forthcoming), "Towards an Open Functional Approach to Welfare State Change: Pressures, Ideas, and Blame Avoidance," *Public Administration*. We wish to thank the publishers of these journals and Amsterdam University Press for allowing us to re-use the material here. We also thank Philip Manow for allowing us to use material from Kees van Kersbergen and Philip Manow (eds.) (2009), *Religion, Class Coalitions, and Welfare States*, Cambridge: Cambridge University Press. Table 4.3 is adapted from Vrooman (2009: 214–15, table 4.1). Many thanks to J. Cok Vrooman for allowing us to use this table in Chapter 4.

Since we started work on this book project, we have each experienced a life-changing event. Barbara gave birth to a little girl, Rena, whose mere presence, but especially her way of looking at the world, puts everything in a new – and better – perspective. The unfailing support and love of her partner, Pim, has been indispensable throughout the entire project. Kees changed countries, moving from the Netherlands to Denmark, which puts *almost* everything in a new – and better – perspective. Such a radical change can work out well only if there is at least some constancy – in Kees's case, his wife Inger, without whose support he would not even have begun the project.

I

Introduction

The Political Opportunities and Constraints of Welfare State Reform

Thursday, 1 December 2011: in Greece schools are closed, hospitals are staffed with emergency personnel, and public transport has come to a near standstill as a result of the first strike against a new and broad coalition government, which aims to push through a tough retrenchment and welfare state restructuring program in an attempt to come to terms with the country's sovereign debt crisis.

Wednesday, 30 November 2011: 29 unions in the United Kingdom (UK) organize one of the biggest nationwide strikes in 30 years. Approximately 2 million public sector workers block services (including hospitals and schools) as a protest against the government's plan to retrench pensions.

Sunday, 20 November 2011: the new Danish center-left government presents a budget plan that proposes public investments to kick start the economy and major reforms in active labor market policies to fight unemploymert. Following tradition, the main opposition party supports the law.

Wednesday, 16 November 2011: United States (US) senator Bernie Sanders gives a remarkable speech, which is worth quoting at some length:

There is a war going on in this country.... I am talking about a war being waged by some of the wealthiest and most powerful people in this country against the working families of the United States of America, against the disappearing and shrinking middle class of our country. The reality is that many of the nation's billionaires are on the warpath, they want more, more, more. Their greed has no end.... The reality is tnat many of these folks [the wealthy] want to bring the United States back to where we were in the 1920s. And they want to do their best to eliminate all traces of social legislation, which working families fought tooth and nail to develop to bring a modicum of stability and security to their lives.... While we struggle with a record breaking deficit and a large national debt, caused by the wars in Iraq and Afghanistan, caused by tax breaks for the wealthy ... caused by the Wall Street bailout, driving up the deficit, driving up the national debt, so that people can say oh my goodness, we have got all of those expenses and then we got to give tax breaks to millionaires and billionaires, but we want to balance the budget. Gee, how are we going to do that? Well, obviously, we know how they are going to do that. We are going to cut back on health care ... education ... childcare ... food stamps, ... we surely are not going to expand unemployment compensation, ... we got a higher priority, ... we have got to, got to, got to give tax breaks to billionaires.[1]

Welfare state reform occurs in all advanced capitalist democracies, but not everywhere to the same extent and degree, in identical ways, or with similar consequences. In some welfare states, such as a couple of continental European countries (see, e.g., Palier 2010a; Hemerijck 2013) or in Denmark (Larsen and Andersen 2009), social policy adjustments have been radical and path-forming (Hay 2011) by breaking with habitual courses of development and by taking groundbreaking new directions. In other cases, such as in most other continental countries, reform has been smaller, slower, derivative, and very often incomplete – in short, path-dependent. In yet other cases, such as the United States, policies have been allowed to "drift" (Hacker 2004; Hacker and Pierson 2010) as a result of deliberate political decisions to abstain from adjusting social policies or tax policies even if the social outcomes – for instance, high and still rising inequality – are clearly not in congruence with the original policy goals. Interestingly, in some cases, as the examples of the United Kingdom, the United States, and Greece signify, welfare state reform is accompanied by deep social conflicts and harsh political struggles, whereas in other cases, such as in Denmark but also Sweden, reform seems a relatively smooth and balanced process of policy learning and comparatively consensual politics (for a review of the literature, see Starke 2006).

What explains these differences? In this book we try to uncover, map, and explain the political opportunities and constraints of contemporary welfare state reform in advanced capitalist democracies. Welfare states come in different shapes and sizes; they are constructed on diverging conceptions of social rights and duties; some stress equality and solidarity, others freedom; and the range of policy objectives is vast and widely dissimilar. Still, we agree with Barr (2004: 7) that in a general sense welfare states exist "to enhance the welfare of people who (a) are weak and vulnerable, largely by providing social care, (b) are poor, largely through redistributive income transfers, or (c) are neither vulnerable nor poor, by organizing cash benefits to provide insurance and consumption smoothing, and by providing medical insurance and school education." Enhancing the welfare of vulnerable groups of people in society and offering or facilitating social protection for all is what a welfare state is about.

We define welfare state reform in a similarly broad manner, namely, as change, in any direction, in the organization and implementation of the amalgam of

---

[1] http://euwelfarestates.blogspot.com/2011/11/inequality-and-politics-of-welfare.html (Accessed December 2011).

social policies (benefits and services) that make up a nation's welfare arrangements and that are to enhance welfare and offer protection. Welfare state reforms have many appearances. One is *retrenchments*, which roll back social protection and other welfare state interventions and are meant to increase citizens' market dependence. The lowering of benefits and the tightening of eligibility criteria of social insurances are examples of this. We regard as a subcategory of retrenchment those reforms that aim at *containing the rising costs* due to rising demand of a program (e.g., sick pay) or of an entire sector (e.g., health care). Furthermore, there are *adaptations* that are meant to modify existing policies so that they can continue to do what they have been doing. Another form concerns social policy *updates* or *recalibrations* (Pierson 2001a) that aim to amend or renew the existing policy instruments in an attempt to respond to new social risks or political demands. The expansion of family policies to facilitate the growing participation of women (mothers) on the labor market is an example of updating. *Restructuring* is the broad term that we use to indicate the type of reorganization of benefits and service delivery that is undertaken to redefine the relations of power that govern a program, amend the rights and duties of stakeholders and clients, or terminate a policy entirely. An example of restructuring is the transformation of governance arrangements of social security programs, including privatization and marketization. Subsumed under restructuring is what others call *dismantling*, that is, the diminution of the number of policies, the reduction of instruments, and the lowering of intensity (e.g., instrument settings and scope, administrative capacities) (Bauer and Knill 2012: 33–35; Pierson 1994). Increasingly, welfare state reforms involve more than one dimension (Häusermann 2010; Bonoli and Natali 2012a). Häusermann (2010), for example, focuses on the dimensions of benefit levels (retrenchment), the financing mechanisms (capitalization), the privileges of specific occupational groups (targeting), and gender-equality (recalibration) to explain the politics of pension reforms in Continental Europe.

As indicated, *policy drift* may also lead to welfare state reform, usually in the direction of a deterioration of the status quo, but it is an effect of the conscious decision *not* to reform and thus not to adapt policies and instruments to changing circumstances. Hacker and Pierson (2010), for instance, explain the, comparatively speaking, dramatic rise in inequality in the United States in the past decades as a result of such intentional policy drift: "policy change often occurs when groups with the ability to block change effectively resist the updating of policy over an extended period of time in the face of strong contrary pressure and strong evidence that policy is failing to achieve its initial goals" (168). Intentional policy drift, then, is the "politically driven failure of public policies to adapt to the shifting realities of a dynamic economy and society" (170). Unlike simple inaction, which may stem from, for example, a relative unawareness of the changed social and economic circumstances, intentional policy drift assumes knowledge of policy failure and implies that "policy makers fail to update policies *due to pressure from intense minority interests or political actors exploiting veto points in the political process"* (170, emphasis in original). This is what Bauer and Knill (2012) define as *dismantling by default*, a strategy of social policy dismantling, which is not based on an overt decision and has low visibility, but which nevertheless has harsh consequences in the long run. For instance, not adjusting benefits to inflation and the increase in wages for a protracted period of time reduces the real value of benefits considerably (Green-Pedersen et al. 2012).

To account for the variation in the politics of welfare reform across countries and over time, we adopt a broad perspective and ask and answer "big" questions about the welfare state. Why did we need a welfare state in the first place? How did we get it? Why did we get different worlds of welfare and do we still have them? What does the welfare state actually do? Why do we need to reform the welfare state? Why is reform so difficult and electorally risky but why does it nevertheless happen? Can and will the welfare state survive the current financial, economic and debt crisis? By focusing on such big questions, for which current comparative welfare state research already offers some – admittedly controversial and in any case still scattered – answers, this book not only brings together central findings of various research fields but also aims to make its own substantial contribution by presenting recent data and new analyses. In other words, the book is explicitly conceived and designed as a cross between a text- or reference book that informs the reader comprehensively about the state of the art in the field of welfare state studies and an academic research monograph that aims to contribute theoretically and empirically to the ongoing debate on the politics of welfare state reform.

Our leading idea is that the opportunities and constraints of welfare state reform depend crucially on the welfare state's architecture, on its positive and negative social and political feedback mechanisms, on the functional demands placed on it, on the distribution of (political) power, and on the capacity of political actors to design reform packages that are not only functional (i.e., economically efficient and/or socially desirable) but also politically feasible. Moreover, and in marked contrast to that part of the literature that has considered welfare state *stasis* the main explanatory problem, we propose that welfare state *reform* is what has been happening all along. This observation derives from the following counterfactual argument: the fact that the welfare state has survived several crises and so many critical changes in its environment (as we discuss in more detail in Chapters 2, 7 and 8), must mean that it has been permanently reforming (i.e., retrenching, adapting, updating, or restructuring) so as to cope with these changes. If such reform had not occurred, we would be observing much more policy drift or dismantling than we actually do. Welfare state reform is thus not something that only appeared recently, as some suggest (Palier 2010b: 19). As Ringen (1987 [2006 edition]: xlvi) wrote more than 25 years ago, "The welfare state is reform on a grand scale. It is an attempt to change the circumstances individuals and families live under without basically changing society. No less; no wonder it is controversial. *If the welfare state works, reform works"* (our emphasis). This means that in order to understand welfare state reform, we need to retrace the welfare state's history and functioning. Specifically, we need to appreciate the origin of the welfare state, why we have different worlds or regimes of welfare, how these regimes function, what the pressures in favor of reform are, why reform is so difficult and politically risky, and why it nevertheless happens. We introduce a broad and *open functional approach to welfare state reform* (see Chapter 2 and more extensively Chapter 6), which stresses that "objective" challenges and pressures for reform emerge from key changes in the international environment (especially globalization) and the domestic context (e.g., the postindustrialization of the labor market). The politics of welfare state reform is the struggle to respond to such pressures and challenges and deal with them.

We draw on a very large body of accumulated welfare state research and related literature to help us uncover, map, and explain the political opportunities and constraints of contemporary welfare state reform in advanced capitalist democracies (for an exhaustive overview of the whole field, see Castles et al. 2010). If we look back at more than four decades of welfare state research, four types of relatively detached fields of research emerge: (1) approaches that focus on the causes of the emergence, expansion, and cross-national variation of welfare state regimes; (2) theories of the "crises" of the welfare state; (3) studies that explain the political and institutional resilience of social policy arrangements, in spite of mounting pressures to change; and (4) attempts to understand the conditions under which reforms take place, in spite of resilience and political and institutional sclerosis (see van Kersbergen 2002; Green-Pedersen and Haverland 2002; Starke 2006; Häusermann et al. 2013). This characterization roughly represents the historical development of welfare state research (say, from the 1960s to the present) and also provides an impression of which research problems have been predominant. This book builds on the conviction that to understand the politics of welfare state reform, we can learn and must benefit from a critical exchange with all four fields of research, aiming at a workable integration of the main insights, and adding to it our open functional approach.

Our broad and open functional approach to welfare state reform is therefore different from many recent and excellent studies of welfare state reform that tend to adopt a narrower focus, for example, by examining a very specific empirical puzzle (e.g., why radical retrenchment occurs, as in Starke 2008; why the welfare state persists, as in Brooks and Manza 2007; or how politics and policies shape insider–outsider divides, as in Emmenegger et al. 2012), by looking at a limited number of countries (e.g., Green-Pedersen 2002; Clasen 2007; Stiller 2010; Afonso 2013; Arndt 2013), by singling out specific welfare state programs (such as pensions, e.g., Lynch 2006; Häusermann 2010), by focusing on differences between parties (Seeleib-Kaiser et al. 2008), or by studying the regulation of unemployment in postindustrial labor markets (as in Clasen and Clegg 2011a). Our approach also differs from those studies that are of a normative-theoretical nature and do not pay much attention to empirical substantiation (e.g., Olson 2006), or are really more preoccupied with other issues, such as globalization and neoliberalism (e.g., Ellison 2006), than with the politics of welfare state reform per se. By answering our "big" questions, we map and restate what we know from these and like studies about the politics of welfare state reform. We do so by covering the narrower foci, of course in less detail than more specific studies do, and by integrating them into a single coherent approach. We illustrate our approach empirically and offer a framework that researchers can readily apply for more detailed empirical work.

1.2. THE STRUCTURE OF THE BOOK

The welfare state embodies a remarkable transformation in how nations deal with the economic and social problems generated by modernization, in particular industrialization and the emergence of capitalist markets, and most recently globalization and postindustrialization. In Chapter 2, we highlight the notion that capitalism is an extremely dynamic system that persistently tends to penetrate noneconomic areas and permanently generates new "facts" (social needs, risks, disruptions, issues, conflicts) to which political actors must react (Streeck 2012). Moreover, capitalism has an inbuilt tendency to economic fluctuation and crises, which constantly produce new challenges to the welfare state's status quo. The prolonged period of stagflation of the 1970s and 1980s was but one example of this. It inspired many to question whether the welfare state was capable of surviving capitalism's dynamics and crises. But the welfare state turned out to be politically and institutionally resilient and much more adaptive than expected. Although many studies focused on explaining the absence of change, we argue that political and institutional resilience and stability should not be confused with the absence of change. In fact, the kind of stability that welfare states displayed can only be understood as a result of a substantial amount of reform, very often in response to compelling pressures to adapt social policies to new requirements (i.e., adaptation) so as to maintain the proper functioning of existing arrangements. To capture this, we introduce our open functional approach, which we elaborate in theoretical detail in Chapter 6.

In Chapter 3, we elaborate what welfare states are for by explaining the welfare state's different rationales or logics. The use of rationales or logics is a methodological and analytical device that allows us to simplify and stylize the complex political interconnections between the motivations of social and political actors (ideas, interests, power, etc.), driving forces (demographics, democratization, globalization, etc.), public policy considerations (security, health, efficiency, affluence, etc.), values (equality, solidarity, freedom, autonomy, etc.), and causal mechanisms (power mobilization, elections, policy learning, etc.), linking functional demands and pressures to reform. This, in turn, enables us to understand the broader context of the political opportunities and constraints of welfare state reform. We distinguish four such rationales or logics. First, the logic of socioeconomic development and modernization, which explains why and how the dynamics of capitalist development tend to challenge and break up existing social arrangements and hence generate functional requirements and pressures to adapt and find a new balance for societal integration. Second, the logic of political integration and state-building, which demonstrates that social policy is also a major instrument of social control and political community and identity building in the hands of ruling elites. Third, the logic of need satisfaction and risk reapportioning, which clarifies that welfare state intervention primarily serves the function of pooling and redistributing social risks. Fourth and finally, the logic of class compromises and redistribution, which shows that the power of social classes and their representatives as well as the political coalitions between them influence the degree and shape of welfare state intervention.

In Chapter 4, we turn to the "big" question of why we developed different worlds or regimes of welfare and assess whether we still have them. First, we describe that Esping-Andersen's (1990) seminal regime approach developed out of the theoretical and empirical literature on welfare state development, particularly the social democratic variant of the power resources model. This explains the centrality in the regime typology of the concept of decommodification that is meant to capture the extent to which the state substitutes for the market in guaranteeing a decent livelihood. Second, we discuss the methodological tool of a typology, clarify the terms of the debate around Esping-Andersen's three worlds of welfare capitalism, solve some of the controversies that arise as a result of a flawed understanding of what a typology is or should be, and describe the regime types empirically. Third, we show that the regime classification, with some qualifications, still makes sense analytically and empirically. Finally, we argue that the regime classification lacks a proper theoretical foundation that can explain why we have different worlds of welfare. We defend the classification but provide a better theoretical and historical substantiation.

Chapter 5 asks the "big" question of what welfare states actually do. We show empirically that – perhaps to a remarkable degree – most welfare states do surprisingly well in what they set out to do and all of them provide protection against major social risks, fight poverty, and redistribute wealth from the rich to the poor. Still, there are important and systematic differences across the various regimes, which we map empirically.

In Chapter 6, we pick up the theoretical theme from Chapter 2 and present our open functional approach to welfare state reform in more detail. We explain that functional pressures and demands (i.e., requirements) generate a selective context in which some actors, interests, and ideas are more likely to prevail than others. We take issue with that part of the increasingly recognized constructivist literature that starts from the assumption that ideas by themselves are capable of provoking welfare state reform and that also holds that economic and social interests have no separate analytical status. We acknowledge that ideas as causal beliefs matter, but we stress that they only do so in a context characterized by functional requirements. In addition, we argue that strategies, which political actors employ to avoid the blame for unpopular reform, at least partly help explain the fate of welfare state reforms in the context of "objective" pressures. Blame avoidance strategies link an idea to a reform.

The next two chapters identify and map the functional pressures for the different types of welfare state reform. Chapter 7 focuses on a largely exogenous pressure, namely, globalization. We discuss the main perspectives on globalization and show that no matter whether one evaluates its impact positively or negatively, it is a crucial functional pressure "from the outside" that any explanation of welfare state reform needs to take into account. We present descriptive data to show that globalization's pressure has increased over time but that its impact differs between countries and welfare state regimes. Chapter 8 focuses on endogenous pressures, especially the postindustrialization of labor markets and aging populations, which have revolutionized the traditional, postwar underpinning of welfare states. The exogenous and endogenous pressures discussed in these two chapters constitute the functional pressures for reform.

Even if functional pressures have been building up, and even if politicians recognize the need for reform and can overcome the institutional resistance against it, there is still no guarantee that the job will be done. Politicians still face the high political hurdle of having to convince the electorate of the prudence of reform or to find strategies to let policies drift. Welfare state reform is electorally risky business. How do the politicians cope with the pressures if the reforms that are needed contradict their electoral ambitions? In Chapter 9 we explain why different types of electorally risky welfare state reform occur in spite of electoral stumbling blocks. We draw on prospect theory (Kahneman and Tversky 1979, 2000) to argue that governments will only undertake risky reforms if they consider themselves to be in a losses domain, that is, when their current electoral and policy situation is unacceptable. This is the case when governments face socioeconomic losses (such as deteriorating growth rates or increasing levels of unemployment) and/or political losses (like lower approval ratings or vote losses at an election). Only under such losses will governments accept the electoral risk involved in unpopular, risky welfare state reform. In addition, governments use blame avoidance strategies to reframe the voters' domain from gains into losses so as to change their risk-attitude from risk-averse (i.e., opposed to reform) to risk-accepting (i.e., accepting of reform). If successful, this greatly limits the political risk of implementing the type of drastic welfare state reforms that are functionally required but not guaranteed.

In the final chapter, we bring together the findings of the book, summarize the answers to our "big" questions and ask the final one: can and will the welfare state survive the financial, economic, and debt crisis that started in 2008? We apply our open functional approach empirically to assess the impact of the financial, economic, and debt crisis and its aftershocks on six selected welfare states that represent different welfare state regimes (the United States, the United Kingdom, the Netherlands, Sweden, Germany, and Denmark; see Chapter 2). Have the financial crisis and the negative economic repercussions since 2008, the Great Recession (Bermeo and Pontusson 2013), added up to such a force that the welfare state's edifice is undercut? If ever there was a momentum to reform the welfare state radically, it is the (aftermath) of the financial crisis of 2008–9. All existing theoretical perspectives within comparative welfare state research suggest that radical reform is likely under this circumstance. But does it also happen? Countries were facing similar problems, and their initial response to these problems has been similar, too. In line with our open functional approach to welfare state reform and our prospect-theoretical account, yet contrary to extant perspectives' expectations, rather than increased retrenchment we observe a first phase of emergency capital injections in the banking sector and a second period of Keynesian demand management and labor market protection, including the (temporary) expansion of social programs. However, and again in line with our hypotheses, the contours of a third phase have become increasingly apparent, especially once budgetary constraints started to force political actors to make tougher choices and introduce austerity policies. The functional pressures that financial markets and international agreements exert have made themselves felt. Although perhaps not the only game left in town (Armingeon 2013), retrenchment and restructuring have become the dominant themes of welfare state reform.

2

The Welfare State

Dynamic Development, Crisis, Resilience, and Change

2.1. SOCIAL NEEDS, RISKS, AND DISRUPTIONS IN PERMANENTLY MODERNIZING CAPITALIST NATIONS

The history of the welfare state and its reform is a history of political actors struggling to cope with social needs, risks, and disruptions caused by rapid social and economic development. Paying attention to the "objective" problem pressure to which political actors respond is crucial for explaining past and contemporary welfare state reform. History may never repeat itself, but in many ways and irrespective of regime form or level of development, the problems of societal disruption, social needs, and risks that tend to emerge in the wake of what we conveniently call "modernization," as well as the social and political struggles to deal with them, are strikingly similar across time and space (Wilensky and Lebeaux 1965 [1958]; Flora and Alber 1981; Flora and Heidenheimer 1981b). Take as an illustration the following quotation from a recent study of social policy in China and read it while keeping 19th-century Britain or Germany in mind:

Chinese leaders should ... be ashamed of a high degree of capitalist exploitation and class suppression in the process of economic modernisation. Over the past three decades, China's economic growth has been achieved at the expense of the well-being of hundreds of thousands of members of deprived groups: poor rural residents are always worried about medical care and retirement; urban migrant workers have been excluded from accessing urban public services; many factory workers are working long hours in extremely hazardous work environments; farmers whose land was expropriated have not received proper compensation; and thousands of poor patients are unable to afford treatment. The commonly perceived "gradual economic reforms" have actually brought about tremendous changes in welfare provisions and have rapidly destroyed China's socialist welfare system, leaving millions of poor people unprotected. There is obviously a gap between China's economic development and its social development. (Chan et al. 2008: xiii)

The social needs, risks, and injustice described are not identical with but are still very similar to what we see described in, say, Marx's analysis of the struggle over the working day in *Das Kapital* (1867, chapter 10), in Engels's examination of the suffering of the working class in Victorian England in *Die Lage der arbeitenden Klasse in England* (1844), or, much later, in Polanyi's study of the impact and the reaction to the social dislocation caused by the unrestrained capitalist free market in *The Great Transformation* (1944).

In a sense, the political and public policy history of many a modernizing nation in the 20th and 21st centuries could be described, without much exaggeration, as the history of the increasing presence of the state in the daily life of its population to deal with the social needs, risks, and disruptions inherent to modern industrial and postindustrial capitalist market economies. Most remarkably, in this period the state rapidly moved far beyond its classic functions of, say, securing law and order when it started to initiate, take over, reorganize, and expand key social, economic, and cultural tasks, including education and social protection. In the case of the communist experiments of the 20th century, the state even assumed the functions of production and distribution, a task left largely to the (albeit regulated and socially embedded) market in the evolving democratic capitalist states in Western Europe, North America, and the Antipodes. In the last areas, a welfare state gradually emerged, expanded, matured, and became firmly entrenched as a vital component of a nation's political economy.

The welfare state as we know it today has transformed radically the ways that societies are organized socially, economically, and politically: from a state primarily engaged in policing its population and defending its territory at the beginning of the 20th century, to a state effectively blending capitalism and democracy and currently devoting to public spending roughly between 17 percent (Ireland) and 30 percent (France) of gross domestic product (GDP) and between 44 percent (US) and 64 percent (UK) of total public spending to welfare-related activities (OECD 2008; see Obinger and Wagschal 2010).

This development is rooted in and must be attributed to the immense dynamics of international capitalism. Capitalism is an extremely energetic economic system that is continuously transforming its technological base, the organization of its enterprise ownership structures, and the distribution of income between capital owners and others (see, e.g., Scherer 2010). The engine of the capitalist dynamic is competition, "which since its origin in the 17th–19th centuries has been revolutionizing the human way of life" (Becker 2009: 15).

Capitalist societies are permanently modernizing societies. Capitalism's competition-induced structural dynamics cause "more or less permanent material change in the form of new competitors (in global competition), new production methods and tools as well as new consumer goods and services" (Becker 2009: 168). Moreover, as Polanyi (1944 [1957]; see Chapter 3) argued, capitalism continually tends to transfer its economic logic to other sectors of society. According to Streeck (2012: 2), we must therefore speak of capitalist *society*: "it is … a society [that is] at risk of the social relations governing its economy penetrating into and taking possession of previously non-capitalist social relations." Most crucially for our purposes, the dynamics of capitalism permanently generate new economic and social problems, needs, risks, and conflicts by ceaselessly transforming the social structure, the constellations of interests, and thus the power relations in society. As a result, capitalism's dynamics also permanently ask for new solutions to the new problems, needs, risks, and conflicts, especially because the capitalist market economy has an in-built tendency toward economic fluctuations, with recession and crises as inevitable phases in an innovation and investment cycle that Schumpeter (1976 [1942]: 83) labeled "Creative Destruction" and defined as "the essential fact about capitalism."

Some demands for new solutions are *functional pressures or requirements* to the extent that not responding adequately to such demands implies an existential threat: the distinct risk of a breakdown of the (social) system. The financial crisis of 2008, its economic aftermath, and the sovereign debt crisis that followed are the most recent but also the most momentous cases of how markets generate functional pressures for radical action and change. The sovereign debt crisis of Greece since 2009 is an extreme example demonstrating that financial markets have the capacity to force a political system to accept painful reforms that were dictated from the outside (the Euro countries and the International Monetary Fund, IMF) and that such a system never would have agreed to under more normal circumstances. This could happen only because Greece was coping with threats of an existential nature: the country faced the collapse of its economy, while bankruptcy, and hence a possible (forced) exit from the common European currency (the Euro), were distinct possibilities.

The solutions for such existential crises – and to functional pressures more generally – always consist of some combination of a novel mobilization of power resources and innovative social and political coalitions that back up the ideas that are to be translated into collective action in the form of reformed public policies. In the context of democratic politics, the dynamics of capitalism thus become an inexhaustible source of politically relevant new facts, issues, and conflicts that both enable and limit the options available for the different types of welfare state reform we distinguish. In fact, under extreme conditions, such as during the Greek debt crisis, outside forces may even put a limit to democracy itself. An example is when both the pressure of the financial markets and the leaders of the Euro countries effectively blocked a referendum on the radical reform package imposed on Greece in the fall of 2011. Apolitical technocrats rather than elected politicians were asked to lead the government in Greece (Lucas Papademos) as well as in Italy (Mario Monti) toward drastic reforms, signaling that, in this case, the political system was incapable of processing functional pressures with conventional means.

2.2. CRISIS AND COLLAPSE?

In a sense, therefore, it seems that the welfare state has always been in crisis as it develops in and through the dynamics of capitalism. In fact, to say that the welfare state is in crisis has become a cliché (Garrett and Mitchell 2001: 145). The welfare state in today's advanced capitalist societies operates under very different conditions from the ones in existence when its basic social programs emerged and expanded. This has resulted in an increasing mismatch between the arrangement of tra⁴itional social policies and the (new) social needs, risks, and disruptions that the welfare state, in some combination with the market and the family, is supposed to take care of. Or as Esping-Andersen (1996a: 3) put it eloquently already more than 15 years ago:

The advanced Western nations' welfare states were built to cater to an economy dominated by industrial mass production. In the era of the "Keynesian consensus" there was no perceived trade-off between social security and economic growth, between equality and efficiency. This consensus has disappeared because the underlying assumptions no longer obtain. Non-inflationary demand-led growth within one country appears impossible; full employment today must be attained via services, given industrial decline; the conventional male breadwinner family is eroding, fertility is falling, and the life course is increasingly non-standard.

It all started in the wake of the disruptive oil shocks of the 1970s. The prolonged period of stagflation, the ensuing sky-high budget deficits, and the advent of an increasingly strong, anti-interventionist and anti-welfare state neoliberal political hegemony in the 1980s all seemed to make the further expansion or even the simple prolongation of major welfare states programs precarious, unlikely, or outright impossible. In the 1980s, a dominant theme in the welfare state literature concerned the crisis of the welfare state and ultimately its probable crumbling.

Yet scholars disagreed as to what caused the crisis. Neo-Marxists pointed to the inherent contradictions of postwar welfare capitalism as the root cause of the crisis. The social democrats figured out that the once golden formula, which mixed a capitalist market economy with Keynesian demand management, could no longer guarantee the sustained economic growth necessary to uphold the welfare state. It seemed clear to all, however, that new and theoretically unexpected economic phenomena, such as the coincidence of a stagnating economy and inflation, had led to failing government responses to social needs and risks. The period of continuous economic growth, low inflation, full employment – and the social peace enabled by this – had come to an end. The belief that "things cannot go on like this" was endorsed by both the left and the right (Offe 1984).

Although the market was supposed to be self-regulating (see Chapter 3), the state intervened extensively to ensure and restore its proper functioning. Some, however, agued that this state intervention was the problem. It caused new economic fiascos, which led to further interventions, an "overburdened state," and the "ungovernability" of capitalist societies. While the obligations and responsibilities of the state as well as the public's expectations were continuously rising, the state's capacity to intervene and steer could not keep up (Offe 1984: 67–73). The welfare state's main contradictions came to light. On the one hand, burdening taxation and the regulation of capital hampered investment. On the other hand, workers' social rights and enhanced social power implied a disincentive to work or "at least to work as hard and productively as they would be forced to under the reign of unfettered market forces" (Offe 1984: 149). Taken together, this meant that "while capitalism cannot coexist with, neither can it exist *without*, the welfare state" (Offe 1984: 153, emphasis in original).

Publications of some three decades ago reflected this preoccupation with the welfare state's growth to limits, its crisis, and probable ultimate collapse (see Schmidt 1983; Mishra 1984; Panich 1986; Alber 1988; Moran 1988). Allegedly there was a fiscal crisis (O'Connor 1973), a crisis of governability caused by overload (Crozier et al. 1975; King 1975; Birch 1984), a crisis of legitimacy (Habermas 1976; Wolfe 1979, see Offe 1984), a crisis of liberal democracy (Brittan 1975; Crozier et al. 1975; Bowles and Gintis 1982), and a crisis of culture (Bell 1979) and "utopian energies" (Habermas 1985). Titles such as *Contradictions of the Welfare State* (Offe 1984), *Growth to Limits* (Flora 1986–87), *Beyond the Welfare State?* (Pierson 1991), *Dismantling the Welfare State?* (Pierson 1994), *The End of the Welfare State* (Svallfors and Taylor-Gooby 1999), and *The Survival of the European Welfare State* (Kuhnle 2000) further illustrate the point. Many sweeping statements and general predictions about the welfare state's gloomy fate were made, but usually without any projection of when these were to occur. Moreover, the empirical evidence for the proclaimed collapse was scanty or entirely absent. In fact, the welfare state in all its various forms not only continued to exist, but to a large extent precisely kept doing what it was meant to do (see Chapter 5).

2.3. ABSENCE OF CHANGE?

Recognizing the challenges and pressures and observing that radical welfare state reform was remarkably scarce, most research attention by the mid-1990s shifted to the puzzle of the *absence* of radical welfare state change. Very much inspired by the work of Pierson (especially 1994 and 1996), a whole generation of researchers wondered why – in spite of mounting pressures for change and direct political attacks (by, for instance, Ronald Reagan in the United States and Margaret Thatcher in the United Kingdom in the 1980s) on core social programs – the welfare state "under siege" did not give way. Why, in spite of the predictions of doom and expectations of (occasionally) an apocalyptic sort, did welfare states prove to be so surprisingly resilient? Why and how was the welfare state capable of surviving such a fierce combination of economic, fiscal, political, and – later – demographic attacks? As Pierson (1996: 174, emphasis in original) stressed in the mid-1990s: "What is striking is how hard it is to find *radical* changes in advanced welfare states. Retrenchment has been pursued cautiously: whenever possible, governments have sought all-party consensus for significant reforms and have chosen to trim existing structures rather than experiment with new programs or pursue privatization." Hence, the issue of the political and institutional "stickiness" of the welfare state became the dominant explanatory problem, and public opinion and institutionalist approaches moved to the forefront of the scholarly debate to account for the phenomenon. Let us give a summary – admittedly somewhat simplified but hopefully not unfair – of the main explanations of the absence of radical reform (see also Van Kersbergen 2000, 2002).

New Politics: Political Resilience

The core social programs of the welfare state (say pensions) are so tremendously popular among the electorate that any plan to strike fundamentally at such established social rights will die a premature death in the fear of a fierce electoral backlash. The politics surrounding the welfare state nowadays is a "new" kind of politics. Because of "permanent austerity" (Pierson 2001a), both left-wing and right-wing governments face budget constraints and a constituency that has grown attached to the welfare state. The consequence is that left-wing governments can no longer pursue their preferred policies and expand the welfare state because budget restraints do not allow it. Right-wing governments can no longer pursue their preferred policy of welfare state cutbacks either, because their own constituencies have also become welfare state clients (for instance as pensioners).

The politics is *new* because the welfare state's defense against attacks does not depend anymore on the old forces who built up the welfare state – for example, social democracy, Christian democracy, and labor unions. One important cause is that a social program, once established as the status quo, breeds its own powerful lines of defense by creating and nourishing consumer groups, providers, and organized interests, whose very existence depends on the continuation of the program. Another reason is that electoral competition turns virtually every political party into a pro-welfare state force. No political actor can claim credit for expanding the welfare state, but all have to avoid the blame (Weaver 1986) when undertaking cutbacks. In the new politics context, then, left-wing and right-wing governments become almost indistinguishable because budget constraints preclude expansion, and electoral constraints prohibit radical cutbacks. In fact, so the new politics argument goes, neither type of government will pursue any cutbacks at all unless they have an opportunity to avoid the blame associated with such measures. The reason is simply that the public cherishes key social programs so strongly that any government that retrenches or radically reforms the welfare state openly will be severely chastised.

Is it correct to assume that voters are attached to key social programs? Research demonstrates that the welfare state is indeed well entrenched in national political cultures (Sihvo and Uusitalo 1995; Svallfors 1995; Ferrera 1997; Goul Andersen 1997; Becker 2005; Mau and Veghte 2007; Jaeger 2009, 2012; Svallfors 2012). Public opinion research has consistently reported that the public's support for the welfare state is considerable and that there has been little, if any, decline in public attachment to the national social systems. A survey by Boeri et al. (2001) of welfare state opinions in France, Germany, Italy, and Spain, for example, shows that the majority of citizens opposes cutbacks in the welfare state, but also opposes further expansion. In other words, the status quo is the majoritarian outcome: the public wishes to preserve the welfare state precisely as it is. Svallfors (2011) shows a remarkably robust and even increasing support for the welfare state in Sweden between 1981 and 2010. Even though Eger (2010) finds that immigration has had a negative impact on welfare state support in Sweden, her data too (and in agreement with Svallfors) indicate an aggregate increase in support. A study of Denmark (Sniderman et al. 2013) shows that support for welfare provisions, which are particularly beneficial for immigrants (and integration), remains high if people feel immigrants make an effort to meet their duties as citizens. Rehm et al. (2012) show that cross-national variation in support for the welfare state is explained by the structure of disadvantage (low income) and risk: the more they overlap, the more support for the welfare state is concentrated among the insecure and disadvantaged and the more opposition to the welfare state is found among the secure and advantaged (see also Lupu and Pontusson 2011).

Just as a way of illustrating support for the welfare state further, we look at data from the European Values Surveys (EVS) of 1999–2000 and 2008. Figure 2.1 displays citizens' concern with the unemployed (top panel) and the elderly (bottom panel) in a selection of European countries for which data were available in both waves of the EVS. The EVS survey questions unfortunately do not tap citizens' attitudes regarding the welfare state equally well as, for instance, the questions in the work of Boeri et al. (2001), but the answers still offer some interesting insights. Overall, the EVS data corroborate the findings of earlier studies.[1] On average, citizens in these countries are concerned with the unemployed and the elderly, that is, typically people who receive welfare state benefits. A higher score in Figure 2.1 indicates less concern. In five of the 11 countries in Figure 2.1, the concern for the unemployed increased

---

[1] The same holds for the responses to the survey questions on government's responsibility for providing a living standard for the unemployed and for the elderly from the International Social Survey Programme (ISSP 1996, 2006). The questions on the role of the government are often used to assess citizens' support for the welfare state or for the degree to which they consider the welfare state legitimate. Especially the latter is multidimensional in that citizens may endorse, for example, a substantial role for the government in the provision of welfare, but at the same time may be critical of such provision. But the "role of government" questions seem closest to the measurement of overall perceptions of welfarism (Van Oorschot and Meuleman 2011).

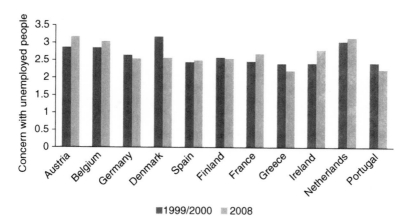

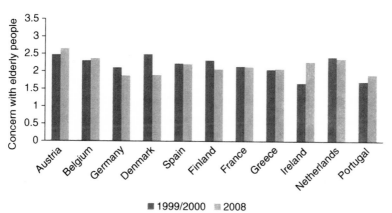

FIGURE 2.1. Concern for unemployed and elderly, selected European countries, 1999/2000 and 2008.

Notes: Are you concerned with: the unemployed / the elderly? (1 = very much; 2 = much; 3 = to a certain extent; 4 = not so much; 5 = not at all).

Source: European Values Survey (1999/2000, 2008).

between 1999–2000 and 2008 (Germany, Denmark, Finland, Greece, and Portugal). This signals (increasingly) positive attitudes of respondents to this welfare state program, which may at least partly be a consequence of the financial crisis and its economic aftershocks (Hemerijck et al. 2009) at the time (see also Chapter 10). In the six other countries, the concern with the unemployed decreased somewhat (Austria, Belgium, Spain, France, Ireland, and the Netherlands), but stayed fairly positive nonetheless. Compared to concern for the unemployed, the average concern with the elderly is somewhat higher. This is in line with what theories of deservingness would predict (see Petersen et al. 2011) because the elderly are typically seen as "more deserving" of their benefit

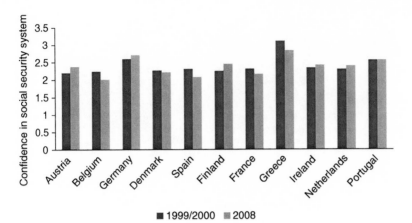

FIGURE 2.2. Confidence in social security system, selected European countries, 1999/2000 and 2008.

Notes: How much confidence do you have in the social security system (in your country)? Higher scores indicate less confidence (1 = a great deal; 2 = quite a lot; 3 = not very much; 4 = none at all).

Source: European Values Survey (1999/2000, 2008).

than are the unemployed. Between 1999–2000 and 2008, the concern for the elderly increased in six countries (Germany, Denmark, Spain, Finland, France, and the Netherlands), and decreased somewhat in the other countries (Austria, Belgium, Greece, Ireland, and Portugal). In six countries at least, citizens typically appreciate this welfare state program and increasingly so.

Another piece of evidence on the enduring support for the welfare state is the degree of confidence citizens have in the social security system. Figure 2.2 displays data on this for the same countries. Higher scores in the figure indicate less confidence in a country's system of social security. Overall, citizens' confidence in the system is fairly high, with the averages in most countries being closer to "quite a lot" of confidence than to "not very much." In this respect, Germany, Portugal, and especially Greece differ from the other countries, with average confidence tilting toward "not very much" support. In five of the 11 countries from Figure 2.2, confidence in the system of social security increased between 1999–2000 and 2008 (Belgium, Denmark, Spain, France, and Greece), and stayed the same in one (Portugal). In the five other countries (Austria, Germany, Finland, Ireland, and the Netherlands), citizens' confidence dropped somewhat over this period, but confidence levels still remained fairly high.

Overall, the data presented in Figures 2.1 and 2.2 support the findings of the existing surveys that citizens have positive attitudes toward the welfare state. If politicians' aim is to avoid voters' wrath, it thus seems safest to abstain from large-scale cutbacks of the welfare state. This holds especially true for social democratic and Christian democratic parties, the parties that have been involved in the construction of the welfare state (Vis 2010; Schumacher 2012;

Schumacher et al. 2013; Arndt 2013). Still, there is an increasing body of literature that casts doubt on the assumption that welfare state reform always is electorally risky. Armingeon and Giger (2008), for example, demonstrate that voters punished the governing parties only when retrenchment was a key issue during the election campaign. This happened in around 25 percent of the 30 cases in which benefits were cut by at least 5 percent, and in those cases, the governing parties lost at least 5 percent of the votes because of the retrenchment. Since it is not known beforehand whether the welfare state will emerge as a top issue in an election campaign, the risk involved in pursuing unpopular measures thus still seems high. Moreover, Giger and Nelson (forthcoming) show that only voters with favorable welfare state attitudes who do not believe that the welfare state hampers the economy punish retrenching governments. This result offers a micro-foundation for an earlier finding that religious and liberal conservative parties may even gain votes after retrenchment (Giger and Nelson 2011). Schumacher et al.'s (2013) results corroborate Giger and Nelson's conclusion that the risk of reform varies across parties: reform is electorally risky especially for the so-called pro-welfare parties, which were involved in the buildup of the welfare state.

Institutional Resilience

In addition to the political hurdle to welfare state reform, there are institutional hindrances fostering resilience. A social program typically progresses in an institutionally path-dependent way (lock-in) that eschews sudden large deviations. The reason is that long-term commitments make any fundamental change of its rules and regulations (e.g., radical retrenchment or restructuring) extremely costly, risky, and uncertain and therefore unlikely. Path dependence refers to self-reinforcing processes that exhibit increasing returns (Pierson 2000b, 2004: chapter 1). Increasing returns imply that once a path is chosen, the probability of further steps along that same path rises with each move down the path. The reason is that the costs of reversal (suddenly taking a different path) are rapidly becoming prohibitively high (see Swank 2001). Imagine, for instance, that policymakers at some point decided to introduce an unfunded pension system, which pays benefits directly out of current workers' social security contributions and taxes (pay-as-you-go). With population aging, that is, a rising number of pensioners and a decreasing number of contributors, the pay-as-you-go system gets into financial trouble. Changing to a funded system (contributions are invested in funds and future returns are to cover benefits), however, would be exceptionally costly because the current generation of workers and employees would not only have to provide the contributions for the current retirees but also the payment for their own future retirement. Hence, such path-breaking reforms are exceedingly difficult, even when they are deemed to be prudent or even necessary. As Jochem (2007: 262) further explains, political institutions introduced earlier in history "have specific effects on policy making processes at later points in time, even if the political basis which led to the introduction of these institutions years ago [is] no longer in place." Path dependence suggests that all change is bounded (see Pierson 2001a; Streeck and Thelen 2005), although this should not be taken to mean that no change is possible (Mahoney and Thelen 2010).

The welfare state's institutional rigidity also derives from rule-governed veto points that enhance actors' capacity to obstruct reform. Veto points are institutionally defined "instances in the policy making process at which a suitable coalition of actors can prevent the adoption of a given piece of legislation" (Bonoli 2001: 238; see Immergut 2010: 232–236). Hence, countries with the fewest veto points, and therefore the highest degree of power concentration, should display the highest degree of welfare state reform. For instance, the capacity for welfare state reform should be greater in Westminster countries like the United Kingdom than in political systems with a high level of power fragmentation (a low level of power concentration) such as Switzerland and the United States. Table 2.1 presents data on the institutional veto points and veto players (the so-called partisan veto points; see Tsebelis 1995, 2002) in seven countries that we selected as representatives of different types of welfare states for illustrative purposes in this book.[2] The United Kingdom has both the lowest number of institutional veto points and the lowest number of partisan ones. The United States has the most institutional veto points of these seven cases, but shares the bottom position with the United Kingdom with respect to partisan veto points (i.e., veto players). Italy, a country with a relatively low number of institutional veto points, has the most partisan veto points. Also the rank-order of the other cases differs somewhat across the two types of veto points, though not as dramatically as in the cases of Italy and the United States. This variation indicates that it matters which type of veto points are considered for the conclusions drawn. Most empirical work in welfare state research focuses on institutional veto points rather than veto players (but see e.g., Becher 2010).

Some quantitative macro-comparative empirical studies support the hypothesis that countries with a low number of veto points reform more than countries with a high number of veto points (e.g., Swank 2001; see Van Kersbergen 2006: 390–391). However, the reverse relationship is also plausible: the higher the level of power concentration, the lower the degree of welfare reform (Ross 1997). The argument then is that political systems concentrating political power also concentrate political accountability. Consequently, "voters know very well

---

[2] We explain the concept and measurement of welfare state regimes in detail in Chapter 4. The selected countries here are the United Kingdom and the United States as liberal cases, Germany as a conservative case, and Denmark and Sweden as the social democratic cases (Esping-Andersen 1990). We also look at the Netherlands as a hybrid welfare state regime (Vis et al. 2008) because this country's welfare state combines traits from both the social democratic and the conservative regimes. Italy is often treated as a conservative case but might also be put into a separate, Mediterranean regime (with Spain, Portugal, and Greece). See section 2.5.

TABLE 2.1. *Veto points and veto players, selected countries, 1980–2005*

Country	Potential institutional veto points	Institutional veto points after absorption	Typical governments	Institutional veto points		Partisan veto points	
				Range	Average	Range	Average
UK	Single member districts	None	Single party	0	0	1	1
US	President Bicameralism Supreme court Federalism single member districts	President House of Representatives Senate	Single party	1–4	3.69	1	1
Germany	Bicameralism Constitutional court Federalism	Second chamber Constitutional court	Multi-party majority	0–2	1.70	2–3	2.56
NL	Bicameralism	First chamber Second chamber	Multi-party majority (minority)	0–2	0.03	2–3	2.43
Denmark	Referendum	Parliament	Multi-party minority	0–1	0.94	1–4	2.64
Sweden	None except parliament	Parliament	Single-party minority or multi-party minority/majority	0–1	0.94	1–4	1.52
Italy	Bicameralism	Chamber of Deputies, Senate	Multi-party minority/majority	0–2	0.24	1–8	5.12

Source: Immergut (2010: 233–235, table 15.1).

who they may blame for unpopular cutbacks, which may lead politicians who want to be re-elected to shy away from welfare state retrenchment" (Starke 2006: 109). In political systems where power is fragmented, conversely, avoiding blame for unpopular measures is easier (Weaver 1986; Pierson 1994), which may result in more – not less – retrenchment. This so-called accountability effect (Bonoli 2001: 244–245) is likely to be stronger in (1) highly competitive systems, because these have a credible opposition party that can step up as an alternative for the government, and in (2) single-member constituencies, because the losses due to electoral punishment have a larger effect on the number of seats in parliament than in proportional representation systems. Furthermore, the accountability effect would also be stronger close to an election, because politicians then focus more on public opinion. The so-called power concentration effect, conversely, would be stronger when the electoral term has just commenced. Consequently, the accountability effect is stronger in the United States than in most European countries. In the latter countries, the accountability effect varies over time due to the combination of the different conditions identified earlier.

It is important to note that the availability of veto points, for instance, in a federalist system, does not mean that these veto points are actually used to obstruct policymaking. Veto points' presumed impeding effect makes sense only if one assumes that the dominant political actors have clearly distinct preferences regarding the welfare state (Manow 2005). Only under this condition can an anti-welfare party use the institutional veto points available in the system to block the spending preferences of the pro-welfare party. This is not always the case. In Germany, for example, both the social democrats and the Christian democrats were in favor of welfare state expansion, whereas "what hinders reform efforts is not so much the blocking effect of federal structures, but rather the dynamics of inter-party competition" (Manow 2005: 225).

The influence of veto players on the duration of the adoption and the outcome of social entitlement bills also depends on who initiates the bill (Däubler 2008). The following factors delay the adoption of bills initiated by government parties in parliament: (1) a larger number of coalition parties; (2) a greater ideological distance between them; (3) a second, upper chamber, which is controlled by opposition parties and when this chamber's approval is necessary; (4) a situation where the most left-wing veto player is actually quite right-wing; and (5) a bill that deals with expansionary or so-called mixed policies (i.e., policies mixing retrenchment and expansion). Interestingly, these factors have no bearing on the bills initiated by the cabinet. This does not exclude the possibility that veto players have been important during the pre-parliamentary phase, because probably they have been consulted during the preparatory stages of the cabinet bill. It is also very likely that their wishes, at least to some extent, have been taken up in the cabinet bill. However, whereas we would not dismiss a possible effect of veto players, it may make sense to disentangle what the cabinet proposes and does at the meso level, and what individual government parties propose and do.

Power sharing (i.e., the existence of veto players) is reconcilable with high reform capacity if the government controls the policy areas included in the reform (Lindvall 2010). Veto players will also have to be confident that they remain veto players in the future. In general, the empirical track record of pension reforms in Europe fails to lend support to the argument that veto points can only hinder reform or that a low number of veto points facilitates reform. However, in countries with a high number of veto points, reforms tend to take the form of package deals, including side payments (i.e., these reforms are multidimensional; see Chapter 1).

From the mid-1990s up to the early 2000s, many a scholar walked in the footsteps of Paul Pierson and Gøsta Esping-Andersen – and others – by examining the remarkable stability of developed democracies' postwar welfare states. The combination of the political hindrances and the institutional difficulties discussed earlier impedes reform, so the theoretical argument goes. And if this argument is correct, the lack of reform in turn strengthens these obstacles to reform.

Given the strong reasons for the absence of reform and against the backdrop of the earlier predictions of welfare state crisis and collapse, it may not be surprising that for a long time, comparative welfare state scholars were interested almost exclusively in explaining the remarkable lack of reform. Pierson (1996: 179) ended his analysis of welfare state resilience with the following assessment and prediction:

Governments confronting the electoral imperatives of modern democracy will undertake retrenchment only when they discover ways to minimize the political costs involved. But ... such techniques are hard to come by. While this analysis suggests some of the possible keys to variation in policy outcomes, the most significant finding concerns not variation but commonality. Everywhere, retrenchment is a difficult undertaking. The welfare state remains the most resilient aspect of the postwar political economy.

Pierson (1998) came to characterize welfare states as "immovable objects" that remained fortresses of stability in spite of the "irresistible forces" that were pushing for change. More recently, Pierson (2011: 15) stressed that given "acute demographic and economic pressures over a period of more than three decades, along with a broad decline in the power resources of organized labor," we should have seen much more dramatic changes in benefit levels and social spending than actually occurred. Pierson still underscores the fact that when one looks at the coverage and replacement rates of major social schemes over the long run since the golden age of the welfare state, stability is by far the welfare state's most striking feature. Although none of the welfare state regimes was expected to display major reforms at the time, some variations across regimes were envisioned. Particularly, the conservative welfare state regime was considered the most prone to stability. In the words of Esping-Andersen (1996b: 66–67), the conservative welfare states were "frozen" and "immune to change".

2.4. EXPLAINING WELFARE STATE REFORM
BY INSTITUTIONAL CHANGE?

The institutionalists are correct that welfare states have been remarkably resistant to the types of assaults assumed to stem from demographic and economic pressures and from political actors who favor the dismantling of the welfare state. In addition, there were also powerful economic reasons that worked against cutbacks (cf. Glennerster 2010: 692–693). The first economic factor concerns market failure. The very same logic that incited state intervention to ensure social risks in the first place is now at work as a shield against radical cutbacks. The state intervened to cover, for instance, the risk of unemployment, precisely because markets failed to do so. The retreat of the state for budgetary reasons from this social insurance and from other social risk provisions (including pensions) does not make much sense precisely because private solutions are known to have failed and are certain to fail again. Hence, it is not likely that radical retrenchment or restructuring will take place here.

Another economic reason for the difficulty of welfare state cutbacks and restructuring is that the privatization of labor-intensive services does not help to contain costs, but increases the price of such services:

private human services typically sell ... *more* intensive staffing by *higher* qualified more expensive staff. Private schools sell small classes and good staffing quality. In the United Kingdom between 1996/7 and 2001/2 school fees rose by 34 per cent. From 2001/2 to 2006/7 they rose by 39 per cent. This not only outstripped general inflation but was more than *twice* the increase in earnings of those in professional and managerial jobs. The private sector has thus barely grown. Health cost inflation is similarly a problem for private health insurance companies and employers worldwide. (Glennerster 2010: 692, emphasis in original)

Note that welfare state resilience does not imply the absence of reform. In fact, many of the institutionalist studies inspired by Pierson's work failed to identify the small, but – once accumulated – ultimately significant reforms that have been implemented over the past decades. Moreover, the institutionalist analyses encountered large explanatory difficulties when they discovered the – sometimes radical and restructuring – reforms that also have been occurring in most welfare states. Concentrating on the unexpected phenomenon of the absence of change and in spite of Pierson's stress on historical dynamics, the institutionalist school became entirely preoccupied with the *statics* of the welfare state. At the same time, however, the very real *dynamics* of ongoing reform were producing not only piecemeal solutions of a sort for adaptive problems, with sometimes dramatic consequences, but institutional and pathbreaking reforms (i.e., restructuring) as well.

One of the major puzzles for welfare state research, therefore, came to revolve around the question of why reforms can and do take place in spite of the institutional mechanisms and political resistance that seem to work against them (see Palier 2010a, b). Moreover, how much adjustment is there? In which direction are changes moving? The blindness of institutionalist approaches to the real changes that have been occurring also teaches us something about what we should have been studying all along, namely, how the welfare state, taken as a complex amalgam of social policies, institutions, programs, and interests, has continuously been adapting to the endogenous and exogenous challenges and threats it faces. As we stated in Chapter 1, welfare state reform is not something that appeared only recently but must be seen as a permanent feature. Given that the welfare state's environment has changed so much over time, the welfare state should have been reformed along with these changes; if not, we would be observing much more policy drift (i.e., policies that clearly malfunction in terms of social outcomes but that continue because of the conscious decision not to change them) than we actually do. Theorizing welfare state resilience only in terms of the absence of reform thus seriously underestimates the real amount of change that has been going on.

More recently, we have seen a wave of studies that examine welfare state reform rather than its stability. In these contributions, institutions typically still play some explanatory role, but now usually supplemented with an actor-centered account of power and political choice. This holds, for example, for Vail's (2010) study of social and economic policy reform in France and Germany since the 1970s. Vail identifies newly emerging coalitions that stimulate reform and argues that the context of austerity alters the political dynamics of reform in two ways. First, and leading to the new coalitions, the traditional political arrangements can no longer cope with the contemporary socioeconomic challenges. Simultaneously, the traditional models of welfare capitalism are no longer able to manage the social and political unrest resulting from the socioeconomic changes and, especially, the declining economic performance. It is thus the combination of "political and economic pressures for reform and the failure of inherited arrangements to fashion coherent responses to them" that allow for new models of governance to arise in France and Germany (Vail 2010: 11).

Institutions also still play a role in Häusermann's (2010) study of pension reform in three continental countries – France, Germany, and Switzerland – between the 1970s and 2004. However, Häusermann shows that with institutional veto players it is the degree of coalitional flexibility (i.e., the capacity of political parties, trade unions, and employers' organizations to join reform coalitions) that influences the capacity and opportunity for policy change. In the presence of institutional veto players, policy change can come about only as a result of coalitional flexibility. If there are no institutional veto players, such large coalitions are not necessary. Häusermann argues that "power fragmentation in the corporatist and partisan arenas enhances the chances for reform, because this fragmentation allows for more variable coalition formation" (91). Reform capacity in this regard depends on the interaction between institutional veto players and coalitional flexibility. Häusermann's analysis demonstrates

that a high number of veto players is not necessarily an institutional impedi-
ment to reform but may actually strengthen the potential for reform.

[I]n a context where any government has to foster encompassing coalitions (with formal or de facto veto players, in parliament, or in the ranks of their own party) as a precondition for successful policy changes, countries with a tradition of consensus politics
and negotiation may have a comparative advantage. Thereby, a high number of veto
points (i.e., a high number of power-sharing institutions) may turn from an obstacle to
an asset for a country's reform capacity. (Häusermann 2010: 202–203)

For Häusermann (2010: 7), an important motive for reform is institutional
misfit, i.e., "a clash between evolving structures and stable institutions [that]
generates institutional friction." The actors suffering from this misfit have a
clear incentive to pursue reform, while those not suffering from it do not have
such an incentive or have a stronger preference for the existing status quo.
This amounts to the different reform dimensions mentioned earlier that, in
turn, allow for different crosscutting conflict lines that split social interests
(e.g., labor versus capital on one dimension and insiders versus outsiders on
another). This, finally, enables political exchange. Summing up, "successful
welfare state modernization in continental Europe depends on the capacity of
policy makers to build encompassing reform coalitions in a multidimensional
policy reform space. And this capacity, in turn, depends on their strategies of
coalitional engineering and on the institutional framework within which they
deploy these strategies" (Häusermann 2010: 7).

Similarly, Engeli and Häusermann (2009) stress governments' room for
maneuvering even within stable institutions. The degree to which a government can successfully implement policy change depends on the facility of coalition engineering. Two features of every policy – (1) its multidimensionality (by
serving multiple goals and purposes) and (2) the heterogeneity and instability
of actor coalitions – affect governments' capacity to engage in strategies of
coalition engineering. There are three such strategies, of which the use depends
on the number of veto points in the system as well as on the configuration
of actors and interests. The first line of attack is to try to divide the opposition through political exchange and by confronting veto players with a policy
reform consisting of various nonsubstitutable elements. A second technique is
to try to reach ambiguous agreement on an "ambiguous" compromise with
which most actors agree, even though they may vary in their policy goals. The
third strategy consists of the attempt to exclude and delegitimize the opposition to foster a winning coalition (1–2, 8ff).

We agree with Engeli and Häusermann that far-reaching welfare state reform
can be achieved in more ways than through external shocks (particularly crises) only, as most institutionalist analyses and policy studies hitherto assumed.
We also agree that not only endogenous dynamics and "change agents" drive
the incremental institutional changes, implying that the extent and direction of
the change are not inherent in the institutions. Governments have more options

to create their own room for maneuvering and to engineer reform. In other words, there is more room for reform than is often suggested in the literature. But there is something missing in Engeli and Häusermann's theory, namely, an answer to the question of what triggers governments to try to find the room to maneuver and implement different types of reforms. Though potentially successful, each of the three strategies for coalition engineering clearly involves quite a bit of hassle, to say the least. So why go about doing that? Here is where our open functional approach will offer a more complete picture because it also helps to identify the triggers for reform, that is, the answer to why governments would want or feel the need to go through all this trouble at all.

The description of extreme stalemate by a large part of the institutionalist literature fails to characterize well the period of the 1990s, arguably the pinnacle of institutional confinement and political gridlock, especially in continental Europe, for it completely ignored the very real changes that – even in *reformstau* Germany – were permanently going on (Van Kersbergen 2012). The institutionalists are to be blamed here for what we can now identify – admittedly with some benefit of hindsight – as a misleading approach to the development of welfare states. While the very real political dynamics of ongoing reform were producing solutions for adaptive problems or, alternatively, fostered policy drift, the institutionalists studied the statics of the welfare state. The occurring reforms as well as the conscious decision not to respond to the changing context of social policies, of course, created a mass of anomalies for the institutionalists. By now it has become clear that research should have been focusing on why and how welfare states are continuously adapting to the endogenous and exogenous challenges they face. Explaining welfare state reform, we claim, involves recognition of the extent to which reform in its various guises is a response to functional pressures. For this, we introduce our open functional approach.

2.5. INTRODUCING THE OPEN FUNCTIONAL APPROACH TO WELFARE STATE REFORM

We propose an open functional approach (see Becker 2009) to welfare state reform. This approach recognizes the causal effect of political agency and ideas on policy change, but it preserves the notion that it is first and foremost the selectivity of the functional context of political action that controls which political actors are likely to prevail and which reform ideas will matter and how. This open functional approach allows us to examine the socioeconomic, institutional, and political opportunities and constraints of reform; explain how such opportunities and constraints emerge; and discuss which consequences they have. We adopt and build on important insights from mainstream comparative welfare state research, particularly (1) the challenges-capabilities-vulnerabilities approach advanced in the contributions to the seminal Scharpf and Schmidt (2000) volumes; and (2) the policy learning approach, originally proposed by Hall (1993) and further developed by, among others, Visser and Hemerijck (1997: chapter 3), Hemerijck and Schludi (2000), and Hemerijck (2013). Much more explicitly than in these approaches and in sharp contrast to constructivist approaches, however, we stress that "objective" pressures for change, which stem from the international and domestic environment, are vitally important in accounting for the qualities of the context in which political actors make decisions or nondecisions on different types of welfare state reform.

Our open functional approach understands the challenges that welfare states face as functional demands for policy change whenever such challenges can be shown to threaten social policy arrangements existentially. These are "objective" problem pressures because they do not depend on political choice. However, because it is difficult to determine that a social policy arrangement faces an existential threat, we place the term "objective" between inverted commas. The point we wish to stress is that the functional problem pressure controls which political actors are likely to make a difference for policymaking and which range of ideas they are willing and/or able to consider. The "objective" problem pressure generates a selective context that tends to facilitate the adoption of certain ideas and the neglect or abandonment of others. These ideas, in turn, affect the type of reform that political actors will pursue. Different ideas may thus lead to different reform proposals, but not all ideas are equally feasible in a given functional and necessarily selective context.

Whether welfare state reform, especially a major departure from customary social policy practices and well-entrenched arrangements (i.e., radical reform such as restructuring or severe retrenchment), can be implemented or not hinges on the extent to which political actors (political parties, policymakers, governments) are capable of circumventing the social and political resistance against the reform. One important way of achieving this is via blame avoidance strategies (e.g., Pierson 1994; Vis and Van Kersbergen 2007, see Hood 2011), like finding a scapegoat to blame for the measures taken. Another would be to invoke a crisis imperative (Kuipers 2006) to make the blame-avoiding case that no matter which party or government rules, a radical reform will have to take place. Blame-avoidance strategies are politically needed because welfare state reform is typically an electorally risky endeavor that may cost the governing party or parties votes, as we discussed earlier. This holds a fortiori for radical reform. Whereas there are various mechanisms that link objective pressures to welfare state reform, we argue that blame avoidance is a particularly important strategy for political actors aiming at radical reform.

Functional pressures require that political actors respond; they are compelling forces. However, this does not imply that political actors will indeed always react or will always respond functionally. On the contrary, the neglect to reform, the conscious decision not to act (policy drift), and erroneous responses are all distinct possibilities. But inadequate responses will cause the system to falter and it is this particular feature of functional linkages that embodies a very powerful incentive for reform. Functional requirements are therefore critical aspects or components of the structural context of political behavior: they are constraints on political actors. Such constraints are selective and restrictive to the extent that they favor certain actors over others, limit the policy options that actors can choose from and enact, and encourage certain rather than other actions or nonactions. But they can also be enabling and powerful drivers to the extent that they open up new options and opportunities for reform by enhancing certain actors' capacity to act and by inciting them to action.

This theoretical lens helps us to explain why there can still be different responses, including nonresponses, to the same types of functional demands – the reason that our functional approach is defined as "open." Any explanation of different types of welfare state reform solely in terms of functional pressures would be incomplete. This is because we must also provide an account for the mechanisms that link the actual reform strategies that actors choose and the functional demands that make themselves felt within the context of political action. In other words, we still wish to explain how and when welfare state reform takes place (or not) that is functional (or not).

Welfare states, in one form or the other, have come about in all advanced capitalist democracies (Flora and Heidenheimer 1981a). Our open functional approach applies primarily to such countries. These are the countries that arguably have experienced a "full circle" of development, starting with a few tentative social programs to cater to specific needs and risks, such as an industrial accident scheme, to fully fledged, encompassing welfare states. All the countries that we examine here – Australia, Canada, Ireland, New Zealand, the United Kingdom, the United States, Austria, Belgium, France, Germany, the Netherlands, Italy, Switzerland, Denmark, Finland, Sweden, and Norway – have done so in a context of democracy and capitalism. In this regard, the welfare states that are rapidly arising and taking shape in more recently developed countries and newly emerging economies differ substantially from these older ones (see, e.g., Jones 1993; Glatzer and Rueschemeyer 2005; Walker and Wong 2005; Segura-Ubiergo 2007; Haggard and Kaufman 2008; Chan et al. 2008; Schubert et al. 2009; Castles et al. 2010; Huber and Stephens 2012; Hudson and Kühner 2012; Kam 2012). The verdict is still out as to whether or to what extent the theories and approaches that explain the developments in advanced capitalist democracies also hold for these newer and developing welfare states, but we hope that the open functional approach to welfare state reform we advance in this book may be of some use.

Whereas all advanced nations have become welfare states, they have not emerged in identical forms. The variation is vast in such features as levels of social spending, risk coverage, institutional makeup and financing structure, effectiveness, political entrenchment, and popularity among the public. However, the observed variation is not random but distinctly patterned. Anticipating our justification in Chapter 4 and acknowledging possible converging trends in most recent times (see Schmitt and Starke 2011), we hold that Esping-Andersen's (1990, 1999) classic cataloging of welfare states in different types or regimes – namely, a liberal, conservative, and social democratic regime, and possibly a fourth Southern European or Mediterranean regime – is still useful for empirical and heuristic purposes (for important updates of Esping-Andersen's work, see Scruggs and Allan 2004, 2006, 2008; Paetzold 2012; for exhaustive empirical analyses of regime characteristics, see Goodin et al. 1999; Vrooman 2009: chapter 4; Ferragina and Seeleib-Kaiser 2011; Ferragina et al. 2012). In the chapters that follow, we therefore group the countries according to regime type and pay special attention to the United Kingdom and the United States as illustrative liberal cases, to Sweden and Denmark as representative members of the social democratic cluster, to Germany as the leading exemplar of the conservative regime, and to Italy as perhaps belonging to a fourth Mediterranean regime. We look at the Netherlands as a hybrid case that is difficult to place in one of the typology's categories (see Vis et al. 2008 and Chapter 4).

2.6. CONCLUSION

Historically, industrialization and the emergence of capitalist markets are the macro-developments against which the rise of the welfare state must be explained. The welfare state was the way in which society came to terms with the consequences of modernization. The enormously dynamic character of capitalism implies that political actors are permanently confronted with new social, economic, and political issues to solve. Since the capitalist system has an inbuilt tendency to claim noncapitalist sectors of society and to produce periodic crises, the welfare state must respond and seems to move from crisis to crisis too. Its demise has been predicted more than once. Yet, in the light of the permanently changing circumstances of development and recurring economic tribulations, the welfare state's survival skills have proven to be remarkably well developed.

The welfare state is still around, but this fact and sign of stability should not be taken to mean that it has resisted the pressure to reform. On the contrary, we take this notable accomplishment of survival "against all odds" as an indication that, in fact, reform must have been a requirement of the welfare state's continued existence. To uncover in which crucial areas and under what constraints reform must have taken place so as to guarantee the welfare state's persistence, we need to focus on the complex political interconnections between the motivations of social and political actors, the driving forces of development, the sorts of public policy considerations actors struggle with, the values that underpin their choices, and the mechanisms of power that relate these. This is the task we take up in the next chapter.

3

The Logics of the Welfare State

Why Did We Need a Welfare State in the First Place and How Did We Get It?

3.1. INTRODUCTION

Looking back at history, we have a tendency to impute values to welfare state arrangements that were not necessarily part of the motivation of political actors when they designed and implemented social policy. For instance, for many people the first and foremost association with the welfare state concerns values such as equality, solidarity, and social justice. And surely, socialists used to underpin their reform proposals with references to these values. For others, however, the welfare state is primarily about collective solutions to social needs and misery, and about social order. And indeed, many of the liberal, conservative, and Christian social reformers saw themselves as pragmatic politicians experimenting with social laws that would substitute for charity and other traditional forms of social security. Still others tend to stress the social control and discipline that are exerted through social legislation. And yes, the rich did see poverty and deficient urban sanitation as threats to their own safety and health, and they did fear the revolting masses and hoped to quiet them down with social policy. Such considerations can be seen as social actors' motivations or as important *effects* and *forms* of modern social policy in the welfare state.

With the benefit of hindsight and with better theoretical understanding of developments in various nations, we may be able to capture what we propose to call the *rationales* or *logics* of the welfare state: a conscious reconstruction by us as researchers of what we consider to be the main motivations, driving forces, considerations, values, and causal mechanisms behind welfare state development. With the idea of a rationale or logic, we do not claim any historical specificity or possibility of social scientific generalization. Rather, we introduce a heuristic device that can help us reveal and stylize analytically the complex political interconnections between the motivations of social and political actors (ideas, interests, power, etc.), driving forces (demographics, democratization, globalization, etc.), public policy considerations (security, health, efficiency, affluence, etc.), values (equality, solidarity, freedom, autonomy, etc.), and causal mechanisms (power mobilization, elections, policy learning, etc.). With these logics, we can sketch the broader context of the political opportunities and constraints of welfare state reform and answer the first big question: why did we need a welfare state in the first place and how did we get it? Analytically, we distinguish four rationales or logics that are, however, interconnected and partly overlapping:

1. *A logic of socioeconomic development and modernization,* whose dynamics tend to challenge and break up an existing social equilibrium, hence generating functional requirements and pressures to adapt and find a new balance for societal integration. Typical elements and keywords of this reasoning are capitalist development and dynamics, the making of markets, industrialization, postindustrialization, tertiarization, and (re-) commodification;

2. *A logic of political integration and state-building,* where social policies appear as major functional instruments of social control and political community and identity building in the hands of ruling elites. The representative vocabulary includes social policy as statecraft, social rights and citizenship, political legitimacy, national and territorial integration, social policy as power mobilization, and equality and solidarity;

3. *A logic of need satisfaction and risk reapportioning,* where welfare state intervention primarily serves to pool and redistribute social risks in such a way that key social needs are satisfied and that risks are covered collectively. Examples of the characteristic terminology are equality and equity, market failure, adverse selection, moral hazard, compulsory social insurance, and (new) social risks;

4. *A logic of class politics and redistribution,* where the power of classes and their representatives as well as the political coalitions among them determine the extent and type of welfare state intervention. Here we characteristically find such terms as stratification, mobilization, power resources, decommodification, redistribution, and the democratic class struggle.

3.2. LOGIC I: SOCIOECONOMIC DEVELOPMENT AND MODERNIZATION

Which societal forces drove the welfare state's emergence and historical development? To which emerging needs was welfare state intervention an answer? Why did traditional forms of social protection become obsolete? What is the relationship between socioeconomic growth and social policy development? The answers to such questions should help us understand better whether, under which conditions, and to what extent the forces that have been responsible for the welfare state's emergence and growth still shape the opportunities and constraints of welfare state reform.

Widespread poverty has been a major impetus for the development of the welfare state (Alber 1982). By no means was the problem of the poor a phenomenon of modernity per se. Before the industrial revolution, Poor Laws, which were introduced between the 16th and the 18th centuries, were already catering to the poor in agrarian societies, where markets were not dominant (Rimlinger 1971: 36). In medieval Europe, poor relief in the form of charity had been relatively uniform, although after the Reformation the attitude toward the poor came to depend on the specific Christian denominations dominant in a society (Heclo 1974: 49; Kahl 2009). The traditional view was that because of the privileged position of the poor in Christ's teaching, poverty in principle was an acceptable or, as in the case of monks and – most extremely – the hermits, even a desirable state of being. "In Christian doctrine, poverty could be considered a virtue and begging an accepted means of livelihood" (Heclo 1974: 47). Christianity worked according to the precept that one feeds one's poor brother, but also followed the imperative that paupers work for their bread. And in practice, the poor were usually looked upon as a major nuisance and accordingly pestered, punished, and forced to work.

The Christian obligation to assist the poor became differentiated after the Reformation, and the differences among Roman Catholicism, Lutheranism, and Calvinism have left their imprint on contemporary systems of social assistance (Kahl 2009). Roman Catholicism remained closest to a charitable "feed the poor" attitude. In the course of the Counterreformation, the "Council of Trent [1545–1563] confirmed the traditional principles of poor relief and disapproved of the repression of begging. Because people were justified by faith in Christ and by a life of good works, almsgiving remained an individual act and begging was not forbidden" (Kahl 2009: 279). Calvinism, in contrast, squarely embraced a harsh work ethic. "Calvin excoriated begging and instead insisted that beggars should work, and that indulgences and almsgiving were emblematic of the corruption of the Church. He condemned those who 'live by others' instead of 'labouring with their own hands' as 'no better than a violent man and a robber'" (Calvin cited in Kahl 2009: 274). And Lutheranism defined a position somewhat in between, uplifting the status of work to an activity pleasing God and as a means to escape poverty. This implied that not working meant poverty and this meant displeasing God. The poor had to work, but "once they do, they have a right to a minimum standard of living; if they cannot work or if there is no work, they should still be supported" (Kahl 2009: 271).

Conversely, the nonreligious, mercantilist economic tradition stressed that the poor were valuable because they provided labor (Rimlinger 1971: 14–15). For society's best interest it was crucial that the poor continued working; otherwise they would not provide benefits for a wealthy society. The poor had to be kept poor and numerous, but their natural inclination was to remain idle if they were not forced to work (Rimlinger 1971: 17–18). So, here poor relief was primarily creating work for the poor and their children, accompanied by repression and subsidized wages (Rimlinger 1971: 19).

Although the emergence of the welfare state typically has been interpreted as a radical break with the preindustrial poor law tradition, Kahl (2009: 281–282) has argued that this is a simplistic interpretation at best: "Rather, poor relief was historically foundational for the welfare state because it was the first realm of public redistribution toward the needy and constituted a central part of early modern state capacity. The design of poor relief also conditioned to which extent state involvement in social assistance was morally acceptable and institutionally feasible." Welfare state interventions in the wake of the industrial revolution and the spread of markets, especially for labor, typically occurred as additions to existing relief systems. The Lutheran countries, which had developed nationally centralized and tax-based relief systems, were the first to introduce social insurance as a response to modernization.

Poverty in itself did not arise because of modernization, but the technological progress and new social structure emerging due to the industrial revolution and capitalist dynamics profoundly uprooted traditional social relations and, with that, the habitual ways in which poverty was dealt with. This is but one of the events by which modern Western societies were shaped by the industrial revolution that spread throughout Western Europe during the 18th and 19th centuries (Hobsbawn 1962, 1979). The industrial revolution transformed the face of poverty itself and made all existing arrangement to deal with it obsolete. According to the liberal economists, including Malthus, the existing poor laws, tailored to agrarian poverty, tended to have negative effects on economic growth and speeded up population growth (Rimlinger 1971: 39) and therefore had become dysfunctional. Relief of poverty not only harmed society at large but also the poor themselves. Relief reduced the incentive to work, made the poor dependent on relief, and reinforced their miserable situation. Malthus in England, like many others elsewhere, concluded that abolishing the poor laws was the only way to discipline the poor into work (Rimlinger 1971: 40). The notorious Speenhamland poverty relief system (introduced in 1795), for instance, guaranteed a worker an addition to his wage to make a sufficient family income (depending on the number of children and the price of bread), but created a poverty trap. In this system, employers had no incentive to pay higher wages and workers had no incentive to be productive. The Poor Law Commissioners' Report of 1834 called the system "a bounty on indolence and vice" and a "universal system of pauperism" (as cited in Deane 2000: 151). The new Poor Law fitted the emerging economic orthodoxy of laissez-faire capitalism that helped to create the free market and forced the poor to work, either in the market or in the workhouses.

The modernization perspective picks up from here and stresses that the starting point for welfare state development is modernization and its correlates industrialization, secularization, and democratization. The advent of industrial capitalism and the free labor market were causing large-scale disruption, and masses of people had to rely exclusively on the utterly insecure labor market to try to earn an income sufficient to survive, while the traditional means of social protection, including church-organized charity, were being annulled. The dynamics of industrial capitalism unleashed such transformative forces that the very cohesion and stability of society were at stake. Societal disruption, disorder, misery, and poverty pressed for intervention, while public protest and social and political movements demanded it.

But the revolution was more profound than that; it created a whole new social category of the laboring poor, that is, men, women, and children who, although they worked long and hard hours, could not make enough money to provide for themselves a decent living, or just a living for that matter. Some rebelled and some made it into the middle class. The majority of workers, however,

faced with a social catastrophe they did not understand, impoverished, exploited, herded into the slums that combined bleakness and squalor, or into the expanding complexes of small-scale industrial villages, sank into demoralization.... Towns and industrial areas grew rapidly, without plan or supervision, and the most elementary services of city life utterly failed to keep pace with it: street-cleaning, water supply, sanitation, not to mention working-class housing (Hobsbawn 1962: 241).

As a result, the laboring poor were not just poor; they were usually also ill – of cholera, typhoid, typhus, and tuberculosis.

Modernization, then, increased the pressure and demand for social protection, and state intervention through social policy not only expanded tremendously the state's physical and financial presence in society but also revolutionized the very character of the state itself as it gradually came to embrace as its major new tasks the relief of poverty, protection against the social risks of industrial society, and, finally, provision of social services (Flora and Heidenheimer 1981b: 23). A whole generation of welfare state scholars came to emphasize the causal link between industrialization (or modernization more generally) and welfare state development (Wilensky and Lebeaux 1958; Kerr et al. 1960; Cutright 1965; Pryor 1968; Rimlinger 1971; Jackman 1975; Wilensky, 1975).

However, the emergence and rapid spread of a fully fledged and self-regulating labor market in the 19th century, rather than industrialization, were the main forces responsible for the destruction of traditional social protection and the large-scale misery.[1] As Polanyi (1944 [1957]: 40–41) explained:

[O]nce elaborate machines and plant(s) were used for production in a commercial society, the idea of a self-regulating market was bound to take shape.... Since elaborate machines are expensive, they do not pay unless large amounts of goods are produced.

---

[1] The paragraphs on Polanyi are based on Manow and Van Kersbergen (2009). Many thanks to Philip Manow for allowing us to make use of this work.

They can be worked without a loss only if the vent of the goods is reasonably assured and if production need not be interrupted for want of the primary goods necessary to feed the machines. For the merchant, this means that all factors involved must be on sale, that is, they must be available in the needed quantities to anybody who is prepared to pay for them. Unless this condition is fulfilled production with the help of specialized machines is too risky to be undertaken both from the point of view of the merchant who stakes his money and of the community as a whole which comes to depend upon continuous production for incomes, employment, and provisions.

Recall that Polanyi argued that the capitalist market economy had the in-built tendency to transfer the market logic to all social spheres. A market *economy* could only function in a market *society* and such a society could not tolerate any interference: it had to be a self-regulating market *system*. "Self-regulating implies that all production is for sale on the market and that all incomes derive from such sales. Accordingly, there are markets for all elements of industry, not only for goods (always including services), but also for labor, land, and money" (Polanyi 1944 [1957]: 69). In other words, all goods and services became commodities.

The problem of the self-regulating market for labor was that it treated workers and their labor power as if they were nothing but commodities. The capitalist market had *commodified* labor. But Polanyi stressed that labor was obviously not produced for the sole purpose of selling. It was a fictitious commodity that was forced to function on the labor market as if it were a commodity. It was subject to the forces of supply and demand and subject to the price mechanism. But the problem was that physically labor could not function as a real commodity because if it really did so on an unrestrained market, it would destroy society.

For the alleged commodity "labor power" cannot be shoved about, used indiscriminately, or even left unused, without also affecting the human individual who happens to be the bearer of this peculiar commodity. In disposing of a man's labor power the system would, incidentally, dispose of the physical, psychological, and moral entity "man" attached to that tag. Robbed of the protective covering of cultural institutions, human beings would perish from the effects of social exposure; they would die as the victims of acute social dislocation through vice, perversion, crime, and starvation. (Polanyi 1944 [1957]: 73)

Labor needed to be subjected to the logic of the market, and the logic of the market had to be exported to the rest of society, which, as a result, became an "accessory of the economic system" (Polanyi 1944 [1957]: 75). The commodification of labor had disastrous consequences and "human society would have been annihilated but for protective countermoves which blunted the action of this self-destructive mechanism" (75). In other words, the commodification of labor was necessarily followed by its *decommodification*. This "double movement" of commodification and decommodification epitomizes the social history of the 19th century: "society protected itself against the perils inherent in a self-regulating market system" (76). The countermovement against commodification first took the form of labor legislation and later of modern social protection laws and explains their emergence. All modernizing countries experience first a phase in which the self-regulating labor market emerges, spreads, and causes pervasive dislocation and misery in society, and an ensuing stage in which destitution and other social maladies provoke the response of labor legislation and social protection measures.

The self-regulating market and its destructive forces establish an important functional demand for welfare state intervention that stresses that the commodification of labor power under capitalist markets involves a huge pressure to decommodify, which explains that all modernizing nations sooner or later develop social protection laws. Polanyi (1944 [1957]: 147) himself made a historical-comparative statement to demonstrate that a variety of social and political actors operating in very different regime types were all forced to save the capitalist market from itself:

Victorian England and the Prussia of Bismarck were poles apart and both were very much unlike the France of the Third Republic or the Empire of the Habsburgs. Yet each of them passed through a period of free trade and laissez-faire, followed by a period of antiliberal legislation in regard to public health, factory conditions, municipal trading, social insurance, shipping subsidies, public utilities, trade associations, and so on. It would be easy to produce a regular calendar setting out the years in which analogous changes occurred in the various years.

Polanyi (147–148) provided such a calendar or list and subsequently observed how diverging the supporting forces had been:

[I]n some cases violently reactionary and antisocialist as in Vienna, at other times "radical imperialist" as in Birmingham, or of the purest liberal hue as with the Frenchman, Edouard Herriot, Mayor of Lyons. In Protestant England, Conservative and Liberal cabinets labored intermittently at the completion of factory legislation. In Germany, Roman Catholics and Social Democrats took part in its achievement; in Austria, the Church and its most militant supporters; in France, enemies of the Church and ardent anticlericals were responsible for the enactment of almost identical laws. Thus under the most varied slogans, with very different motivations a multitude of parties and social strata put into effect almost exactly the same measures in a series of countries in respect to a large number of complicated subjects.

What we learn from these approaches is that a free and unregulated labor market in industrial capitalism generates insecurities and risks that require state intervention, that is, if such a market is to continue to exist and function. Intervention in the form of labor legislation is a *functional requirement* to the extent that a self-regulating market for the fictitious commodity labor would otherwise, to repeat Polanyi's words, cause human beings to perish from the effects of social exposure. The theory does not specify, however, which social and political forces actually take up the challenge of functional decommodification and under which conditions. It is for such insights that we turn to the other logics of the welfare state. We start with the logic of political integration and state-building, in which social policies emerge as major functional instruments for the ruling elites of social control and the building of political community and identity.

3.3. LOGIC II: POLITICAL INTEGRATION AND STATE-BUILDING

As Polanyi showed, around 1850 most industrializing capitalist countries already had some version of a modern poor law and had started to introduce labor protection measures. Social security or insurance policies, however, are of a more recent date. It was the Prussian state that had experimented with social insurance (health funds; see Hennock 2007) since the 1840s, but imperial Germany first introduced mandatory social insurance on a grand scale (Kuhnle and Sander 2010), such as a sickness insurance in 1883, an industrial accident scheme in 1884, and an old age and invalidity insurance in 1889. Other countries followed, some early (Austria), others comparatively late (the Netherlands). It has become a convention to date the welfare state's birth as 1883, when Bismarck introduced the first modern social insurance. Bismarck's social policy rationale was strongly anti-socialist in that it was consciously designed to temper the workers' revolutionary potential and to supplement the earlier repressive but ultimately unsuccessful antisocialist laws (*Sozialistengesetze*) from 1878 (Rimlinger 1971). It was an attempt to buy the workers' loyalty to the state.

Bismarck's etatism was a conservative state-building strategy (see Van Kersbergen and Kremer 2008) of granting social rights to enhance the integration of a hierarchical society, to forge a bond between workers and the state so as to strengthen the latter, to maintain traditional relations of authority between social and status groups, and to provide a countervailing power against the modernist forces of liberalism and socialism. This social policy strategy was accompanied by a cultural policy directed against Catholicism that was to combat the supranational or "ultramontane" orientation toward Rome of the Catholic *Reichsfeinde*. Here etatism led to the principle of "monarchical socialism," that is, "an absolutist model of paternal-authoritarian obligation for the welfare of its subjects" (Esping-Andersen 1990: 40).

Such etatism was translated into Bismarck's anti-socialist policies, into the political intention of his social policies, and into his proposal for a centralized state administration of the social schemes. Other conservatives stressed corporatist or romantic quasi-feudal solutions to the social question, familialism in policy, and, like the liberals, a general commitment to a limited state. But Bismarck's main worry was to turn the new *Reich* into a viable and strong nation-state and he therefore stressed etatist policies to counter pressures from liberals and conservatives alike. As Esping-Andersen (1990: 59) correctly noted:

When Bismarck promoted his first social-insurance schemes, he had to battle on two fronts: on one side against the liberals, who preferred market solutions, and on the other side against conservatives who sponsored the guild-model or familialism. Bismarck desired the primacy of etatism. By insisting on direct state financing and distribution of social benefits, Bismarck's aim was to chain the workers directly to the paternal authority of the monarchy rather than to either the occupational funds, or to the cash nexus.

Etatist social policy was state-building policy. The pioneering Bismarckian social policies, the major model for other countries on the European continent, were explicitly designed to attach the politically alienated working class directly to the state in order to tone down its revolutionary potential. The idea was that once the security of workers' income depended on the stability of the state, they would understand that revolutionary action was in fact alien to their own real interest. Such loyalty demanded state compulsory insurance and state subsidy so that workers would directly realize that it was state support that they were enjoying (Rimlinger 1968, 1971; Beck 1995). Bismarck saw a real political danger in a corporatist road, in which the state's support was only indirect, because he was convinced that to safeguard social order and to control the working class, it was necessary to let the state's presence be felt in the workers' life in a direct and clearly recognizable way. Unlike Bismarck, the upper bourgeoisie favored stateless corporatism because this offered the perfect moral model: social policies would not alter the status or income differentials and would at the same time reaffirm the hierarchical relationship between employers and employees within one institution under the employers' control. Faced with opposition from his closest allies, Bismarck understood that his pure etatist setup would never receive enough support to be implemented. The model was then adjusted somewhat in the corporatist direction. Employers were given the right to administer the social insurance schemes, but the state was to supervise. In the case of pensions, Bismarck managed to introduce his politically crucial state subsidy. "I will consider it a great advantage," Bismarck said in a debate on the 1889 old-age and invalidity pensions act, "when we have 700,000 small pensioners drawing their annuities from the state, especially if they belong to those classes who otherwise do not have much to lose by an upheaval and erroneously believe they can actually gain much by it" (as cited in Rimlinger 1968: 414).

Bismarck's social policy innovations are the main example of the etatist rationale underlying social policy and the welfare state. State-building efforts through social policy can more generally be interpreted according to an idea rooted in Marshall's (1964) theory of the codification and gradual extension of citizenship rights to increasingly larger segments of the population. Who counted as a citizen and would reap the fruits of social policy were crucial issues in the struggles over the building of the national state. Marshall had proposed viewing citizenship as consisting of civil, political, and social rights that corresponded to successive phases of the history of state-building:

The civil element is composed of the rights necessary for individual freedom – liberty of the person, freedom of speech, thought and faith, the right to own property and to conclude valid contracts, and the right to justice. By the political element I mean the right to participate in the exercise of political power, as a member of a body invested with political authority or as an elector of the members of such a body. By the social element I mean the whole range from the right to a modicum of economic welfare and security to the right to share to the full in the social heritage and to live the life of a civilized being according to the standards prevailing in a society. It is possible, without doing too much violence to historical accuracy, to assign the formative period in the life of each to a different century – civil rights to the eighteenth, political to the nineteenth and social to the twentieth. (Marshall 1964: 78, 81)

Civil rights, then, emerge as the rights of the individual to be free, particularly in the economic realm. *Political* rights are conceptualized as strengthened individual civil rights that both permitted groups to perform as legal individuals (as demonstrated by recognition of the right of collective bargaining) and established universal suffrage. The development of *social* rights was a consequence of trying to make civil rights actually work, of removing the barriers that blocked the full and equal exercise of civil and political rights. Capitalist market relations, poverty, and inadequate education tended to reduce these rights to mere formal capacities, a contradiction that created the necessity for social policy. The final phase of state-building was the development of social programs, which guaranteed that the members of a national community as citizens became inclusively entitled to the *material* promises of civil freedom and political equality.

The development of the welfare state was the final step in the territorial consolidation of the nation-state, because it was "the creation of territorial economic solidarity through measures to equalize benefits and opportunities both across regions and across strata of the population" (Flora 1999: 58). Rokkan (1975: 572, original emphasis) spoke of "the growth of *agencies of redistribution*, the building of public welfare services, the development of nationwide policies for the equalization of economic conditions, negatively through progressive taxation, positively through transfers from the better-off strata to the poorer, from the richer to the backward regions." In this view, the welfare state was essentially an answer to two problems of political development: "the formation of national states and their transformation into mass democracies after the French Revolution, and the growth of capitalism that became the dominant mode of production after the Industrial Revolution" (Flora and Heidenheimer 1981b: 22).

We already saw that the welfare state responded to the demands for social and economic security and that to the extent that the state intervened to deal with the destructive forces of the self-regulating capitalist labor market, its nature was transformed. States tended to become welfare states, albeit at a differing pace and in various forms (see Chapter 4), partly as a consequence of social and economic modernization. But politically, the welfare state started to play an important role in stabilizing the internal order of the democratizing national state. Following Rokkan's lead on "bounded structuring," Ferrera (2003: 618) has put it well:

This stabilization occurred through the anchoring of people's life chances to state-national institutions via the creation of explicit entitlements to (a modicum of) material resources. System-specific social rights became new, important ingredients of national membership spaces. Their introduction accelerated the fusion between the concept of citizenship and that of territorial identity. The basic duo cultural identity cum political participation – within a demarcated territory – was complemented with a novel social sharing component ..., reinforcing, on one hand, those feelings of "we-ness" that are a crucial underpinning of the national state construct and offering to national elites, on the other hand, new tools for differentiating between insiders and outsiders.

An additional advantage was that "we-ness" as a new foundation of the national state reinforced the ideological and emotional power resources on which the ruling elites could draw. The Rokkanian analysis reminds us that social policy was a crucial instrument for state formation. In fact, social policy has been a critical instrument of statecraft in the welfare state (Banting 1995) that has the capacity to foster loyalty to the national state. Governments of national states, in addition to guaranteeing territorial integrity, attempted to nourish the population's political commitment to their rule by providing social security, thus reorganizing the struggle over power as a positive-sum game and introducing clear benefits that affect people's interests also positively.

The social integration of the national state as part of territorial consolidation has nowhere emerged spontaneously and mechanically. The formation of national welfare states has been generally characterized by fierce social and political struggles, by failed attempts to appease class and ethnic wars, and by violent clashes over the construction of national solidarity (see Stjernø 2004). It was after the second world war that in Western Europe effective mechanisms of social redistribution were properly institutionalized and that the legitimacy of large-scale redistribution became fairly well entrenched.

Many analysts readily mention legitimacy as perhaps the *politically* most advantageous aspect of the welfare state. In an interesting but largely forgotten chapter, King (1983: 22) analyzed the welfare state as a bulwark of political stability and a cushion of change: "If it did not exist, political conservatives would have to invent it." Kuhnle (2003: 54) holds that "developed democratic welfare states are quite good at making adjustments of public policies in such a way that the legitimacy of the system can be preserved at the same time as new vitality and transformations in the economy can be brought about." The challenges-capabilities-vulnerabilities approach (see Chapter 2) advanced by Scharpf and Schmidt (2000: 3) even started from the assumption that work and welfare are so important for citizens' life chances that democratic polities' political legitimacy critically depends on the good performance of the welfare state. From a Marxist point of view, the welfare state's role or function was defined in terms of a "peace formula" and the political solution to major societal contradictions (Offe 1984: 147).

At some point, political actors may have recognized the beneficial political consequences of social policies – perhaps originally unintended – and begun to reinforce such effects to their own interest. One prominent example of how these political effects were cherished and buttressed concerns Scandinavian social democracy, where the social citizenship state became one of the most important power resources of the political movement (Esping-Andersen 1985a). The socialists saw social citizenship as a goal in itself but also as a means to power mobilization. Universalist social policy created inter-class solidarity and helped to build a national collective identity. Moreover, social policy liberated workers from the disciplinary whip of the labor market and made them stronger vis-à-vis employers. Finally, social policy advanced equality, a precondition for the other socialist goals. Esping-Andersen (1985a: 148–149) expected

the long run political fate of social democratic labor movements to be contingent on their ability to implement solidarity, decommodification, and equality through social legislation. Conversely, failure to implement a socialist alternative to liberal or conservative reformism would weaken the capacity for working-class political unity and social democratic power mobilization.

Another example would be Christian democracy's project of "social capitalism" as both a medium for and outcome of power mobilization in countries such as Germany, Italy, and the Netherlands. Cross-class coalitions, both among the electorate and within the parties, have distinguished Christian democratic parties. The cross-class appeal and the integration of various social groups have been important for building cross-class coalitions. This happened through exchange among groups, social compensation, and maintenance of extensive relations with affiliated social organizations. The sources of the welfare state's tax-benefit system provided the means for the so-called politics of mediation, that is, the ideologically (and in the case of Christian democracy also religiously) inspired, institutionally rooted, and politically practiced conviction that conflicts of social interests can and must be reconciled politically to foster solidarity (social democracy) or to restore the natural and organic harmony of society (Christian democracy), and helped to build cross-class political coalitions beneficial to Christian democracy (Van Kersbergen 1995, 1999).

   This reasoning in terms of the functional requirements and pressures of societal and political integration helps to disclose the two pivotal and beneficial integration effects of the welfare state as a structural component of postwar advanced industrial democracies. The first is *social integration* and concerns the variable extent to which social policies and welfare arrangements effectively mediate, regulate, and reconcile social conflicts – particularly, but not exclusively, class conflicts. The second is *national or territorial integration* and involves the extent to which the welfare state successfully and positively constructs and reinforces a national political community by redistributing means from the rich to the poor (both people and regions). Both effects have been critical for the continuation of nation-building, territorial reconsolidation, and the rebuilding of the political legitimacy of the nation-state after World War II (Milward 1992).

A social and political order can never be assumed to be inherently stable because social, economic, and political conditions change continuously, creating a permanent need to adapt (see Chapter 2). The reconciliation of social conflicts and the construction of a national political community have never been fixed properties of a polity because they are always built on social and political alliances whose institutionalization will be challenged. What we can learn for our purposes, then, is that social and political integration with the help of social policies is an adaptive process that is continuous, dynamic, and contingent. National welfare states, however stable they may have been and still seem, must constantly reaffirm and reinforce societal and political integration. Attempts to reform the welfare state, then, imply not only a change of policies but also the always politically risky job of redefining or reorganizing the once beneficial links between social policy and political order and legitimacy. The success of social policy, as an aid to nation-building and the construction of national identities, contributes to the political legitimacy of the welfare state through positive feedback mechanisms and is part of the reason that drastic welfare state reform is so difficult.

3.4. LOGIC III: SATISFACTION OF NEEDS AND RISK REAPPORTIONING

Regardless of whether political actors were carrying out the countermovement of decommodification (logic I) or were building nations and states (logic II), they still needed to formulate social policies that actually addressed the existing social needs, demands, and political goals of their societies. In line with Baldwin (1990) and Esping-Andersen (1999), we argue that the welfare state's rationale in addressing such needs and requirements has been less about socioeconomic equality and the redistribution of wealth from the rich to the poor, as many observers have supposed, than about the pooling and redistribution of social risks. A risk is defined as the probability of an event's occurring (e.g., an accident) times the impact of that event (say, income loss). We define a social risk as the – admittedly difficult to estimate – probability of a welfare loss associated with one's position in society and the life cycle. Thus Baldwin (1990: 1) argued:

Applying the instruments of social insurance on behalf of increasing numbers of citizens to ever greater varieties of risks and ill fortune, the welfare state decisively advanced society's ability to treat each of its members equally. It did so, however, less by redistributing wealth than by reapportioning the costs of risk and mischance. Insurance translates the effects of fate, luck and iniquitous social circumstance into the common denominators of cash, kind and services, then reallocates them so that the stricken bear no more than an average burden and those spared assume responsibility for events not directly affecting them. In terms of misfortune's consequences, all who are members of a common risk pool stand equal.

Welfare states, then, are supported by some idea of risk equality in the specific sense that Baldwin stresses, although the particular notions vary. Some welfare states put emphasis on individual *equity* with traditional, contribution-defined social insurance or status segmented insurance, whereas others stress *equality* with universal schemes that are designed to eliminate differences in class and status (Esping-Andersen 1999, see Chapter 4). Baldwin's lesson is that despite such differences, all welfare states aim at the protection against social risks. Equality first and foremost concerns whether individuals face similar risks that they can pool: "Risk categories," writes Baldwin (1990: 12), "are actors identified and given interests in common by their shared relations to the means of security, by their stake in or against the redistribution of risk promised by social insurance." This is what Baldwin called the possibility of solidarity: equality in real terms of people sharing risks.

But why and when does the state assume the responsibility to promote, organize, or even guarantee protection against social risks? How was this task taken up by social and political actors? What *is* the rationale here? We know from established welfare regime theory that the family, the market, and the state all play a role in the provision of work, welfare, and the protection against social risks. And we also know that these major institutions are not simply functional equivalents in the sense that they can deal with social risks interchangeably (Esping-Andersen 1990, 1999). A major reason for state intervention in the social distribution of risks, which complements the political integration and state-building argument discussed as logic II, is that the market and the family fail in covering social risks.

Market failure and market inefficiency are well-known phenomena (see Barr 2004).[2] According to the "invisible hand theorem" (Barr 2004: 73), markets clear if and only if all the model's so-called standard assumptions hold. The first assumption is *perfect competition*: "economic agents must be price-takers; and they must have equal power" (Barr 2004: 73). Market inefficiencies occur if price-taking is violated by, for instance, economic monopolies, or if power is unequally distributed. The second assumption is *the absence of market failures*, which is violated (1) in the case of public goods, which the market, inter alia, because of the free rider problem, cannot provide; (2) when external effects occur, that is, when costs (or benefits) conferred by A on B are not compensated (from A to B) (or paid by B to A); and (3) when there are increasing returns to scale for a firm or producer that force competitors without such an advantage to exit the market.[3] The model's third assumption is *perfect information* of the

---

[2] This section also gratefully makes use of De Beer et al. (2009).

[3] The most important characteristic of a public good is that those who do not pay for it cannot be excluded from its consumption. Someone who profits from a public good or service but does not contribute to covering the costs is a free rider. Increasing returns to scale occur when a producer increases resources as input, say, a doubling of labor and capital, but the output increases by more than double.

good's quality and price. This assumption is also often violated. In health care, for instance, evaluating quality as "good" (care, treatment) typically requires highly technical knowledge that is possessed only by the ones selling the good (e.g., doctors, specialists). Information is therefore costly to acquire and is not readily available. Moreover, there may be extremely high costs (e.g., in terms of health damage) resulting from poor or unavailable information and bad choices. Comparing prices is difficult if not impossible for most services, so here too, there is no perfect information. Finally, especially with a view to insuring future contingencies, perfect information about the future is obviously nonsensical. There is an important counterfactual rationale for the welfare state here. If we lived in a world of certainty, there would hardly be a welfare state. As Barr (2004: 79) summarizes the state of affairs in such a situation,

- Insurance is unnecessary, since there is no risk.
- People provide for their old age through voluntary saving and finance their education by borrowing in perfect capital markets. Thus consumption smoothing takes place through voluntary action using private institutions.
- Transient (i.e., temporary) poverty is also dealt with by borrowing or saving.... Dealing with poverty for someone who is not lifetime poor is more akin to consumption smoothing than to traditional poverty relief.
- The only reason for a welfare state in such a world is to provide poverty relief for a person who is lifetime poor.

The model's final assumption is *complete markets*, which "would provide all goods and services for which individuals are prepared to pay a price that covers their production costs" (Barr 2004: 74). This often does not occur, most famously in the case of public goods, but most relevantly here in the case of (almost) uninsurable risks, like unemployment. Failure of any of these assumptions leads to inefficiency and is (or might be) a justification for state intervention. The rationale of the welfare state thus emerges from a world that does not behave according to the invisible hand theorem.

Unemployment insurance is perhaps the clearest example to illustrate the economic theoretical rationale. The problem with insuring the risk of unemployment is that it is not a random or universal risk. In the case of unemployment, there are systematic externalities. A person's risk of unemployment is not independent of another person's risk of becoming unemployed. In periods of economic downturn, for example, many workers are laid off simultaneously. Still, the incidence of unemployment is difficult to predict, as is its duration and level. The uncertainty involved makes social risks special, because the probability of individual risks is hard to estimate or to calculate in an actuarial sense. As a result, an insurance company would need to create a very large financial buffer to cope with the possibility of a large number of insured individuals becoming unemployed at the same time. The contribution for the unemployment scheme would become prohibitively high.

Individual employees can estimate their own risk of unemployment to at least a reasonable extent. They know how they are doing in their jobs and how their firm or organization is doing (are future layoffs likely?). An insurance company can hardly estimate such individual risks and therefore cannot differentiate contributions (i.e., information asymmetry with employees having more information than insurance companies). This leads to "adverse selection," a situation in which an individual who is a poor risk can conceal this fact from the insurance company (Barr 2004: 109, 389). The insurance company would want to attract low risk employees ("good risks") and it offers a low contribution/low coverage/low benefit insurance, which is not attractive for the high risk group that prefers a higher risk coverage. The low risk employees leave the high coverage alternative, and as a result, the contribution is further raised. This causes even more employees to leave the high coverage scheme and choose the lower coverage option, causing more low risk employees to opt for insurance with an even lower coverage, and so on. The market for unemployment insurance fails as a consequence.

Generally speaking, insurance has the problem of "moral hazard: a situation in which an insured person can affect the insurance's company's liability without its knowledge" (Barr 2004: 111, see 392). Less formally put, moral hazard is the phenomenon in which people become less risk averse for a risk they are insured against. Losing your job is less serious when you can claim a benefit. The incentives for employees (and employers) to avoid unemployment become less strong, and so does the incentive to seek another job.

Because of adverse selection and moral hazard, private unemployment insurance is unlikely to develop. *Compulsory insurance* is a solution to adverse selection, where the "good risks" are made to contribute to covering the "bad risks" and the "bad risks" are compelled to participate. Differentiated contributions in the compulsory scheme can help to solve the problem of moral hazard. However, compulsory insurance does not solve the problem of the interdependence of individuals' unemployment risks as *social risks*, as a result of which insurance companies must keep large financial buffers or the state must guarantee benefits when insurers are in danger of going bankrupt. The conclusion is that a private insurance market for risks like unemployment is unlikely to develop or will cover only the least vulnerable fraction of workers. The solution to this problem was the development of a *public*, compulsory insurance with equal contributions,[4] which solves the problem of solidarity by avoiding adverse selection and the problem of prohibitively large financial

---

[4] We are disregarding a third option here: the labor union model or Ghent-system, primarily because historically these systems have all been absorbed by the state for reasons similar to why the private market option fails. The labor union model fails also because it necessarily excludes those outside the labor market, concentrates strongly correlated individual risks, and is financially unsustainable. In countries where a variant of the Ghent-system survived, it did so because the state (local government) subsidizes either the benefit (Belgium) or the contribution (Denmark) (see Alber 1981).

buffers because contributions can be increased retrospectively (in theory, if not necessarily in practice – as demonstrated by the debt crisis in Greece since 2009 – the state cannot go broke). In a word, the solution consisted of compulsory social insurance, which differs from private insurance in two crucial ways. As Barr (2004: 117, emphasis in original) argues:

First, because membership is ... compulsory, it is *possible* ... to break the link between premium and individual risk; a pooling solution is therefore an option. Second, the contract is usually less specific than private insurance, with two advantages: protection can be given against risks that the private market cannot insure ... ; and the risks can change over time.... [S]ocial insurance, in sharp contrast with actuarial insurance, can cover not only *risk* but also *uncertainty*.

Obviously, the problem of moral hazard is not solved by a public scheme. In fact, a passive public unemployment scheme with no challenger that competes on price (insurance contribution) reinforces moral hazard because there is no incentive to reintegrate workers into the labor market as soon as possible. The result is that a public unemployment insurance that fosters solidarity also tends to lead to higher levels of unemployment. For these reasons policymakers experimented with differentiation of contributions according to risk of individuals and sectors, with introducing some element of competition in the implementation of policies, and with setting eligibility criteria and other conditions (level of benefit, duration, waiting days, means tests) in such a way that they minimize job-seeking disincentives.

In sum, in terms of dealing with social needs and requirements, welfare is first and foremost about pooling and redistributing social risks. Compulsory social insurance emerges because social risks have special features that prohibit the development of private insurance markets. Some major social risks, such as illness and old age, are not class-specific (see Esping-Andersen 1999: 41–43) and are more generally associated with the life course. Here risk pooling is a distinct option for all and redistribution primarily takes place horizontally between risk categories. Some social risks, however, are strongly associated with one's position in the social structure. This holds particularly strongly for social class. Class risks, such as unemployment and work accident–related disability, are highly distinctive, because they demand a pooling of risks that also involves a politically contentious vertical redistribution of wealth and income, which brings us to the final logic of the welfare state: class politics, coalitions, and redistribution.

3.5. LOGIC IV: CLASS POLITICS, COALITIONS, AND REDISTRIBUTION

"Welfare states exist to meet the needs of their citizens. While this is only one of the welfare state's many raisons d'être, it would seem odd to defend a welfare state that did not at least do that: satisfy needs" (Zutavern and

Kohli 2010: 169). The modernization theories discussed under logic I (section 3.2) are *functionalist theories* that explain welfare states' origins and emergence by reference to the needs they fulfill. "Functionalist explanations," argue Zutavern and Kohli (2010: 169), "stand or fall with their specification of the needs they assume to be the responsibility of the welfare state." The main criticism of this type of explanation is that it fails to distinguish between a developmental *pull* or need for intervention and the social and political *push* for expansion exerted by social and political actors. As a result, functionalist theories tend to be silent about the differences or variations that arise out of the differential successes and failures of social and political actors to have their demands fulfilled. Or in the apt analysis and words of Zutavern and Kohli (2010: 174), "the consequences of social and economic transformations for human needing must be articulated as problems for the welfare state if they are to trigger policy changes." The latter is precisely what our open functional approach to welfare state reform sets out to do. The fourth and final logic of the welfare state that we draw on in this regard is that of class politics, coalitions, and redistribution.

The power resources approach to the welfare state was formulated as a critique of functionalist accounts. According to this approach, socially (e.g., unions) and politically (parties) organized interests, particularly of the working class or wage earners more generally, struggled to articulate their demands (preferences) and interests as problems that welfare states had to deal with. Still, such an interest-based or preference-based approach partly identifies the interests on a conception of need. Assuming rationality, this is because "it is rather implausible that they [organized interests] would want something which they do not also need" (Zutavern and Kohli 2010: 174).

There is a problem of history with the power resources approach, though. The power of the wage earners' movement cannot be linked directly to the origins of modern social policy. After all, recall that Bismarck, the pioneer of compulsory social insurance, was a conservative state-builder, not a social reformer concerned about the dire fate of industrial workers. Still, the connection can be argued to be indirect, because Bismarck's anti-socialist laws, complemented by his social insurance experiments, were a reaction to the so-called workers' or social question as well as to early socialist mobilization. Even if the socialists were not the prime movers themselves, they were still pushing for reforms in the context of pulling societal needs. The welfare state's expansion and distributional impact clearly cannot be explained without at least reference to this political logic of the strength of the socialist or social democratic labor movement.

Usually, the power resources approach is characterized as causally linking the level of social democratic organization of wage earners (organization being the major power resource of the working class) to the high level of universalism, solidarity, and redistribution of the welfare arrangements. Through the welfare state, social democratic power produces a high level of social equality.

The political efficacy of left-wing parties to bring about such egalitarian out-comes in capitalist society depended on the extent to which they could count on the support of strong trade unions and on facilitating institutions, including a centralized, corporatist industrial relations system.

The starting point of the power resources logic of the welfare state is the conviction that employment relations and labor markets determine to a large extent a society's social stratification. There may be other cleavages relevant for the distribution of life chances, but the class cleavage is by far the dominant one in capitalist society. As the "father" and main protagonist of the approach, Korpi (2006: 172) argued:

Employment relations and labor markets form the core of socioeconomic stratification. In labor markets and in employment relations, actors engage two basic types of power resources: economic assets and labor power, or human capital. The major difference between these assets turns on the fact that unlike human capital, economic resources can be divested from their owners and transferred to other actors, with the result that economic resources are typically concentrated to a much higher degree than is human capital. In employment relationships, individual employees relying primarily on their human capital are therefore generally subordinated to employers, who ultimately derive their power from control over various forms of capital.

For human capital to become a source of power of some significance, collective action is necessary. Hence, the struggle for labor power is the struggle for enhancing the conditions under which collective action is possible. As Marx would have put it, if labor in capitalist society is to exert any influence at all, the working class *an sich* must become a class *für sich*, conscious of its position and its needs, organized as such, and thinking and ready to act in terms of class struggle.

The link between social class and the welfare state is that

[S]ocioeconomic class generates differences in risks to which citizens are exposed during the life course. While some life-course risks are generated by universal processes, most risks, such as those associated with aging, illness, work accidents, unemployment, poverty, and rearing of children, are instead unequally distributed among individuals occupying different positions in socioeconomic class structures. Furthermore, class is also related to citizens' resources for coping with these life-course risks, making for the generation of negative correlations between risks and resources. Thus, citizens more exposed to risks tend to have lesser individual resources for coping with them. Differences in types of power resources controlled by actors involved in employment relations and in labor markets are therefore expected to make class a major basis for distributive strife. (Korpi 2006: 173)

Surely, there are other sources of social and political identity (religious denomination, ethnicity, occupational status) that have an impact on collective action and distributional struggles and outcomes. However, the power resources approach assumes that class-related distributional struggles prevail. "The extent to which cross-cutting cleavages are mobilized is affected by structural factors," says Korpi (2006: 173), "but distributive strife is also focused on influencing the relative importance of these competing lines of cleavages."

The main point about the welfare state is that it was a class project of the organization of the working class: social democratic parties and unions. However, as Przeworski and Sprague (1986) have argued, the socialists never managed to mobilize an electoral majority on their own anywhere, at least not for prolonged periods of time. To implement any type of social policy and to succeed, they needed the support of another class, and other social organizations and political parties, which they also had to convince of the lofty socialist goals of equality, social justice, workers' better living conditions, and decommodification. Esping-Andersen therefore correctly adjusted the crude version of the approach and argued that "the history of political class coalitions [is] the most decisive cause of welfare state variations" (Esping-Andersen 1990: 1; see Chapter 4).

According to this perspective, the emergence and expansion of the welfare state are driven by the social and political struggle of classes and the coalitions they engage in. The relations of power between the social (unions versus employers; see Ebbinghaus 2010b) and political (social democratic versus other parties; see Schmidt 2010) organizations of classes determine the variation in welfare state development. Crudely put, the higher the level of organized power of the working class, the larger will be the welfare state.

As we show in Chapter 4, in which we further elaborate and amend the power resources approach, the idea that conflict and coalitions are paramount to understanding welfare state variation implies that there cannot be a linear relationship between social democratic power and welfare state development. Other political forces, most notably Christian democracy (Van Kersbergen 1995; Kalyvas and Van Kersbergen 2010) draw upon the support of various classes, including the working class. The crucial issue for explaining the variation of welfare state arrangements is determining what kinds of coalitions are forged and whether and how the middle class is included in or excluded from such a pro-welfare state coalition with the working class and its representatives.

3.6. CONCLUSION

In this chapter, we discussed four logics or rationales of the welfare state that enable us to examine the intricate connections of the driving forces behind welfare state development, actors' motivations, and the causal mechanisms linking the functional demands and welfare state reform. Taken together, the logics also allow for painting the broad context of the political opportunities and constraints of welfare state reform. Let us summarize each of the logics and indicate what they teach us for the opportunities and constraints of contemporary welfare reform.

In a general sense, all logics address the "big" question of why we needed a welfare state in the first place and also to some extent how we got it. The first logic of socioeconomic development and modernization specifically points to which societal developments and forces were driving the welfare state's origins and development. We have seen that poverty was an important factor. The old Poor Laws were designed to deal with agricultural poverty, but they proved ineffective in dealing with the widespread destitution that emerged after the industrial revolution. Both the risk of industrial labor and the needs of the poor were elements pushing for new measures catering to these needs. Modernization hereby changed the face of privation as well as how poverty was dealt with. According to the modernization perspective, the social dislocation, misery, and poverty pressed for intervention, while simultaneously public protests demanded it. This is what we learn from the modernization perspective. However, we cannot assume that the growth of the welfare state is a direct result of the growing needs of industrial society. We argue, following Polanyi, that the development of the welfare state in the 19th century can best be viewed in terms of the creation of a self-regulating market, the social dislocation to which the commodification of labor led, and the counteraction in social protection this process spurred. It explains why all countries have the same troublesome experience with the self-regulating market and the commodification of labor and why these exert a functional pressure to respond. So, we acknowledge the logic of the self-regulating market, also for the "fictitious" commodity labor, but disagree that the decommodification of labor is in any sense an automatic response. Social and political actors, acting under diverging conditions, respond to the challenge of commodification in different ways. In other words, what the modernization perspective is lacking is an account of what connects functional pressure to reform to an actual reform. Different from the functionalist modernization perspective, our open functional approach does not assume that a response will always occur or take the same form across all countries facing the pressure.

The second logic of political integration and state-building provides a helpful addition to the first logic precisely in this regard, because it introduces an important specification: namely, that under certain conditions political actors use social policies as instruments of social control and for building a political community and national identity. The pioneering social policies that Bismarck established and that were "copied" by many other European countries aimed at creating a dependence of the working class on the state so as to reduce this class's revolutionary potential. With social policies in place, their income would depend – at least partly – on the state, making revolutionary action against this state contrary to their interests. Importantly, more than a century later, we note that tying workers (and citizens more broadly) to the state has been an extremely successful strategy and helps to explain why under conditions of the continuing popularity of the welfare state its reform is such a difficult endeavor. What we learn is that the welfare state has become so entangled in individuals' and families' lives that retrenching welfare programs hurts them often directly. So, what in the 19th century was an impetus for developing the welfare state, nowadays may very well act as a constraint on reform, or at least on some kinds of reform.

What we take from the third logic of the welfare state of need satisfaction and risk reapportioning is that welfare states first and foremost address the problem of social needs and social risks by risk pooling and risk redistribution. Because the world does not behave in line with the invisible hand theorem, that is, because markets fail, there is a rationale for the welfare state's existence. Markets cannot insure social risks such as unemployment satisfactorily, nor can this risk be covered by the family. It is the state that has to step in by compelling people of the same risk categories but with different risk profiles to join the same type of social insurance. With regard to the opportunities and constraints of welfare state reform this teaches us that when the social risks that need addressing change – for instance, because of the postindustrialization of labor markets – social policies catering to these risks need to change as well (see Chapter 8). Because of market failure as well as family failure, it is once again the state that needs to reapportion the new social risks.

The fourth and final logic of class politics, coalitions, and redistribution offers further insights into the (collective) actors pushing for welfare state development and reminds us that some social risk categories overlap with other groups, such as social classes. Redistribution of wealth and income may not have been the welfare state's primary goal or instrument but it has not been unimportant either. Here we find social classes and other groups and their social and political representatives struggling to mobilize power to support a redistribution of income to their interest. The same actors that once won distributive battles and came to promote the welfare state and redistribution nowadays are likely to be strong defenders of the status quo and act as a constraint on reform. At the same time, new distributional coalitions emerge that offer the main political opportunity for radical welfare state reform (see Häusermann 2010; Bonoli and Natali 2012a and Chapter 8). Before we examine the contemporary politics of welfare state reform, we now turn to the big questions of why we have different worlds of welfare and whether they have changed over time (Chapter 4). After that we ask yet another big question: namely, what do the different types of welfare states actually do (Chapter 5).

4

Welfare State Regimes

Why Did We Get Different Worlds of Welfare and Do We Still Have Them?

In Chapter 3, we discussed the rationales or logics of the welfare state in order to grasp its various driving forces. So far, we have largely abstracted from the substantial empirical differences between welfare states. This chapter explains that there is no such thing as *the* welfare state, but that there are distinctive worlds of welfare. We analyze the differences between welfare states and their social and political origins, foundation, and development. We ask two big questions: (1) why did we get different worlds of welfare, and (2) do we still have them? Answering these questions enables us to understand welfare state variation.

The field of comparative welfare state research is dominated by, and greatly indebted to, the work of Gøsta Esping-Andersen, whose landmark study *The Three Worlds of Welfare Capitalism* (1990) revolutionized the way social scientists look at the welfare state. Two innovations were particularly powerful. First, Esping-Andersen introduced the concept of a welfare *regime* that allowed a much broader and better understanding of the variety of ways in which the major institutions of society (state, market, and family) interacted to produce specific patterns of work and welfare. In this way he not only helped to remove the field's exclusive and theoretically unsatisfying preoccupation with social spending as the indicator of welfare state generosity (for a discussion of this so-called dependent variable problem, see Green-Pedersen 2004 and Clasen and Siegel 2007) but also opened up a whole new area for systematic comparative research. Second, Esping-Andersen introduced, documented, and explained the qualitative variation in welfare regimes (as the dependent variable), showing how these regimes (as the independent variable) were systematically related to differences in social outcomes that really matter, particularly in terms of employment structure and labor market behavior – and recently also at the micro-level of welfare state outcomes (e.g., Kammer et al. 2012).

Much intellectual effort has been invested in further developing, testing, adjusting, criticizing, and, in various ways, applying the regime typology. Hundreds of books and papers have been published that successfully make (critical and serious) use of the regime typology as a classificatory and heuristic research tool. The regime typology has become a paradigmatic one (cf. Arts and Gelissen 2010: 569). Based on a review of empirical studies that use Esping-Andersen's regime typology Arts and Gelissen conclude that "in spite of all kinds of conceptual, operationalization, and data problems that must be solved ... his typology is promising enough for work to continue on welfare state models" (581). They add, however, that further progress will very much hinge on the ability to devise a firmer theoretical foundation of contemporary and future welfare state models (understood not as normative ideals but as explanatory categories). This resonates well with Powell and Barrientos's (2011) thesis that the "welfare modeling business" (a term originally coined by Abrahamson 1999) has been paying too much attention to empirical intricacies and has not focused enough on further theoretization. This is one of the tasks we take up here.

There have always been critical assessments of the analytical utility and empirical status of the typology (e.g., Kasza 2002; Ferragina and Seeleib-Kaiser 2011; Van der Veen and Van der Brug 2013), and the approach has recently come under increasing attack because of its supposedly limited ability to explain contemporary developments and welfare state reform. Although we take these criticisms seriously, we also take issue with them and hold that the three worlds typology is still a useful device, at least for heuristic purposes and for the time being.

First, we describe how the regime approach developed out of the theoretical and empirical literature on welfare state development. The regime approach took its main inspiration from the social democratic variant of the power resources model. Our review of the field shows why the concept of decommodification is so crucial for the regime typology and why the other regimes are defined in terms of how they differ from the social democratic regime.

Second, one critical problem with the debate about the regime concept, and a great source of confusion, concerns the term "typology" and its theoretical status (see Aspalter 2013). We discuss this methodological issue, clarify the terms of the debate, solve some of the controversies that arise as a result of a flawed understanding of what a typology is or should be, discuss the criteria for good typologies, and describe the regime types.

Third, we examine whether and to what extent the regime classification still makes sense empirically. We make use of data gathered on the quality of welfare state arrangements (Scruggs 2004; Scruggs and Allan 2006; Vrooman 2009; Van Vliet and Caminada 2012) to show that the regime approach is still analytically useful and empirically valid. Esping-Andersen's regime classification was primarily based on an index of decommodification, that is, the degree to which individuals can maintain a livelihood without reliance on the market. The updated data provided by Scruggs and Vrooman provide evidence that – apart from a misclassification due to computing errors in the original classification and some other anomalies – the updated country rankings and other analyses actually reinforce the "three-worlds" typology. The regimes clearly come to the fore in these replication studies. For instance, the social democratic states occupy the first places in the decommodification rank order. The continental welfare states occupy the middle ground. And the liberal welfare states (except Canada) still occupy the lowest positions. Generally speaking, there is good evidence to support the thesis that the three worlds typology is still a useful classification device. This indicates that important institutional, political, and perhaps cultural differences clearly differentiate the various welfare states.

However, since welfare states are in a permanent stage of adaptation to a continuously modernizing environment (see Chapter 2), the question is whether within-regime differences have been increasing or declining. Using different techniques and more recent data and in spite of reforms, it is striking to note that the empirical evidence still suggests the continued relevance of the typology (Scruggs and Allan 2006; Vrooman 2009).

What explains why we have different worlds of welfare? This is the fourth and final issue we discuss in this chapter. Although we accept the regime classification, we agree with some of the critics that the regime typology as originally formulated by Esping-Andersen lacks a solid theoretical foundation of why and how different class coalitions produce different regimes. Therefore, we provide a better theoretical and historical substantiation that draws on Iversen and Soskice (2006) and Van Kersbergen and Manow (2009). The power resources approach, which we elaborate and amend in our literature review, stressed that the history of the welfare state is driven by class conflict and political class coalitions. We agree, but we hold that the crucial issues are whether the middle class is included in or excluded from the pro-welfare state coalition and which party represents the middle class in politics. These variables to a large extent determine the redistributive quality of a welfare state regime.

4.2. WORLDS OF WELFARE CAPITALISM: THE INTELLECTUAL ROOTS

Welfare states have been analyzed and discussed using empirical typologies practically since systematic welfare state research became a major branch of comparative social policy analysis. Wilensky and Lebeaux's (1965 [1958]) functionalist study of how industrialization affected social welfare in the United States, for instance, introduced early the highly influential distinction between two types of welfare. The first kind they characterized as a *residual* version, in which "social welfare institutions should come into play only when the normal structures of supply, the family and the market break down" (138). The second model they called the *institutional* variety because it assumes "welfare services as the normal first line function of industrial society" (138).

Titmuss (1968: 113, 128), who actually wrote a review of the Wilensky and Lebeaux book (1965 [1958]), initially used a similar twofold typology that distinguished between universal (later labeled universalist) and selective models of social services and redistribution. Titmuss was very much concerned with how social policies could avoid the kind of social stigma that had been so characteristic of the New Poor Law in England (1834). As Timuss (1968: 113) stressed: "The framers of the New Poor Law deliberately intended the system to operate as an assault on personal dignity and self-respect. Shame was needed to make the system work; many techniques were to hand, the inquisition of the relieving officer being only one." One crucial reason to adopt the universal principle in social policy was "the aim of making services available and accessible to the whole population in such ways as would not involve users in any humiliating loss of status, dignity or self-respect. There should be no sense of inferiority, pauperism, shame or stigma in the use of a publicly provided service" (129). In his later work, Titmuss (1974) came to promote a classification of welfare states as existing in three forms: (1) a residual type that intervenes only in cases of serious market and family failure, (2) an industrial-achievement-performance model in which a person's performance on the labor market is decisive for his or her social entitlements, and (3) an institutional redistributive variety that is encompassing and egalitarian. As Esping-Andersen (1999: 74, fn. 1) himself indicated, his and Titmuss's typologies are similar.

The intellectual roots of the regime approach that Esping-Andersen developed can be traced back to a double critique. First, there had been long-standing dissatisfaction with the functionalist literature for its failure to explain the huge observed differences in welfare effort (generally measured in terms of social expenditure) between equally advanced and industrialized capitalist countries. Second and similarly, the alternative median-voter view that democratization explained the expansion of the welfare state did not fare much better because it also could not account for the variation in social spending among democratic nations.

Starting with the latter, the basic political economy model for how democracy leads to income redistribution was presented by Meltzer and Richard (1981), who argued that when income inequality rises, the demand for income redistribution among voters also rises. Typically, the income distribution is right-skewed. Figure 4.1 shows an example of such a right-skewed distribution, namely, the number of households (Y-axis, × 1,000) according to the level of (equivalized) household income (X-axis, € × 1,000) in the Netherlands in 2010. In such a distribution, the income of the median household (€ 21,000) is below the average income (€ 23,300).

The Meltzer/Richard model holds that the median voter has an interest in redistributing income toward the average income and will vote for the party that promises to do that. The more unequal the distribution, the louder will be the demand for income redistribution. And the more poor people vote, the higher will be the degree of redistribution. So the explanation for the growth

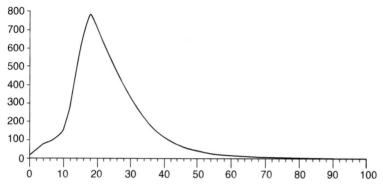

FIGURE 4.1. Example of a right skewed distribution.
Note: Number of households (Y-axis, × 1,000) according to the level of (equivalized) household income (X-axis, € × 1,000) in the Netherlands in 2010.
Source: CBS (2012: 21).

and variation in welfare state development with redistributive policies was found in the introduction and extension of democracy. In short, democracy leads to redistribution via the welfare state.

This democratization theory focusing on the median voter was criticized for two major shortcomings. First, equally democratic countries tended to have widely diverging levels of welfare effort. Second, the most unequal societies did not redistribute the most. In fact, the relationship between inequality and redistribution seemed inverse: countries that already had relatively modest wage differentials were also redistributive leaders (say Sweden), while highly unequal countries (such as the United States) were welfare state laggards. The power resources critique, to which Esping-Andersen contributed, stressed that democracy was a necessary condition for the possibility and the potential extent of redistribution, but that (party) political struggles and coalitions decided which paths countries followed in their redistributive efforts. A large number of studies corroborated the thesis that it was primarily politically organized labor (social democracy and labor unions) that spurred the redistributive qualities of welfare states. The political representative of labor, social democracy, emerged as the single strongest actor behind welfare state expansion and high levels of redistribution (classic studies are Hewitt 1977; Korpi 1983; Stephens 1979; Hicks and Swank 1984; Esping-Andersen 1985b; Hicks 1999. For an encompassing study see Huber and Stephens 2001).

However, the social democratic impact on redistribution could be questioned too because universalism and generosity did not necessarily imply redistribution from the rich to the poor but were very much favorable for the middle classes (Esping-Andersen 1990; Korpi and Palme 1998; see also our discussion of the paradox of redistribution in Chapter 5). One major source of inspiration for the formulation of the regime typology was tapped when researchers began looking for the social democratic effect not so much in welfare *effort* and the *level* of redistribution (quantity), but increasingly in the variation in the *quality* of welfare arrangements that social democrats promoted, measured specifically in terms of universalism, state-guaranteed social rights, and high protection against the whims of the market (i.e., decommodification or protection from market forces), full employment, and lenient conditionality.

The new line of research ran into some theoretical and empirical trouble almost instantly because early welfare state reforms of this type were rarely if ever introduced by social democrats, but rather by conservatives (e.g., Bismarck in Germany) and liberals (the liberal reforms between 1906 and 1914 in Britain; see Hay 1978; Mommsen and Mock 1981). Another problem was that several countries (e.g., the Netherlands) seemed to pursue social democratic-like policies under Christian democratic rule (see Van Kersbergen and Becker 1988). In other words, as a theory of the origins and variation of welfare states, the social democratic model fared poorly. Christian democracy, too, acted as a pro-welfare force, matching social democracy in terms of generosity and social spending (for a recent overview of the partisan impact, see Schmidt 2010). The electoral competition between social democracy and Christian democracy for the workers' vote appeared to have a strong effect on governments' welfare effort (see Van Kersbergen 1995; see also Jensen 2010: Häusermann et al. 2013).

Emphasizing political agency against the functionalist approaches, the development of the social democratic model helped a good deal in explaining the substantial variation in social spending and in the quality of welfare states. However, this strand of literature tended to overemphasize the role of political struggles and the impact of political parties by losing track of the social and economic processes and events that are beyond the direct control of single political actors, including demographic aging, deindustrialization and the rise of the service economy, and the built-in tendency of public sector growth (Van Kersbergen and Manow 2011). While all advanced welfare states have to cope with such secular challenges, their vulnerabilities and opportunities in coping with them vary according to their politico-institutional setup. And it is precisely here where Esping-Andersen's seminal contribution to the study of the welfare state comes in. Esping-Andersen's regime approach and typology offered a powerful critique of the – at the time dominant – quantitatively oriented studies that tended to look at welfare state expansion and variation solely in terms of social spending, usually expressed as some percentage of gross domestic product (GDP). Esping-Andersen's respecification of the welfare state concept with reference to qualitative features radically changed the field's orientation. Starting from the view that "expenditures are epiphenomenal to the theoretical substance of welfare states" (1990: 19) and the reflection that "it is difficult to imagine that anyone struggled for spending *per se*" (1990: 21, emphasis in original), Esping-Andersen suggested that the study of welfare states had much to gain by looking at three dimensions that typify a welfare state regime. First, he underlined the importance of the quality of social rights. How good are welfare states actually at shielding people from the uncertainty of markets and against social risks associated with the life course? Second, he advised looking at the typical patterns of stratification that social policies foster. Do social policies distinguish between classes of people and do all have equal social rights? Do social policies overcome or reproduce status and other relevant social differences? Third, he emphasized that it is not just the state that produces welfare, but that the market and the family are always inextricably involved as well. How do these major public and private institutions of society interact to form a welfare regime that shapes a nation's work and welfare?

By empirically mapping various indicators that capture these three dimensions, Esping-Andersen was able to distinguish three types of welfare state regimes: a social democratic, a liberal, and a corporatist or conservative regime. The regimes differed with respect to the major institutions guaranteeing social security (the state, the market, or the family); the kind of stratification systems upheld by the institutional mix of these institutions (the extent of status and class differentiation, segmentation, and inequality typically implied in social security systems); and the degree of decommodification, that is, "the degree to which individuals, or families, can uphold a socially acceptable standard of living independently of market participation" (Esping-Andersen 1990: 37).

4.3. THE TYPOLOGY OF WELFARE REGIMES

To explain the three-worlds typology well and to be able to evaluate the criticisms, it is necessary to start our exposé with a short discussion of the analytical status of typologies. In our view, a typology, unlike the theoretical device of ideal types, is an empirical classificatory device that reduces observed complexity by cataloging existing cases as meaningful representatives (types) of some concept of interest. This is done by using relatively arbitrarily chosen values of theoretically relevant features as criteria for placement in the cells of the classification scheme, that is, the typology. Cases that have similar or nearly identical scores on the variables are classified as belonging to the same type.

Although a typology is necessarily constructed on the basis of some implicit or explicit (proto-)theory, it is at heart simply a classification device that helps to arrange the observable empirical "mess" of phenomena into a more ordered, transparent, and therefore comprehensible manner. A good typology, in addition to being efficient and reliable in reducing complexity, should be exhaustive and mutually exclusive. That a typology should be exhaustive implies two things: (1) all theoretically relevant dimensions should be included in the construction of the types; and (2) it should be possible to assign all existing cases to one of the types. For a typology to be mutually exclusive means that an empirical case can be assigned to one type only. In sum, a typology is designed for conceptual and descriptive purposes.

Applied to the welfare state regime typology, this implies that the theoretically relevant dimensions of variation must be identified. Esping-Andersen (1990: 21), following Marshall (1964), defined the core idea of the welfare state as social citizenship, embodied in the granting of decommodifying social rights (first typological dimension) and the extent to which stratification is upheld or modified by such rights (second typological dimension). In addition, the third dimension of variation relevant for the construction of the typology concerns the extent to which the state's welfare activities are interconnected with the market's and the family's contribution to social welfare. On each of these dimensions, Esping-Andersen compared the existing worlds of welfare and found that welfare states were systematically clustered around specific values of the identified dimensions.

To operationalize the decommodification potential of social rights (pensions, sickness insurance, and unemployment benefits), Esping-Andersen looked at (1) the rules of access to benefits (eligibility and restrictions on entitlements, such as contribution record and needs test); (2) the level of income replacement offered; and (3) the duration of entitlements. The decision on how to draw a line between a high, medium, and low level of decommodification was not theoretically justified but technically solved on the basis of one standard deviation below (low) or above (high) the mean (medium) (Esping-Andersen 1990: 54, Appendix). However, the final ranking of countries was based "roughly on how nations cluster around the mean" (Esping-Andersen 1990: 51). Table 4.1 shows the rank order of countries along the decommodification dimension of the typology. On the basis of these data, Esping-Andersen (1990: 51) inferred that we can distinguish three groups of countries: "the Anglo-Saxon 'new' countries are all concentrated at the bottom of our index; the Scandinavian countries at the top. In between these two extremes, we find the continental European countries, some of which (especially Belgium and the Netherlands) fall close to the Nordic cluster."

Stratification, the second dimension of the typology, was theoretically specified by arguing that one needs to look at how social policies affect the social structure. One type of welfare state "may cultivate hierarchy and status," writes Esping-Andersen (1990: 58), as is done in conservative social policy; "another dualisms," as is characteristic for the liberal type; "and a third universalism," which is the distinctive feature of the social democratic variety. The stratification dimension of the typology was operationalized in this way:

The corporatist model is best identified by the degree to which social insurance is differentiated and segmented into distinct occupational- and status-based programs [status]. In this case we would also expect large variations between the bottom and top in terms of benefits. To identify etatism [hierarchy], the simplest approach is to identify the relative privileges accorded to civil servants. In contrast, we would identify liberal principles in terms of welfare states' residualism, especially the relative salience of means-testing; in terms of the relative financial responsibility accorded to the individual insured; and in terms of the relative weight of voluntary, private-sector welfare. And to capture the socialist ideals, the

TABLE 4.1. *The rank order of welfare states in terms of combined decommodification, 1980*

	Decommodification score
Australia	13.0
United States	13.8
New Zealand	17.1
Canada	22.0
(Japan)	(22.3)
Ireland	23.3
United Kingdom	23.4
Italy	24.1
France	27.5
Germany	27.7
Finland	29.2
Switzerland	29.8
Austria	31.1
Belgium	32.4
Netherlands	32.4
Denmark	38.1
Norway	38.3
Sweden	39.1
Mean	26.9
Standard deviation	7.8

Note: Note that Japan was originally mistakenly given an additive score of 27.1 and was placed in the middle group after Italy. The correct score is 22.3, so Japan should have been located between Canada and Ireland as in this table (see Scruggs and Allan 2006). The mean and standard deviation are corrected accordingly.
Source: taken from Esping-Andersen (1990: 52, table 2.2).

relevant measure is clearly the degree of universalism. The socialist regime ought to exhibit the lowest level of benefit differentials. (Esping-Andersen 1990: 69)

Corporatism was measured as the number of occupationally distinct public pension schemes, *etatism* as expenditure on pensions to government employees, *means testing* as means tested poor relief as a percentage of total public social expenditure, *individual responsibility and private sector dominance* as private pensions as a percentage of total pensions and private health spending as a percentage of total health spending, and *universalism* as program universalism measured as the averaged percentage of population (aged 16–64) eligible for a sickness, unemployment, and pension benefit, and as average benefit equality measured as average net, after-tax differential between basic and maximum social benefits for sickness, unemployment, and pension benefits.

Esping-Andersen (1990: 75, table 3.3) then constructed a table, again roughly based on the mean scores and standard deviations of the cumulated index scores, to indicate the extent to which countries show strong, medium, or low regime attributes. He concluded that the three clusters clearly come to the fore.

The nations which score high on our summary index of conservatism (Italy, Germany, France, and Belgium) all score low, or at best, medium on our indices of liberalism and socialism. In turn, the countries characterized by strong liberalism (Australia, Canada, Japan, Switzerland, and the United States) score low or medium on conservatism and socialism. Finally, the socialism cluster includes the nations of Scandinavia, and the Netherlands, all countries which score low (or medium) on the two other regimes-clusters. (Esping-Andersen 1990: 76)

The third dimension of the typology was theoretically meant to capture a nation's specific mix of state, market, and family in the provision of social welfare, but Esping-Andersen empirically and exclusively looked at the public-private mix in pension policies. Surprisingly, the conspicuous exclusion of the family from the analysis of this dimension of the typology is not justified in the *The Three Worlds*.[1] Pensions were argued to be the logical choice, because they are the largest and most important part of social transfers: "pensions constitute a central link between work and leisure, between earned income and redis-tribution, between individualism and solidarity, between the cash nexus and social rights. Pensions, therefore, help elucidate a set of perennially conflictual principles of capitalism" (Esping-Andersen 1990: 79–80).

Theoretically, a distinction was made between (1) different types of *public pensions*, including both state legislated pension schemes and publicly mandated private sector schemes; (2) *civil-service pensions* that are not to be counted as public, but as occupational, and that indicate the legacy of etat-ism and corporatism rather than the granting of social rights; and (3) *private pensions*, including both occupational plans, which are a type of collective or trade-union insurance, and real individual annuities. The public-private mix in pensions is measured by looking at total expenditure by program category and by the sources of income among aged households. The first indicator reveals that those nations that provide low social security pensions have an expanded private pension sector. In addition, the etatist and corporatist countries are the only countries that have very big public-employee pensions. The liberal coun-tries have by far the most advanced private pension schemes and the social democratic the least developed ones. Three pension regimes emerge from the classification (confirmed by the data on the second indicator, source of income), (Esping-Andersen 1990: 85–87):

> Corporative state-dominated insurance systems, in which status is a key element in the pension-program structure. In this regime, the private market is generally marginal, and social security tends to be highly

[1] The family and the changing role of women later became the main focus of Esping-Andersen's work (1999 and 2009).

TABLE 4.2. *A summary overview of welfare regimes' characteristics*

	Liberal	Social democratic	Conservative
Role of:			
Family	Marginal	Marginal	Central
Market	Central	Marginal	Marginal
State	Marginal	Central	Subsidiary
Welfare State:			
Dominant mode of solidarity	Individual	Universal	Kinship Corporatism Etatism
Dominant locus of solidarity	Market	State	Family
Degree of decommodification	Minimal	Maximum	High (for breadwinners)
Modal examples	US	Sweden	Germany Italy

Source: Taken from Esping-Andersen (1999: 85, table 5.4).

occupationally segregated with particularly pronounced civil servants' privileges: Austria, Belgium, France, Germany, Italy, and Japan, with the possible inclusion of Finland.

Residualist systems, in which the market tends to prevail at the expense of either social security or civil-service privilege, or both: Australia, Canada, Switzerland, and the United States.

Universalistic state-dominated systems, in which population-wide social rights eradicate both status privilege and markets: New Zealand, Norway, Sweden, with the possible inclusion of Denmark and Holland.

This overview shows that Esping-Andersen meant his typology to be a classificatory device that reduces the empirically existing complexity of many worlds of welfare to three. It also seems clear that the boundaries between the three types occasionally are drawn in a theoretically relatively arbitrary way, but cases end up as representatives of one of the types because of similar scores on the various variables. Summing up, according to Esping-Andersen, the worlds of welfare come in three regime types. Table 4.2 presents the regimes' characteristics, as originally conceived.[2] Table 4.3 offers a more exhaustive overview of regime features that was skillfully composed by Vrooman (2009: 214–215, table 4.1).

The liberal regime of countries such as the United States, the United Kingdom, Australia, and New Zealand relies on low and flat rate benefits for which very strict eligibility or access criteria are formulated and applied. Benefits are

---

[2] This overview thus does not take into account the sometimes radical changes that have taken place in the welfare state regimes.

TABLE 4.3. *An extended overview of welfare regimes' characteristics*

Characteristics	Welfare regime type		
	Liberal	Conservative	Social-democratic
Collective benefits			
– coverage (main target group)	limited – the poor without means	selective and hierarchical – professional groups	universal – all residents
– entry conditions	very strict – incapable of work – means-testing	fairly strict (actuarial) – employment history – contributions paid	only strict if work-related – residency for a certain number of years – job search behavior – participation in training or workfare programs
– limitation of duration	strict – benefit paid only as long as recipient cannot work	(quasi-)actuarial – long benefit duration if sufficient rights accrued	not too strict benefit continues as long as risk is manifest
– level of benefit	meager – subsistence minimum	high – wage related	high – adequacy social minimum and/or wage related
– collective schemes for specific occupational groups	few – civil servants	many – status groups – civil servants (high level)	none
– level of contributions	low	fairly high	high
– method of funding	general taxation	mainly through contributions	general taxation
Private benefits			
– coverage	high (for middle classes) – stimulated through tax benefits/credits	low	low
Employment			
– minimum wage	absent or very low	high	high

– (dis-)incentives to employment of women	no disincentives – low level of benefits → *fairly high labor participation*	many disincentives – breadwinner benefits – generous motherhood and child allowances – few childcare facilities → *low labor participation*	many incentives – individual benefit entitlement – elaborate leave arrangements for care tasks – extensive childcare facilities – high contributions force both partners to work → *high labor participation*
– (dis-)incentives to employment of older people and disabled	no disincentives – no collective retirement schemes → *high labor participation*	many disincentives – collectively funded schemes for early retirement, disability and unemployment → *low labor participation*	few disincentives use of collective retirement schemes is discouraged – active reintegration of disabled → *high labor participation*
– collectively guaranteed employment	virtually absent	limited – sheltered employment for handicapped persons	extensive
– postindustrial employment	extensive dual structure – good jobs in professional business services – low skilled "junk jobs"	few	extensive government sector – welfare, care, social security, education – large share of middle-ranking posts occupied by women
Stratification – differences between groups of citizens which are promoted by regime	reinforcing distinctions – welfare clients/working poor – middles class – privileged classes	reproduction of stratification – occupational groups – gender – household type	none – universalist
– expected future development	proletarianization	insider/outsider problem – contrast between working/nonworking	private/collective problem – contrast between females working in collective sector and males employed in private firms
decommodification – extent to which a regime promotes an acceptable living standard, independent of one's market value	low, depending on: – stringency of means-testing – minimum benefit level	medium, depending on: – – replacement rates – stringency of actuarial principles – scope of social assistance	high, depending on: – benefit levels

Source: Adapted from Vrooman (2009: 214–215, table 4.1).

means tested, low, primarily meant to prevent or alleviate poverty, and for the most part tax-financed. If citizens wish more than basic protection – for instance, life insurance or a private pension scheme – they need to purchase that on the market or acquire it via the employer. Such arrangements are often stimulated through tax exemptions and allowances. Public social spending is comparatively low. The regime has limited collective provisions and is service-lean. The welfare state solely targets the poor, the extremely vulnerable, and the neediest. It reinforces social differences, particularly among welfare recipients, the middle classes, and the privileged, and between the well-paid professionals and the underpaid underclass of the working poor. In short, this is a tight-fisted welfare state that offers little protection and does not interfere much with the inequalities generated by the market.

The social democratic regime as found in the Scandinavian countries is also tax-financed but much more lenient in its eligibility rules (no means testing) and generous in the provision of benefits and services; it works with compulsory social insurance with earnings-related benefits. It aims to offer a high level of social protection through benefits and services as a matter of rights to all citizens. It is an expensive welfare type, and public social spending and tax levels are high. As a result, maximum labor market participation of all groups is highly valued, not just as a commendable goal in itself, but also as necessary for upholding the universal and expensive welfare state. This regime excels in the provision of public social services (social care, health, labor market, and education). The role of the market is downplayed. The social democratic welfare state itself is a big employer, where particularly women find jobs. In Scandinavia, income redistribution is an important component of the welfare edifice and because of its universal features, the regime greatly diminishes social distinctions.

The conservative regime stresses that social rights are earned on the basis of one's economic contribution to society (employment) or one's social function in the family (primarily housewife). Hence, social benefits are financed through payroll contributions and those who have no job, especially women in their role as mothers, are entitled to benefits via their relationship with an employed person (husband, father, or other family members). Eligibility is strict to the extent that actuarial principles link performance (e.g., contribution period and employment) to entitlements. Unlike the other regimes, the conservative welfare regime discourages female employment and the employment of the elderly and disabled. The level of social benefits depends on former income and contributions to the insurance funds. There are usually many different collective schemes, with special treatment of civil servants. Also in this regime, the market plays a relatively limited role. The particularist features of the regime tend to reproduce existing social stratification, reinforcing differences between occupational status groups, men and women, and types of families. This regime is a minimal service provider (e.g., underdeveloped childcare) and primarily relies on cash transfers through a myriad of occupationally distinct schemes.

4.4. THE QUALITY OF THE TYPOLOGY AND CONFUSING TYPES AND IDEAL TYPES

Does Esping-Andersen's typology fit the criteria of a good typology we outlined above, that is, is it efficient and reliable in reducing complexity as well as exhaustive and mutually exclusive? Regarding efficiency in reducing complexity, the typology does a proper job by condensing the 18 welfare states (for which data were available) down to three regimes. Notwithstanding some arbitrary choices (discussed later), it does so reliably. Moreover, the typology is arguably exhaustive, first, because decommodification, stratification, and the public-private mix are the relevant dimensions that needed to be included, and second, because roughly all 18 cases could be classified in one of the types. The single largest missing aspect in the classification exercise concerns the role of the family in the public-private mix of social provision.

The typology cannot be qualified unambiguously as mutually exclusive, however, because several marginal borderline cases emerged that could not clearly be assigned to one of the three types. For instance, as Esping-Andersen (1990: 51) honestly reports and judging from Table 4.1, Belgium, the Netherlands, and Austria have high levels of decommodification and are put together with the social democratic countries. However, the distance between Austria (the lowest of the high scores) and Denmark (the lowest of the social democratic countries) is 7 points (38.1–31.1), exactly the same distance as between Austria and Italy (the lowest in the medium group) (31.1–24.1). So, should Austria be placed in the conservative or in the social democratic group? The criterion actually used for the classification is unclear. If the one-standard-deviation-from-the-mean rule had been applied, there would be two very distinctive clusters, namely, Australia, the United States, and New Zealand with one standard deviation below the mean (= 19.1), and Denmark, Norway, and Sweden with one standard deviation above the mean (34.7), and one large indistinct remaining group that includes all the continental countries, but also Canada, Ireland, the United Kingdom, Japan, and Finland.

We encounter similar classification difficulties with respect to the typology's other dimensions, such as the problem of the high degree of universalism of benefits in the liberal countries Canada and Switzerland[3] and the high degree of social democratic regime attributes in the Netherlands. In all cases, Esping-Andersen points to the problematic issues and cases, although he does not

---

[3] Van der Veen and Van der Brug (2013) argue that there is a problem with the validity of Esping-Andersen's model: the indicators used do not seem to be valid measures of the three regimes, particularly because the model mixes institutional indicators and outcome measures. Their alternative social insurance model, which includes only institutional variables to specify the regimes, replaces the dimension "socialism" with "universalism" and leads to some changes in the classification of countries, notably Canada and Switzerland, which are classified as "hybrid" cases. The construct validity problem, moreover, may have caused some studies to draw invalid inferences about the causal impact of regimes.

always justify well the choices he had to make to ensure that all cases could be assigned to one of the three types, and to one type only.

In any case, Esping-Andersen clearly struggled in placing some of the cases in an attempt to meet the "mutually exclusive" criterion. In fact, in his reexamination of the three-worlds typology, Esping-Andersen (1999: 73ff) explicitly states that his typology was primarily a classification device and exercise. He further explains that typologies are useful because they allow for parsimony, may highlight underlying patterns and causalities, and help to generate hypotheses that can be tested. He also defends the typological approach against various criticisms.

In trying to decide whether the typology remains robust and valid, Esping-Andersen (1999: 86) confusingly argues that since typologies "are, in a sense, ideal types, there are bound to be ambiguous cases" and he mentions the Dutch case as an example of a country that is sometimes social democratic and sometimes conservative. In the context of the typological method, however, it is not possible and is therefore incorrect to label cases as ambiguous, because empirical cases are what they are and cannot be ambiguous. The only thing that might be ambiguous is the way the researcher classifies a case as a certain type. If it is difficult to categorize a specific case – for instance, because the scores on the relevant dimensions allow for assignment to more than one type – the typology clearly is not mutually exclusive. It is the typology that is ambiguous, not the case.

The problem is that Esping-Andersen is confusing his typological method with both the ideal type approach and cases with types, a misunderstanding subsequently and often uncritically reproduced in the literature (e.g., Vrooman 2009: 217; Arts and Gelissen 2010: 572ff; Aspalter 2011; Powell and Barrientos 2011; Aspalter 2013; Rice 2013; see Becker 2009: 8ff). An ideal type is a theoretical construct that has no empirical cases that fit any of the types, whereas – as we argued earlier – a typology is a classification device in which all empirical cases must find a place as belonging to one of the types and to one type only. In a typology, an empirical case either belongs to a type or not. In ideal-typical analysis, the question concerns not whether an empirical case fits the theoretical ideal, but the extent or degree to which it does. The question of "goodness of fit" makes sense only when working with ideal types.

In the three-worlds typology, the Dutch case must thus be classified either as representative of the conservative type or of the social democratic type. If this can be done only by violating what the data on the relevant dimensions really indicate, then there are only two options. Either the typology must be adjusted so that it meets the demands of being "exhaustive" and "mutually exclusive" and the Dutch case can be classified properly,[4] or the classificatory strength

---

[4] This is in fact what we did elsewhere in a co-authored paper with Uwe Becker (Vis et al. 2008). There we proposed a more encompassing method of distinction that identified also the regulating or guiding assumptions underlying the ways in which countries deal with market risks

of the typology must be compromised by admitting that the Dutch case cannot be properly placed. In the latter case, it is perfectly allowed (although the terminology is somewhat confusing perhaps) to speak of the "hybrid" Dutch case, but only on the condition that this is explicitly taken to mean that on the dimensions of the typology this specific case cannot be classified unambiguously by the researcher. "Hybrid" in this context must not be taken to mean that the case diverges from any ideal type or mixes features of different ideal types (see Becker 2009: 8ff).

The distinction between a typology and an ideal type is important because it helps to distinguish between constructive and to-the-point criticisms of the original regime typology and not very useful (because ill-conceived) attacks on the three worlds as ideal types and between adequate and deficient replies to criticism. For example, a valid criticism would be that the regime typology is not exhaustive because it did not include all the theoretically relevant features of welfare states in the tool box of classification, including the institution of the family or household and social services (Esping-Andersen 1999: 73); as a result, it does not capture well the important differences and similarities between the regimes.

Potentially equally valid is the criticism that the chosen dimensions for the construction of the typology make it impossible to classify all the existing cases of welfare states in the correct categories. We already mentioned the problematic Dutch case. Moreover, Castles and Mitchell (1993) early proposed to broaden the three-way typology by including the so-called wage-earner model that guarantees income through another dimension of empirical variation, namely, the wage arbitration system. As a result of the focus on public policies, the three-worlds typology underestimates the income guarantee (and therefore decommodifying) quality of the welfare regime of Australia and New Zealand that is much less liberal than would appear in the Esping-Andersen classification. The counterargument that Esping-Andersen (1999: 89) provides is that, in fact, since the 1990s, this model was effectively dismantled by large-scale market liberalization, turning these welfare regimes into fully fledged cases of the liberal regime.

Some argued that it would be useful to add a Mediterranean type (Leibfried 1992; Ferrera 1996) because southern welfare states are special in one

---

and market (and family) failures. We took into account the relationship between politics and the market, the makeup of society (hierarchical, socially egalitarian, or individualist), the locus of responsibility for welfare (elites, society, or citizens), the centrality of freedom, equality of opportunity, and equality of condition. Based on these criteria, we proposed a typology of welfare systems, in which Esping-Andersen's conservative category was split into a paternalist and a communitarian version (because both might be conservative but are still very distinctive) and two additional categories (one with clientelistic traits and a rudimentary category). We argued that the Dutch welfare state until the 1960s belonged to the paternalist type where "the strong" are distinguished from "the weak" and where the latter are cared for by the "caring state" (Dutch: *verzorgingsstaat*).

dimension: they have only residual social assistance programs. This point did not convince Esping-Andersen either. Unless the regimes of countries such as Spain and Italy could be shown to have some specific features that the three worlds classification did not yet pick up, there was no reason to sacrifice parsimony. But because the underdevelopment of social assistance seemed to be an expression of the strong familialism of these countries, this might be a reason to introduce a fourth world. Ultimately, however, this option was rejected for empirical reasons, because the distinction between the conservative and Mediterranean model was too small to be considered germane.

Others have taken up the task of developing and expanding the regime typology beyond the world of advanced welfare states by exploring the extent to which distinct patterns can be discerned among welfare states outside Europe, North America, and the Antipodes. There is a lively debate on the characteristics of an emerging Asian or Confucian regime (e.g., in Japan, South Korea, and Taiwan) (see Peng and Wong 2010), on the distinct trajectory of Latin American public policies and their similarity to the conservative and Mediterranean regime (see Huber and Bogliaccini 2010), and on the possible emergence of a distinct postcommunist regime in Eastern Europe and Russia (see Cook 2010). If anything, these debates underscore the heuristic prolificacy of the regime typology.

An ill-conceived criticism of the typology is the argument that the worlds of welfare are far too complicated and have changed too much to be captured by any typology. This is the position taken by Schubert et al. (2009), who argue that we need to take a step back to a precomparative stage so as to be able to document and highlight the real complexities of social and welfare policies. As a result, studying the diverse European Union systems of welfare necessarily means studying 27 individual countries on as many variables as possible. That, as realized by Schubert et al. (2009: 21), is also a step back analytically, and after 27 single-country chapters, Bazant and Schubert (2009) unsurprisingly have to conclude that there is no such thing as *the* welfare state or *the* European social model, and no systematic pattern of variation in the key dimensions of spending, financing, actors, and *leitmotifs* (guiding principles). The main conclusion of the exercise is that "it is neither possible to ratify any of the existing groupings we know from the relevant literature ... nor to identify clear-cut new clusters" (533).

This type of criticism of typological work obviously misses the whole point of what a typology is about: a meaningful, efficient, and reliable reduction of complexity for analytical and comparative purposes. It also misses the point that every typology that reduces complexity does so by necessarily simplifying reality. That is not a disadvantage; it is what typologies are *meant* to do. Therefore, to criticize a typology for not doing justice to the full complexity of empirical reality is entirely beside the point. What we end up with in the approach of Schubert et al. is a complete loss of analytical power without real gains in empirical accuracy (see Arts and Gelissen 2010: 581).

Esping-Andersen's welfare regime typology has been by far the most influential and fruitful classification and it has been successfully orienting research to the present day. Just to give an example, on the basis of a rough count in the Social Science Citation Index 2012, we found that the 1990 *The Three Worlds* book was cited more than 3,000 times and the 1999 *Social Foundations* book more than 1,000 times. Google Scholar gave approximately 16,500 and 4,800 quotations.

The original typology was designed with data from around 1980 and made a pretty strong case that there are three worlds of welfare capitalism. There have been many attempts to test the adequacy of the empirical typology with different techniques, but the results have been mixed and have sometimes indicated the likely utility of additional types (for an exhaustive overview, see Arts and Gelissen 2010; see also Powell and Barrientos 2011; Aspalter 2011). The robustness of the typology was corroborated by Scruggs and Allan (2006), who replicated Esping-Andersen's original study with new data (see Table 4.4).

Scruggs and Allan first of all found that several countries seem to have been misplaced originally and that the coherence within the clusters of countries is less strong than Esping-Andersen proposed. On the basis of their new data, they concluded that there is limited empirical support for the regime classification. This, however, is a somewhat surprising inference in the light of the data they themselves present. If we look at Table 4.4, which compares the classification of Esping-Andersen (left panel) with the Scruggs and Allan generosity index, the strength of the clustering of countries by regime type is striking. This conclusion can also be drawn from the relatively high correlation coefficients between Esping-Andersen's original data and the replication data of Scruggs and Allan that Table 4.4 also displays (ranging from 0.70 for pension generosity to 0.95 for sick pay generosity).

The liberal countries – Australia, United States, United Kingdom, and New Zealand – were classified as the least decommodified in 1980, and the new data list them still as the most residual welfare states. Japan now occupies a place among the liberal welfare states; it should have been classified as such in 1980 (see Table 4.1 above) but was not because of a calculation error in the original classification. Also the most decommodified welfare states of 1980 (Denmark, Norway, and Sweden) are still at the top if we look at the generosity index. The conservative welfare state regime (Austria, Belgium, and also France, Germany, and the Netherlands) is quite stable, too. The major puzzles are Switzerland, a country which is supposed to belong to the liberal regime but whose decommodification score looks social-democratic or top-conservative; Finland, a Scandinavian country that moves in the direction of the social-democratic regime but does not quite reach the appropriate level of decommodification; Italy, a country whose score is so low that it ends up close to the liberal countries; and Canada, usually grouped with the liberal welfare states but really more akin to the (not so generous) members of the conservative regime.

TABLE 4.4. *Decommodification and benefit generosity indices, 1980*

	Unemployment	Sickness	Pension	Total decommodification[a]
Australia	4.0	4.0	5.0	13.0
United States[b]	7.2	0	7.0	13.8
New Zealand	4.0	4.0	9.1	17.1
Canada	8.0	6.3	7.7	22.0
Ireland	8.3	8.3	6.7	23.3
UK	7.2	7.7	8.5	23.4
Italy	5.1	9.4	9.6	24.1
Japan[a]	5.0	6.8	10.5	27.3
France	6.3	9.2	12.0	27.5
Germany	7.9	11.3	8.5	27.7
Finland	5.2	10.0	14.0	29.2
Switzerland	8.8	12.0	9.0	29.8
Austria	6.7	12.5	11.9	31.1
Belgium	8.6	8.8	15.0	32.4
Netherlands	11.1	10.5	10.8	32.4
Denmark	8.1	15.0	15.0	38.1
Norway	9.4	14.0	14.9	38.3
Sweden	7.1	15.0	17.0	39.1
Mean	7.1	9.2	10.7	27.2
Standard deviation	1.9	4.0	3.4	7.7
Coefficient of variation	0.27	0.44	0.32	0.28

Correlation between programs
Unemployment – Sickness r = 0.44
Unemployment – Pension r = 0.23
Sickness – Pension r = 0.72
Cronbach's α = 0.72

	Unemployment	Sickness	Pension	Total decommodification[a]
United States[b]	7.4	0	11.3	18.7
Japan	4.5	6.2	9.4	20.0
Australia	5.0	5.0	10.1	20.1
Italy	3.2	7.3	10.0	20.7
Ireland	6.9	6.2	8.3	21.4
United Kingdom	7.2	7.2	8.5	22.9
New Zealand	5.0	5.0	13.3	23.3
Canada	7.2	6.4	11.4	25.0
Austria	6.9	9.7	11.2	27.8
France	6.3	9.5	12.0	27.8
Finland	4.9	10.0	13.0	27.9
Germany	7.5	12.6	8.7	28.8
Netherlands	10.6	9.7	11.5	31.8
Switzerland	9.2	11.0	12.0	32.2
Belgium	10.2	8.6	14.0	32.9
Denmark	8.6	12.6	11.8	32.9
Norway	8.5	13.0	11.9	33.4
Sweden	9.4	14.0	15.0	38.4
Mean	7.1	8.6	11.3	27.0
Standard deviation	2.1	3.5	1.9	5.8
Coeffient of variation	0.29	0.41	0.17	0.21
Correlation with original scores	0.87	0.95	0.70	0.87

Correlation between programs
Unemployment – Sickness r = 0.45
Unemployment – Pension r = 0.36
Sickness – Pension r = 0.30
Cronbach's α = 0.59

[a] Total decommodification score is amount in table 2.2 of Esping-Andersen (1990), not the sum of program scores.
[b] The United States has no sickness program.
Source: Adapted from Scruggs and Allan (2006: 68).

Recently, Vrooman (2009) applied a categorical principal component analysis to 54 characteristics of social security systems with data from the early 1990s. This analysis clearly revealed three major clusters of regime features (but also an outlying indicator: entitlement to a disability scheme) and two dimensions: a scope of social security dimension (from residual to extensive social rights) and a degree of universalism dimension (from particularistic to universalistic features). Looking at the object scores (the values attributed on the two dimensions to countries on the basis of the optimal scaling procedure) and corroborated by various other techniques (e.g., cluster analysis), Vrooman's analysis shows that Esping-Andersen's three regimes unambiguously hold. There is one case (the Netherlands) that is defined as an outlier because the scope of social security looks very social-democratic, whereas the degree of universalism is much lower than usual in the social-democratic regime (Vrooman 2009: 231; see Vrooman 2012).

Do the three regimes still exist? In other words, how robust is the classification over time? Vrooman, in collaboration with others (Soede et al. 2004) applied the same kind of analysis using data for 1998–2000 and found exactly the same clustering. Reviewing a host of other empirical analyses and summarizing his own analyses, Vrooman (2009: 232) concludes: "Taken together, these studies corroborate for the period 1980–2000 the existence of the 'worlds' as originally proposed by Esping-Andersen. Because both the underlying dimensions and the clustering of countries are fairly constant, it may be assumed that the classification is empirically valid during these two decades" (but see Van der Veen and Van der Brug 2013). He also makes an interesting observation as to the possibilities and constraints of radical reform:

Of course … this does not guarantee that the different regime types will continue to exist in the future. On the other hand, path dependence could play a decisive role. The material and social costs of complete regime shifts may be quite high, the cognitive frames and interests of policy makers could stand in the way, and the informal rules of the electorate may set limits to the direction and degree of change that is attainable. (Vrooman 2009: 232)

These are issues to which we return in the following chapters.

Summing up, it made sense to reduce the complexity of the very varied worlds of welfare by grouping countries into three distinct regimes. Various empirical analyses that use a wide range of techniques largely confirm (with some exceptions, such as Japan) the correct assignment of countries to one of the three types, and they also confirm the robustness over time of the regime clustering. Although it seems sensible to discuss the usefulness of adding types to the classification scheme (a Mediterranean one?) or accepting the existence of cases that are difficult to classify (the Netherlands?), the robustness of the three-worlds typology over time has been corroborated. Moreover, it may very well be that decades of social policy reforms necessitate the development of a new typology. Be that as it may, it is important to remember that a typological classification has the function of effectively grouping together empirically the many worlds of welfare capitalism and rearranging them into distinct types so as to reduce complexity for analytical and comparative purposes. Nothing more, nothing less.

4.5. EXPLAINING VARIATION: POLITICAL CLASS COALITIONS AND WELFARE REGIMES

Now that we have established the theoretical and empirical background of the regime typology in some detail, let us answer the "big" question of why welfare states come in different types. What caused the very pronounced institutional and regulatory variation? This question is important, because we expect the political opportunities and constraints for reform to depend on the varying political power constellations of the regimes.

Politically, the variation in welfare regimes is explained by how strongly the middle class joins with the working class to back the welfare state, and which party represents the pro-welfare coalition. If the middle classes are not included in receiving welfare benefits, the result is a residual welfare regime. If the middle classes are included, the state will offer more extensive and generous social policies. In summary, we find a residual, liberal regime in countries where the middle class opposes the welfare state; an encompassing (universal), social democratic welfare state in countries where the middle class is an integral part of a firm pro-welfare state coalition; and an in-between, conservative regime in countries where only parts of the middle class are incorporated.

But why does the inclusion of the middle class vary so radically across the regimes – from not included (liberal) to conditionally incorporated (conservative) to fully integrated (social democratic)? As one of us has argued elsewhere (Manow and Van Kersbergen 2009),[5] we need to determine the logic by which political class coalitions are formed and made stable. Why does the middle class in some cases join forces with the working class to support a more generous distributional regime, and in other cases ally with the upper class to guarantee a low tax-benefit regime? Iversen and Soskice (2006) have offered an explanation of why different political class coalitions bring about different types of distributional regimes. Their point of departure is the intriguing observation that in advanced capitalist democracies since World War II, the left has governed more often in multi-party systems and the right more often in two-party systems. The middle class (or the middle class voter) has more to lose if the left governs in a two-party system and more to gain if it enters a coalition with the left in multi-party systems.

In a two-party system, the middle class fears – if the left governs – that the government will tax both the upper and the middle classes to the exclusive

---

[5] This section is based on Manow and Van Kersbergen (2009). Many thanks to Philip Manow for allowing us to make use of this work.

benefit of the lower class. If the right governs, the middle and upper classes will not be taxed, and, as a consequence, redistribution will be marginal. In this two-party setting, the middle class has the choice of either receiving no benefits but being taxed for them if the left governs, or receiving no benefits but *not* being taxed for them if the right governs. Obviously, it would prefer not to be taxed. However, in a proportional representation (PR), multi-party system, the middle class choice is different. By forming a coalition, left parties and middle-class parties together can tax the rich and credibly commit to divide the revenue. The prediction then is that in multi-party systems the left will be in a governing position more often, redistribution will be higher, and the welfare state more generous. In majoritarian, two-party systems, conversely, the middle class will more frequently vote for the center-right party, governments will more often have a conservative composition, the welfare state will remain residual, and redistribution will be marginal.

This Iversen-Soskice model explains very well the difference between the liberal-residual welfare state in the Anglo-Saxon countries and the generous welfare state in Scandinavia. However, the approach fails to account for the substantial differences between the Scandinavian regime and the equally generous, yet profoundly different continental, conservative welfare states. The empirical typology clearly demonstrates the existence of three worlds, not two, as we showed earlier. So we need a theoretical account for the three-way variation, and it is here that the importance of elements other than class come in, especially religion.

Majoritarian electoral rules are associated with a two-party system, and in these systems the middle class more often votes for center-right parties. In such two-party systems, the labor-capital split dominates politics. All other cleavages – including, for instance, the religious and center-periphery ones, even if they continue to be politically salient – remain latent or are incorporated in the basic labor-capital cleavage. So the basic Iversen-Soskice mechanism applies: under majoritarian electoral rules, two parties predominantly represent the economic split, and within this setting the middle class more often votes for conservative parties. The welfare state remains residual (liberal).

In PR systems, in contrast, a larger (effective) number of parties allows for the political representation of more than the dominant labor-capital division. The kinds of additional cleavages represented in the party system depends on the structure of the country in question. Here the distinction between the Nordic and the continental countries and their welfare regimes achieves particular relevance. In the north of Europe, religion did not become politicized and translated into party politics because these societies were not religiously heterogeneous and the "national revolution" did not lead to strong state-church conflicts. Instead, the primary-secondary (rural-urban) economy division assumed political relevance.

In marked contrast to the Catholic church in southern Europe, the northern Lutheran state churches did not feel fundamentally threatened when the new nation-state started to take over those responsibilities that previously had fallen under the responsibility of the church. Anti-clericalism never became a strong political current in Scandinavia. Instead, it was the cleavage between agrarian and industrial interests that became politicized and relevant in party politics, because the agrarian sector was still very strong at the moment of mass democratization in late industrializing Scandinavia. Only in Europe's north did strong parties of agrarian defense emerge and receive a substantial share of the votes over the entire postwar period. The strong position of the agrarian parties explains why almost all accounts of the historical development of the Nordic welfare state stress the importance of workers-farmers (red-green) coalitions for the formation and the subsequent expansion of the welfare state.

The political space occupied by agrarian parties in the north is occupied by Christian democratic parties on the European continent. These parties have their roots in political Catholicism and are the offspring of the fierce state-church conflicts of the late 19th and early 20th centuries (see Kalyvas 1996; Kalyvas and Van Kersbergen 2010). In the religiously mixed or homogenously Catholic countries, it is the state-church conflict, which – in addition to the left-right cleavage – is prominently represented in the party system. Parties of *religious*, not agrarian, interests therefore developed in continental Europe. And these parties became social democracy's most important ally in the major welfare state-building enterprise that took place after World War II.

This history of political class coalitions explains why we find liberal welfare states in countries with a majoritarian electoral system (exemplary case: the United Kingdom). But it also explains the generous social democratic welfare states in the north of Europe, the result of a coalition between social democratic parties and parties of agrarian defense. One important precondition for the emergence of a red-green coalition has been *the absence* of a strong religious cleavage, so that parties of religious defense did not enter the Scandinavian party systems. On Europe's continent, in turn, we find conservative welfare states that are the product of a coalition between social democracy (red) and Christian democracy (black), if the welfare state was not the product of Christian democracy alone, as for instance in a country like Italy, where the left was too weak and divided to exert much influence on public policy. In these continental countries the second cleavage represented in the party systems, besides the dominant left-right or labor-capital split, has been the religious one.

In sum, Iversen and Soskice correctly stressed the importance of class coalitions between lower and middle class as the driving force behind the redistributive quality of welfare regimes. However, only by also taking into account the different cleavage structures of the Nordic and continental countries in their impact on the emerging party systems can one identify *which type* of middle class party entered into a coalition with social democracy. This insight allows us to explain theoretically the three types of welfare regimes to which these different political class coalitions have led. This account thus offers a theoretical underpinning of the existence of three regimes that was absent in Esping-Andersen's work.

4.6. CONCLUSION

We conclude that it is important to remember that Esping-Andersen's story of the three worlds of welfare capitalism is, for all intents and purposes, a typological classification that effectively grouped together empirically the many worlds of welfare capitalism and rearranged them into three distinct types. To a considerable degree this seminal typology, so the data tell us, is still relevant for understanding the various worlds of welfare capitalism today. The logic of class coalitions under different electoral systems (majoritarian versus PR) explains why the middle class was sometimes included in the pro-welfare coalition and sometimes excluded from it. If excluded, the welfare state remained very much a residual system that predominantly catered to the needs of the poor, as in the liberal welfare regime. If the agrarian middle class and its party forged a bond with the working class's representative social democracy, a much more encompassing and redistributive system evolved, as in the social democratic regime of Scandinavia. If Christian democracy took the lead in bringing the middle class into the welfare state, the result was a much less universal, much less redistributive, but also much less residual welfare state, as in the conservative welfare regime of continental Europe. In the next chapter, we map and document empirically what these different regimes actually did. And we expect and highlight substantial differences between regimes in social and economic outcomes, because clearly the different regimes do very distinctive things.

5

What Do Welfare States Actually Do?

How Welfare States Protect against Social Risks and Fight Poverty and Inequality

5.1. INTRODUCTION

What are welfare states for? What do they do? These are the "big" questions we take up in this chapter. We again (see Chapter 1) quote Barr (2004: 7), who defines the raison d'être of the welfare state as follows: "The welfare state exists to enhance the welfare of people who (a) are weak and vulnerable, largely by providing social care, (b) are poor, largely through redistributive income transfers, or (c) are neither vulnerable nor poor, by organizing cash benefits to provide insurance and consumption smoothing, and by providing medical insurance and school education." This describes in a general way what welfare states do: enhancing the welfare of vulnerable groups of people in society and offering or facilitating social protection for all.

In Chapter 4, we showed that welfare states come in different shapes and sizes. They are founded on diverging conceptions of social rights and duties, prioritize different values (freedom, equality, solidarity), and set out to accomplish different objectives. There we mapped the crucial dimensions of variation according to which the various welfare regimes do very different things. We therefore expect the various welfare regimes to deal differently with the general objective of enhancing the welfare of the vulnerable and providing social protection for the population at large. The Anglo-Saxon, liberal, market-oriented, and targeted welfare states pledge to take care of the weak and the vulnerable. In contrast, the Scandinavian, state-oriented, and universalist systems also wish to take care of the middle class, as they are organized around the ideal of social citizenship. The continental and southern European family-oriented and particularist welfare states hold a middle position. They take care of various occupational groups according to those group's standards but rely strongly on the family for care. Still, Barr's definition describes what, in a general sense, all welfare states (should) do: enhance the welfare of vulnerable groups of people in society and offer or facilitate some level of social protection for all.

Although in Scandinavia redistribution is seen as part and parcel of the welfare state, in the rest of the world, as we argued in Chapter 3, welfare states are more about pooling and reapportioning social risks (e.g., old age, unemployment, and sickness) (Baldwin 1990). The redistribution of wealth and income from the rich to the poor is hardly an explicit goal for the liberal and conservative welfare states. In fact, the social insurance principle is meant to reproduce acquired socioeconomic status and inequality. Moreover, most welfare states characteristically transfer money within income strata, "from those of working age to those of retirement age, from the childless to those with children, from the well to the sick, from the employed to the unemployed, and so on" (Barry 1990: 505). This means that to see what welfare states actually do, we should first examine if and how well welfare states reapportion social risks by insuring major risks. This is the task we take up in section 5.3. Still, we also know that the existence of widespread poverty has been a major impetus for developing social policies in the first place – even if only to curb the poor's revolutionary socialist potential (see Chapter 3). We examine how welfare states address poverty in section 5.4. There is evidence that equal societies have healthier, more trustful, and happier citizens than unequal societies (Wilkinson and Pickett 2009; Stiglitz 2012). A high degree of inequality in a society potentially leads to unhappy voters who may rebel as a response. In section 5.5 we examine how the different types of welfare state regimes actually check inequality.

One important reason that we wish to know what welfare states do is that we expect the welfare state's performance to have an impact on the opportunities and constraints of (further) welfare state reform. Our reasoning here is straightforward. First, if the welfare state does not do what it sets out to do, or not anymore, this can be regarded as policy failure or the failure to adjust (i.e., policy drift), implying that resistance against major reforms would not be too great. In fact, one could imagine that the public at large and the voters in particular find themselves in a situation of large-scale welfare state failure in the fields of poverty and inequality reduction. In such a context, both those who abhor the welfare state already and those who expect much from it but are disappointed would be willing to accept major reforms. The first group aspires for reform to dismantle a costly yet nonfunctioning system. The second group desires for the welfare state to improve its performance in fighting poverty and inequality. This would be the basis for an otherwise unlikely coalition of pro-welfare state reform forces. Second, in the case that the welfare state performs well, the odds for reform would be very different. In that case, those who directly benefit from anti-poverty and anti-inequality policies have a clear vested interest in their continuation, whereas those who loathe the welfare state might still oppose the policies but cannot claim that the state does not deliver. The prospects for a coalition that supports major or radical reforms are then much more unpromising, and any reform effort of this type must be accompanied by proof that the proposed measures do not substantially affect the poverty and inequality moderation effect of the welfare state. Third, if major inefficiencies exist in anti-poverty and inequality policies, a struggle can be expected between those who see this condition as requiring the abolition of the programs and those who wish to turn "vice into virtue" (Levy 1999).

Finally, we build on the counterfactual argument we developed in Chapter 1 (see also Chapter 2): we assume that if welfare states work, this must indicate that they have been permanently reforming, that is, adapting, updating, retrenching, or restructuring, to adjust to their continually changing social and economic environment. If they had not done so, they would not have been able to advance the welfare of the vulnerable and offer social protection. The plausibility of this counterfactual argument is supported by the empirical phenomenon of intentional policy drift, that is, the conscious decision by policymakers *not* to adapt social policies to changing circumstances, as a result of which they not only fail to accomplish their goals but even undermine their set objectives (see Chapter 1).

In this chapter, we compare 18 developed welfare states (grouped according to welfare state regime type) between the mid-1970s and the mid-2000s and add analyses of later points in time if the data are available. The countries included are again Australia, Canada, Ireland, New Zealand, the United Kingdom, the United States (the liberal regime), Austria, Belgium, France, Germany, Italy, the Netherlands, Switzerland (the conservative regime), Denmark, Finland, Sweden, Norway (the social democratic regime), and Japan. Summarizing our findings, we show what welfare states actually do and – given the challenges and threats they face – that they perform surprisingly well. Risk coverage has remained relatively stable over time or, in some cases, has even been improved. For the generosity of social benefits we find a similar result of relative stability, although if one looks at real values especially of unemployment benefits, one observes a gradual decline over time since the early 1980s, as a result of both policy drift and overt political choice (Green-Pedersen et al. 2012). Social expenditure to cover new social risks – those type of risks that are typically not covered by conventional welfare state arrangements like the reconciliation of work and family life (Bonoli 2005, 2006) – has increased and did typically not occur at the expense of old risks' coverage. Welfare states also continue to fight poverty and reduce inequality but seem to have increasing, albeit varying, difficulties in doing this with success. Welfare states work, have remained relatively stable over time, and differ in how good they are in performing their tasks. The social democratic regime is the best performer, the liberal regime the worst, and the conservative regime holds a middle position.

5.2. A METHODOLOGICAL CAVEAT

Before we can assess how the different welfare states and regimes cover social risks, fight poverty, and reduce inequality, we must issue an important methodological caveat. Although it is often routinely done, estimating the welfare states' effect on coverage, poverty, and income inequality, as well as, for instance, labor market participation, is actually tricky (Kenworthy 2004; Esping-Andersen and Myles 2009). The reason is that we need information about the world – say, the primary income distribution or the original poverty level – *before* it is affected by welfare state intervention to be able to estimate the outcome *after* intervention. However, the problem is that welfare states are already implicated in the "free" labor market, the primary income distribution, or the original poverty level. As Esping-Andersen and Myles (2009: 640–641) emphasize, the welfare state affects the original income distribution in two ways. First, the welfare state's very existence induces substantial market inequality "because it produces large populations with low or even zero market incomes, such as pensioners or women on maternity leave." Second, the welfare state influences the original income distribution by providing resources, like education or support to working mothers, which affect individuals' earning potential. This means, so Esping-Andersen and Myles (2009: 640–641) argue, that

to really estimate redistribution we would need to invent a counter-factual "virgin" distribution that was unaffected by social policy altogether. No such distribution exists in the real world. The degree of distortion that ensues from a comparison of pre- and post-redistribution inequalities will vary very much across welfare states. [Moreover], … the provision of social services can have major effects on the distribution of well-being but such effects go unmeasured in income statistics. Since social insurance primarily serves to smooth incomes across the life cycle, its relevant redistributive effects must be related to income on a lifetime basis.

Similarly, Saunders (2010: 528) correctly notes that if welfare state programs did not exist – or not to the same extent – "people's behaviour would change in ways that would 'fill the gap' provided by the government (e.g., individuals would have to work harder and save for their own retirement) … and this would lead to changes in MI [market income], and in its distribution." Esping-Andersen and Myles (2009: 241) advise us to remember that the welfare state's redistributive principles vary, whereby some "may promote more equality of outcomes or of opportunities, while others may actually work in the opposite direction." Moreover, and related to Saunders (2010), they warn us to keep in mind that "the income data that we routinely use pick up only a part of the overall welfare state effect" (Esping-Andersen and Myles 2009: 241). With this caveat in mind, we now turn to how the different welfare states and regimes protect against social risks, address poverty, and deal with inequality.

5.3. TO WHAT EXTENT DO WELFARE STATES COVER SOCIAL RISKS AND HOW GENEROUS ARE THEY?

If the welfare state is about risk reapportioning through compulsory insurance against major risks (e.g., the risk of income loss in old age), then the first simple thing to look at is how well the population exposed to market forces is actually covered by such insurance. Table 5.1 gives the coverage ratios of the four most important insurance programs (old age, unemployment, sickness, and accidents) in 1975 and 2000. Coverage is the ratio of the number of insured persons divided by the labor force (Korpi and Palme 2007). We chose the date 1975 because arguably the expansion of the welfare state had not yet ended around the mid-1970s, although growth had already been slowing down. The first attempts at cost containment and retrenchment were made soon afterward in the wake of the oil crises and ensuing stagflation, but these do not show up in the numbers for 1975. Therefore, 1975 can be taken as a typical representative year of the welfare state in the golden age, that is, the year just before the "silver" age, or the time of permanent austerity, set in (Taylor-Gooby 2002; Ferrera 2008). The latest year for which comparative data for coverage are available is 2000. The programs included in Table 5.1 all grant benefits as a social right through legislation at the national level. Only programs are included that have been created through national legislation and/or programs where the conditions concerning entitlements are regulated by the state, and where the state contributes to the financing. For federal states, programs are included that – despite lacking national legislation – exist in all states (definitions and data are taken from the Social Citizenship Indicator Program [SCIP], see Korpi and Palme 2007).

The coverage data for the four programs in Table 5.1 show that the welfare state provides protection against the major risks for a remarkably large proportion of the labor force, but also that such protection is certainly not all inclusive. On average, coverage ratios are highest for pensions and accidents: 80 to 90 percent of the labor force is covered by insurance for these programs. Pensions cover the risk of labor market exit because of old age, and accident insurance covers the risk of labor market exit due to incapacity to work. This high proportion is probably explained by the fact that the programs insure risks that are furthest away from the labor market and where the incentive to build in work incentives is nonexistent or very low.

Looking at the pattern over time, we see that pension coverage remained high and stable between 1975 and 2000. Interestingly, in three of the liberal countries, pension coverage increased over 10 percentage points between 1975 and 2000 (Ireland, the United Kingdom, and the United States). According to the SCIP 2007 data, pension coverage drops from 100 percent to 0 percent between these two years in Australia. However, this must be a mistake, because neither was the public pension scheme abolished nor was it dramatically reduced (Rein and Turner 2001). To estimate the correct figure, we report the pension take-up rate of those above the retirement age for 2000 (taken from the SCIP dataset). This rate of 81 percent corresponds nicely with the figure of a public pension coverage (82 percent) that Rein and Turner (2001: 114) report.

Looking at the regime averages, the social democratic regime has the highest pension coverage (100 percent in 2000), followed by the liberal regime (84 percent) and the conservative regime (71 percent). In the conservative regime, the

TABLE 5.1. The coverage and generosity of major social insurance programs (proportion of labor force covered), 1975 and 2000

Country	Pension coverage		Unemployment coverage		Sickness coverage		Accident coverage		Generosity		Net UI rr		
	1975	2000	1975	2000	1975	2000	1975	2000	1975	2000	1975	2000	2009
Australia	1.00	.82[a]	.00	.00	.00	.00	.75	.75	17.6	18.4	.47	.64	.54
Canada	1.00	1.00	.90	.78	.90	.78	.79	.80	24.6	25.5	.77	.76	.72
Ireland	.53	.78	.71	.97	.71	1.00	.81	1.00	17.2	26.9	.78	.50	.64
N. Zealand	1.00	1.00	.00	.00	.00	.00	1.00	1.00	22.2	23.7	.63	.57	.47
UK	.58	.69	.74	.83	.78	.90	.90	.83	16.0	21.4	.67	.54	.52
US	.59	.73	.74	.90	.00	.00	.73	.89	16.8	18.8	.59	.57	.52
Aver. LR	*.78*	*.84*	*.52*	*.58*	*.40*	*.45*	*.83*	*.88*	*19.1*	*22.5*	*.65*	*.60*	*.57*
Austria	.66	.64	.66	.66	.80	.76	.95	1.00	23.7	28.9	.48	.72	.68
Belgium	.54	.57	.68	.63	.79	.84	.59	.63	27.5	32.6	.62	.59	.60
France	.53	.60	.61	.62	.85	.82	.79	.79	26.7	28.0	.36	.72	.70
Germany	.62	.60	.73	.69	.71	.73	1.00	1.00	28.3	27.5	.70	.71	.72
Italy	.61	.57	.50	.51	.74	.62	.48	.82	19.2	26.7	.20	.49	.73
NL	1.00	1.00	.77	.84	.77	.84	.77	.84	32.2	35.8	.92	.78	.72
Switzerland	1.00	1.00	.33	.85	.81	.78	.53	.85	25.2	19.6	.81	.82	.83
Aver. CR	*.71*	*.71*	*.61*	*.69*	*.78*	*.77*	*.73*	*.85*	*26.1*	*28.4*	*.58*	*.69*	*.71*
Denmark	1.00	1.00	.44	.77	1.00	1.00	.80	1.00	29.2	35.4	.69	.66	.62
Finland	1.00	1.00	.57	1.00	1.00	1.00	.83	.81	25.5	30.7	.51	.68	.63
Norway	1.00	1.00	.91	.88	1.00	1.00	.94	.88	30.0	41.6	.67	.72	.72
Sweden	1.00	1.00	.75	1.00	1.00	1.00	1.00	1.00	38.9	36.2	.83	.72	.63
Aver. SDR	*1.00*	*1.00*	*.67*	*.91*	*1.00*	*1.00*	*.89*	*.92*	*30.9*	*36.0*	*.68*	*.70*	*.65*
Japan	.74	.82	.44	.50	.57	.52	.64	.72	12.6	20.4	.66	.56	.56
Average	.80	.84	.58	.69	.70	.70	.79	.87	24.1	27.7	.63	.65	.64

a This is the pension take-up rate after the retirement age (Korpi and Palme 2007); see main text for why we report this figure here.

Notes: LR is liberal regime; CR is conservative regime; SDR is social democratic regime; net UI rr is net unemployment insurance replacement rate for a one earner couple with two dependent children.

Sources: Coverage ratios: Korpi and Palme (2007); Generosity data: Scruggs (2004); Net UI replacement rates: Van Vliet and Caminada (2012).

within-regime variation among the countries is more substantial than within the other regimes, with Italy and Belgium having a low coverage rate of 57 percent and the Netherlands and Switzerland a high rate of 100 percent.

With respect to accident coverage, there is an average increase of 8 percent between 1975 and 2000. This rise results mainly from the major boosts in coverage in Switzerland (an increase of 43 percentage points), Italy (plus 34), Ireland (plus 19), and the United States (plus 16). These increases more than offset the reductions in coverage in Finland (minus 2 percentage points), Norway (minus 6), and the United Kingdom (minus 7). For accident coverage, the regime averages are the same as those for pensions, with the social democratic regime having again the highest coverage (100 percent in 2000), followed by the liberal regime (88 percent), and the conservative regime on the bottom (85 percent).

Compared to pension and accident coverage, unemployment coverage is on average much lower in 1975 (58 percent), although it approaches the coverage levels of pensions in 2000 (69 percent). Note that countries with below average coverage typically have relatively strict systems of employment protection, so that in these cases labor market incentives are probably not the overriding objective of low coverage. In fact, there is a trade-off between unemployment benefits and employment protection legislation (Neugart 2008). In any case, we see that over time most countries hardly change their unemployment coverage. The countries that do display a change tend to increase their coverage a lot (US is up 16 percentage points, Sweden plus 25, Ireland plus 26, Denmark plus 33, Finland plus 43, and Switzerland plus 52). Unemployment coverage is on average the highest in the social democratic regime (91 percent), followed by the conservative regime (69 percent), and the liberal regime (58 percent). Note that our focus on two time points hides the possible variation over time. Such variation is particularly pronounced for unemployment coverage. There are only two countries (Denmark and Finland) where the increase in coverage over time is steady, that is, with an increase visible in 1980, 1985, 1990, and so on. In five other countries, the increase in coverage took place between 1975 and 1980 or between 1980 and 1985 and stayed at about the same level thereafter (Switzerland and Sweden), or fell between 1995 and 2000 (UK and Belgium). In Italy, coverage went down between 1975 and 1980 but increased between 1980 and 1985. These patterns indicate that the story is not one of universal expansion from 1975 to 2000 but that many countries display both retrenchment and expansion (or vice versa). However, the overall trend in unemployment coverage between 1975 and 2000 is toward higher coverage levels.

The average for sickness coverage is 70 percent between 1975 and 2000. The variation across the regimes is substantially larger for this program than for the other three. The social democratic countries cover 100 percent, while three of the liberal countries cover 0 percent (Australia, New Zealand, and the United States). The liberal regime's average is consequently low (40 percent in 1975 and 45 in 2000), despite the high coverage in the other three liberal countries. The conservative regime is on average once more in the middle, with sickness coverage at 81 percent in 1975 and 78 percent in 2000. The reduction is mainly due to the 12 percentage point decrease of coverage in Italy; the other conservative countries display only little change.

All in all, with respect to coverage, the welfare state clearly provides protection against risks, although the variation across countries is considerable, especially in sickness insurance. However, coverage ratios do not inform us exactly how *well* the labor force is protected against these risks because they do not offer any information on the benefits' generosity. Table 5.1 therefore also presents the generosity index as developed and measured by Scruggs (2004) and based on Esping-Andersen's (1990) decommodification index (see Chapter 4). The generosity index summarizes information on the coverage of unemployment and sickness insurance but also includes data on how much income a benefit replaces, a benefit's duration, whether there are qualifying periods and waiting days before a benefit is granted, how much contribution employees have to pay, and how many people entitled to a pension benefit actually claim it (i.e., the take-up rate of pensions) (see Scruggs and Allan 2006). The higher the generosity index, the more generous (decommodifying) a welfare state system is.

Theoretically, the generosity index ranges from 0 to 100, with 0 indicating a state in which citizens are fully dependent on the market for their livelihood (i.e., when there is no welfare state) and 100 showing that the welfare state provides everything for citizens' livelihood (i.e., when the market plays no role). Empirically, the generosity index ranges from 11.0 (Japan in 1971) to 45.1 (Sweden in 1983), suggesting that even in the most generous countries, individuals still depend mostly on the market for their livelihood. Average generosity across the 18 developed democracies is 24 in 1975 and almost 28 in 2000. However, the variation across countries and regimes is substantial. In 1975, four welfare states (Ireland, Japan, the United Kingdom, and the United States) score one standard deviation below average generosity, and two welfare states (the Netherlands and Sweden) one standard deviation above it. In 2000, there are again four countries (Australia, the United States, Switzerland, and Japan) that score one standard deviation below the average generosity, and even four (the Netherlands, Denmark, Sweden, and Norway) that score one standard deviation above it. When we examine the regime averages, the social democratic regime enters again in the top position with average generosity of almost 31 in 1975 and 36 in 2000. The conservative regime is next, with average generosity of 26 in 1975 and 28 in 2000. The liberal regime again brings up the rear with average generosity of 19 in 1975 and about 23 in 2000.

Recently, Van Vliet and Caminada (2012) updated the Scruggs data for unemployment insurance net replacement rates (i.e., the percentage of the last earned wage the benefit recipient received, after the deduction of taxes) to 2009. The last column in Table 5.1 presents these data for 1975, 2000, and 2009 for a one-earner couple with two dependent children. It is particularly interesting to look at what happened to unemployment insurance replacement rates in the most recent period to see what the reality of retrenchment is in the 2000s. We know that public opinion research finds that, generally, unemployment benefit recipients are considered to be the least deserving welfare clients. If anywhere, then, it is in unemployment benefits that we expect retrenchment to be pronounced. On average and in many countries, however, this is not what we find. Generally, the conservative regime has the highest net replacement rate in 2009. This rate has increased from 58 percent in 1975 to 71 percent in 2009 – which is also the highest average replacement rate of the three regimes. In most of the conservative countries, the replacement rate has gone up since 1975. This holds particularly for Italy (from 20 percent in 1975 to 73 percent in 2009), France (36 percent to 70 percent), and to a somewhat lesser extent Austria (48 percent to 68 percent). Only in the Netherlands did the net replacement rate for unemployment insurance fall during this period, but from a very high level (from 92 percent in 1975 to 72 percent in 2009). In the liberal and social democratic regimes, conversely, the net unemployment insurance replacement rates dropped between 1975 and 2009 (from 65 percent to 57 percent and from 68 percent to 65 percent, respectively). In the social democratic regime, the fall was largest in Sweden (from 83 percent to 63 percent) and small in Denmark (69 percent to 62 percent); Finland increased its rate between 1975 and 2000 (51 percent to 68 percent) and reduced it between 2000 and 2009 (to 63 percent). Finally, Norway increased its replacement rate between 1975 and 2000 (from 67 percent to 72 percent), and left it at this level. In the liberal regime, almost all countries reduced their replacement rates between 1975 and 2000, and further between 2000 and 2009 (Canada, New Zealand, United Kingdom, and United States). In Ireland, the replacement rate which had been reduced in 2000 (from 78 percent to 50 percent), was increased in 2009 (to 64 percent). In Australia, the replacement rate went up between 1975 and 2000 (from 47 percent to 64 percent), while it had decreased by 2009 (to 54 percent). All in all, the development of net unemployment insurance replacement rates between 1975 and 2009 indicate an expansion rather than retrenchment in six countries. And even though most countries did cut back their replacement rates between 1975 and 2009, on average, the unemployment replacement rate remains at about the same level in 1975, 2000, and 2009 (63 percent, 65 percent, and 64 percent).

Summing up, the data in Table 5.1 seem to warrant the conclusion that welfare states offer protection against social risks and pure market dependence. Not all countries cover all social risks equally well, or course, and the programs' generosity also varies substantially across countries and types. But most remarkably and perhaps unexpectedly, the average coverage and overall generosity of all programs *increased* between 1975 and the 2000s, despite retrenchment and restructuring that many programs were experiencing at that time. This suggests that over time welfare states have actually become *better* at social protection.

However, at this point we must mention another caveat with coverage and generosity data, namely, that the numbers hide the extent to which different groups are covered by the programs. In general, most programs cover the full-time employed with no job interruptions, while the coverage of individuals outside the labor market (say, housewives) or people with an atypical employment profile (e.g., those who have job interruptions or work part-time) may be substantially poorer (see Emmenegger et al. 2012). Also, these data do not tell us much about the protection against the new social risks (see Bonoli 2005, 2006), for instance, the problem of reconciling work and family life. Given that atypical employment and new social risk profiles have actually become much more normal in most countries (see Chapter 8), this is an important point when the coverage ratios of traditional risks are evaluated.

A final issue concerns the difference between gross and net benefits. In judging the relative generosity of regimes, we need to take into account whether benefit recipients receive extra income or have to pay taxes. If we do, we observe that the difference between the generosity of the social democratic and conservative regimes vis-à-vis the liberal regime is not so large (Adema 2000; see also Esping-Andersen 2005). Those countries with higher direct expenditures (particularly Denmark, Finland, and Sweden) claim back a larger share of these expenditures through the tax system than do countries that spend less. The average difference between net and gross expenditures in the social democratic regime was no less than 9.6 percentage points in 1995. This difference was reduced to 5 percentage points in 2005. In the conservative regime, the difference between gross and net expenditures is substantially lower, but still large. Because of changes mainly in the tax system, net expenditures in the conservative regime were on average higher than gross expenditure in 2005, albeit only slightly so. Interestingly, the net expenditures in the countries of the liberal regime are always *higher* than the gross expenditures. This probably stems to a large extent from the lower value added tax (VAT) in the liberal regime than in the conservative and, especially, social democratic regimes. The difference in the United States is especially striking. In this country, which in 1995 was the lowest gross spender, with 17 percent of GDP on gross social expenditures, the net rates are almost 7.5 percentage points higher than the gross rates. Consequently, in net terms, the United States is almost as generous as the Netherlands – a country that used to be known for its welfare state generosity. In 2005, net expenditures are even 11 percentage points higher in the United States than are gross expenditures, as a result of which the United States is *more* generous than, for instance, the Netherlands in net terms. Because of these differences, the averages of the three regimes in terms of net rates are much closer than those of the gross rates (data taken from Adema 2000: 194, table 1; Adema and Ladaique 2009; authors' calculations).

5.4. TO WHAT EXTENT DO WELFARE STATES REDUCE
POVERTY?

Most scholars, and probably policymakers and citizens too, agree that reducing poverty is a – or perhaps even *the* – central aim of the welfare state (e.g., Fraser 1994; Kenworthy 1999). Actually, as Barry (1990: 503) notes, to a large extent, welfare state policies not only *relieve* poverty; they primarily *prevent* it by "providing money to people who qualify for it … in such a way that poverty does not as a matter of fact arise." Yet, poverty is an enduring phenomenon that even the most generous welfare states need to deal with it. Table 5.2 lists the percentage of people at risk of poverty and exclusion in selected European countries in 2009. The measure concerns the number of persons with an equivalized disposable income below the risk-of-poverty threshold, which is set at 60 percent of the national median equivalized disposable income (after social transfers). The equivalized income is "a measure of household income that takes account of the differences in a household's size and composition, and thus is equivalised or made equivalent for all household sizes and compositions" (http://epp.eurostat.ec.europa.eu/statistics_explained/index.php/Glossary:Equivalised_income, accessed October 2011). These Eurostat data show that there are welfare states that are not particularly good at fighting poverty, especially the Mediterranean countries. But even the best welfare state in this respect (the Netherlands) still has 11 percent of its population at risk of poverty, even after social transfers.

So, if preventing and reducing poverty are crucial goals of the welfare state, why is it so difficult to achieve them fully? Drawing on Kenworthy (1999) and Hill (2006), we identify a first reason in that money spent on social policies may not, or not enough of it, reach the poor but rather end up in the pockets of the higher income strata. This is the so-called biblical Matthew effect, that is, "for unto every one that hath shall be given, and he shall have abundance: but from him that hath not shall be taken away even that which he hath" (Matthew 25:29). Some recent studies indicate that the Matthew effect may be considerable, especially in education, but also in pensions and services that cater to new social risks (Cantillon 2010, 2011: 5; but see Vandenbroucke and Vleminckx 2011), while other studies seem to indicate that social investment policies that cover new social risk are (or at least can be) of an egalitarian nature too (Vaalavuo 2010; Hemerijck 2013: chapter 10; but see Cantillon 2011).

A second reason that the welfare state may not lower poverty is that redistributive policies may foster welfare dependency and, by extension, poverty. It is true that welfare policies may involve work disincentives, but empirically there does not seem to be a direct relationship between (generous) benefits and welfare dependency. The comparatively low poverty rates in the most generous welfare states, such as the Scandinavian ones, are an indication of this. Also the relationship between *declining* generosity and *rising* poverty in the United States suggests that there is no one-on-one link between the two.

TABLE 5.2. *People at risk of poverty after social transfers; percentage of total population, 2009*

	People at risk of poverty (% of total population)
Ireland	15.0
United Kingdom	17.3
Average LR	*16.2*
Austria	12.0
Belgium	14.6
France	12.9
Germany	15.5
Greece	19.7
Italy	18.4
Netherlands	11.1
Portugal	17.9
Spain	19.5
Switzerland	15.1
Average CR	*15.7*
Denmark	13.1
Finland	13.8
Norway	11.7
Sweden	13.3
Average SDR	13.0

Notes: LR is liberal regime; CR is conservative regime; SDR is social democratic regime.

Source: Eurostat, available from http://epp.eurostat.ec.europa.eu/tgm/table.do?tab=table&plugin=1&language=en&pcode=tessio10 [accessed October 2011].

A third and related reason that the welfare state may not reduce poverty is that generous benefits inhibit economic growth. This is the well-known equality-efficiency trade-off hypothesis, which holds that higher levels of progressive taxation and generous welfare benefits lower the incentives to invest and work and thereby limit economic growth (e.g., Okun 1975, but see Brady 2003, 2005; Kenworthy 1999; Scruggs and Allan 2006). A seemingly plausible argument against the positive impact of the welfare state on the reduction of poverty thus holds that although the welfare state reduces poverty, it does so only in the short run, and if poverty is defined in relative terms (e.g., as the number of people in a country with a certain percentage of the median income in that country). Whether a relative measure of poverty or an absolute level should be preferred is a matter of considerable academic debate (see Kenworthy 2008: chapter 2). Many studies focusing on the developed countries use a relative measure of poverty – typically 50 or 60 percent of the median income (e.g., Brady 2003, 2005). The "official" poverty line of the European Union is 60 percent of the median national equivalized income, which is the figure that we employed earlier. Using a relative measure for these countries makes sense, because whether someone is poor in developed countries is influenced by the specific conditions in that country as well as by the normal expenditure patterns (Nolan and Marx 2009). Across the 27 EU countries, for instance, the national at-risk-of-poverty thresholds for a household consisting of two adults and two children younger than 14 varied between 34,661 purchasing power standards (PPS) in Luxembourg to 5,882 in Bulgaria in 2008 (Atkinson et al. 2010). PPS is a measure that converts amounts expressed in a national currency to an artificial common currency, equalizing the purchasing power of different national currencies (including those countries sharing a common currency).

A problem with a relative measure of poverty is that welfare programs' dynamic effects become invisible, especially "the possibility that such programs reduce the society's growth rate and therefore hurt the poor over the long run" (Kenworthy 1999: 1123). If welfare policies lower work or investment incentives in the longer run, as the equality-efficiency trade-off thesis posits they do, the longer run effect of welfare policies on the poor may be detrimental – despite any short-run positive effect. If a researcher is interested in such longer run effects, an absolute measure of poverty is therefore to be preferred. Researchers typically measure absolute poverty by looking at post-tax/post-transfer household income, adjusted for the number of persons in the households (because there are usually economies of scale in a household) in some country (very often the United States) and make a choice as to the percentage (say, 50 percent) of the median income, which is the poverty line. This is then the standard for other countries (adjusted for inflation, using purchasing power parities to convert various currencies into US dollars). In developing countries, conversely, the notion of absolute poverty is typically used to assess households' inability to obtain the essentials for their livelihood. The standard in this regard is the World Bank's categorization of those persons living on less than $1 a day as "extremely poor" and less than $2 a day as "poor" (see Ferreira and Ravallion 2009).

Although it matters whether a researcher employs a relative or an absolute measure of poverty, most empirical evidence suggests that welfare state policies lower both types of poverty. Focusing on absolute poverty, Kenworthy (1999) finds that the reduction effect of social policies on poverty is robust even if the indirect and dynamic effects are taken into account. Similarly, Scruggs and Allan (2006) find that more generous welfare entitlements lower both relative and absolute poverty rates. The most recent research available stresses that there is a strong relationship between the size of the welfare state (level of social spending) and the reduction in relative poverty among the working age population (see Figure 5.1). Different welfare states may combat poverty in different ways, but, as Nolan and Marx (2009: 329–330) also highlight, the data

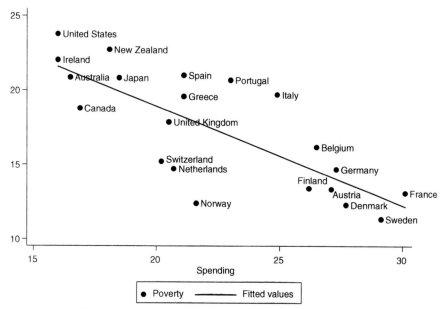

FIGURE 5.1. The relationship between social spending (% GDP) and poverty (% of total population < 60 % of median income), mid-2000s.

Notes: Regression coefficient: –0.67; Beta: –0.77; Adjusted R²: 0.57.

Source: OECD dataset, http://stats.oecd.org/Index.aspx?DataSetCode=POVERTY and http://stats.oecd.org/Index.aspx?DataSetCode=SOCX_AGG (Accessed February 2013).

portrayed in Figure 5.1 show that low levels of poverty are nowhere achieved without high levels of social spending.

There are therefore grounds to question the empirical validity of the assertion that more equality leads to inefficiency (i.e., lower economic growth). Efficiency and equality can go hand in hand. Welfare benefits can, for example, stabilize consumer demand and offer increased training opportunities for the poor. For a long time, scholars and policymakers alike considered only two models viable: the "bad" liberal regime's neoliberal model or the "good" Scandinavian regime's social democratic one (the conservative regime's model was considered to be the "ugly" one; see Esping-Andersen 2002; Manow 2004). However, the liberal countries seem to have most difficulty coping with the aftershocks of the financial and economic crisis of 2008, whereas some of the conservative countries, like Germany, perform comparatively well (see Chapter 10).

In any case, taken as a goal in itself, poverty reduction is a task of the welfare state and although nowhere poverty is prevented, the welfare state's impact is considerable. Esping-Andersen and Myles (2009: 656–657) present compelling data on the poverty reduction through the welfare state for a group

TABLE 5.3. *Poverty (< 50 % median equivalent income) reduction in families with children, mid-1990s*

	Market poverty	Post-redistribution poverty	Percent reduction of poverty
Australia	32	17	47
Canada	29	16	45
Ireland	28	15	46
United Kingdom	39	21	46
United States	31	26	16
Average LR	32	*19*	*40*
Belgium	31	6.0	81
France	40	10	75
Germany	31	12	61
Italy	37	21	43
Netherlands	25	8	68
Average CR	33	*12*	*66*
Denmark	30	6.0	80
Finland	18	3.0	83
Norway	29	5.0	83
Sweden	39	4.0	90
Average SDR	29	*5.0*	*84*

Notes: LR is liberal regime; CR is conservative regime; SDR is social democratic regime.
Source: Esping-Andersen and Myles (2009: 656, table 25.3); averages are authors' calculations.

at risk of poverty – families with children – in the mid-1990s. They measure poverty relatively as less than 50 percent of the median equivalent income. Table 5.3 presents the data.

Table 5.3 shows that, perhaps somewhat surprisingly, pre-redistribution poverty rates hardly vary across the welfare regimes. On average, market poverty is almost identical in the liberal and the conservative regimes (32 and 33 percent) and only slightly lower in the social democratic regime (29 percent). The variation across countries is also modest, with market poverty ranging from a high 40 percent in France and low 18 percent in Finland. Esping-Andersen and Myles (2009: 656) note that there seems to be even more child poverty in Sweden than in the United States, but explain that this is due to the "artificiality of the 'original' income distribution [discussed in section 5.2]. The universality of paid maternity leave in Sweden and the lack thereof in the USA implies a large number of zero-earner mothers in Sweden compared to the USA."

Once we enter redistribution, clear differences emerge across the regimes. The social democratic regime is by far the most redistributive, reducing market poverty by 84 percent to only 5 percent on average. The conservative regime holds the middle position, having on average a reduction of market poverty of 66 percent leading to post-redistribution poverty of 12 percent. The liberal regime, finally, is the least redistributive with an average reduction of market poverty of 40 percent – half the average redistribution in the social democratic regime – resulting in post-redistribution poverty of 19 percent. Looking at the individual countries, we see a large variation in post-redistribution poverty in the conservative regime (from a high of 21 in Italy to a low of 6 in Belgium). The variation within the other two regimes is substantially lower (from 15 in Ireland to 26 in the United States in the liberal regime, and from 3 in Finland and 6 in Denmark in the social democratic regime).

How can we explain the variation across countries in poverty rates? Nolan and Marx (2009: 328ff.) identify several factors that help account for this variation. First, a high employment rate generally helps to avoid poverty, although it is not a sufficient condition. Those welfare states that create jobs are best at fighting poverty. Second, if a household is capable of generating more than one income, the risk of poverty declines. Here the type of welfare state plays an important role because some welfare states include policy-induced obstacles to multiple earners, such as restrictions on part-time work, as well as work-entry disincentives implied by benefits, dual earner penalties in tax-benefit systems, or insufficient childcare facilities. Some countries would have a much lower rate of poverty if they had a more equal distribution of work among households (rather than individuals). Again, this is partly a welfare state effect, because welfare state policies can stimulate and facilitate (or hinder) female labor market participation. Third, employment of lone mothers dramatically decreases child poverty (see also Esping-Andersen 2009: 124–125). Of course, whether a single mother is capable of taking a job depends on whether the market, the family, or the welfare state helps with childcare needs. Because child poverty is concentrated in low income families, it is likely that the market in this case will fail to provide (enough) care: there is just not enough money to buy good quality childcare. The family is likely to fail, too, especially among low education and low income couples that have higher divorce rates. Hence it is the welfare state that must do the job. Those welfare states that provide good childcare for low income families, and especially lone mothers, fight poverty best. Fourth, policies that aim to provide work incentives by lowering benefits do not help to fight poverty. Retrenching benefits actually produces higher poverty. To control poverty, then, benefits simply need to keep up with living standards.

In addition to the variation in poverty rates across countries, there is also variation in poverty across groups within a country. Generally, the households or individuals at highest risk of being poor include those "with low levels of education and skills, the low paid, the unemployed, people with disabilities, lone parents, large families, the elderly, children, ethnic minorities, migrants, and refugees" (Nolan and Marx 2009: 326). Christopher (2002) has analyzed how the welfare state reduces poverty among the largest subgroup of lone parents: single mothers (see Table 5.4). As for poverty in general, the social democratic regime reduces poverty among single mothers (as well as mothers in general) the most, followed by the conservative regime, and with the liberal

TABLE 5.4. *The percentage reduction in poverty rates due to tax/transfer system, mid-1990s*

	Single mothers	Mothers
Australia	44.2	43.3
Canada	31.4	38.5
United Kingdom	56.9	49.3
United States	14.0	13.3
Average LR	36.6	36.1
France	63.7	69.2
Germany	28.0	28.6
Netherlands	73.2	53.4
Average CR	55.0	50.4
Finland	86.3	79.2
Sweden	89.1	89.8
Average SDR	87.7	84.5

Notes: LR is liberal regime; CR is conservative regime; SDR is social democratic regime.
Source: Christopher (2002, table 2).

regime once more doing the least. The United States especially does little to reduce the poverty of single mothers and reduces poverty only by 14 percent (compared to the almost 90 percent reduction in Sweden). Within the conservative regime, Germany stands out for its fairly limited reduction of poverty among single mothers (28 percent), as well as among mothers in general (almost 29 percent).

5.5. TO WHAT EXTENT DO WELFARE STATES REDUCE INCOME INEQUALITY?

We now turn to the question of income inequality: how much do welfare states limit this? Table 5.5 provides an overview of income inequality across countries, welfare regimes, and time, using the Gini coefficient after taxes and transfers. The higher the Gini coefficient, the more unequal is the distribution of income in a society. Specifically, a Gini coefficient of 0 indicates perfect equality (all individuals or households have identical incomes) and a Gini coefficient of 1 means perfect inequality (one individual or household has all the income whereas the rest has none). Comparing the data from the mid-1970s and mid-1980s to those for the mid-2000s, we see that on average, inequality has increased in all welfare regimes and in most individual countries as well. Only in Ireland and Belgium does inequality stay the same throughout this period and only in France does it fall. The largest increase in inequality between the mid-1980s and the mid-2000s takes place in New Zealand (from .27 to .34), followed by Finland (from .21 to .27), Norway (from .23 to .28), the United States (from .34 to .38), Italy (from .31 to .35), and Germany (from .26 to .30).

Remarkably, these fairly large rises in inequality take place in each of the three regimes. On average, the social democratic regime has remained nearest to equal over time, with a Gini coefficient of .25 in the mid-2000s. Norway stood out with the highest inequality among the Scandinavian countries in the mid-2000s, but recent data indicate that inequality has been decreasing again since 2005, with the Gini coefficient standing at .24 in 2009, that is, perfectly in line again with the average of the Scandinavian countries.[1] The conservative regime is once more second in line with a Gini of .29. Within this regime, Italy stands out for its relatively high inequality (.35 in the mid-2000s), suggesting that this country may perhaps be better seen as part of a fourth, Mediterranean regime (see Chapter 4) that, primarily due to family failure and the absence of (adequate) social assistance programs, does not cope with poverty as efficiently as the conservative regime (Ferrera 2005). The liberal regime's income distribution, finally, is on average the most unequal, with a Gini coefficient of .34. Within this regime, and thus also overall, the United States is clearly the country with the most unequal income distribution, which a Gini of .38 in the mid-2000s signifies.

A study by the Organisation for Economic Co-Operation and Development (OECD) (2008) on income distribution demonstrates that the world has been growing more unequal in the past decades. The main findings are that inequality is on the rise and significantly so in Canada, Germany, the United States, Italy, and Finland. This is mainly because the top of the income distribution has fared much better than the middle and the bottom. More unequal countries also have higher poverty rates, and poverty among the elderly is declining but rising among the young and families with children. However, the OECD study also reports that inequality has actually decreased in some countries, notably in the United Kingdom and Australia. A final finding worth noting is that the poor in inegalitarian yet high per capita income countries (such as the United States) are worse off than the poor in lower mean income yet more equal societies (say Sweden). The rich are better off in inegalitarian countries with a low mean income (e.g., Italy) than in high mean income countries that are more egalitarian (such as Germany).

One of the notable features of the OECD inequality study is the overall positive evaluation it gives to the welfare state's role in safeguarding equality and fighting poverty, for instance in the following counterfactual statement: "If governments stop trying to offset the inequalities by either spending less on social benefits, or by making taxes and benefits less targeted to the poor, then the growth in inequality would be much more rapid" (OECD 2008: 16). Moreover, "the key policy message," writes the OECD (2008: 19), "is that – regardless

---

[1] See http://www.ssb.no/english/subjects/05/01/iffor_En/tab-2011-03-11-02-en.html, accessed October 2011.

TABLE 5.5. *Inequality in welfare states in Gini coefficients (after taxes and transfers), mid-1970s–mid-2000s*

	Mid-1970s	Mid-1980s	Around 1990	Mid-1990s	Around 2000	Mid-2000s
Australia	..	..	..	.31	.32	.30
Canada	.30	.29	.29	.29	.32	.32
Ireland	..	.33	..	.32	.30	.33
New Zealand	..	.27	.32	.34	.34	.34
United Kingdom	.28	.33	.37	.35	.37	.34
United States	.32	.34	.35	.36	.36	.38
Average LR	.30	.31	.33	.33	.34	.34
Austria	..	.24	..	.24	.25	.27
Belgium	..	.27	..	.29	.29	.27
France	..	.31	.30	.28	.28	.28
Germany	..	.26	.26	.27	.27	.30
Italy	..	.31	.30	.35	.34	.35
Netherlands	.25	.26	.28	.28	.28	.27
Switzerland	..	..	..	..	.28	.28
Average CR	.25	.28	.29	.29	.28	.29
Denmark	..	.22	.23	.21	.23	.23
Finland	.23	.21	..	.23	.26	.27
Norway	..	.23	..	.26	.26	.28
Sweden	.21	.20	.21	.21	.24	.23
Average SDR	.22	.22	.22	.23	.25	.25
Japan	..	.30	..	.32	.34	.32

Notes: LR is liberal regime; CR is conservative regime; SDR is social democratic regime.
Source: OECD (2008).

of whether it is globalisation or some other reason why inequality has been rising – there is no reason to feel helpless: good government policy can make a difference."

Indeed, as the descriptive data in Table 5.5 and Figure 5.2 show, there is a negative relationship between welfare state spending and the degree of inequality: the higher social spending is, the lower the level of inequality in that nation tends to be. Yet the relationship does not hold in all countries to the same extent, and the level of social spending can only partly explain the reduction in inequality. For instance, we can see that the Netherlands achieves a considerably lower level of inequality than Spain and Greece with slightly less social spending. And we see that Italy has a much higher level of inequality than Norway with even more social spending. Esping-Andersen and Myles (2009: 644–645) computed that a 10 percent increase in social spending results in an additional 1 percent reduction of inequality, but this is what we would expect if the characteristics of the different welfare states

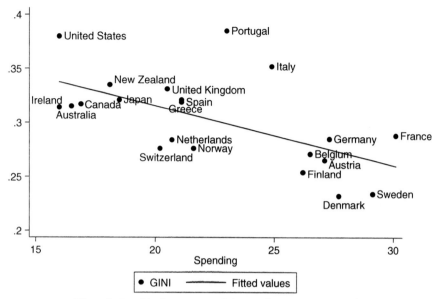

FIGURE 5.2. The relationship between social spending (% GDP) and inequality (Gini coefficient after tax and transfers), mid-2000s.
Notes: Regression coefficient: –0.01; Beta: –0.60; Adjusted R²: 0.32.
Source: OECD dataset, http://stats.oecd.org/Index.aspx?DataSetCode=INEQUALITY and http://stats.oecd.org/Index.aspx?DataSetCode=SOCX_AGG (Accessed February 2013).

matter. A linear estimation of the impact of spending on inequality distorts the picture, because the institutional organization of welfare states (e.g., how the money is spent and for what purposes) is more important for the stratification in society than just the amount of social spending. The OECD (2008: 119) finds that the "redistributive effect of the welfare state is generally larger for public cash benefits than for household taxes – except in the United States, which achieves more redistribution through the tax system than through the transfer system. Similarly, the degree of redistribution to the lowest income quintile varies widely across countries, and is greatest in Australia and the Nordic countries."

Many people naturally associate social policies and the welfare state with redistribution and equality. However, it is important to realize that redistribution does not always imply more equality. For instance, life-cycle redistribution does not take place from the rich to the poor. With respect to equality, the intellectual debate has revolved around the issue of whether social policies targeted at specific groups (e.g., the working class, the poor, women, or migrants) have the effect of reducing inequalities or whether universalism in social policy, that is, "the provision of a single, relatively uniform service or benefit for all citizens regardless of income or class" (Hill 2006: 192), actually does a better job.

The kind of redistribution that is offered is important because the different welfare regimes vary precisely in this respect, with the social democratic model using a universal system of benefits and the liberal regime using the most specific targets. Moreover, in all regimes, but especially in the conservative regime, social inequalities and status differentials are intentionally reproduced in the welfare system, through occupational and earnings-related social insurance schemes. Inequalities are also reproduced in the universal schemes because the better-off and better educated people with higher skills and competences are much more capable of taking advantage of universal services (health care, or education) than poorer and less educated people.

At face value, it seems that targeting is ultimately better for the poor or the less well-off, primarily because social policies are designed exclusively for those who need it most. Redistribution via targeting, moreover, is fair and efficient because it does not waste resources by transferring money to people who do not need aid. However, targeting is a kind of Robin Hood strategy ("stealing" from the rich, giving to the poor) that antagonizes the rich and provokes them to defect from the system. As Korpi and Palme (1998: 672) explain: "By discriminating in favor of the poor, the targeted model creates a zero-sum conflict of interests between the poor and the better-off workers and the middle classes who must pay for the benefits of the poor without receiving any benefits."

An alternative is a simple egalitarian system with flat-rate benefits for all, giving relatively more to the poor than to the better off. However, this system (known as the Beveridge system) also has incentives for the middle classes to opt out and look for private insurance. Finally, there is the evangelical Matthew strategy (described in section 5.4) of earnings-related provision that gives relatively more to the rich than to the poor. The Matthew-effect is most pronounced in services – for instance, in (higher) education, where the rich profit much more than the poor, not only because they get most of the service but also because education greatly advances their earnings capacity.

When we compare welfare state regimes empirically, we find the paradox of distribution: "The more we target benefits at the poor only and the more concerned we are with creating equality via equal public transfers to all, the less likely we are to reduce poverty and equality" (Korpi and Palme 1998: 681–682). So-called encompassing models, which are found in Finland, Sweden, and Norway, combine a simple egalitarian system with the Matthew strategy and are the most redistributive systems that also have a high level of political support and legitimacy. This is because the scope of the welfare state is much bigger and because this model brings low-, middle-, and high-income groups together in one system, fostering coalitions between social classes and precluding the exit of the better-off stratum. "By providing sufficiently high benefits for high-income groups so as not to push them to exit, in encompassing institutions the voice of the better-off citizens helps not only themselves but low-income income groups as well" (Korpi and Palme 1998: 672).

Similarly, Smeeding (2005) shows that the targeting countries, especially the United States, have the highest levels of poverty and inequality and that this is a political effect. Speaking about the United States, Smeeding (2005: 980) says that "if one decides to make poverty or inequality an active policy goal, one can make a difference. We have more inequality and poverty than other nations because we choose to have more." Smeeding also argues that when the distance between the rich and the less well-off becomes too great, as happens in a targeted system, the rich opt out and look out for themselves: they get private insurance, get the best health care, and make sure their children get the best education available. This reproduces and even reinforces social divisions. As Smeeding puts it (2005: 980), "higher income inequality produces lower levels of those publicly shared goods that foster greater equality of opportunity and greater upward mobility: income insurance, equal educational opportunity, and more equal access to high-quality healthcare."

Empirical research underscores the differential impact of various welfare state regimes on equality and poverty (e.g., Kenworthy 1999; Korpi and Palme 2003; Brady 2005; Scruggs and Allan 2006; Esping-Andersen and Myles 2009; see also earlier discussion). Although some find that the welfare state, regardless of the period or the type one studies, strongly reduces poverty (e.g., Brady 2005: 1354), there seems to be a consensus that universalism in particular produces the most pronounced effects. The mechanisms behind this are manifold (see Hill 2006: 192–194). For instance, good benefits and services (especially education and health care) tailored to the standards of the better off rather than to the poor are good for the poor and increase social mobility. Also, fragmented, targeted, or particularist systems (i.e., separate systems for separate groups) actually reinforce inequality and may imply that the state or politics is associated with the promotion of inequality, causing severe problems of legitimacy. In addition, universal provision of services protects both the poor and the better off from sudden attacks on their budgets (e.g., health care), so that the poor get the service they otherwise would be forced to give up. Simultaneously, the incomes of the better off are protected so they do not become poor. Finally, some universal transfers, such as child benefits or family allowances, serve society at large, even for those people who have no children, because other people's children will contribute to their pension (see Esping-Andersen 2009). This explains why an earlier generation of comparative (quantitative) studies failed to find a linear relationship between welfare state and post-tax and post-transfer income equality, but when we account for the different types of welfare states and understand the paradox of redistribution, this finding is no surprise. Still, Esping-Andersen and Myles (2009: 652–653) conclude that there is

no doubt that welfare states redistribute in an egalitarian direction. Post-redistribution Gini coefficients, decile ratios and poverty rates are systematically lower than for primary income distributions. What is also clear is that welfare states do it differently and vary substantially in their degree of equalization.... [I]t is clear that the Anglo-Saxon group is systematically far less redistributive than the other two, which, in turn, appear surprisingly similar within such aggregate comparisons. But when one excludes the elderly population, the convergence disappears and the Continental European welfare states begin to look more "liberal." ... The Continental European countries' tax-transfer system is far more pensioner-biased.

As discussed in section 5.2 on the methodological caveat, one major way in which the welfare state already influences the primary income distribution is through services (such as education, health care, training, and support to working mothers). The impact of services is always in an egalitarian direction, regardless of regime type, but less so than transfers. In terms of the redistributive effect, the Scandinavian welfare states stand out, as here family services and elderly care contribute substantially to inequality reduction: 18 percent in Denmark, 8 percent in Finland, 16 percent in Norway, and 21 percent in Sweden (average 16 percent), compared to an average of a mere 4 percent in the liberal regime and 3 percent in the conservative regime (Esping-Andersen and Myles 2009: 654, table 25.2).

A final issue is that inequality is typically phrased in terms of income and market position and in this sense can be said to address especially the class issue in social divisions and stratification. Feminist critiques have pointed to the more general weakness of class analysis, namely, that class theory had great difficulty in dealing with the class position of women, particularly of housewives who are not active in the labor market. The feminist critique of Esping-Andersen's work, for instance, stressed that if one wants to understand the working of the regimes in terms of market, state, *and* family, one also needs to develop theoretical tools that can make sense of the gender dimension of social stratification and how social policies presuppose and affect the relations between men and women (see, e.g., Bussemaker and Van Kersbergen 1994).

Social policies assumed the distribution of labor between men and women and tended to reinforce these (Fraser 1994). For the position of women, a crucial point is whether they are entitled to benefits as individuals or whether their rights are tied to families in which men are often the sole or main income earner. Also, women may have different types of risks and needs (e.g., think of pregnancy and single parenthood). As a result, the outcomes of welfare state interventions in terms of equality and poverty and in terms of labor market behavior are markedly different for men and women. Let us give just three examples. First, in the European Union (except in Finland and Sweden), although the welfare state reduces the risk of poverty everywhere, the poverty risk for women is considerably larger than for men (European Commission 2004: 188). Second, only in the social democratic welfare regime does the rate of employment of women approach the male rate. Third, women earn less than men everywhere.

A final remark is that in the golden age of the welfare state, the income security and redistribution that the welfare state offered was not only considered to be a matter of social justice but also one of macro-economic efficiency. Welfare state expenditures could be viewed as part of the Keynesian demand management logic that helped to maximize economic performance, particularly economic growth and the prevention of unemployment. Many of the welfare state's programs contribute to the supply of labor. It is no exaggeration to say that the welfare state's jobs and programs (such as childcare, parental leave, and sickness benefits) have played a crucial role in increasing the supply of female labor (see Esping-Andersen 2009). Or, put differently, the welfare state has helped women enter the labor market at a scale that would have been impossible without it.

Summing up, despite an overall increase in inequality since the mid-1970s, all welfare states reduce inequality and poverty to some extent, but the variation across welfare state regimes and individual countries is substantial. At any rate, the welfare state in all regimes plays an indispensable role in moderating market-induced inequalities and poverty, with the social democratic regime outperforming the conservative regime (to some degree) and the liberal regime (to a considerable extent).

5.6. CONCLUSION

With the methodological caveat in mind that it is difficult to measure the exact impact of the welfare state on poverty and inequality, we can now answer the "big question": what does the welfare state do? The welfare state covers citizens against the major "old" social risks of old age, unemployment, sickness, and accidents, and also is providing protection against new ones. The social democratic regime covers the largest part of its population and offers the most generous benefits. The conservative regime holds the middle position on coverage and generosity. For almost all programs, the liberal regime has both the lowest coverage and the lowest benefit generosity. The only exception here is coverage of accidents in 2000, where the liberal regime is on average second in line. Still, even in the liberal regime, most major social risks are covered to some extent. Welfare states reduce poverty and income inequality, at least somewhat, in the same order as for coverage and generosity. We also find again substantial variation across individual countries, but all welfare states do reduce poverty and lower inequality.

In short, welfare states provide protection against risks and reduce poverty and inequality. Interestingly, even those welfare states that are not explicitly aiming at equality, such as the United States, produce outcomes that move their societies in a somewhat more egalitarian direction. We have also demonstrated that there are clear and distinct differences between the regimes. The liberal welfare regime is the least redistributive and the weakest in fighting poverty. The social democratic welfare regime clearly stands out as the most comprehensive, redistributive, and effective anti-poverty regime among the various worlds of welfare. The conservative regime holds the intermediate position on both the reduction of poverty and the curbing of inequality.

Even though we also observe that many people are still not properly insured against social risks, that there is still poverty, and, most remarkably, that inequality has been on the rise for a couple of decades, the counterfactual argument we follow leads us to conclude that there must have been much welfare state reform (adaptation, updating, cost containment, retrenchment, or restructuring) in many countries and little intentional policy drift (the deliberate decision not to reform a policy and let it drift). Welfare states not only continue to perform but in some respects have actually improved their records, especially if we look at the coverage of major social risks until the 2000s. With respect to new social risks, welfare states have started to cover these, too.

Regarding the opportunities and constraints of welfare state reform, we infer that because welfare states perform relatively well, their capacity to cope with the permanent changes in their environments has been considerable. Just how substantial this capacity is depends on how great the pressures on and challenges to welfare states have been. This is partly a theoretical issue that we turn to in Chapter 6, before we examine the empirics in Chapters 7 and 8, and ask to what extent welfare states keep doing what they were doing under increasingly difficult circumstances (Chapter 10). We now introduce our open functional approach in more detail, an approach that stresses the importance of functional demands and requirements for explaining welfare state reform – adaptation, updating, cost containment, retrenchment, or restructuring.

6

Toward an Open Functional Approach to Welfare State Reform

6.1. INTRODUCTION

In Chapter 5, we mapped and documented the persistent but also variable performance of welfare states. We developed the counterfactual argument that because welfare states have been performing their tasks remarkably well, there must have been a large amount of reform to adjust the existing architecture to the changing social and economic context of welfare politics. Surely, some policy drift – the conscious decision not to update existing social policy arrangements to respond to changing circumstances – must have occurred everywhere. However, the empirical documentation of how well welfare states worked shows that, with the exception of inequality, policy drift seems actually to be limited. Rather than suggesting that stability and the absence of change have been the main features of the past decades until the onset of the financial crisis, this observation implies that welfare states have shown the capacity to update social policies and to adapt to permanently changing circumstances. Since there must have been plenty of welfare state adaptation, updating, retrenchment, and restructuring – that is, reform – this has helped to secure the welfare states' ability to perform their tasks. But, as we will document extensively in Chapters 7 and 8, functional stress has been building up steadily. Hence, we are expecting to see a great deal more reform pressure and policy adaptation, updating, retrenchment, and restructuring. Ultimately, the question is whether welfare states can continue to function, especially in the wake of the financial, economic, and debt crises since 2008 (see Chapter 10). In this chapter, we develop the theoretical tools for answering such questions. What is the best way to think about why and how welfare states should adjust to their continuously changing social and political context?

We present an open functional approach to welfare state reform to theorize about the role of endogenous and exogenous functional pressures, on how such pressures are translated into reforms, and under which conditions reforms are likely to be successful. We immediately wish to underscore that the conscious decision to reform or not reform social policy arrangements and in what way to do this is ultimately always a political one. In a democratic capitalist environment, this means that governments, political parties, voters, firms, labor unions, interest organizations, and others are all involved in the decision-making process and, to a greater or lesser extent, influence the outcome through what is essentially a power struggle over ideas and their implementation. This happens either through deliberate choices for reform or by calculated decisions not to reform ("non-decisions" that produce policy drift). We build our approach on the conviction that to understand the political opportunities and constraints of welfare state reform, we can learn and must benefit from the accumulated comparative welfare state research of the past four decades. Hence, in section 6.2 we discuss the literature relevant to this purpose, highlighting what we consider the most relevant findings and insights.

We draw on the recent ideational and constructivist literature (e.g., Blyth 2002; Schmidt 2008, 2011; Hay 2011; Stiller 2010; Wincott 2011) to argue that ideas are a central factor in explaining the variation in welfare state reform. However, in section 6.3 we explain why we do not consider ideas to be the key causal factor; rather, ideas as causal beliefs are important for understanding why policymakers pursue some types of policies rather than others. "Men make their own history," Marx famously wrote in 1852 in *The Eighteenth Brumaire of Louis Bonaparte*, "but they do not make it as they please; they do not make it under self-selected circumstances, but under circumstances existing already, given and transmitted from the past."[1] These already existing circumstances establish the socioeconomic and institutional context of political action that constrains actors and ideas, determining which ideas matter, and how. We adopt and build on important insights from mainstream comparative welfare state research in which structural factors or problem pressures play a role, particularly (1) the challenges-capabilities-vulnerabilities (CCV) approach (Scharpf and Schmidt 2000); and (2) the policy learning (PL) approach, originally proposed by Hall (1993), but further developed in Visser and Hemerijck (1997, chapter 3), Hemerijck and Schludi (2000), and Hemerijck (2013). Exogenous and endogenous pressures generate a strategically selective context (Hay 2002) in which some actors, interests, and ideas are more likely to prevail than others.

In sharp contrast to the constructivist approaches and more explicitly formulated than in CCV and PL, our argument is that the existing "objective" problem pressure influences the range of ideas that political actors consider for reform. Pressures to reform are objective to the extent that they threaten the existential conditions of a system's survival. The objective pressure tends to

---

[1] "Die Menschen machen ihre eigene Geschichte, aber sie machen sie nicht aus freien Stücken, nicht unter selbstgewählten, sondern unter unmittelbar vorgefundenen, gegebenen und überlieferten Umständen" (http://www.mlwerke.de/me/meo8/meo8_115.htm, accessed July 2011).

facilitate the adoption of certain ideas and the neglect or abandonment of others. These ideas, in turn, affect the type of reform that political actors pursue. Different ideas may thus lead to different reform proposals, but not all ideas are feasible. While political preferences, normative ideas, and world culture also affect which ideas are on actors' minds (see Campbell 2002: 22–26), the objective problem pressure is key here.

We illustrate our theoretical considerations in section 6.5. We show how the identification of a functional requirement and a specific idea can be taken to explain a drastic social policy reform – in our case, the drastic restructuring of the disability scheme in the Netherlands in the 1990s. We conclude (section 6.6) that ideas as causal beliefs are important for explaining welfare state reform, but that they can assume this explanatory role only if one recognizes that functional requirements are "objective" constraints on the behavior of political actors and their ideas. Such constraints, as Giddens (e.g., 1984: 179) would put it, not only limit, but also enable action, as a result of which "all explanations will involve ... reference both to the purposive, reasoning behaviour of agents and to its intersection with constraining and enabling features of the social and material contexts of that behaviour."

6.2. INTEGRATING THEORIES AND APPROACHES

There are economic, financial, social, and political challenges and pressures that stem from the dynamics of capitalism (see Chapter 2) and that seem to necessitate (radical) adjustments in developed welfare states' core policies and institutions. The large body of comparative welfare state literature has emphasized this time and again. The increased internationalization of economies (globalization), for instance, provides perhaps gains from trade, but such macro-level gains could be offset by micro-level losses like job relocations and labor shedding. Simultaneously, political and economic constraints, such as limited fiscal and monetary autonomy due to regional integration (as in the European Union), inhibit governments to accommodate the political demands that such losses spur. Also, globalization may exert a downward pressure on tax rates and government spending. Consequently, higher levels of globalization might lead to lower levels of welfare effort. The financial crisis of 2008–9 hit all welfare states hard precisely because national economies are so intensely interconnected. The financial and economic aftershocks of the crisis are aggravating the already dismal situation of some welfare states (say, the southern European countries) and are making welfare politics in all welfare states exceedingly difficult. However, looking at the history of the welfare state in the past decades gives us some reason to believe in the distinct possibility that these states, by adapting, updating, retrenchment, and restructuring, can adjust to the rapidly changing context. In any case, whether viewed positively or negatively, the forces unleashed by globalization create functional pressures for reform (see Chapters 7 and 10).

But the challenges to the welfare state not only come from the outside or only from the dynamics of capitalism. Endogenous transformations, like the revolution of women's roles, although linked to capitalist developments (e.g., via the increasing demand for female labor in the postindustrial labor market), have their own dynamics and have also been rapidly altering the foundation of postwar welfare states in such a way that continuation of existing social policy arrangements seems increasingly unlikely if not impossible (see, e.g., Esping-Andersen 2002, 2009). Such challenges as aging and the postindustrialization of labor markets also may add up to functional pressures for adaptation, updating, retrenchment, or more radical reform (see Chapter 8).

From studying the *causes of the emergence, expansion, and cross-national variation of welfare state regimes,* we can learn that social policies are always formulated in response to societal needs and demands that tend to present themselves as pressing (functional) requirements of state intervention (see Wilensky and Lebeaux 1965 [1958]; Flora and Heidenheimer 1981a). But we also know that the nature, shape, and effectiveness of such responses depend on a nation's prevalent power structure (see, e.g., Korpi 1983; Esping-Andersen 1985a, b). Similar demands are addressed by different social and political actors who – in various types of coalitions – respond with distinctive interventions or deliberate noninterventions (see Chapter 3). Moreover, initial state interventions are inclined to take on a life of their own, causing path dependency. They are likely to become the mold for further social policy development and ultimately tend to become institutionalized as social policy configurations or regimes with characteristic patterns of mutual dependencies and complementarities. Distinctive welfare state regimes can therefore be expected to create and cultivate unique capacities as well as inabilities for reform (Esping-Andersen 1990, 1996a, 1999).

From the various *crisis literatures* (see, e.g., O'Connor 1973; Ginsburg 1979; Gough 1979; Offe 1984; Flora 1985, 1986–87; OECD 1981, 1985; see Chapter 2) we infer that there are certain limits to growth and that welfare state development in the context of a capitalist democracy is incessantly generating tensions if not internal contradictions and legitimacy problems. Moreover, we learn that various endogenous and exogenous challenges, including population aging, globalization, regional (European) integration, and the postindustrialization of society, involve a destabilization of the existing architecture of welfare states and entail the rise of new social risks and needs (Armingeon and Bonoli 2006). Welfare states, we therefore acknowledge, are dynamic entities that are continuously confronted with and reacting to changes in the economic, social, and political context that represent challenges, if not threats.

As we discussed in Chapter 2, researchers were very puzzled by observing that welfare states apparently were moving very little in response to the strong forces that pushed for change and the crises that were expected to undermine their foundations. Welfare states kept on doing what they were doing. However, one cannot infer that therefore there has been no change. Welfare state resilience does not imply the absence of reform (say, retrenchment) or radically changing social outcomes, such as increasing inequality or poverty (Hacker 2004). We criticized those institutionalist studies that did not acknowledge the – perhaps small, but not insignificant – continuous reforms that were being implemented. Also, the more radical and institutional reforms that could be observed could not be explained in the strict institutionalist framework. In short, institutionalist analyses placed too much attention on the statics of the welfare state, whereas the dynamics of ongoing reform constituted the real puzzle.

But this criticism does not imply that we cannot learn from the *institutionalist approach* to welfare state resilience. Our message – like Pierson's (2011) – is that the welfare state has kept on functioning amazingly well (see Chapter 5), in spite of the major threats to its continued existence and the massive forces that not only push for change but even seem to threaten its core modus operandi. The institutionalist literature (see extensively Vrooman 2009: chapters 2 and 3) teaches us that welfare states are remarkably "sticky" and resilient and that there are distinct political reasons for this. Pierson's famous claim that the new politics of retrenchment is radically different from the old politics of welfare state expansion still needs to be taken seriously, even though we also know that the old politics still matters (Scarbrough 2000; Schumacher et al. 2013) and that welfare state reform is not only about austerity or retrenchment (see, e.g., Weishaupt 2011; Bonoli and Natali 2012b; Hemerijck 2013). Still, the rapid expansion of welfare programs in the post-1945 period did create new program-specific constituencies of clients and professional groups that developed an interest in these programs' continuation and further expansion. In addition, many social policies did become and have remained tremendously popular among voters. As a result, any political manifesto that explicitly aims at radically retrenching cherished arrangements may not be absolutely doomed to fail (Giger and Nelson 2011), but implementing it will be exceedingly difficult in the face of potential voter retribution.

From the latest research results *on the conditions under which reforms take place*, in spite of resilience and political and institutional sclerosis (Starke 2008; Häusermann 2010; Palier 2010a; Stiller 2010; Vis 2010; Hemerijck 2013), we welcome the insight that institutional "stickiness" and political popularity of welfare programs may be hard and exasperating facts in the lives of reform-minded actors, but that nevertheless radical reforms have been put into practice in many welfare states. The major puzzles of contemporary welfare state research revolve around the questions of why reforms can take place in spite of the institutional and political mechanisms that seem to work against them, and in which direction changes are moving.

In line with (and inspired by) former research (e.g., Scharpf and Schmidt's 2000 CCV approach), we observe that contemporary welfare states are facing pressing challenges as a response to which policies are formulated that, depending on institutional conditions, are effective or deficient in adapting while retaining distinctive aspiration levels in terms of employment, social security, and equality. Against this backdrop, we assert that the capacity to reform the welfare state and the direction of policy changes (adaptation, updating, retrenchment, restructuring, or policy drift) crucially depend on the welfare state's architecture, the character of the challenges it is facing, the positive and negative social and political feedback mechanisms it is generating, and the distribution of (political) power. As argued in Chapter 2, the constant stream of politically relevant new facts, issues, and conflicts generated by capitalist dynamics shape the opportunities and constraints of contemporary welfare state reform. But these also hinge on the actors' ability to design reform packages to adapt, update, retrench, or restructure the welfare state that are not only deemed economically efficient and socially desirable but politically feasible as well – and the conscious decision not to act is always an option too.

Recently, we have seen an ideational and constructivist turn (Blyth 2002) in comparative political science in general and comparative welfare state research in particular (for overviews, see Campbell 2002; Béland 2005; Taylor-Gooby 2005; Schmidt 2002, 2008; Béland and Cox 2011). Constructivists stress that the ideas policymakers adopt in their attempts to solve social problems are the key factor in accounting for the variation in the type and success of welfare state reform. We agree that ideas matter, but we disagree in some critical respects with some of the inferences constructivists make from this postulation. As this is a growing and increasingly important literature from which much is to be learned, we proceed by first explaining our position in this debate on the role of ideas in policymaking before we lay out more extensively our open functional approach to welfare state reform. We acknowledge that ideas can have a causal impact on social policy change, but we hold that functional pressures take precedence as causes because they are a crucial part of the strategically selective context of political action that constrains which actors and ideas carry weight and how.

6.3. THE ROLE OF IDEAS IN WELFARE STATE REFORM: HOW TO ESTABLISH CAUSALITY

The ideational turn has also reached the field of comparative welfare state studies. The constructivist literature is increasingly prominent in the debate about what explains welfare state reform, not in the least, we assume, because of the institutionalist literature's failure to do so (Blyth 2002; Schmidt 2008, 2011; Hay 2011; Stiller 2010; Wincott 2011). We are not convinced about the explanatory potential of the ideational approaches because they tend to suffer from a kind of *post hoc ergo propter hoc* justification. To put it briefly, and admittedly not doing full justice to the quality and richness of many of these studies, the (implied) argument is very often that when reform takes place, ideas or discourse have been, at least partly, responsible. If a reform attempt fails, conversely, the correct ideas and discourses have not been employed properly.

Such analyses leave unexplained why some policymakers act on a specific idea and discourse while others do not. Moreover, it remains unclear whether such an approach is capable of discovering and explaining policy drift, which is the result of a deliberate choice not to act, in the awareness of failing policy and the presence of ideas on how to remedy the defect. Also, why do some ideas and discourses succeed while others fail? For example, Schmidt (2008: 313) suggests that "discourses succeed when speakers address their remarks to the right audiences (specialized or general publics) at the right times in the right ways." But how does one establish the right audience, the right time, and the right way? In addition, Schmidt's (2008, 2011) discursive approach, like ideational approaches more generally, is silent about the *types* of reforms, such as unpopular versus well-liked reforms or radical reforms, and the various strategies used to implement reforms, including blame avoidance (for more on blame avoidance, see Chapter 9).

Similarly, Cox (2001) posits that focusing on the social construction of the need for reform helps to explain why welfare state reform has happened in the Netherlands and Denmark, but not in Germany. The argument is that the Dutch and Danish leaders, but not the German ones, were able to construct a new discourse by carefully framing issues to that effect. In Schmidt's terminology, the former used a communicative rather than strategic discourse – with success. Cox's argument can help to explain the diverging reform experiences in the 1990s, but leaves important questions unanswered. For instance, why were the Danish and Dutch leaders able to construct a new discourse while the German leaders were not? Were they facing similar pressures in comparable contexts? We would need to establish this before we can estimate what role ideas play factually. It also begs the question of why shortly after (in the 2000s), very significant welfare reforms (the Hartz reforms) were suddenly possible in Germany (see Chapter 9).

Instead of opting for a wide notion of discourse or one of the other existing definitions of ideas (see, e.g., Schmidt 2008: 306; Carstensen 2010) and because we are interested in developing a theoretical framework to explain welfare state adaptation, updating, retrenchment, restructuring, or drift, we adopt the definition of *ideas as causal beliefs* (Goldstein and Keohane 1993; Béland and Cox 2011: 3–4). The definition consists of several components. First, ideas are products of our cognition, hence *beliefs*. Second, ideas connect things and people in the world, hence *causal* beliefs. Here causality can either refer to an actual connection between two events or to an assumed connection, that is, a connection an individual believes to be present. Finally, a causal belief – or idea – makes individuals act by suggesting *how* to address challenges or problems, including the decision not to act so as to let things take their "natural" course. This does not mean, however, that causal beliefs tell us *which* solution is needed. Note that this definition of ideas allows these to be both cognitive ideas, which could be based on failure induced learning, and normative ideas, which are based on learning before failure takes place.

We dispute the notion that ideas *by themselves* create the incentives for action or inaction and that interests have no separate analytical status. Hay (2011), for instance, solves the problem of the relationship between material interests and behavior by arguing that only constructions of interests exist. But can ideas on their own produce an outcome, such as a reform? Does the context, of which material interests are a part, not influence the range of ideas that may affect outcomes? We would rather stress that the challenge or problem that an individual faces offers the starting point for action or inaction. This might also help to solve the puzzle that not "all holders of alternative political ideas act on them" (Lieberman 2002: 698). The context matters crucially. What the constructivist, ideational literature needs is a theory of what it is that ideas refer to (what are they about?) as well as a better elaboration of the mechanisms through which different types of ideas affect policymaking (do they prescribe action or inaction?) (Campbell 2002; Mehta 2011).

Some recent work tries to solve some of the theoretical lacunae. Stiller's (2010) study of the role of ideational leadership in German welfare state reforms, for instance, combines ideational factors and political agency into a single explanatory concept: ideational leadership (see also Schmidt 2008: 309ff.), but it does not theorize about decisions not to act. An ideational leader is motivated toward action (policy) rather than power and displays four communicative or behavioral traits. First, the leader exposes the drawbacks of the policy status quo. Second, the leader makes consistent efforts to legitimize the principles of the new policy. Third, the leader confronts opponents by suggesting that their resistance is problematic. And finally, the leader tries to build political consensus to gain support for the proposed reform. The major contribution of Stiller's work is that it presents a mechanism for moving from an actor's idea to the implementation of a reform, which opens the black box in, for instance, Schmidt's account. However, Stiller does not explain where ideas come from and does not develop an account of their cognitive and normative content.

Jacobs (2009) offers a theory of social policy reform that is based on mental models and attention. A strong point is that he explains how preexisting ideas influence the decisions (but not the nondecisions) of reform-motivated decision makers. A study of three key episodes in German pension politics from the 1880s to the 1950s demonstrates that ideas direct actors' attention to specific options. Specifically, an actor's mental model – that is, "a simplified representation of a domain or situation with moving parts that allow reasoning about cause and effect" (Jacobs 2009: 257) – directs an actor's attention toward certain causal logics and away from others. For example, in the mid-1880s under Bismarck, when Germany was the first country to erect a pension scheme, decision makers operated under a so-called insurance mental model. With this mental model in place, even the actors opposed to the system of funding proposed by the legislators did not refer to potential dangers outside this dominant way of thinking, such as inflationary pressures (Jacobs 2009: 266). Ideas come to shape actors' preferences among options, with those options that fit the mental model weighing more heavily and those outside the mental model being discounted or even ignored altogether, as in the Bismarck example. Identifying and analytically establishing the relevant mental model is challenging empirically, but can be done, as Jacobs (2011) shows. Most important, some mental frames help to overcome so-called inter-temporal dilemmas that politicians face: the need to impose certain costs (e.g., higher social contributions) in the short run for goals to be achieved in the long run (e.g., pension security). One could imagine that a similar short-term /long-term dilemma emerges with policies that deal with new social risks and with social investment policies more generally. In terms of viability and effectiveness, such social policy innovation, such as activation, normally takes on a longer time perspective (effects are not immediate) but may involve pursuing short-term retrenchment, say, in unemployment benefits (whose effects are immediate). In short, social policy solutions in the longer run may come at the cost of social protection in the short run and the challenge is to establish how and to what extent ideas (in the form of mental models) are capable of solving the dilemma.

Blyth (2002) argues that the social democrats in Sweden had clear political ideas in the 1920s but no economic ideas. Since there were no alternatives to classical economics yet (in the words of Jacobs: no alternative mental model), social democrats behaved like conservatives when in power. By the end of the 1920s, new economic ideas had developed within the social democratic party that could act as the "weapons" by which classical economics could be challenged (Blyth 2002: 101ff.). Blyth's analysis makes clear that individual politicians are crucially important for new ideas to gain ground, combined with supportive socioeconomic circumstances, such as the high unemployment despite the recovery in exports in Sweden in the mid-1920s. For Blyth (2002: 270), "it is only in those moments when uncertainty abounds [that is so-called Knightian uncertainty in which agents' interests are structurally underdetermined by nature] and institutions fail that ideas have this truly transformative effect on interests." Blyth, in other words, offers an elegant analysis of how a transformative idea emerges and affects interests, but he does not connect the idea to an outcome.

Schmidt (2008, 2011) proposes a new type of institutionalism, discursive institutionalism, which treats institutions simultaneously "as given (as the context within which agents think, speak, and act) and as contingent (as the results of agents' thoughts, words, and actions)" (Schmidt 2008: 314). This focus makes institutions internal to the actors and there is no such thing as an objective interest, because "one cannot distinguish objective interests from ideas; all interests are ideas, ideas constitute interests, so all interests are subjective" (317). This, however, does not mean that there is also no such thing as a material reality. A material reality exists as the setting within which, or as a response to which, actors can consider their interests (320).

It is precisely on this point that Hay (2011) criticizes the institutionalist constructivists for their ontological inconsistency. To concede to the possibility of a materialist conception of an actor's interest that is determined by the actor's context is "to deny the agency, autonomy, individuality, and identity of the agent. It is to reduce the agent to the status of a mere bearer, rather than a shaper, of systemic logics" (79). Hay advises that constructivists dispense altogether with the concept of material self-interests and, by implication, with the notion that an actor's context also consists of material constraints and objective interests (79). In our view, Hay's proposal seems an overly radical and unnecessary ontological inference from the presumption that ideas as causal beliefs matter for behavior.

6.4. TOWARD AN OPEN FUNCTIONAL APPROACH
TO WELFARE STATE REFORM

We propose to employ an open functional approach (see Becker 2009) to welfare state development and reform that recognizes the potential independent causal effect of many variables, including most crucially ideas, but gives preference to the notion that the context of political action constrains what other variables matter and how.

In line with the work of, among others, Scharpf and Schmidt (2000), Pierson (2001), and Esping-Andersen (2002), our approach starts from the conviction that all welfare states face internal and external challenges that require policy adjustments, updates, and restructuring (Scharpf and Schmidt 2000; Pierson 2001a; Esping-Andersen 2002). This holds irrespective of whether actors perceive these challenges as such, because welfare states' continuation depends on their reform. The exogenous challenges primarily concern increasing economic internationalization, regionalization, and (financial) interdependence, which force policymakers to react continuously to new facts and which are, strictly speaking, outside their domain of influence (see Chapter 7). The endogenous changes concern population aging and declining fertility, sluggish economic growth, mass unemployment, changing family structures and gender roles (e.g., atypical families, lone parents), the transformation of life cycle patterns (e.g., longer education, later childbirth, increasing divorce rates), the shift toward a postindustrial labor market (e.g., no steady lifetime jobs, increasing female labor force participation) (see Chapter 8), and the transformation of traditional systems of interest intermediation and collective bargaining.

Welfare state reform has sometimes been portrayed as a trial and error process of policy learning to respond to such challenges (Hemerijck and Schludi 2000; Casey and Gold 2005; Fleckenstein 2008). This literature stresses that past policy profiles, initial policy responses to external shocks, policy learning in the wake of policy fiascos, and coordination capabilities determine the type of policy ideas and learning that can occur and the conditions of their successful adoption and application (Hemerijck and Schludi 2000: 129). In the definition of Hall (1993: 278), policy (or social) learning is "a deliberate attempt to adjust the goals or techniques of policy in response to past experience and new information. Learning is indicated when policy changes as the result of such a process." Even though there may be limits to the degree to which political actors (can) actually learn (see Chapter 9), the policy learning approach is well equipped to map actual reform processes. Hemerijck (2013: 102–112), for instance, mentions functional pressures as potential triggers of policy change (they indicate failure), but analytically these pressures do not play a central role in his explanatory analysis. Hemerijck's approach is particularly strong in identifying and describing the various kinds of welfare recalibration, that is, "all initiatives that aim to transform the welfare state into a new configuration, far beyond core social insurance programmes, with the intent of being better able to cope with ... adaptive challenges" (104). The main shortcoming we see in the learning approach is that there may be too little theoretical foothold to answer the question of exactly *when* (rather than how) learning occurs and under which conditions policy drift, a phenomenon difficult to grasp in terms of learning, is likely. Why are some countries often considered to be good learners (such as Denmark and the Netherlands), while other countries are usually viewed as poor ones? Why are some countries' experts excellent policy learners in some periods but not in others? Why do some actors not act, even if it can be shown that they have learned from past mistakes and are aware of likely future adversity? What, if anything, forces policymakers to learn?

We argue that exogenous and endogenous challenges appear as functional demands for policy change insofar as they jeopardize the existence of systems of social protection by debilitating the degree to which the various components of the systems are functionally integrated. This weakens what Becker (2009), following Demerath III (1966), calls a configuration's level of "systemness." For example, a crisis of some sort may cause social insurance contributions to become insufficient to cover the demand for benefits. Or an insurance's eligibility rules may prove to be formulated in such an indistinct manner that – under stress – they fail to discriminate between just and unjust (in the light of the original frame of the scheme) claimants, leading to excessive demand. Also, failing supply of benefits in one social insurance or provision may spill over and increase demand elsewhere in the system, causing a further decline in the functionality among parts of the wider social system.

Under such conditions, policymakers either learn how to respond adequately and adapt, update, retrench, or restructure the scheme, or they fail to do so, either because they are unaware of the functional demand or because they wish to produce drift by not acting, including blocking reforms. In other words, and to some extent in line with the policy learning approach (Hemerijck 2013), but in sharp contrast with recent developments in the constructivist literature (see Hay 2011), we hold that there exist certain requirements pushing for reform that logically, for reasons of system continuity and integration, need to be fulfilled – they are *functional* requirements. However, to avoid lapsing into functional*ist* rather than our function*al* reasoning, we hasten to add that one cannot jump from functional demands to adequate functional responses, because fulfillment of needs or requirements is never automatic or in any other way guaranteed. Learning is possible, but policy drift is a distinct possibility too. In the case of neglect, functional demands will ultimately reinforce the existential threat to the system of social protection.

This open functional reasoning helps to construct a causal account of welfare state reform by, first of all, elaborating the specific demand or requirement a reform reacts or should respond to (Becker 2009: 24). This establishes the goal for which a reform is functional. Becker makes the useful distinction between the existential and politically contested dimensions of such functional goals. Some goals of system-like configurations are existential because they are conditions of material survival. To the extent that such goals have to be met for reasons of survival, they may be labeled "objective" (Becker 2009: 25), because they do not depend on political preferences. Political goals of a system-like configuration, by contrast, are not existential and may be identified as "subjective" (Becker 2009: 25). In other words, "objective" problem pressures constitute functional demands for reform to the extent that nonfunctional responses, including drift, cause system defects in the sense described.

Surely, systems – albeit to varying degrees – always have flaws; therefore, when exactly these become functional pressures remains debatable, and explains our quotation marks for "objective." Because the onset of these pressures is difficult to establish, a functional argument ultimately must refer to the well-functioning (a functional level of "systemness") or continuation of the system. If the working or continuation of the system is threatened, the demands for action that follow from it can be understood as functional demands. Second, a causal account of welfare state reform is crafted by specifying the mechanism bringing about the reform. Functional*ist* explanations are unacceptable not only because they assume that requirements will always be met, but also because they typically fail to provide a causal mechanism in the case a demand is actually met. Conversely, a functional reasoning that is open is useful because globalization, aging, financial crises, mass unemployment, and others entail functional pressures and requirements to which political actors must respond. This is not to say that such actors will always respond in a functional manner, because pressure to change does not tell us which reform is selected or that actors will learn. But the message of the functional pressure is that to continue as before is impossible.

Our reasoning is *open* and *nonfunctionalist*, then, as we do not assume that political actors always will react or that their responses are necessarily functional in that they succeed in reaching an intended goal (e.g., increasing labor participation rates) that is functional to the system. Hence, similar pressures do not automatically lead to identical responses in the various worlds of welfare (cf. Scharpf and Schmidt 2000), nor do they unavoidably break up

path-dependent developments. Pressures can be dealt with in various ways –
and these may be effective or futile – or not dealt with at all, whether as a
result of a conscious decision or not. An open functional approach to welfare
state reform, then, prescribes that we need to determine where the functional
demand comes from as well as an account of the causal mechanisms producing
the response to such demand.

We favor an approach that explains under what conditions (the functional
requirements) and how (through which causal mechanisms) specific welfare
state reform takes place (or not) that is functional (or not). And in this approach
we think ideas as causal beliefs (Goldstein and Keohane 1993; Béland and
Cox 2011) should play a prominent role. Ideas provide a key link or mechanism between the functional demand and the action, such as welfare reform.
However, ideas on their own are not capable of explaining the success or failure
of a reform because this is also a matter of how actors organize power behind
their ideas (see Hemerijck and Schludi 2000). Political actors need strategies to
formulate and implement ideas in the light of potential resistance, especially in
cases of radical reform.

The point where our open functional approach differs most from the constructivist approaches concerns how we look at the *context* in which ideas
assume their status as causal beliefs. In fact, we disagree with Schmidt and Hay,
who equate interests and ideas. For one, Schmidt's conclusion that all interests
are subjective does not follow from the theses that all interests are ideas and
that ideas constitute interests. Hay's plea for abolishing the notion of material
interests is not only unnecessary but also unproductive for analyzing the role
of ideas in welfare state reform.

We would rather allow for the possibility that some interests constituted by
the ideas of some actors appear not as ideas, but as "objective" material constraints in the context in which other actors find themselves. The context of
political action consists partly of a constellation of interests. Constructivists
hold that interests are historical, social, and political constructions and we
agree. And, as Schmidt argues, ideas constitute interests. However, this does
not imply that, once constructed, such interests are contingent in the sense
that they can be changed and reconstructed as one sees fit according to some
idea. Once constructed and embedded in the context, interests are transmut-
able only within limits, namely, the limits set by the other interests that form
part of the same context. This is what makes interests appear as "objective"
interests within the context or at least as limits to the maneuvering room for
some actors. A particular context constrains and enables the political behavioral options more for some actors than for others. Some material forces in
the social world, and ideationally constructed interests functioning as such,
make themselves felt no matter how they are interpreted or socially constructed. In this sense, we do not adopt the ontological position that the
social world is constructed if this is taken to imply that ideas *only* determine
social reality.

We build on the challenges-capabilities-vulnerabilities (CCV) approach and the policy learning (PL) approach and propose that exogenous and endogenous pressures generate this context. The context is strategically selective because "it favours certain strategies over others as means to realise a given set of intentions or preferences" (Hay 2002: 129). Although outcomes are not determined, some outcomes are more likely than others and some demands are felt harder than others. For example, ideas do not construct the functional requisites of capitalism. Social order, efficiency, profitability, and competitiveness are requirements without which the system would collapse, or at least the level of integration of the system ("systemness") would decline (Becker 2009: 27). These requirements are contestable in that political actors may normatively oppose them. However, while a communist is against goals like profitability, that does not mean that he or she would contest that this is a system requirement for capitalism, the very system that he or she rejects. The bottom line is that even though political actors may oppose the functional requirements of a system such as capitalism or the system of social security, these requirements are the "objective" requirements to which some policies are less and others more functional responses. When these functional requirements are not met, or no longer met, the system is put under strain and its goal attainment is in danger. We therefore label these "objective" pressures for change.

Where ideas as causal beliefs matter is in determining the frame, the political strategies, and the public policies to realize or adjust to these functional requirements. We agree that outcomes are strategically selected, as for instance in the case of the political economy of globalization. As Hay (2002: 130) puts it:

Given near-universal perceptions amongst policy-making elites of the increased mobility of capital, it is unlikely ... that liberal-democratic states will increase the tax burden on corporations.... Heightened capital mobility ... makes credible previously implausible capital exit strategies. Consequently, states which wish to retain their revenue base will find themselves having to internalise the preference of capital for lower rates of taxation and more deregulated ("flexible") labour markets.

In Hay's formulation, however, it seems that politicians' room to maneuver is solely determined by their *perception* that capital has become more mobile and their *belief* that they have to give in to corporate demands. Our point would be that capital's mobility appears as an objective actuality with which to reckon, because disregarding this fact has immediate consequences of an existential nature (e.g., relocation of production and investments and galloping unemployment). This observation, however, does not imply that lowering corporate taxes is the only policy option. In fact, empirical evidence indicates that governments have other, perhaps even better options available, such as public investment strategies in material infrastructure (say, roads or glass fiber telecommunication) and cognitive infrastructure (say, education). But it does imply that governments, although they have several options, must work in the contextually given presence of a real exit threat of mobile capital. This social fact of the context has to be taken into account, although the context does not determine how this will or must be done. After all, some capital does relocate and markets, especially the financial market as the sovereign debt crises since 2009 illustrate, respond vehemently to political incapacity and instability, forcing unorthodox acts, including unlikely and unpromising spectrum-wide "grand coalitions" (Greece 2011), or replacing politicians with technocrats as policy-problem solvers (as in Italy in 2011).

So, some contextual elements appear as objective pressures to act. How and why politicians perceive which acts are functional and which are not is an open question. Or as Larsen and Andersen (2009: 243) state, "what is perceived as 'necessary' depends very much on the diagnoses of the problems and on the concomitant cause-effect beliefs of actors." But we think that, for instance, the political economy of globalization demands adjustment and reform policies that are usually difficult to turn into electoral assets, if only because they call for a change of the status quo of welfare state–related established social rights and conventions. Policy ideas, too, can be identified to be well-adapted or ill-adapted to the functional demands that appear as "objective" pressures. For instance, some welfare state reforms (say, an increase in retirement age) may not correspond very well to the demands of important voter groups (those who expected to retire relatively soon), which would perceive such reforms as opposed to their interests based on their interpretation of the world (e.g., retirement as an earned right). Consequently, reform-oriented politicians are confronted with an objective constraint on their behavioral options to which they must react. One reaction could be to ignore the fact, in which case the consequences may be felt at the next election. If they choose to go ahead with an unpopular measure, while recognizing the potential electoral retribution, they have an incentive to seek ways to avoid electoral punishment. Knowing, or assuming to know, that a reform may have negative electoral repercussions, a political actor whose idea would require pursuing a reform may want to turn to a blame avoidance strategy. This makes blame avoidance strategies moderating variables between ideas and reform in our approach (this is elaborated in Chapter 9).

6.5. ILLUSTRATING THE ARGUMENT: THE DUTCH DISABILITY CRISIS OF THE 1990S

Here we wish to illustrate the value of our open functional approach that links an objective problem pressure to an idea and to reform. We take as our example the early 1990s reform of the Dutch disability insurance scheme (*WAO, Wet op de Arbeidsongeschiktheidsverzekering*) because this case illustrates the value of our approach well. It is not our goal to offer a new or better explanation of this reform (for excellent studies, see Visser and Hemerijck 1997; Green-Pedersen 2002; Kuipers 2006). Our aim is more modest: illustrating our open functional approach.

The objective problem pressure or functional requirement is our point of departure. The Dutch social insurance of 1968 covered the risk of disability and was meant to provide benefits for, initially, a maximum of 155,000, and later, after an extension, a maximum of 285,000 people. Expenditure for the scheme hovered between 3.5 and more than 4 percent of gross domestic product. The number of disabled persons as a percentage of all insured persons exploded, from 6.1 percent in 1975 to 11.4 percent in 1990. Because the number of insured persons also increased in this period, the trend in absolute number was even more alarming. By 1990, almost 900,000 people received a benefit out of a labor force of 6 million. Without action, the scheme would drift and would quickly absorb a million people (Van Gestel et al. 2009: 76; Adviescommissie Arbeidsongeschiktheid 2001: 24; SCP 2001, Table B2.1; Kuipers 2006: 150) – that is, three and a half times the scheme's original capacity.

This massive influx of benefit recipients existentially threatened the insurance to the extent that not radically reforming the institutional rules of the scheme (e.g., by tightening the eligibility criteria and improving prevention and reintegration) would indubitably have caused the scheme to collapse. Moreover, the malfunctioning of the disability scheme contributed strongly to the vicious circle of "welfare without work," further policy drift, and other negative spillovers. High wages force entrepreneurs to seek labor-saving techniques that increase productivity. This leads to a round of shedding less productive labor to save costs, which, in turn, increases social security expenditure (early exit, disability, unemployment). This forces up social security contributions and thereby further increases the already high wages. "These necessitate further productivity increases in competitive firms as a result of which another round of reductions in the workforce begins and so on" (Hemerijck et al. 2000: 109). As a consequence, the crisis of the disability system endangered the entire wage and social security system. As Visser and Hemerijck (1997: 117) stress, the financial problem of the disability scheme in effect became a system-wide governability emergency. This, in our view, constitutes an "objective" functional requirement and the context for radical reform.

However, as argued earlier, functional requirements and pressures do not cause their own fulfillment. In fact, not intervening and therefore allowing policy drift were distinct possibilities at the time, and political actors could have chosen this option. Yet it is highly plausible that the insurance scheme would have fallen apart without drastic action. To understand why things started moving toward a radical reform that included harsh retrenchment and the restructuring of power relations and responsibilities, we argue that the role of ideas is crucial. In the case of the disability reform, one very specific idea turned out to have a momentous transformative capacity: the idea that it was possible to express in one single number how many benefits society was capable of sustaining. This number was the inactivity/activity ratio (i/a ratio). The measure was developed by the Ministry of Social Affairs and expresses the number of economically inactive individuals as a proportion of the economically active ones. The economically inactive include the benefit recipients of 15 years and older in benefit years. The active population includes those individuals with a job of 15 years and older in full-time equivalents. Since the 1990s, the i/a ratio has become a key criterion for assessing the sustainability of the system of social security. The notion that the i/a ratio does this constitutes an idea as causal belief because (1) it is a product of our cognition; (2) it connect things in the world – the number of benefit recipients, the working population, and the system's sustainability; and (3) it makes individuals act, as a high and/or increasing ratio offers a motive for action.

It had been shown, among others by the Dutch Council for Scientific Research (WRR) (1990), that the high percentage of disability benefit claimants contributed massively to a high i/a ratio. Consequently, this scheme could be targeted to reduce entry into the scheme and to facilitate exit. In addition, the message had to be conveyed that there was no other option but to reform drastically, that is, further policy drift was a political impossibility. This job was prepared by the Dutch Prime Minister Ruud Lubbers, who, in a speech in September 1990 to a layman audience stated that "the Netherlands is sick," implying that drastic reform was an absolute necessity. The role of ideas is decisive here, because when voters accept the idea of both the alarming indicator – in this case, the i/a ratio – and the idea of the unavoidability of drastic reform, they adopt the same causal belief as the government, maximizing the chances for implementing the reform.

Lubbers's promise that he would resign as prime minister if the number of disability benefit claimants reached 1 million helped the government to convince the public of the cause-effect relationship of their idea. If the i/a ratio was not lowered by drastically curbing access to the disability pension scheme and boosting claimants' exit out of it, the system would disintegrate. What also helped was the unanimous recommendation of the Social Economic Council (SER), consisting of independent experts, trade unions, and employer organizations, to curb the increase of the disability scheme. Higher participation rates would – in their view – partly solve the problems the Dutch economy was facing (WRR 1990; Visser and Hemerijck 1997, Green-Pedersen 2002).

However, these developments did not remedy the negotiation problems of the parties that made up the government (the Christian democrats and the social democrats). The two coalition parties could not agree on the content of the reform, with the Christian democrats being willing to abolish the disability scheme altogether and the social democrats assuring their electorate that no drastic changes were upcoming (Kuipers 2006: 152–153; Green-Pedersen 2002). At this point, the cabinet asked the SER to come up with a wide variety of reform options. However, the SER was also unable to reach a consensus, and the employer organizations and the expert members advised making the level of disability benefits dependent on the claimant's age and tightening the eligibility terms so that only those who were "disabled to do any work" could qualify for a benefit. The government took over the SER's proposal on the eligibility criteria but also made the duration of the benefit dependent on the number of employment years prior to disability (Kuipers 2006: 154). Because of resistance from the unions and the social democrats, the government parties in the end agreed on a less drastic proposal (Kuipers 2006: 156ff.).

The other conspicuous reform concerned a major organizational transformation to restructure radically the relations of power and responsibilities that governed the scheme (suggested by the Buurmeijer Commission on Social Security Reform, building on a report from the Dutch Audit Office [*Rekenkamer*]). This committee pointed to the fuzzy tripartite corporatist institutional structure that had caused the ungovernability of the Dutch social security system in general and the disability scheme in particular. The power of the social partners in the administration of social insurance funds was curbed. The ensuing institutional overhaul effectively dismantled the corporatist governance structure of the Dutch social security system.

This short illustration of the 1990s reform of the disability scheme in the Netherlands underscores the merit of our open functional approach to welfare state reform. First, we identified the source of the functional demand, namely, the exceedingly large number of disability benefit claimants that was rapidly approaching three and a half times the intended number of claimants and exhausting the scheme's capacity. Drastic reform was a functional requirement as the scheme would not have continued to exist without it, endangering also the continuation of the entire system of social security. These facts effectively precluded further policy drift. Second, an idea as causal belief was that the scheme caused an extremely high inactivity rate and contributed to the vicious "welfare without work" cycle, whereas a high activity rate was vital for the Dutch economy. This idea offered the guide to act: the inactivity rate had to decrease drastically by curbing the inflow of claimants and by stimulating the outflow out of the disability scheme. It is the functional pressure that prompted the government to select certain types of drastic reforms that, so our counterfactual reasoning would hold, in different circumstances would have been inconceivable and impossible to implement: a firm restriction of access to the disability scheme accompanied by a complete overhaul of the organizational structure so as to take away power from the unions and employers and restore the control of the government over the disability insurance program.

6.6. CONCLUSION

Building on our discussion in the previous chapters, in this chapter we drew on insights from comparative welfare state studies and integrated these into an open functional approach to welfare state reform. From the modernization perspective, we adopted the view that societal needs and demands make themselves felt as functional requirements of state intervention (see also Chapter 3). From the power resources approach, we learned that whether and how such requirements are picked up depends on a nation's prevalent power structure.

The studies of the welfare state's crises taught us that the expansion of the welfare state in the context of a capitalist democracy has clear limits and that mixing political democracy with economic capitalism creates contradictions and problems of legitimacy. Moreover, we took over from various sources of inspiration that there are many challenges that threaten to knock off balance the existing construction of welfare states and that new social risks and needs have emerged that are not, or only badly, covered. The institutionalist analyses pointed us to the remarkable resilience of welfare states and to the institutional and political reasons for "stickiness." The recent literature showed that institutional stickiness and political resistance can be overcome and that radical welfare state adaptation, updating, retrenchment, and restructuring are more characteristic features than resilience and stability. The major puzzles we are confronted with is why such reforms can take place and in which direction they are tending.

Our theoretical starting point is that welfare state reform is formulated, proposed, and implemented in response to the pressing challenges that contemporary welfare states face. Institutional conditions and political power struggles determine the extent to which these responses are effective or deficient in how the reform helps to adjust the welfare state's arrangements to new challenges and to allow it to continue performing by securing socially and politically acceptable levels of employment, social security, and equality.

Constructivist studies have convinced us that ideas matter in welfare state reform. The major difficulty in showing *how* ideas matter concerns the problem of establishing causality (see also Kangas et al. 2013). We identify one of the major problems as the assumption that ideas by themselves create the incentives for action. We take issue with this view and argue that ideas on their own do not produce outcomes such as drastic welfare state reform. We need to take into account the broader context, of which ideas are a part, to explain how ideas affect outcomes.

The open functional approach we developed takes these major insights from the literature seriously and proposes to understand the challenges that welfare states face as functional demands for welfare state reform whenever the challenges can be shown to threaten the actual existence of the social policy arrangements. In such cases, demands for reform need to be met; if they are not met, the schemes will collapse, effectively blocking deliberate further policy drift. In this sense, the challenges entail functional pressures and requirements to which political actors must respond. However, this does not mean that political actors will indeed always learn and react, or will always respond functionally. But nonreform or bad reform will cause the system to falter, no matter what the ideas are. Functional requirements are therefore important aspects or parts of the context of political behavior: they are "objective" constraints on political actors. Such constraints are restricting to the extent that they limit policies that actors can enact. They can also be enabling in that they open up new options and opportunities. This explains why there can be different responses to the same type of functional demands and why we stress that our functional approach is open.

We stressed further that explaining welfare state adaptation, updating, retrenchment, and restructuring solely in terms of functional pressures would be incomplete. We also must account for the mechanisms that link the actual reform strategies that actors choose and the functional demands that make themselves felt in the context. This is because we still wish to explain how and when welfare state reform does or does not take place and whether it is functional. Here ideas as causal beliefs play a prominent role. In our analysis of the reform of the Dutch disability scheme, which illustrated the value of our approach, we made plausible that absorbing three and a half times more beneficiaries than the scheme originally was devised for threatened the very existence not only of the arrangement itself but also – through spillovers and interlinkages – the social security system at large. As a result drastic reform became a functional requirement. However, it was an idea that linked the functional demand to the political act of reform. We found that the idea of the inactivity crisis as embodied in an alarming statistic (the i/a ratio) and in the metaphor of the sick Dutch society was capable of preparing the way for political action.

Still, welfare state reform, even under conditions of functional pressures and ideas, remains difficult because it almost invariably conflicts with established pro-welfare state preferences and interests among the public. Welfare state reform is almost never an electoral asset (Giger and Nelson 2011, forthcoming; Schumacher et al. 2013). In terms of our open functional approach, the functional requirements of the economic system are likely to conflict with the demands of the political system. Welfare state reform is a risky business, and when it takes place, the political actors who choose to reform the system drastically must devise and apply blame avoidance strategies. This is the issue we pick up and elaborate in Chapter 9. But first we map and document in the next two chapters the actual functional pressures that welfare states are facing.

7

Why Do We Need to Reform the Welfare State?

Part I: Globalization as a Functional Pressure Coming from the Outside

7.1. INTRODUCTION

In the previous chapter, we outlined our open functional approach to welfare state reform. In this approach, "objective" functional pressures play a key role. What are those pressures and how hard are they pushing? This chapter examines a key pressure coming from the outside, globalization; Chapter 8 focuses on the pressures from within.

What functional pressure for welfare state reform arises from globalization? Globalization, the increased interconnectedness of economies, is generally seen as a by-product or even an inherent feature of capitalism. It was two centuries ago that the first globalization or "free trade thinkers," Adam Smith (in 1776 [2003]) and David Ricardo (in 1817), wrote their seminal work, and the debate on (the effects of) globalization is still going on. With the onslaught of the financial crisis in 2008 and the sovereign debt crises since 2009, the voices against unlimited capitalism have become much louder, although protests against globalization and international financial capital (e.g., the occupy movement that started in 2011) have been occurring since the late 1990s. For example, in 1999 violent protests took place in Seattle, the place that has been labeled the "birthplace of the 'backlash against globalisation'" (*The Economist* 2000: 97). According to the anti-globalists – a label that has gone somewhat out of vogue lately – globalization is a bad thing because it only makes the rich (relatively) richer and the poor (relatively) poorer. This view contrasts squarely with that of Smith and Ricardo, who saw increased trade openness as – what we now would call – a win-win situation. They argued that globalization's possibly negative effects in the short run could easily be compensated by its positive effects in the longer run. International trade increases the available resources for all; it enlarges the economic pie. In the words of Ricardo (2004 [1817]: 77):

No extension of foreign trade will immediately increase the amount of value in a country, although it will very powerfully contribute to increase the mass of commodities, and therefore the sum of our enjoyments.

This larger pie would make it possible to reduce the gap between the rich and the poor instead of enlarging it, as the anti-globalist would have it. The relationship between economic openness and economic growth suggests a similarly glossy perspective. Most empirical studies find a positive although typically weak relationship (Dollar 1992; Bhagwati 1995; Sachs and Warner 1995; Harrison 1996; Edwards 1998; Frankel and Romer 1999; Dreher 2006). These studies, however, also met with a substantial amount of criticism, mostly directed at the methods and the definitions of key variables used (Levine and Renelt 1992; Rodrik 1999; Rodríguez and Rodrik 2000). So, what does globalization do?

In this chapter, we study the effect of globalization (typically measured as increased trade openness or capital openness) on the welfare state (usually measured as welfare effort, that is, social spending) so as to identify the extent of functional pressures stemming from it. We show that the distinct views of the anti-globalists and the free trade thinkers are also prominent in the theoretical and empirical literature on the relationship between globalization and the welfare state. Each of the two prominent, and conflicting, perspectives on this relationship – the efficiency hypothesis and the compensation hypothesis (discussed later) – posits that globalization produces a functional pressure to reform. However, the direction in which this effect is pushing varies. The lion's share of the existing literature corroborates the compensation hypothesis that higher levels of globalization and welfare state effort reinforce one another. More recent studies, however, find support for the efficiency thesis, indicating that greater globalization is inhibiting welfare effort. Each of the strands of literature makes clear that globalization is a key functional pressure for welfare state reform to reckon with, one that is likely more important than the sectoral shifts in employment (from agriculture to industry and from industry to services) that have occurred at the same time.

We present descriptive data on the level of globalization showing that this pressure has increased over time, but also that there is substantial variation across countries and welfare state regimes. To what extent the pressure deriving from globalization is felt depends on the so-called type of trade that dominates (intra-industry trade or high-wage trade versus inter-industry or low-wage trade). Based on a general measure of trade openness, we find that the pressure for welfare state reform is strongest in the conservative regime. However, this pressure is curbed by the fact that this trade is overwhelmingly of the intra-industry type. In the social democratic regime, conversely, the level of intra-industry trade is substantially lower – though still topping 50 percent – adding to the "objective" functional pressure to reform because of globalization. The latter conclusion also holds for Ireland, the most "globalized" country we examine: only 55 percent of the Irish trade is of the intra-industry type, which leads to a rather high pressure to reform.

7.2. TO WHAT EXTENT DOES GLOBALIZATION AFFECT THE WELFARE STATE?

What is the theoretical link between globalization and welfare effort? (For overviews of findings, see Brady et al. 2005: 922–925 and Swank 2010.) There are contrasting views on this, but in a nutshell they can be subsumed under two headings: the efficiency hypothesis and the compensation hypothesis. Both hypotheses suggest that globalization comes with an "objective" functional pressure to reform the welfare state, that is, to adjust, update, or restructure it. Where they differ is in the expected *direction* of welfare state reform: retrenchment or expansion. The *efficiency hypothesis* relates to a neoliberal idea of good governance (cf. Glatzer and Rueschemeyer 2005: chapter 1), in which the voices of Smith and Ricardo echo. To put it briefly, the argument is that globalization fosters increased wealth and well-being all across the globe. Increased openness leads to more specialization, tougher competition, and more choice for consumers. This, allegedly, makes the world a better place because higher openness also comes with more market transparency, less distortion, and more productivity-enhancing activities. Overall, the expectation is that this leads to better government performance because bad governance is penalized by lower economic growth, whereas good governance is rewarded by higher economic growth. The role of the market thus increases and the possibility for political intervention by other means than the market diminishes concomitantly. Consequently, according to this perspective, there is a tension between globalization and welfare effort. To use the words of Glatzer and Rueschemeyer (2005: 3ff.), generous social provisions become a "burden and a drag on national performance and international competitiveness." Globalization puts downward pressure on tax rates and government spending and obstructs new developments in social policy. According to this neoliberal perspective, government spending generally has a detrimental effect on international competitiveness. Consequently, the efficiency hypothesis posits that higher levels of globalization lead to lower levels of welfare effort.

Conversely, the *compensation hypothesis* posits that globalization and welfare efforts are mutually reinforcing. The compensation that society demands for the larger risks in a more open economy, such as a greater chance of job relocation, can and will be provided by governments. It is the inter-relationship between the state and the market that produces this positive condition. Politically, it is precisely the welfare state system that enables the larger role of the market under globalization. Rieger and Leibfried (2003) even go as far as to suggest that the welfare state made globalization possible in developed democracies. As we show in the next section, there is quite a lot of empirical evidence suggesting that the compensation hypothesis is correct. The seminal study by Cameron (1978), for example, was one of the first to show that the relationship between social spending and trade openness is positive. Precisely those countries that have the most open economies also have big governments (i.e., high social spending) (see also Katzenstein 1985 and Becker 2011).

Nonetheless, it is unclear if this correlation also indicates causation. The compensation hypothesis has both a supply-side mechanism and a demand-side mechanism to it (Walter 2010: 404). The demand side concerns the compensation that citizens request from their government in return for the higher risks they face in a globalized economy. The supply side involves whether governments translate these demands into actual social policymaking that offers the compensation requested. This implies that when studies find no effect on the macro-level and hence the compensation hypothesis does not seem to hold, it remains unclear if this is because of a lack of demand for compensation or because governments do not deliver the social compensation that the public asks for (see also Brady et al. 2005: 923; Jahn 2006). Based on World Values Survey data for Switzerland for 2007, Walter (2010) shows that the losers from globalization are more likely to feel economically insecure, increasing their preferences for welfare state expansion. These preferences and demands result in a higher likelihood of voting for the social democrats, which in Switzerland is the party that caters most to the preferences of globalization's losers.

Despite the plausibility of the micro-level foundation of the compensation hypothesis, it could still very well be that these demands are not heard or are ignored at the macro-level where the compensation policies are made. What is the effect of globalization on welfare state policy output? And is this effect stable over time? An increasing number of scholars argue and empirically demonstrate that the answer to the latter question is *no* (e.g., Kittel and Winner 2005; Jahn 2006; Busemeyer 2009). Jahn proposes a theoretical mechanism linking globalization to welfare effort that combines an economic competition model with learning and emulation theory. In this model, governments intervene extensively in their economies for social and political purposes if there is no international competition. With international competition, conversely, governments have to change their behavior so as to take the decisions of other governments into account. They will particularly watch those economies with which their economy is most closely linked (like the Dutch watching the German policies). Without globalization, domestic factors are the main focus point; with globalization, international factors are. Whereas domestic factors expand social expenditures, retrenchment is so to speak enforced by international, external factors. Diffusion is thus a necessary condition for welfare state reform, especially for retrenchment (see Obinger et al. 2013). A second, different model places globalization before structural interdependence by stating that financial openness enables structural interdependence. Financial openness leads to diffusion, which in turn leads to a re-orientation of politics. In this mechanism, diffusion is a coping strategy; when times are uncertain, the behavior of others who are similar or have a similar goal is mimicked so as to reduce the level of uncertainty. In all these three theories, there has to be one central country, the focus country that others copy or follow.

The extensive literature on attitudes toward trade among voters typically finds that less-educated, blue-collar workers display the highest level of support for trade restrictions, that is, they oppose globalization (e.g., Scheve and Slaughter 2001; Mayda and Rodrik 2005). This finding is in line with the Stolper-Samuelson theorem, which states that trade openness benefits the owners of factors of production with which an economy is relatively well endowed (in developed democracies, these are the high skilled) while hurting others (the low skilled). According to Hainmueller and Hiscox (2006), this effect might work through education. In the United States, for example, voters with college or university education have a more favorable attitude toward globalization because they are more exposed to (economic) ideas about the gains from trade.

Quinn and Toyoda (2007) spell out a different mechanism. Their empirical analysis of 82 countries from 1955 to 1999 shows that domestic conditions and ideological shifts partly drive financial globalization policies, measured as changes in capital account regulation. If anti-capitalist ideology is widespread, visible in high levels of votes for communist parties, regulation on international financial transactions is more restrictive. If liberal, pro-capitalist ideology is widespread, that is, when communist parties receive no or only a small share of the vote, regulation is less restrictive. The mechanism through which ideology affects policymakers' decision making is the following. The global ideology, that is, the support for or opposition against openness on the global level, influences government officials' incentives and opportunities for implementing globalization policies. It does so, because the "forces that shape belief formation among individuals globally can be assumed to influence political elites" (Quinn and Toyoda 2007: 345–346). The causal mechanisms of the compensation thesis and the efficiency thesis might be different, but this does not mean that the mechanisms cannot be invoked at the same time (Genschel 2004: 626). In other words, globalization could lead simultaneously to more tax competition (the efficiency thesis) and to an increase in the demands for compensation for the higher risks and consequent government compensation (the compensation thesis). The net effect of these two mechanisms is indeterminate. By analyzing the party manifestos of 21 developed democracies between 1960 and 1998, Burgoon (2006: 25) found that partisan politics is important for the net effect: "left parties do tend to champion welfare compensation as an answer to international economic risks more than do non-left parties; and right parties tend to look less to such compensation as an answer to globalization's risks."

7.3. DOES GLOBALIZATION REALLY AFFECT THE WELFARE STATE?

As we saw, both the compensation hypothesis and the efficiency hypothesis suggest that globalization exerts an "objective" functional pressure for welfare state reform to which political actors may respond or not. So far, most studies find a positive, but typically small effect of globalization on welfare state effort, supporting the compensation hypothesis (e.g., Cameron 1978; Katzenstein 1985; Rodrik 1997, 1998; Garrett 1998; Hicks 1999; Adserà and Boix 2002; Meinhard and Potrafke 2012; see e.g. Brady et al. 2005: 922–925). As Walter (2010: 405) correctly notes, despite this support at the macro-level, micro-level support for the compensation hypothesis is lacking. Given that the causal mechanisms of the compensation thesis lie at the micro-level (see earlier discussion), the lack of such support means that the causal relationship between globalization and the welfare state is still not fully understood.

Until recently, the empirical support for the efficiency hypothesis has been much more modest and has led Castles (2004) to dismiss as a myth the possible negative effect of globalization on the welfare state. The best-known study that does find support for the efficiency thesis is Garrett and Mitchell's (2001). They show that total trade negatively and significantly influences government spending. This study has received a substantial share of criticism. Kittel and Winner (2005), for instance, argue that Garrett and Mitchell's statistical model fails to be well-behaved and that proper modeling leads to the conclusion that globalization has little to do with government spending. Instead, such spending is driven by the state of the domestic economy (see also Plümper et al. 2005). More recent studies are more supportive of a negative relationship between globalization and welfare state effort, typically finding that when we take a longer time period, specifically if we include the 2000s, economic openness relates negatively to public spending, hence supporting the efficiency hypothesis (Busemeyer 2009). If scholars employ data that go beyond the mid-1990s, which the older studies do not do, they are more likely to find a negative effect of globalization. The reason for this is that the negative effect may have needed a longer period to play out. Moreover, as Jahn indicates (2006: 402), "new data are important because the effects of globalization are in flux." Social expenditures increased substantially in the OECD countries from 1990 until 1993, especially in those countries where the expenditure levels were already highest. As of 1993 onward, these very same countries reduced social expenditures substantially, lowering the OECD average over the 1993–2000 period. Remarkably, over the same period, the countries with low levels of spending increased this level, diminishing the gap between the highest and lowest social spenders. By 2001, this trend toward lower spending of the high-spending countries came to an end. The 1980s were thus a very stable period, while the 1990s were much more in flux. It is exactly this distinction that produces the support for the compensation thesis in studies with data up to the mid-1990s.

However, the key features of the different types of welfare state regimes have not been altered, nor has the rank order of countries changed according to the generosity of benefits. The social democratic regime remains the most encompassing and the liberal regime the leanest. The work of, for example, Adelantado and Calderón Cuevas (2006) picks up data that further support the notion that the association between globalization and welfare effort is in flux. They show that pressures arising from globalization have wrought a "convergence to the middle" among 14 European welfare states in terms of public expenditure, social protection expenditure, income inequality, and the risk of poverty. Specifically, they demonstrate that while in absolute terms social expenditures have risen between 1992 and 2001, in relative terms they have fallen. Moreover, as Busemeyer (2009) shows, social spending of the high-spending countries has decreased and that of the low-spending countries has picked up, overall amounting to a convergence of spending levels.

But there is some doubt as to whether convergence is really occurring. Brady et al. (2005) report inconclusive results that inspire the conclusion that we should be skeptical about any bold claim about globalization, irrespective of the direction in which this claim goes (expansion, retrenchment, or convergence). In a similar vein, Dreher et al. (2008a) show that none of the various expenditure categories they used has been robustly influenced by any of the globalization indicators. This suggests that "either the hitherto neglected interaction effects blur the two direct effects to a rather large extent, or governments throughout the world have not rearranged their expenditure shares as a result of globalization" (Dreher et al. 2008a: 265). Conversely, Adserà and Boix (2002) argue that foreign direct investment (FDI) by multinational corporations is an important source of worker insecurity. With FDI, these corporations can more easily substitute factors of production away from workers in a particular country. Multinationals' elasticity in the demand for labor thereby increases from FDI. Adserà and Boix find a positive correlation between FDI activity in the industries in which individuals work and their (individual) perception of economic insecurity.

As mentioned, both the supporters of the compensation hypothesis and those of the efficiency thesis agree that globalization produces greater domestic economic volatility (risk) that translates into a functional pressure to adapt, update, retrench, or restructure policy. They differ in their opinion of whether the government can or cannot compensate the demands spurred as a consequence. Based on economic theory, Down (2007) even questions this shared assumption. Greater trade openness could just as well lead to lower domestic economic volatility. Whether it does depends on the size and depth of markets. First, trade openness leads to integration in larger, deeper, and thus more stable markets. Second, trade openness diversifies risks, for example, through more trading partners or by trading to economies whose business cycle is not fully synchronous. The importance of the size and depth of markets suggests that smaller economies should exhibit more domestic economic volatility as a result of their market rather than as a result of trade (openness). Consequently, these are likely to be the countries that compensate the most, which is visible in, for instance, a higher level of generosity of their welfare states. The empirical finding of a link between trade openness and big government may thus be a spurious one, resulting from the empirical fact that the smallest economies are typically also the most open ones (later we report the data).

There are also scholars who theoretically argue and empirically show that an effect of globalization on the welfare state is probably small at best. Within this body of research, the work of Iversen and Cusack (2000) is best known. Iversen and Cusack's point is that deindustrialization rather than globalization produces an "objective" pressure for welfare state reform by increasing need and causing growing electoral demands for welfare compensation. We see much merit in Iversen and Cusack's argument but do not think that either globalization or deindustrialization is what propels welfare state reform. As we argue in some more detail in the next chapter, it is plausible that higher levels of globalization push for welfare state reform, but that deindustrialization plays a role too.

7.4. FURTHER EMPIRICALLY MAPPING GLOBALIZATION AND ITS EFFECTS

Has the level of globalization increased over the last years? The so-called KOF index (Dreher 2006), which captures three main dimensions of globalization (economic, political, and social integration) suggests that the answer is clearly *yes*. This index combines variables measuring the actual flows of trade and investment, the restrictions of international transactions, the degree of political integration, the extent of personal contacts with people living in foreign countries, the trans-border flows of information, and the degree of cultural integration. Figure 7.1 displays the development of the KOF index for our seven selected countries between 1970 and 2010. In all countries, globalization – as measured by the index – has increased substantially since 1970. The increase is largest in Germany, which becomes 66 percent more globalized. The United Kingdom follows with an increase of 48 percent, Italy with 45 percent, Sweden with 32 percent, Denmark with 29 percent, the United States with 28 percent, and the Netherlands closes the line with a 27 percent increase. Denmark and the Netherlands, and to a lesser extent also the United States, already had very high levels of globalization in 1970. The figure shows that the level of economic, political, and social integration has risen substantially since 1970. This conclusion can be upheld also if the other OECD countries are included and if we examine all 123 countries for which data are available (see Dreher et al. 2008a: 271). Figure 7.1 also indicates that, probably because of the financial, economic, and debt crises, the increase in the degree of globalization over time is no longer self-evident. While globalization continues to rise in the United

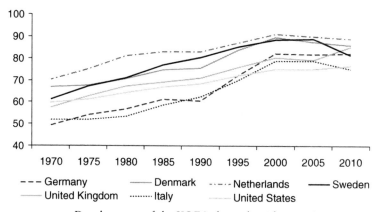

FIGURE 7.1. Development of the KOF index, selected countries, 1970–2010.

Notes: KOF stands for *Konjunkturforschungsstelle*, which is the German word for the Business Cycle Research Institute of the Swiss Federal Institute of Technology (ETH) in Zurich.

Source: Dreher (2006 [updated in Dreher et al. 2008b]) (http://globalization.kof.ethz. ch/, Accessed March 2013).

States and remains at about the same level in Germany, it has fallen in the Netherlands, Italy, and Sweden in recent years.

Chinn and Ito (2008) looked at data on trade openness and capital openness between 1970 and 2007 to measure the extent of globalization. They measured trade openness by imports plus exports in current prices as a percentage of GDP. Capital openness is an index of (1) the presence of multiple exchange rates, (2) restrictions on current account transactions, and (3) the requirement of the surrender of export proceeds. The finding is that the higher the index for capital openness, the more open an economy is.

Before we can draw any firm conclusions – to the extent that this is possible at all – on the "objective" functional pressures arising because of globalization, we first need to address the issue of the *type* of trade. Most existing studies use an aggregate measure of trade openness, such as import plus export as a share of GDP. Given the availability of data on this indicator, this focus is understandable, but from a theoretical perspective it is problematic. The reason is that economic theory suggests that the effect of trade openness on economic risks varies across types of openness and that the consequent compensation that citizens demand varies as well. More precisely, new trade theory (Krugman 1992, 1995) proposes the so-called *smooth adjustment hypothesis* that informs us that the labor market adjustment costs, such as job losses or the need for workers to relocate or retrain, are substantially smaller under so-called intra-industry trade than under inter-industry trade (see, e.g., Balassa 1966; Cabral and Silva 2007). Intra-industry trade is trade that is caused by increasing product differentiation with scale economies (Lee 2004: 6), which means that it is basically trade between developed countries – for example, German shoes for Italian suits. Inter-industry trade, also known as low-wage trade, is trade that is caused by changes in the pattern of comparative advantage (Lee 2004: 6), which means that it is basically trade between developed and less-developed countries – for example, Chinese textiles for Swiss watches.[1]

A second problem of the extant literature is the (implicit) assumption that the impact of trade openness is similar across countries. However, we have seen that it makes theoretical and heuristic sense to differentiate between a liberal, a conservative, and a social democratic (and possibly a Mediterranean) welfare state regime (see Chapter 4). Consequently, it is plausible that the effect of trade openness on welfare effort diverges across welfare regimes as well. The postwar era until the 1970s indeed displays a clear pattern: the most advanced welfare states developed in the most open economies, while the more residual welfare states clustered in relatively protected countries. According to Esping-Andersen (1996a), the answer to this puzzle lies in the way domestic institutions facilitate broad consensual solutions or fail to do so. With the substantial increase in openness from the 1970s onward, lean welfare states and open economies were no longer mutually exclusive. Understanding the new pattern requires going beyond pure domestic explanations.

Do the different welfare state regimes display different levels of and changes in the two kinds of trade openness: low-wage trade and intra-industry trade? Figure 7.1 already shows that there has been a rise in trade openness in general, that is, in openness conventionally measured as import plus export as a percentage of GDP. Table 7.1 shows that this trade ratio increases from 1970 onward. All countries except Ireland display a drop in the level of trade openness between 2008 and 2009 due to the financial crisis and its economic aftermath (see Chapter 10). For examining the variation across the welfare state regimes, we therefore focus on the 1970–2008 period, because this period is not affected by the crisis. The liberal regime's trade ratio rises on average by 30 percent in this period. The conservative regime's trade ratio displays on average an even higher increase, namely, 44 percent, and also the level of trade openness tops the liberal regime (71 versus 103 in 2008). The on average increase in the social democratic regime, finally, holds the middle position with 36 percent. Also in terms of absolute levels, the social democratic regime holds the middle position with a trade ratio of 84 in 2008. Within the liberal regime, Ireland is the outlier, a so-called super-trader that exports much more than it imports and thus has a trade ratio (way) above 100. The trade ratios of the other countries in the liberal regime are much lower, especially in the United States. The variation in the conservative regime is also substantial. Here we have a number of super-traders (Belgium, the Netherlands, Austria, and

---

[1] Note that Garrett and Mitchell (2001 link) find no support for the hypothesis that inter-industry trade – which they label low-wage trade – is damaging to the welfare state.

TABLE 7.1. *Trade ratio, selected OECD countries, 1970–2009 (export plus import as percentage of gross domestic product in current prices)*

	1970	1980	1990	2000	2008	2009	Change 1970–2008
Australia	26	32	33	45	45	39	+19
Ireland	78	107	109	184	158	167	+80
New Zealand	47	61	53	69	63	55	+16
United Kingdom	44	52	51	58	61	58	+17
United States	11.3	21	21	26	30	25	+19
Average LR	41	55	53	76	71	69	+30
Austria	60	74	78	90	113	97	+53
Belgium	101	118	138	166	171	143	+70
France	30	43	44	56	55.6	48	+26
Germany	39	52	54	66	89	77	+50
Italy	32	46	39	53	58	48	+26
Netherlands	90	104	105	135	134	121	+44
Switzerland	63	73	71	87	102	92	+39
Average CR	59	73	76	93	103	89	+44
Denmark	57	66	67	87	107	91	+50
Finland	51	66	47	77	89	72	+38
Norway	74	80	75	76	78	70	+4
Sweden	48	60	59	87	100	90	+52
Average SDR	58	68	62	82	94	8	+36

Notes: Changes are in percentage points. Changes and averages are the authors' calculations. LR is liberal regime; CR is conservative regime; SDR is social democratic regime.
Source: Heston et al. (2011).

Switzerland in 2008) but also countries in which the trade ratio comes closer to the typical liberal country (like France and Italy). The across-country variation is smallest, though certainly not absent, in the social democratic regime. These data indicate that the smaller countries generally display the highest levels of trade openness. This also means that these are the countries in which the pressure stemming from globalization is felt the hardest; the "objective" pressure to reform as a result of globalization is thus the highest here. The larger the level of trade openness and the higher the increase in trade openness, the more governments are confronted with these pressures.

The data in Table 7.1 tell us that trade openness in general increased between 1970 and 2008, but do not differentiate between different types of trade openness. Table 7.2 displays data for our first type of trade openness, intra-industry trade. The level of intra-industry trade is determined by the most widely used measure, the Grubel-Lloyd index (1975), which has a minimum of 0 if all trade is of the low-wage type, that is, if all trade is between developed and less-developed countries, and a maximum of 100 if all trade is of the intra-industry type, that is, if all trade is between developed countries. Although this

TABLE 7.2. *Intra-industry trade, selected OECD countries, 1959–2000*

	1959	1964	1967	1988–1991	1992–1995	1996–2000
Canada	28	35	48	74	75	76
Ireland	..	..	..	59	57	55
United Kingdom	32	40	69	70	73	74
United States	40	40	49	64	65	69
Average LR	33	38	55	66	68	68
Austria	..	..	..	72	74	74
Belgium[a]	53	60	63	78	78	71
France	45	60	65	76	78	78
Germany	39	42	46	67	72	72
Netherlands	55	58	56	69	70	69
Italy	..	..	..	62	64	66
Average CR	48	55	58	71	73	72
Denmark	..	..	..	62	63	65
Finland	..	..	..	54	53	54
Norway	..	..	..	40	38	37
Sweden	..	..	..	64	65	67
Average SDR	..	..	..	55	55	56

[a] For 1959, 1964, and 1967, plus Luxembourg.
Notes: LR is liberal regime; CR is conservative regime; SDR is social democratic regime.
Sources: Data for 1959, 1964 and 1967: Grubel and Lloyd (1975, table 3.5); data for 1988–1991, 1992–1995 and 1996–2000: OECD (2002, table VI.I); averages are authors' calculations.

sounds relatively simple, the level of intra-industry trade is in fact fairly difficult to calculate. This is probably another reason that most scholars stick to the simple import plus export measure. Some authors, such as Marvel and Ray (1987) and Brülhart et al. (2004), maintain that the Grubel-Lloyd index does not adequately measure the level of intra-industry trade and suggest even more complex measurements (see also Lee 2004). However, for the purpose of comparing the levels of different types of trade openness across welfare regimes and across time, the Grubel-Lloyd index suffices.

The variation across countries in the level of intra-industry trade is considerable, as Table 7.2 demonstrates. In addition, the upward trend in most countries supports Balassa's finding of the prevalence of intra-industry specialization under higher levels of trade openness. Notwithstanding the individual countries' variations, the patterns the welfare regimes display are fairly distinct. Over the entire period 1959–2000, which is the period for which data are available, the ranking of regimes in terms of intra-industry trade levels is stable: the conservative regime has the most intra-industry trade, the social democratic regime the least (although for the latter, no data are available before 1988), and the liberal regime holds the middle position. This stability in terms of intra-industry trade is thus similar to the general openness measure presented earlier.

The data in Table 7.2 further tell us that already in 1950 the conservative regime's level of intra-industry trade was relatively high (48 percent). By 1964, over 50 percent of all trade was of the intra-industry type. The liberal regime only surpasses this 50 percent "threshold" three years later but with a higher speed than in the conservative regime. From 1967 onward, there seems to be some convergence between the conservative and liberal regimes regarding levels of intra-industry trade. As stated, the social democratic regime is the intra-industry trade laggard: from 1988 onward around 55 percent of all trade is intra-industry trade, with Denmark and Sweden having substantially more intra-industry trade (60 to 65 percent) than Finland (around 53 percent) and, especially, Norway (around 38 percent). Since intra-industry trade is trade between similar products, the possible effects on a country's labor market are less detrimental. This indicates that whereas overall trade openness suggests that the pressure to reform the welfare state is felt most severely in the conservative regime, this pressure is limited by the fact that most of this trade is of the intra-industry type. In the social democratic regime, conversely, the level of intra-industry trade is substantially lower – though still topping 50 percent – augmenting the "objective" functional pressure to reform due to globalization. The latter conclusion also pertains to Ireland, the biggest super-trader among the countries presented here: only 55 percent of this trade is of the intra-industry type, making the requirement to reform rather high.

Our second type of trade openness, low-wage trade, is the mirror image of the first intra-industry trade, so that an x percent level of intra-industry trade corresponds to a $(1-x)$ level of low-wage trade. The results of the analysis of low-wage trade in the three welfare regimes are hence analogous: the conservative regime displays the lowest level of low-wage trade; the social democratic regime the highest. A commonality between the regimes is the stable level of intra-industry and low-wage trade from 1988 onward. This indicates that if trade openness affects welfare programs and politics in a certain way, this is likely to continue in the years to come. Because of the expected larger impact on welfare effort under low-wage trade, the material presented in this section suggests the largest impact of trade openness on welfare effort in the social democratic regime.

The preceding discussion indicates that the effects of the two types of trade on demands for welfare compensation are very different, with the effects of low-wage trade (inter-industry trade) being generally more harsh – and thus also requiring more compensation. Because the rise of China and India spurs low-wage trade, the effect of globalization on welfare effort is likely to have changed over the last years. Examining the influence of different measures of globalization allows for identifying the possibly varying impact of different types of globalization.

7.5. CONCLUSION

In this chapter, we examined how globalization, the main pressure coming from the outside, affects welfare state reform. We argued that both the compensation hypothesis and the efficiency hypothesis suggest that globalization produces an "objective" pressure to reform the welfare state, but that the expected direction of this reform (either expansion or retrenchment) varies. Most of the existing literature supports the compensation thesis; higher levels of globalization and welfare state effort typically seem to reinforce one another. More recent studies, however, corroborate the efficiency thesis and report that greater globalization puts a downward pressure on welfare state effort. What both bodies of literature show is that globalization is an important functional pressure for welfare state reform to reckon with, probably of more importance than the sectoral shifts in employment (from agriculture to industry and from industry to services) that have been taking place in the same time span. The descriptive data of the level of globalization we presented indicate that this pressure has been getting stronger over time, but also that there is substantial variation across countries and welfare state regimes. In addition, we showed that the type of trade matters for whether and to what extent welfare states feel the pressure of globalization.

In addition to the functional pressures for welfare state updating, adaptation, retrenchment, or restructuring from the outside, there are also functional pressures pushing for reform from within, pressures that according to some scholars are pushing harder than those from the outside. In the next chapter, we probe the functional pressures for welfare state reform that come from among other factors changing labor markets and the increased participation of women in the labor market.

8

Why Do We Need to Reform the Welfare State?

Part II: Post-Industrial Society and the Functional Pressures to Reform Coming from Within

8.1. INTRODUCTION

As we discussed in Chapter 1, welfare state reform, that is, updating, adaptation, retrenchment, or restructuring, is not a recent phenomenon. Still, it is increasingly capturing the agenda of governments in developed democracies, albeit in varying degrees of prominence. Where does the need to reform come from? In the previous chapter, we examined a key pressure coming from the outside, globalization, which pushes for welfare state change by exerting a functional pressure for reform. However, there are also domestic changes or pressures from within that add to this need and that influence actors' ideas on how to respond and which type of reforms to undertake. The pressures from within stem from the shift toward a postindustrial society and comprise new social risks. We assess how this shift influences the need for welfare state reform by analyzing descriptive quantitative data on such diverse phenomena as the makeover of the employment structure and the demographic and household transformation. Moreover, we offer an extensive discussion of the different challenges from within that current welfare states face, including population aging and declining fertility, mass unemployment, changing family structures and gender roles, the transformation of life cycle patterns, and the shift toward a postindustrial labor market.

We show how the still ongoing changes have altered the foundation of the postwar welfare states in such a way that continuation of existing arrangements seems increasingly unlikely, if not impossible. Specifically, various previously well-functioning arrangements, such as pension or disability systems, are facing mounting inefficiencies, including burgeoning benefit claims (as in the Dutch disability scheme discussed in Chapter 6) and declining revenues, a combination of challenges that threatens their existence. Moreover, societal and economic changes cause *new* social risks to emerge, which existing welfare states are not yet covering, or at least not covering adequately. These newly arisen risks add up to a functional pressure for reform. As we argued (especially in Chapters 2 and 6), we do not assume that these functional pressures always translate into welfare state adaptation, updating, retrenchment, or restructuring. However, they do form a key point in our account of welfare state reform.

In discussing the various pressures from within, we assess how the different welfare state regimes deal with them. We demonstrate that the type of shift determines which welfare state regime caters best to that change. Overall, however, the social democratic regime has developed much more extensive policies than the conservative regime and – to an even larger extent – the liberal regime to address new social risks, particularly those stemming from women's increased labor force participation and the problem of youth unemployment. This variation in the development of new social risk policies results at least partly from the timing of the postindustrial changes (Bonoli 2007). If these changes occurred early, that is, in the 1970s, there were no (substantial) competing claims yet from, for instance, population aging. As a result, there was space to develop social policies covering the new social risks. Conversely, if postindustrial changes occurred later, say in the 1990s, welfare states already faced large financial burdens from, among others, aging populations. As a result, at that time, there simply was no room left for implementing policies catering to new social risks.

The chapter is structured as follows. First, in section 8.2, we argue why domestic changes matter for welfare state reform. Subsequently, we focus on the most important of these changes and the new social risks that have emerged. Next, in section 8.3, we turn to the politics involved in catering to these new social risks. In the final section 8.4, we summarize how the ʒ pressures from within and the politics of new social risks affect the opportunities and constraints of welfare state reform.

8.2. WHY ENDOGENOUS CHANGES MATTER (TOO) FOR WELFARE STATE REFORM

Up until the late 1990s and early 2000s, scholars studying the causes of welfare state reform directed their attention almost exclusively to external changes, such as increasing trade openness and capital mobilization (see Chapter 7). Pierson (2001b) was one of the first to indicate clearly that most of the potential strains governments face in the context of required balanced budgets are not so much due to globalization as to changes taking place *within* advanced democracies (see also Esping-Andersen 2005). Pierson presented a highly useful counterfactual: if there had been no globalization, would welfare states still face the pressures for updating, adaptation, retrenchment, or restructuring they currently face? In his view, the answer to this question was a straightforward *yes*.

The pressures for reform stem mainly from postindustrial development, which involves a "declining weight of goods production – manufacturing, farming, and mining – in total employment" (Block 1990: 10) and growth in the importance of services in the economy. Postindustrial societies increasingly have service-based employment profiles. A second important feature of postindustrial society concerns the microchip revolution and the ensuing computer-based and automated production, which effectively obliterates unskilled industrial labor and boosts the required skills and attention requirements of jobs. A third development may be labeled the (still incomplete, see Esping-Andersen 2009) women's revolution, earlier identified by Block (1990: 10) as "the decline of patriarchy and the breakdown of the linear life course." This is most dramatically exemplified in the massive entry of women into the labor force, the substantially changed composition and volatility of households and partnerships, and a host of associated consequences, not in the least the dramatic fall in fertility, adding to the already sizable demographic pressure due to longer life expectancy. Such developments clearly conflict head-on with, and therefore challenge, the very assumptions and conditions under which postwar social policies were formulated and implemented and have been performing relatively well. These developments are therefore responsible for many of the pressures contemporary welfare states face. Welfare states are still continuously required to respond to a permanently changing environment, but many welfare state arrangements are, partly because of political reasons (see section 8.3), simply still not well adapted to the new demands and requirements of postindustrial society. These we will analyze now. Note that because of the sometimes pronounced variation within the conservative regime, we look at the southern countries as a separate (Mediterranean) regime in this chapter.

The Shift toward a Postindustrial Labor Market

Societies have changed their employment profiles considerably in the post-1945 period. The transformation is characterized by a shift from agricultural and industrial employment to service employment, also called deindustrialization (Iversen and Cusack 2000; see Wren 2013). During 1962–93, the share of agricultural and industrial employment in total employment declined by 16 percent on average across the welfare state regimes. In our selection of countries, the numbers were the following: Denmark 21 percent; Germany 15.4 percent; the Netherlands 13.3 percent; Sweden 17.7 percent; Italy 19.5; the United Kingdom 15.6 percent; and the United States 5.3 percent (Iversen and Cusack 2000: 315, table 1). Because such employment loss could only be absorbed imperfectly by the public and private service sectors, the welfare state stepped in, either to help improve the skill level of former industrial and agricultural workers or to provide benefits to compensate for income loss, adding to the expansion of the welfare state. As one of us argued more extensively elsewhere (Manow et al. 2013), it matters whether the employment losses occur in industrial employment or agricultural employment because this influences if and how the welfare state stepped in.

In the immediate period after World War II, agricultural employment in the center of the European continent was already much lower than in the southern part. About 20 percent of the labor force was still employed in agriculture in Italy and France, while Belgium, Germany, and the Netherland had shares between 6 and 15 percent. In Scandinavia, average agricultural employment was around 20 percent, but here a rapid transformation toward service employment occurred earlier than in the other countries. In most countries, employment in manufacturing began to decline in the 1970s and 1980s. The decline in agricultural and industrial employment and the need to adapt (make ready) and transfer a large number of people from these sectors to the service sector were major incentives for the growth of welfare state intervention (Manow et al. 2013).

In the shift toward the postindustrial society, it is the slowdown in productivity growth in services that is a key factor pushing for welfare state reform. It was precisely the rise in productivity that produced the substantial increase in economic growth, first after the industrial revolution in the late 18th century and early 19th century and – much later – also after World War II, accompanied by the drastic shift in the employment structure. Pierson (2001b: 83ff.) convincingly argues that it is difficult, to say the least, to blame the slowdown in productivity growth on globalization. If increased openness has any effect on productivity, it would be a positive one. Increased openness (at least theoretically) makes the available pie larger, among other things by helping to allocate resources to where they yield the most. This process increases productivity rather than lowers it (see Chapter 7).

The exact reason for lower productivity growth remains somewhat of a puzzle, although we have some clues about its possible cause. In the mid-1960s, Baumol (1967) already informed us that the service industry (which he labels technologically nonprogressive) would be unable to match the productivity growth in the manufacturing sector (which he labels technologically progressive), a situation that is known as Baumol's cost disease. Baumol's conclusion on what this would result in was anything but rosy.

Unbalanced productivity growth [with one sector's productivity increasing faster than the other sector's] ... threatens to destroy many of the activities that do so much to enrich our existence, and to give to others over into the hands of the amateurs (Baumol 1967: 422).

The slowdown of productivity growth is one of the reasons for the emergence of the so-called *new social risks*, those situations in which individuals-cum-citizens experience welfare losses because of the transformation toward a postindustrial society, especially the shifts in employment structure and skill requirements, the growing entry of women into the labor force, and the strong increase of the elderly segment of the population. The risks are considered "new" because they hit different groups than before (e.g., women as workers, youth, elderly, and other minorities; see Schmidt 1993; Esping-Andersen 1999;

Goodin et al. 1999; Daly 2000) and larger groups (e.g., the retiring and aging population; see Ebbinghaus 2000). In spite of the welfare states' remarkable adaptive capacity, such risks are generally still not well served (see Bonoli 2006; Armingeon and Bonoli 2006; Bonoli and Natali 2012b). As we elaborated in Chapter 3, the welfare state is more about pooling and reapportioning social risks than about equality and redistribution. The existing social policy arrangements pool the kinds of risks typical for employment careers and life cycles in industrial society. The functional pressure on the welfare state, therefore, concerns the demand for new ways of pooling and reapportioning the new social risks of postindustrial society.

One group that is hit particularly hard by the transformation to a postindustrial labor market is low-skilled individuals. In the early postwar years, low-skilled workers were primarily employed in the manufacturing industry and saw their wages increase with this sector's rising productivity. This has changed substantially. Now, low-skilled individuals have either no job at all or are employed in low value-added industries such as retail sales, cleaning, or catering. These are precisely the industries that are notorious for their lack of productivity growth. In Baumol's terminology, these are nonprogressive industries. When wages are fully market based, workers in industries in which the productivity growth is less than the (inter)national average have full-time jobs that no longer pay a living wage, causing in-work poverty (see Andreß and Lohmann 2008; Cretaz 2011; Fraser et al. 2011; Marx and Nolan 2012).

In countries where wages are controlled by the government and/or the social partners, such as in the Scandinavian countries and the Netherlands, the wages in the nonprogressive industries are kept artificially high so as to enable an adequate level of subsistence. However, since there is hardly any growth in these types of jobs, an increasing number of low-skilled individuals are unemployed (Bonoli 2005), although there is substantial variation across countries in the labor demand for the low skilled (Maselli 2012). In 2009, the Netherlands had the lowest in-work poverty risk among the countries studied here. Still, in this year 5 percent (as compared to 4.4 percent in 2006 and a European average of 8 percent in 2008) of all employees were at risk of poverty while employed, that is, they had an equivalized income below the poverty threshold of 60 percent of the Dutch median income after social transfers (Eurostat 2011; see Chapter 5). Employees with a low level of education have a slightly higher risk of poverty when employed, while single parents are the most vulnerable group, with in-work poverty risks varying between 13 and 22 percent in the 2000s (Kruis and Blommesteijn 2010: 3, table 1.1).

In postindustrial society, then, being low skilled (and a single parent) implies a high risk of unemployment and poverty. Increased educational demand is a *new* social risk, because the level of education one now needs to attain a longterm job is much higher than it was during the golden age of industrialism. In the Netherlands, for example, only a high school diploma from either the highest or the second highest level qualifies as a so-called start qualification that would be enough to get a first-time job. However, over half of Dutch youth receive a diploma from a high school of a lower level. Only those who – in addition to this high school diploma – have also finished intermediate vocational training of a sufficient level are considered qualified for a long-term job, leaving around 10 percent of the Dutch youth without sufficient preparation to get any job at all.

Population Aging and Declining Fertility

Two other related pressures from within that are pushing welfare state reform are aging populations and declining fertility. Starting with the latter, the data in Table 8.1 show that the total fertility rate – the number of children per woman – has decreased in all OECD countries since 1970. The OECD average was still 2.7 in 1970, but it had fallen to 1.6 by 2005. Women not only have fewer children but also give birth to their first child at a later age. For the countries for which data are available, the average age for having the first child has risen from 24.2 to 27.5. As Table 8.1 indicates, in many countries a woman's age at first childbirth has increased to around 29. These data mask differences among women, because highly educated women often have their first child much later, often around their mid-thirties. Still, for women of all education levels, the age when they have their first child has increased.

According to Esping-Andersen (2005, 2009), low fertility signals not so much that women want fewer children – the ideal for women in most countries is on average still a little over two children – but rather that most countries have mounting constraints on family formation. Recent demographic research indicates that once countries have reached a certain very high level of development, the downward trend in fertility normally associated with economic and social development is actually reversed (Myrskylä et al. 2009). Although the jury is still out as to the cause of this reversal, it seems likely that "at advanced levels of development, governments might explicitly address fertility decline by implementing policies that improve gender equality or the compatibility between economic success, including labour force participation, and family life" (Myrskylä et al. 2009: 742).

Table 8.1 also shows that an increasingly large number of children are born out of wedlock. On average, almost 31 percent of all children were born to parents who were not married in 2005 as opposed to only 11 percent in 1980. In Sweden and Norway, the share of children born out of wedlock is higher than those born to married parents (55 and 51 percent, respectively), with Denmark, France, New Zealand, and the United Kingdom approaching the 50 percent threshold. These data indicate that in many countries, traditional family patterns have changed quite radically, although in most cases unmarried parents still raise their children while living together in the same home. As announced, because of the special position of the Mediterranean countries on specific indicators such as this one, we look at these countries separately and

TABLE 8.1. *Selected family statistics, OECD countries, 1970–2008*

	Total fertility rate			Mean age of women at first birth			Births out of wedlock		
	1970	2008	Change 1970–2008	1970	2004	Change 2005–1970	1980	2007[a]	Change 1980–2007
Australia	2.89	1.97	−0.92	23.2	..	..	12.4	32.2	19.8
Canada	2.33	1.66	−0.67	23.1	26.3	3.2	..	24.5	..
Ireland	3.87	2.10	−1.77	..	28.5	..	5	33.2	28.2
New Zealand	3.28	2.18	−1.10	23.4	28	4.6	21.5	47.2	25.7
United Kingdom	2.43	1.96	−0.47	..	29.5	..	11.5	43.7	32.2
United States	2.48	2.09	−0.39	24.1	25.1	1	18.4	38.5	20.1
Average LR	*2.88*	*1.99*	*−0.89*	*23.5*	*27.5*	*2.93*	*13.8*	*36.6*	*25.2*
Austria	2.29	1.41	−0.88	..	27	..	17.8	38.2	13.4
Belgium	2.25	1.82	−0.63	24.3		..	4.1	39.0	32.9
France	2.47	2.00	−0.47	24.4	28.4	4	11.4	50.4	39.0
Germany	2.03	1.38	−0.65	24	29	5	11.9	30.0	18.1
Netherlands	2.57	1.77	−0.80	24.8	28.9	4.1	4.1	39.7	35.6
Switzerland	2.10	1.48	−0.62	25.3	29.3	4	4.7	16.2	11.5
Average CR	*2.29*	*1.64*	*−0.68*	*24.6*	*28.5*	*4.3*	*9.0*	*35.6*	*25.1*
Denmark	1.95	1.89	−0.06	23.8	28.4	4.6	33.2	46.1	12.9
Finland	1.83	1.85	+0.02	24.4	27.8	3.4	13.1	40.6	27.5
Norway	2.50	1.96	−0.54	..	27.6	..	14.5	54.5	40.0
Sweden	1.92	1.91	−0.01	25.9	28.6	2.7	39.7	54.7	15.0
Average SDR	*2.05*	*1.90*	*−0.15*	*24.7*	*28.1*	*3.6*	*25.1*	*49.0*	*23.9*
Greece	2.40	1.51	−.089	..	28	..	1.5	5.0	3.5
Italy	2.43	1.41	−1.02	25	..	..	4.3	20.7	16.4
Portugal	3.01	1.37	−1.64	..	27.1	..	9.2	31.6	21.4
Spain	2.88	1.46	−1.42	..	29.2	..	3.9	28.4	24.5
Average MR	*2.68*	*1.44*	*−1.24*	*25*	*2.1*	*..*	*4.7*	*21.4*	*16.5*
Japan	2.13	1.37	−0.78	25.6	28.9	3.3	0.8	2.1	1.3
Aver. OECD	*2.70*	*1.71*	*−.99*	*24.2*	*27.5*	*3.3*	*11.2*	*30.9*	*19.7*

[a] 2005 for Australia, Canada, and OECD average; 2006 for Japan, New Zealand, Portugal, the UK, and the US.

Notes: Changes in percentage points. LR is liberal regime; CR is conservative regime; SDR is social democratic regime; MR is Mediterranean regime.

Source: D'Addio and Mira d'Ercole (2005); OECD (2007a, 2010b).

observe that Italy and Greece are countries that have hardly any out of wedlock births. The same holds for Japan.

The decline in fertility adds to the problem of population aging. Table 8.2 displays the development of the age-dependency ratio since 1980. This ratio measures the population aged 65 and over as a share of the working age population (15–64). In all countries (except Ireland), the age-dependency ratio increases between 1980 and 2010, on average from 19.3 to 25.2. Since the

TABLE 8.2. *Age-dependency ratio, 1980–2050*

	1980	2010	Change 1980–2010	2030	2050	Change 2010–2050
Australia	14.7	20.1	+ 5.4	33.2	39.8	+ 19.7
Canada	13.9	20.5	+ 6.6	38.7	43.7	+ 23.2
Ireland	18.3	17.8	– 0.5	27.1	40.6	+ 22.8
New Zealand	15.7	19.4	+ 3.7	33.7	37.7	+ 18.3
United Kingdom	23.5	24.6	+ 1.1	33.8	38.5	+ 13.9
United States	16.9	19.2	+ 2.3	31.2	32.2	+ 13.0
Average LR	17.17	20.27	+ 3.1	33.0	38.8	+ 18.5
Austria	24.0	26.4	+ 2.4	43.4	54.9	+ 28.5
Belgium	21.9	27.3	+ 5.4	41.9	47.2	+ 19.9
France	21.9	25.4	+ 3.5	39.4	45.8	+ 20.4
Germany	23.7	30.5	+ 6.8	44.3	49.1	+ 18.6
Netherlands	17.4	22.3	+ 4.9	38.2	41.6	+ 19.3
Switzerland	20.8	29.2	+ 8.4	52.5	55.3	+ 26.1
Average CR	21.6	26.9	+ 5.3	43.3	49.0	+ 22.1
Denmark	22.2	25.7	+ 3.5	39.0	41.7	+ 16.0
Finland	17.7	25.7	+ 8.0	44.1	45.5	+ 19.8
Sweden	25.4	29.6	+ 4.2	42.8	46.8	+ 17.2
Norway	23.4	24.0	+ 0.6	38.5	44.4	+ 20.4
Average SDR	22.2	26.3	+ 4.1	41.11	44.6	+ 18.3
Greece	20.5	29.8	+ 9.3	41.8	62.4	+ 32.6
Italy	20.4	31.1	+ 10.7	47.0	65.5	+ 34.4
Portugal	16.4	25.4	+ 9.0	35.2	53.4	+ 28.0
Spain	17.0	26.6	+ 9.6	40.6	67.7	+ 41.1
Average MR	18.6	28.2	+ 9.6	41.2	62.3	+ 34.1
Japan	13.4	35.0	+ 21.6	52.5	72.4	+ 37.4
OECD	19.3	25.2	+ 5.9	39.7	48.9	+ 23.7

Notes: Change in percentage points. LR is liberal regime; CR is conservative regime; SDR is social democratic regime; MR is Mediterranean regime
Source: OECD (2007a).

Irish reduction is only small (minus 0.5), we can conclude that the OECD populations are indeed aging. In some countries and welfare state regimes, the population is already quite gray. This pertains particularly to Japan, where the ratio reached 35 in 2010. In most countries of the social democratic and conservative regimes, the age-dependency ratio also rose to a rather high number by 2010. This pertains less to most countries of the liberal regime and to the Netherlands, where the ratio was around 20 in 2010.

When we examine the predicted change for the period 2010 to 2050, which the last column of Table 8.2 displays, we can see that within 40 years, all other things being equal, the age-dependency ratio will rise quite steeply everywhere. On average, the share of those aged 65 and over will be almost 50 percent by

2050. Again, the Mediterranean regime and Japan, Austria, and Switzerland are special as the share of pensioners in these countries is (much) higher than the share of working age individuals (62 percent on average for the Mediterranean regime, 72 for Japan, 55 for Austria and Switzerland). In some countries from the conservative and social democratic regimes, the 50 percent threshold is approaching rapidly (Belgium, Finland, France, Germany, and Sweden). Although aging is obviously not a "new" social risk, the very high share of elderly in the population with the demands on care this brings certainly is. If welfare states wish to continue to promise the current level of well-being for future pensioners, pension expenditure will need to grow by 50 percent (Esping-Andersen 2005: 4), which comes down to an extra 5 percent of GDP by 2050. Additionally, health care expenditure will need to rise by another 3 or 4 percent of GDP (Esping-Andersen 2005: 5). Irrespective of whether pensions or care are privatized, this means that an extra 10 percent of GDP will have to go to the elderly by 2050, which is for most countries about a third of current spending levels. This may be a prohibitively large increase and thus, by our reckoning, population aging and declining fertility imply a functional pressure to reform.

Homogamy

A further endogenous factor that puts contemporary welfare states under pressure is the increasing degree of homogamy. Homogamy relates to the degree to which social structures in society are open or closed. A society in which individuals marry mostly individuals from the same social group has a high degree of marital homogamy and is closed. Marriages between individuals from different groups, conversely, indicate an open society. Based on an analysis of 65 countries, Smits et al. (1998) find an inverted U-curve between the level of economic development and educational homogamy. Up to a certain level of economic development, the so-called status attainment hypothesis holds, which indicates that individuals marry with those whose educational level is the same as theirs because educational level is a good predictor of socioeconomic status. When a particular level of economic development is reached, conversely, the so-called romantic-love hypothesis starts to work. If societies are developed enough to have, for example, a developed social security system, the partner one marries affects less the extent to which one can maintain an acceptable livelihood. Consequently, parents will have less of an incentive to influence their children's choices in a marriage partner, will be less likely to be able to affect this choice, and the children themselves are more likely to select potential partners with different educational backgrounds. This seems to have been the pattern in the period of the welfare states' golden age and the period up to the 2000s. More recently, however, a new postindustrial pattern seems to be emerging that indicates increasing homogamy again.

Fu and Heaton (2008), for instance, find that the degree of educational homogamy on average still decreased in the United States between 1980 and 2000; but, and important for social stratification in society, the degree of homogamy was highest among the least and most highly educated individuals. This suggests that for low-skilled individuals the possibility of moving up the socioeconomic ladder through marriage was still rather poor, while highly educated couples are increasing their position in terms of family income. Educational homogamy among low-educated couples causes higher economic vulnerability, especially since educational requirements of jobs have been increasing (Gesthuizen and Scheepers 2010). Among higher educated groups, young men increasingly prefer women with the potential for earning a high income (Blossfeld 2009). Because employment and unemployment also tend to come "in couples," growing marital homogamy tends to increase polarization in terms of a rising employment and income gap (Esping-Andersen 2007). Recent data indicate that in the United States, 25 to 30 percent in the increase in inequality since the 1980s is explained by the increase in spouses' earnings among better educated couples (Schwartz 2010). A similar conclusion is reached for the OECD area as a whole, "because of assortative mating and the higher educational levels of spouses, their earnings contribute to widening the distribution of household income" (OECD 2008: 87).

Children from divorced families are more likely to marry with someone who comes also from a divorced family (Wolfinger 2003). These marriages are particularly likely to end up in a divorce, leading to lone parents when there are already children. This so-called family structure homogamy transcends socioeconomic boundaries and suggests that the increasing rate of divorces not only spills over into future generations' divorce rates but also increases these rates. Given that in Scandinavia and in the United States over half of all children do not grow up with both their biological parents (Esping-Andersen 2005: 3), this is a substantial risk indeed (see also Blossfeld 2009).

Mass Unemployment

The transformation of the labor market and the other postindustrial changes coincide with the materialization of mass unemployment. During the late 1980s and early 1990s, the patterns of both employment and unemployment in Europe changed considerably (Esping-Andersen 1996a; Clayton and Pontusson 1998; Clasen and Clegg 2011a). The effects of this changed environment are particularly negative for those individuals who are attempting to enter the labor market and for those who are forced to leave (Therborn 1986; Daly 2000; Hemerijck et al. 2013). Specifically, the reshaping of the welfare state appears to produce "collateral damage" to the younger and older population segments. Table 8.3 displays the development of unemployment between 1985 and 2007, that is, before the effects of the financial and economic crisis started to kick in (see Chapter 10).

The average European unemployment rate displays little change between 1985 and 2007 (from 8.5 percent in 1985 to 7.7 percent in 2007). However, this apparent stability hides the rise in unemployment in Austria, Switzerland, Finland, and Sweden and the (sharp) decline (at least 3 percentage points) in Australia, Canada, Ireland, the United Kingdom, and Belgium. There is also considerable variation across the welfare regimes. The liberal regime displays the highest reduction in unemployment (on average −3.6 percentage points), and the Mediterranean regime follows with a reduction of about 1.5 percentage points. The level of total unemployment in the conservative regime remains roughly the same, while that in the social democratic regime rises with 1.8 percentage points. Despite the reduction between 1985 and 2007, the level of total unemployment in the Mediterranean regime remains by far the highest of the four regimes (almost 12 percent in 2007).

When breaking down the average unemployment figure into demographic categories, we see that the cross-national variation is considerable. It is difficult to interpret unemployment figures exclusively in terms of old and new risks because they are, inevitably, an amalgamation. In Germany, Switzerland, Finland, Sweden, Italy, and Portugal, older men are often unemployed, whereas in, for example, liberal Australia, Ireland, and the United Kingdom as well as "flexicure" Denmark and Mediterranean Spain, this group is getting back to work again. Everywhere, the young find it most difficult to find jobs: 18 percent had no job in 2007. In some countries (Ireland, Belgium, France, Finland, Sweden, Italy, Portugal, and Spain) the traditional insider-outsider structure of labor markets translated into very high percentages (at least 20 percent) of youth unemployment in 2007. In 2000, 40 percent of all unemployed were long-term unemployed (see Emmenegger et al. 2012). Overall, the data presented in Table 8.3 reveal that the chances for work in general have not increased and that unemployment is still a mounting problem. It seems, however, that labor markets in Europe became more inclusive both for the unemployed and the inactive between 1997 and 2007 (Eichhorst et al. 2011), indicating that it has become easier for the unemployed and the inactive to make the transition to any form of employment. Still, and in spite of rapid labor market deregulation and flexibilization, male workers between 25 and 55 continue to be the core of the workforce that, differentiated according to skill level, have the lowest risk of unemployment.

Hence, certain groups in society are hurt more by the changes in employment patterns and income supplements than others. As a result, there is a clear divide between distinctive groups according to the degree of social risks they face. The "outsiders" now include the young, women, older workers, low-skilled workers, and immigrants, and these groups are hit hardest during economic downturns and sectoral transformations. Exactly these groups form political constituencies that are usually under-organized in trade unions and less well represented within the mainstream political parties in government (Scruggs and Lange 2001; Rueda 2007; Ebbinghaus 2010a; Emmenegger et al. 2012). Davidsson and Emmenegger (2012) show that the reform pattern in Sweden and France displays a dualist pattern in job security. These countries

TABLE 8.3. *Pattern of unemployment, 1985–2007*

| | TOTAL | | | Male | | | | | | Female | | | | | | Youth | | |
| | | | | 25–54 | | | 55–64 | | | 25–54 | | | 55–64 | | | 15–24 | | |
	1985	2007	Δ85–07	1985	2007	Δ85–07	1985	2007	Δ85–07	1985	2007	Δ85–07	1985	2007	Δ85–07	1985	2007	Δ85–07
Australia	8.3	4.4	-3.9	5.6	3.0	-2.6	7.1	2.8	-4.3	6.4	3.9	-2.5	3.5	2.6	-0.9	15.2	9.4	-5.8
Canada	10.7	4.4	-6.3	8.9	5.3	-3.6	8.8	5.2	-3.6	9.7	4.7	-5	7.8	4.9	-2.9	16.1	11.2	-4.9
Ireland	16.7	12.0	-4.7	15.0	14.0	-1	9.3	2.4	-6.9	16.8	6.7	-10.1	8.7	1.9	-6.8	23.4	25.9	2.5
New Zealand	4.1	3.7	-0.4	2.3	2.3	0	1.4	1.5	0.1	3.7	3.0	-0.7	1.8	1.4	-0.4	7.9	10.1	2.2
United Kingdom	11.3	7.7	-3.6	9.5	6.8	-2.7	9.7	4.1	-5.6	9.5	5.2	-4.3	6.5	2.2	-4.3	17.8	18.9	1.1
United States	7.2	4.6	-2.6	5.6	3.7	-1.9	4.4	3.2	-1.2	6.2	3.8	-2.4	4.3	3.0	-1.3	13.6	10.5	-3.1
Average LR	9.7	6.1	-3.6	7.8	5.9	-2.0	6.8	3.2	-3.6	8.7	4.6	-4.2	5.4	2.7	-2.8	15.7	14.3	-1.3
Austria	3.5	4.8	1.3	2.9	4.4	1.5	3.8	2.9	-0.9	3.8	4.0	0.2	2.7	3.2	0.5	5.0	10.0	5
Belgium	11.3	7.9	-3.4	6.0	6.7	0.7	4.6	3.6	-1	15.3	6.9	-8.4	6.4	5.3	-1.1	23.5	21.9	-1.6
France	10.2	9.1	-1.1	6.1	7.2	1.1	6.7	5.3	-1.4	9.4	8.2	-1.2	7.6	4.9	-2.7	25.6	22.8	-2.8
Germany	7.1	7.7	0.6	5.7	7.6	1.9	7.4	9.7	2.3	7.4	6.9	-0.5	6.2	11.2	5	9.9	11.0	1.1
Netherlands	4.1	3.9	-0.2	11.6	3.0	-8.6	6.1	4.5	-1.6	9.4	3.3	-6.1	4.5	3.7	-0.8	23.0	7.3	-15.7
Switzerland	1.7	4.1	2.4	0.8	3.3	2.5	1.4	2.6	1.2	2.6	4.1	1.5	0.6	3.8	3.2	7.9	8.2	0.3
Average CR	6.3	6.3	-0.1	5.5	5.4	-0.2	5.0	4.8	-0.2	8.0	5.6	-2.4	4.7	5.4	0.7	15.8	13.5	-2.3
Denmark	7.8	6.0	-1.8	5.5	5.7	0.2	5.8	3.1	-2.7	8.9	4.7	-4.2	6.1	4.1	-2	11.5	11.2	-0.3
Finland	5.1	8.3	3.2	4.6	7.1	2.5	5.8	6.9	1.1	3.2	6.1	2.9	7.8	6.0	-1.8	9.7	21.6	11.9
Norway	2.6	3.2	0.6	1.4	2.9	1.5	1.2	1.1	-0.1	2.6	2.0	-0.6	0.9	0.8	-0.1	6.5	9.2	2.7
Sweden	3.1	8.3	5.2	2.1	6.4	4.3	3.5	4.3	0.8	1.9	6.0	4.1	4.6	3.2	-1.4	7.2	25.0	17.8
Average SDR	4.7	6.5	1.8	3.4	5.5	2.1	4.1	3.9	-0.2	4.2	4.7	0.6	4.9	3.5	-1.3	8.7	16.8	8.0
Italy	10.3	7.8	-2.5	3.3	5.9	2.6	1.6	2.6	1	10.1	8.5	-1.6	2.2	2.1	-0.1	33.9	25.4	-8.5
Portugal	8.6	9.5	0.9	4.6	8.5	3.9	2.3	7.1	4.8	8.7	10.1	1.4	1.8	5.8	4	19.0	20.0	1
Spain	21.0	18.0	-3	15.4	16.2	0.8	12.1	4.9	-7.2	16.3	16.9	0.6	5.2	7.7	2.5	43.8	37.9	-5.9
Average MR	13.3	11.8	-1.5	7.8	10.2	2.4	5.3	4.9	-0.5	11.7	11.8	0.1	3.1	5.2	2.1	32.2	27.8	-4.5
Total average	8.5	7.7	-0.8	6.1	6.7	0.6	5.3	4.2	-1.1	8.1	6.7	-1.5	4.5	4.2	-0.3	18.1	18.1	0.0

Notes: Data for New Zealand and the Netherlands, 1986 instead of 1985; Switzerland, 1991 instead of 1985; Austria, 1994 instead of 1985. All figures are percentages of the total labor force and for the categories mentioned; Δ indicates change in percentage points. LR is liberal regime; CR is conservative regime; SDR is social democratic regime; MR is Mediterranean regime.

Source: Online OECD Employment database (2011) (www.oecd.org/employment/database) (Accessed May 2011).

have deregulated job security for the outsiders (people in atypical or precarious employment and unemployed people) while upholding it for the insiders (people in standard employment). This is a result of the active involvement of the unions, who defended their organizational interests. Similarly, labor market reforms in Germany are in line with this dualization (Eichhorst and Marx 2011), a trend producing welfare states that are "comprised of (less and less) social insurance on the one hand (for the 'insiders'), and more developed targeted assistance and activation schemes (for the 'outsiders') on the other" (Palier 2012: 249).

Reconciling Work and Family Life

The difficulty of reconciling work and family life is a major new social risk that has arisen because of the changes within society. Since the late 1980s, women across the developed world have massively entered the labor market. Table 8.4 shows that in the early 1980s, in most countries for which data are available, the employment rate of women was lower than 50 percent (Ireland, Belgium, Germany, the Netherlands, Greece, and Italy). Only in the United Kingdom (57 percent), France (56 percent), and Denmark (72 percent) did the employment rate of women top the 50 percent mark. By 1990, with data available for more countries, the picture already looked quite different; only Ireland (42 percent), Belgium (46 percent), Greece and Italy (43 percent), and Spain (41) had a female employment rate below 50 percent. By 2009, only Greece (49 percent) and Italy (46 percent) continued to have such a low rate. If we look at the regime averages, we also see a clear upward trend over time. The only exception to this is the social democratic regime, where the employment rate already started out at the highest level of all regimes. The only social democratic country where there was an upward trend, but coming from a lower starting level, is Finland (from 59 percent in 1995 to 68 in 2009). The liberal regime increased its female employment rate on average from 48 percent in 1983 to 62 percent in 2009 – an increase of about 12 percentage points. The increase in the conservative regime is even more pronounced: from 47 percent in 1983 to 66 in 2009 – a rise of 19 percentage points. The Mediterranean regime also displayed a substantial increase over time, although the employment rate of women continued to fall behind the other regimes. With a rise from 39 percent in 1983 to 52 in 2009, on average the Mediterranean regime's female employment rate increased by 13 percentage points.

Figure 8.1 displays the same data, but now zooming in on our selected cases only (Denmark, Germany, Italy, the Netherlands, Sweden, the United Kingdom, and the United States). This figure shows that the increase in the employment rate of women started in the mid-1980s, but has accelerated since the late 1980s and early 1990s. The rise in the employment of women is especially remarkable in the Netherlands: from only 40 percent in 1983 to 72 in 2009, ending up close to the Swedish and Danish rates. It should be noted, however, that in

TABLE 8.4. *Employment rate of women, 1983–2009*

	1983	1985	1990	1995	2000	2005	2009
Ireland	39.8	39.1	41.9	41.6	53.9	58.3	57.4
United Kingdom	57.0	61.0	66.1	61.7	64.7	65.8	65.0
United States	..	..	..	65.8	67.8	65.6	63.4
Average LR	48.4	50.1	54.0	56.4	62.1	63.2	61.9
Austria	..	..	..	59.0	59.6	62.0	66.4
Belgium	44.3	45.1	46.1	45.0	51.5	53.8	56.0
France	56.4	56.7	58.0	52.1	55.2	58.4	60.0
Germany	49.0	51.7	57.6	55.3	58.1	60.6	66.2
Netherlands	40.0	41.1	52.4	53.8	63.5	66.4	71.5
Switzerland	..	..	..	..	69.3	70.4	73.6
Average CR	47.4	48.7	53.5	53.0	59.5	61.9	65.6
Denmark	71.9	74.6	77.6	66.7	71.6	71.9	73.1
Finland	..	..	..	59.0	64.2	66.5	67.9
Norway	..	..	..	..	73.6	71.7	74.4
Sweden	..	..	..	68.8	70.9	70.4	70.2
Average SDR	..	..	..	64.8	70.1	70.1	71.4
Greece	39.2	41.0	42.6	38.1	41.7	46.1	48.9
Italy	39.6	39.7	43.2	35.4	39.6	45.3	46.4
Portugal	..	..	57.1	54.4	60.5	61.7	61.6
Spain	..	..	40.6	31.7	41.3	51.2	52.8
Average MR	39.4	40.4	45.9	39.9	45.8	51.1	52.4
Japan	..	..	..	56.4	56.7	58.1	59.8

Notes: The employment rate is calculated by dividing the number of persons aged 15 to 64 in employment by the total population of the same age group. LR is liberal regime; CR is conservative regime; SDR is social democratic regime; MR is Mediterranean regime.
Source: EUROSTAT data, retrieved from http://epp.eurostat.ec.europa.eu/tgm/table.do?tab=table &plugin=1&language=en&pcode=tsiemo10 (Accessed March 2011).

contrast to these latter two cases, Dutch women typically have part-time jobs, which also holds for childless women. As a consequence, the Netherlands has been labeled a one-and-a-half earner society (see Plantenga 2002).

With women entering the labor market in large numbers, the typical employment profile also changes substantially. No longer is the average worker a white male, who works full-time and continuously from an early age, earning a steadily rising income sufficient to support a family and save for a pension. An increasing number of people tend to have atypical careers that take them from part-time job to part-time job, punctuated by longer or shorter periods of unemployment. Table 8.5 shows that there is quite a bit of variation in atypical employment among our selected countries. If we look at part-time and temporary employment, we see that the Netherlands clearly stands out with over 35 percent of total employment being part-time employment and, somewhat less strikingly, over 18 percent temporary employment. The United States

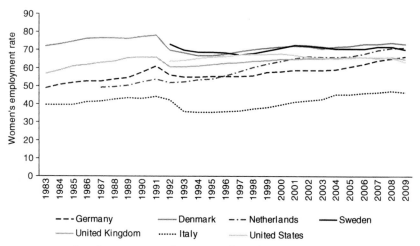

FIGURE 8.1. Employment rate of women, selected countries, 1983–2009.
Note: The employment rate is calculated by dividing the number of persons aged 15 to 64 in employment by the total population of the same age group.
Source: EUROSTAT data, retrieved from http://epp.eurostat.ec.europa.eu/tgm/table.do ?tab=table&plugin=1&language=en&pcode=tsiem0010 (Accessed March 2011).

TABLE 8.5. *Employment profiles, selected countries, 2009*

	Temporary employment as a % of dependent employment 2009	Part-time employment as a % of total employment 2009	Employment protection strictness 2008 (scale 0–6)
United Kingdom	5.7	23.9	1.1
United States	4.5[a]	14.0	0.7
Germany	14.5	21.9	2.4
Netherlands	18.3	36.7	2.1
Denmark	8.9	18.9	1.8
Sweden	15.3	14.6	2.2

[a] The year is 1999; no more recent data available for the US.
Note: Higher scores for employment protection indicate stricter protection.
Source: OECD Key Employment Statistics, OECD webpage: http://www.oecd.org/topic/o,3699,en_ 2649_37457_1_1_1_37457,00.html (Accessed May 2011).

stands out at the other end of the spectrum, with rates being, respectively, 14 percent and 4.5 percent. The forms of atypical work are not exclusively a continental "welfare-without-work" affair because Sweden has a higher percentage of temporary employment than Germany, while the United Kingdom beats Germany when it comes to part-time employment.

In general, part-time labor has been growing everywhere, except in the Mediterranean regime (Greece, Italy, Portugal, and Spain). To what extent part-time labor is a social risk depends, among other things, on the level of job protection, which varies per country (OECD 1999, 2004a). Especially in those countries of the conservative and Mediterranean regimes, where job protection was a major instrument of social security, the flexibilization of labor markets increased the social risk of atypical employment, including part-time work. The regime clustering comes to the fore to some extent in the level of employment protection. Employment protection concerns the regulations on hiring and firing, especially regular procedural inconveniences, difficulty of dismissal, and notice and severance pay (OECD 1999: 50, 2004a: 110–111). The index ranges from 0 to 6, with higher scores indicating stricter employment protection. The liberal regime has the lowest level of employment protection and the conservative cluster the highest. However, Sweden with a score of 2.2 matches the conservative level. The low level of employment protection in the United States and the United Kingdom confirms Esping-Andersen's (1999: 90) observation that over time Britain has become more liberal: "minimal state and maximum market allocation of risks, and the market side of the coin appears increasingly genuinely market."

The point of the new social risk structure is that individuals with atypical employment careers are likely to encounter a social security system that has been designed on the assumption of the full-time (male) worker. The system cannot cope well with atypical workers who have fixed-term contracts, do temporary agency work, or work part-time. Such workers are incapable of building up the social security contribution record that would qualify them for the benefits they need. The old system (see Chapter 4), in other words, fails to offer full protection (unemployment, pensions) to those individuals who do not fit the precise profile of the standard production worker (Bonoli 2005), but who – due to their fragile position in the labor market – need protection the most. We must add to this that women are more likely than men to be in atypical employment, both temporary and part-time and also freelance work. Also, the traditional systems of interest representation and intermediation were designed and still work for the standard worker – employer negotiations – and offer little to nothing for atypical employees, even though these have rapidly becoming more typical in the past decades.

The difficulty of reconciling work and family life is a new social risk (Bonoli 2005). In the old days, mothers typically stayed at home to take care of the children while fathers went out to work and earn a family wage. The degree to which individual countries fit this male breadwinner model (Lewis 2001; Pfau-Effinger 2003; Levine Frader 2008) varied, but this division of labor characterized most countries until at least the 1970s. With women (mothers) entering the labor market in massive numbers, families needed help from the state or the market for finding childcare, or they had to turn to other family members (e.g., grandparents). When families have to find childcare through the state or

TABLE 8.6. *Maternal employment policy index, mid-1980s–2000s*

	2001–2003	1994–1995	1984–1986
Australia	17 (19)	15	6
Canada	30 (15)	21	15
Ireland	20 (17)	14	13
New Zealand	46 (8)	36	..
United Kingdom	18 (18)	15	11
United States	13 (20)	13	4
Average LR	*24*	*19*	*10*
Austria	43 (9)	38	..
Belgium	66 (6)	65	58
France	70 (4)	59	57
Germany	32 (13)	29	28
Netherlands	38 (11)	27	18
Average CR	*50*	*44*	*40*
Denmark	100 (1)	83	74
Finland	76 (3)	53	52
Norway	69 (5)	61	47
Sweden	88 (2)	73	76
Average SDR	*83*	*68*	*62*
Greece	26 (16)	23	24
Italy	53 (7)	51	47
Portugal	35 (12)	32	24
Spain	32 (14)	29	19
Average MR	*37*	*34*	*29*
Japan	40 (10)	29	19

Notes: The maternal employment policy index measures maternity and parental leave and child-care provision from 1984–86, 1994–95, and 2001–3, focusing on maternity and parental leave, publicly provided or subsidized child care for children under three, and early childhood education and care for children from three years to school age. The rank order of the countries for 2001–2003 is indicated between brackets, with 1 being the country with most maternal employment policy and 20 the one with the least. LR is liberal regime; CR is conservative regime; SDR is social democratic regime; MR is Mediterranean regime.
Source: Lambert (2008).

the market they encounter problems. Childcare may not be available in a sufficient quantity; it may be unaffordable; it may not be of sufficient quality; or it may suffer from a combination of these shortcomings. Poor availability of childcare negatively influences how many hours parents – and in most cases (still) women – can work, and this reduces the family's income. It also leaves underutilized at least part of the available human capital. For single-parent families, the problems in this regard are even more severe.

Table 8.6 provides data on the availability and generosity of maternity and parental leave, publicly provided or publicly subsidized childcare for children under three, and early childhood education and care for children from three years to school age between the mid-1980s and the early 2000s (Lambert 2008). A low score means that the country has little or no paid maternity and parental leave and that the government's effort to provide funding for the care of preschool-aged children is low. A high score indicates that the country offers both paid maternity and parental leave benefits and that the government's effort to fund early childhood education and care is high.

The data in Table 8.6 demonstrate that in all countries the provision and generosity of policies that reconcile work and family life increased between the mid-1980s and the early 2000s. This means that in all countries it became easier – which does not mean undemanding – to reconcile work and family life (see Morgan 2006, 2013; Kremer 2007; Kenworthy 2008: chapter 10). In the social democratic countries and the Netherlands, the index rose by at least 20 points in this period. In other countries (like Germany, Greece, or Italy), the increase was much less. Table 8.6 also indicates that the most substantial boost of these reconciliation policies took place between the mid-1980s and the mid-1990s, which relates positively to rising female labor force participation (Jensen 2011b). The rank order of countries and regimes that offer the best reconciliation policies did not change much throughout the entire period.

In the period 2001–3, Denmark was the country with the highest score on the index (100). The United States, conversely, scored the lowest (13). Table 8.6 displays clear regime differences. Comparatively speaking, the liberal regime has the least developed policies to reconcile work and family life (an average of 24 on the index). In fact, New Zealand is the only liberal country scoring in the top 10 of most generous countries in this regard. The Mediterranean regime is on average next in line (37 on the index). Italy, with a score of 53 on the index (rank number 7), is – perhaps remarkably – an exception to the typically low scores on the index for the countries in this regime. The conservative regime scores on average 50 on the index, but the variation across countries in this regime is higher than in the liberal and the Mediterranean regimes. Specifically, Belgium and France have comparatively high scores on the index whereas the Netherlands, Germany, and, to a lesser extent, Austria have less elaborate policies to reconcile work and family life. The social democratic regime clearly has the most developed policies in this area, with all four countries in the top 5 (with an average on the index of 83). This pattern across regimes indicates that the new social risk of reconciling work and family life is highest in the liberal regime and lowest in the social democratic regime. The Mediterranean and conservative regimes hold an intermediate position in this regard.

To sum up, if we view welfare states in terms of the reapportioning of social risks, the substantial changes in the risk structure of society we mapped above clearly seem to warrant welfare state reform. Yet not all welfare state regimes cater to these new risks in similar ways or to the same extent. The social demand and need for reform still must be translated into policies that address the new social risks. And this is intrinsically a political process in which ideas as causal beliefs play a prominent role (see Chapter 6). In the next section, we probe the politics of new social risks.

8.3. POLITICS OF NEW SOCIAL RISKS

With the rise of the new social risks and the correlate demand for welfare state reform, what are the possibilities that political action will address these risks? The prospects do not seem too bright (Bonoli 2005). Women are a vulnerable group in the new risk structure, and although they are increasingly considered an electoral asset (see Fleckenstein and Lee 2012; Morgan 2013), their political power is generally still low. Women, for example, typically constitute a small minority in parliament and government. So-called critical mass theory (Grey 2002, 2006; Thomas 1994) suggests that the percentage of women legislators matters for the development of social policies catering to women's needs, such as maternal employment-supporting policies like childcare or paid maternal leave. A critical mass of women legislators is necessary because maternal employment-supporting policies are typically not electorally popular; the median voter fails to support them. For example, 61 percent of the Swiss electorate voted down a proposal for 14 weeks of paid maternity leave (at 80 percent of the woman's last income) in the late 1990s (Kuebler 2007: 226–227).

Also, the population pyramids of Western democracies leave room to question maternal employment supporting policies' overall popularity (OECD 2007b). The population between ages 25 and 44 – the group benefiting directly from family policy – represents between 26 (Finland) and 31 (Canada) percent of the overall population, and thus is far from a majority. Perhaps even more important, the share of population over 45 years of age – typically not benefiting from the policies – is substantially higher. This proportion ranges from a low 33 percent in Ireland to 46 percent in Italy. These figures indicate that the median voter would not benefit from new social policies taking care of young families' needs. Bonoli and Häusermann (2009) show that political demography is important for social policy development. Based on an analysis of the actual voting behavior on referendum issues in Switzerland, they find that the youngest generation (in their case between 18 and 39 years of age) was two or three times (depending on the referendum) more likely to support maternity insurance than the oldest generation of people (65 years or older).

A large share of women legislators, however, is not enough to tip the balance. Co-authored work by one of us that focuses on the governments of 12 OECD countries between 1980 and 2003 (Koole and Vis 2012), for example, shows that a critical mass of at least 15 percent of women legislators is necessary for high levels of spending on an important maternal employment-supporting policy: parental leave benefits.[1] In addition, other factors such as leftist partisanship,

---

[1] For an overview of the generosity of parental leave policies, measured by their duration and benefit levels, in 21 developed democracies in 2008, see Ray et al. (2010).

the presence of corporatism, openness, and high economic growth also matter to some extent. Naumann (2012) argues that a major change must occur before child care shifts from a marginal policy field into a "key pillar of modern welfare states" (158); only when child care was perceived as "economic policy that fit within the dominant economic paradigm did broad political alliances that promoted the expansion of employment-oriented child-care service provision" occur (159–160). Naumann also reminds us that gender, religion, and class intersect. For example, women for whom religion is important may prefer policies enabling them to stay at home to care for their children rather than policies that address work-child care reconciliation issues. Stated more generally, not all women are in favor of what are often called women-friendly policies.

Typically, the young as a group are also poorly represented in politics: the average (male) parliamentarian is 50 years of age. The young are also hardly represented in trade unions, whose membership consists largely of older men who still approximate the standard production worker. The young depend on nontraditional forms of political action, such as camping in main city squares as they did in the spontaneous youth protest against unemployment in Spain in May 2011. In the Scandinavian countries and the United Kingdom, conversely, women are more likely to be union members than men are. In these same countries, there is also hardly an age-gap in union membership between the young and the old. In general, however, women and the young are less likely to be union members than (older) men. There is also substantial variation in party membership across age groups, with older people being more likely to be member of a political party than the young (Goerres 2009: chapter 5).

Another problem for individuals exposed to a new social risk is that, as a group, they do not have homogenous political preferences comparable to, for example, full-time employed, middle-aged men, and these differences could make them unlikely to join forces politically. Häusermann (2010: chapter 4) distinguishes between two outsider groups: (1) sociocultural professionals, who are high-skilled and typically women with atypical employment profiles (working part-time and/or on a temporary contract), and (2) low service functionaries, who are low-skilled but are similar to sociocultural professionals in that they are most often women with an atypical employment profile (see also Häusermann and Schwander 2012). Häusermann (2010: 40) labels one group of reforms as targeting reforms, that is, measures that "loosen the tight link between contributions and benefits by distributing selective benefits according to specific needs." The introduction of specific insurance conditions for workers with atypical jobs would be an example of this. But because atypical jobs as a rule are held by women, conflicts over targeting are not only about material resources but also about gender equality, individualization, and lifestyle choices. It is this latter dimension that pits the two outsider groups against one another. While sociocultural professionals are typically libertarians who favor gender equality and other lifestyle features, low service functionaries are generally traditionalists who oppose this (Häusermann 2010: chapters 3 and 4).

Although the more women are exposed to new social risks, the more likely they are to vote for parties that express their interests (typically left-wing, social democratic parties), the correlations of the political preferences within the group are rather weak (Bonoli 2005: 440). At the same time, "Third Way" social democratic parties are not necessarily defenders of the traditional income replacement schemes and were forced to balance the budget, too. Hence, determining which party represents the interests of those facing social risks, old or new (see Häusermann 2010: chapter 4; see Rueda 2007; Schumacher 2012; Arndt 2013), is not always easy. It is therefore unsurprising that the empirical findings on the role of partisanship for developing new social risks policies, such as parental leave schemes or active labor market policies, are inconclusive (Häusermann et al. 2013; see also Klitgaard and Elmelund-Praestekær 2013). Regarding the latter, leftist social democratic parties in general favor a larger role for labor market policy than do rightist parties. Social democrats pursue policies that keep individuals in the labor market once they have entered it, for example, by using social policy to protect individuals' investment in specific skills (Iversen 2005; Rueda 2007) or by retraining them when needed. Given social democracy's interest in labor market participation (e.g., Huber and Stephens 2001; Huo et al. 2008), policies that intend to uphold and boost this participation fit this party's ideology well. Most authors find empirical support for the leftist partisanship hypothesis. But some find that the positive effect of leftist partisanship works only in combination with another condition, namely, economic openness (Bonoli 2008). The argument here is that an open economy ties leftist parties' hands with respect to the adoption of strong pro-worker policies because such measures hurt international competitiveness. Active labor market policies offer leftist parties a way to cater to their constituency while simultaneously upholding competitiveness, although the electoral return on the strategy is uncertain (Arndt 2013).

Moreover, as Rueda (2006, 2007) and Lindvall and Rueda (2012) stress, active labor market policies benefit predominantly labor market outsiders but potentially hurt labor market insiders (those with steady employment) through tax effects or wage competition. Since insiders are social democracy's core constituency, the parties will oppose increases in active labor market policies. Rueda thus finds a negative relationship between leftist partisanship and spending on activation (see also Franzese and Hays 2006; Gaston and Rajaguru 2008). However, when the level of unemployment increases, which increases the insiders' vulnerability to unemployment and hence makes them more like outsiders, the relationship between leftist partisanship and increases in active labor market policies becomes positive. In those countries with high levels of corporatism, leftist governments are associated with lower levels of active labor market policies. If there are no corporatist arrangements to protect them, insiders resemble outsiders and consequently are more interested in activation policies. For insiders in corporatist countries, the opposite applies. Since insiders are protected, they are less interested in active labor market policies.

In fact, as one of us has argued elsewhere (Vis 2011a), both research findings may be correct if one takes into account the leftist parties' strategic character. The left faces tough choices between its preferred policies and power (office and/or votes) ambitions, whereby the ever-tighter government budgets intensify the strategic choices to be made (Scharpf 1991 [1987]; see also Kitschelt 1999). Under conditions of decreasing unemployment, rightist partisanship and corporatism foster increased active labor market policies, but in the absence of corporatism leftist governments start to pursue active labor market policies. When decreasing unemployment coincides with economic openness, both rightist and leftist governments favor activation. Leftist governments in non-corporatist countries, however, need economic growth, and they strategically opt for higher spending on activation, but only if they have the budgetary room to do so. Rather than opting for higher spending on active labor market policies when unemployment rises, it is actually decreasing unemployment that does the trick.

Interestingly, the character of new social risks and of the policies that address them make for a distinct set of opportunities for policymaking that were absent during earlier phases of welfare state development (Bonoli 2005: 441ff.; Bonoli and Natali 2012b). While traditional social policies largely intended to decommodify workers, new social risk policies only try to improve the situation where the at-risk workers are. The timing of postindustrialization and the accompanying rise of new social risks led to distinct patterns of welfare state adaptation (Bonoli 2007). When postindustrial changes first occurred (in the 1970s), competing claims from population aging were largely absent. This was particularly so in the social democratic regime. If there is to be successful adaptation or updating of the welfare state, postindustrialization and rising costs from the industrial welfare state should not occur simultaneously. This concurrent occurrence, however, was exactly what happened in the conservative regime in the 1980s and in the Mediterranean regime in the 1990s. These regimes, already facing large financial burdens in the welfare state, simply had no room left to develop policies to help citizens suffering from new social risks.

In other words, the degree to which one type of endogenous change (postindustrialization or population aging) can and will be addressed depends on the timing of the other endogenous change. This pattern of welfare state adaptation and updating as a result of postindustrialization also illustrates that a similar process can be an opportunity for reform (in the social democratic regime) or a constraint (in the conservative and Mediterranean regimes). Bonoli's timing argument, however, does not hold for the liberal regime. This regime confronted postindustrialization around the same time as the social democratic regime did but did not develop policies that could cover the newly emerging risks. In Bonoli's view, this is because the liberal regime is less developed than the social democratic regime. The absence of generous policies addressing new social risks is consistent with the absence of generous policies for industrial workers. Related, but somewhat more specific, we consider the lower development of new social risk policies in the liberal regime largely a consequence of the main locus of welfare provision in this regime: the market. In the context of a market-dominated liberal regime, it is less likely that new social risks, or any risks for that matter, are covered directly by the welfare state (see also Howard 1997).

8.4. CONCLUSION

Summing up, in addition to the pressure for welfare state reform that comes from the outside (Chapter 7), we identify and describe strong pressures pushing for reform that arise from within. It is, so we hold, a given that the contemporary politics of the welfare state has become not one of "permanent austerity" and "irresistible forces" meeting "immovable objects" (Pierson 1998), but rather one of functional pressures driving (almost) permanent reform. The "need" to reform the welfare state has been constant and now evidently has become so pressing that further and perhaps more radical adaptation, updating, retrenchment, and restructuring are to be expected. To understand the massive pressure and the immense reform potential that the changes from within have been generating, we mapped and analyzed in some detail the endogenous changes that constitute the need to reform.

We identified one major source of pressure, namely, the shift toward a postindustrial society and the corresponding new social risk structure. These changes have been revolutionizing the very foundation upon which the various welfare states were erected. This in itself explains why existing welfare state arrangements have come under increasing pressure to adapt further to rapidly changing circumstances. Such pressures constitute a functional demand for change, because if there is no change, this static condition implies an existential threat. Ill-adaptation and new social risks to which the postwar welfare state does not cater ask for permanent reform. With this we do not imply that the still needed reforms will occur, let alone be successful. In fact, the politics of new social risks explains and the empirical trend of dualization illustrates that, under present conditions, the welfare state is not capable or likely to reapportion social risks smoothly and in such a way that a high level of social protection is guaranteed under new circumstances also for those groups most at risk. More radical welfare state reforms may be needed, but there is no guarantee that they will occur or, if they do, that they will be successful. What is necessary may be difficult. Yet, what is difficult may still not be impossible. In the next chapter, we present an account of the conditions under which and how – that is, through which mechanisms – such difficult, because they are politically highly risky, reforms are possible. The next chapter offers the final theoretical step in our open functional approach to welfare state reform.

9

Why and How Do Politicians and Governments Pursue Risky Reforms?

9.1 INTRODUCTION

The previous chapters focused on the "objective" exogenous and endogenous pressures to which politicians and governments must react so as to adapt, update, retrench, or restructure the welfare state. No matter how strong the demands for reform are and how existentially threatening the challenges might be, there is no guarantee that political actors will do the job of reform. And we stress once more that whether reforms should be implemented or consciously abstained from (in the latter case effecting policy drift) and which reforms are considered "necessary" are ultimately political decisions made in the arena of democratic politics. This chapter highlights what is special about the context of democratic politics, and especially the political logic of elections, for the political opportunities and constraints of different types of welfare state reform. Given that the welfare state is politically well entrenched and very popular among citizens and assuming that political parties wish to win elections, why would politicians and governments pursue reforms that may cost votes? So, the big questions of this chapter are why, how, and when do politicians and governments translate the exogenous and endogenous pressures into reform if the new policies that are needed contradict their electoral ambitions?

In this chapter, we draw on our earlier work (Vis and Van Kersbergen 2007; Vis 2009a, b, 2010, 2011b) to advance an explanation for electorally risky welfare state reform that is rooted in *prospect theory* – a descriptively accurate, psychological theory of choice under risk (Kahneman and Tversky 1979, 2000). We propose that political actors act like gamblers who are willing to accept the risk of electoral punishment that comes with welfare state reform if they have been losing heavily in the democratic game. Specifically, prospect theory teaches us that governments – as the main political actor in welfare state reform – will undertake risky reforms only if they consider themselves to be in a losses domain, that is, if their current political prospect for winning elections is gloomy and intolerable. This will be the case when they face socioeconomic losses (such as deteriorating growth rates and/or increasing levels of unemployment) and/or political losses (like lower approval ratings or vote losses at an election). The hypothesis is that only under such losses are governments willing to accept the electoral risk involved in unpopular, risky reform. Governments only respond to the "objective" functional pressures by acting on their ideas that require a risky reform if they are already facing losses, such as dwindling popularity and a high probability of retribution at the next elections. The reform policies are considered to offer a (slight) chance of improving the existing critical condition, which makes it politically worth pursuing a risky reform and politically disadvantageous to let existing policies drift. We illustrate the plausibility of the prospect-theoretical account by discussing the puzzling reform experience in Italy in the 1990s and the well-known Hartz IV reform in Germany in 2004.

After having identified what causes the decision to tackle a problem and to implement a risky reform – the government finds itself in a losses domain – we turn to the strategies that politicians and governments have at their disposal to overcome the resistance against such reform and avoid the blame associated with it. Politicians who cannot get away with policy drift and are forced to action do not passively sit back and wait to see how the voters will react (on how voters react to welfare state reform, see Armingeon and Giger 2008; Giger 2011; Giger and Nelson 2011, forthcoming; Schumacher 2012; Arndt 2013; Schumacher et al. 2013). Rather, politicians actively devise strategies to avoid the potential blame for the reform and minimize the risk of punishment. Blame avoidance strategies have already been well researched (see, e.g., Lindbom 2007; Zohlnhöfer 2007; Hering 2008; Giger and Nelson 2011; Wenzelburger 2011; Bonoli 2012), but we propose a new take on the issue by linking these strategies to the insights derived from prospect theory (cf. Vis and Van Kersbergen 2007). Specifically, we argue that politicians and governments will try to reframe the domain of the electorate from gains to losses with a view to changing the voters' attitude from risk-averse and opposing the reform to risk-accepting and embracing the reform. This would limit the political risk of implementing reform to almost zero. If it works, it is a highly effective strategy for political actors to use.

The strategy comes in two basic flavors. First, *damned if you do, damned if you don't*, which is essentially an attempt to make plausible the position that no matter which party or government rules, the reform will take place because the status quo is untenable. This is, for instance, what the Dutch government, and particular Prime Minister Lubbers, tried to do in preparing the reform of the disability scheme in the 1990s, by stating that "the Netherlands is sick" and by referring to the overly high number of people on social benefits, particularly disability benefits (see Chapter 6). Second, *creative accounting* and *lies, damn lies, and statistics*, which implies redefining the terms according to which the outcomes are measured that are feared to have negative consequences, in order to change the domain of voters from gains into losses. Combining the prospect-theoretical model with strategies of blame avoidance offers new key insights into the constraints and opportunities of different types of welfare state reform. The reform-resistance of voters and politicians is a powerful check on reform, while blame avoidance strategies, used by politicians who find themselves in a losses domain, shift the voters' domain from gains to losses and enhance the possibilities for reform.

9.2. THE PUZZLE

As explained in Chapters 2 and 6, one of the major puzzles of contemporary welfare state research is why and how reforms take place in spite of the institutional mechanisms and political resistance that work against them. It is especially the *why* question for which welfare state studies had no theoretical answer and for which we turned to "objective" functional pressures. In Chapter 6, we presented our open functional approach that helps us to explain the opportunities and constraints of different types of welfare state reform and that offers a partial answer to this "why" question. In this chapter, we take the final, and crucial, step in this endeavor. Our contribution is rooted in two theories. The first one is *prospect theory*, which helps us to identify when political actors are willing to deal with the objective functional pressures by pursuing electorally risky welfare state reform rather than by letting policies drift. Prospect theory is especially well equipped to deal with the problem of decision making under conditions of risk (for reviews, see McDermott 2004; Mercer 2005; Vis 2010: chapter 6), which makes it applicable to the lion's share of decision making on social policy reform. The second is the *theory of blame avoidance*, which inspires us to identify the causal mechanisms that link functional pressures to welfare state reform by explaining how political actors try to avoid the potentially negative electoral consequences of their reform efforts.

9.3. INTRODUCING PROSPECT THEORY

It is intriguing that prospect theory, "the most influential behavioural theory of choice in the social sciences" (Mercer 2005: 3), hardly has had any influence in political science in general and in comparative politics in particular (see Wilson 2011). Some interesting attempts aside, mainly (but not exclusively) in the field of international relations (Weyland 1996, 1998, 2002; Quattrone and Tversky 2000; Bueno de Mesquita et al. 2001; Boettcher III 2004; Taliaferro 2004; Haerem et al. 2011; Perla Jr. 2011, see Levy 2003; Norman and Delfin 2012), this is all the more surprising because prospect theory seems particularly apt for dealing with situations in which decisions have to be made under conditions of risk, which is the situation in which political actors typically find themselves (Vis 2011b). Expected utility theory, as commonly used in economics and in political science schools that employ economic theories such as rational choice institutionalism, conversely, makes predictions that do not adequately describe how people actually make choices under conditions of risk and uncertainty.

Prospect theory, developed by Kahneman and Tversky (1979, see 2000 and Kahneman 2011: chapter 26), was meant as a descriptive model of decision making that would provide an alternative to the normative theory of expected utility. According to Camerer (2005: 129), prospect theory is much more than an alternative for expected utility theory; it is "a perceptual and psychophysical perspective to thinking about money, goods, and risk." In experimental settings, a significant number of people consistently made choices that deviated from the predictions of the model of expected utility. In both expected utility theory and prospect theory, people make choices over gambles, and these gambles are defined over end states in the former and over deviations from a reference point in the latter. Prospect-theoretical experiments also disclosed that people are more likely to choose risky options when they find themselves in the domain of losses, whereas they were risk-averse in the gains domain. In prospect theory, the propensity to take risks is thus not a stable personality trait, with some individuals being prone to take risks while others always steer away from them. This does not exclude the possibility that some people overall are more risk-acceptant or risk-averse than others (for a discussion of the heritability of risk attitude, see Zhong et al. 2009). However, the context (domain of gains or losses) affects the extent of risk all individuals are willing to take. Individuals use a reference point, usually the status quo (discussed later), to determine whether they find themselves in a domain of losses or of gains. The risks an individual is willing to take not only depend on this domain but are also asymmetric. Because individuals are *loss averse*, "losses loom larger than gains" (Kahneman and Tversky 1979: 279) and "losses hurt more than equal gains please" (McDermott 2004: 298, see Akalis 2008), typically two to two-and-a-half times more.

Let us illustrate the original theory[1] with the so-called (hypothetical) value function (see Figure 9.1): "the value function is (i) defined on deviations from the reference point; (ii) generally concave for gains [in the figure denoted by B] and commonly convex for losses [A]; (iii) steeper for losses than for gains" (Kahneman and Tversky 1979: 279).

Figure 9.1 shows that in the domain of gains (i.e., the area right of the reference point) the (positive) value that a person attaches to a gain (say, a pay raise) increases sharply at first, but then levels off quickly. This indicates that people are more pleased with a pay raise of, say, $100 if they earn $1,000 (their reference point) than if they earn $3,000 (and thus have a higher reference point). The pleasing effect declines with every additional $1 at higher income

---

[1] Tversky and Kahneman (2000) have extended their theory into the so-called cumulative prospect theory version that – among other things – applies to uncertain as well as risky prospects with multiple outcomes. There are still significant limitations of the theory, for instance, the lack of applicability to strategic interaction and aggregate behavior (see Levy 1997: 102–105; McDermott 2004: 305).

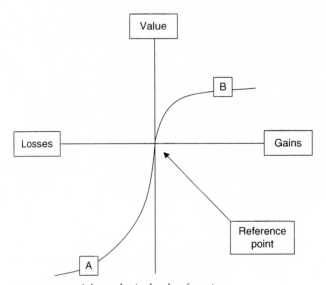

FIGURE 9.1. A hypothetical value function.
Source: Vis and Van Kersbergen (2007: 157), adapted from Kahneman and Tversky (1979: 279).

levels. However, in the losses domain (i.e., the area left of the reference point), the negative value that people attach to a loss (say, a pay cut) increases more sharply than the positive value they attach to a gain. This indicates that losses hurt more than equal gains please. Moreover, the curve in the losses domain does not level off so quickly. This means that people are very displeased with a pay cut of, say, $100 if they earn $1,000 (the reference point) and that they are only slightly less unhappy with a $100 loss if they earn $3,000. The displeasing effect declines with every additional $1 at higher income levels, but not nearly as quickly as the pleasing effect. Expected utility theory cannot explain that losing $100 hurts more than winning the same amount and that losing continues to hurt longer than winning pleases.

Why do the deviations from the predictions of the expected utility theory occur? There are a number of reasons. The first concerns the "negativity effect," which sums up the "losses loom larger than gains" proposition. A negativity effect refers to "the greater weight given to negative information relative to equally extreme and equally likely positive information" (Lau 1985: 119). Second, there is the "certainty effect," which means that "people overweight outcomes that are considered certain, relative to outcomes which are merely probable" (Kahneman and Tversky 1979: 265). In an experimental setup, Tversky and Kahneman (1981: 455) presented 771 subjects with the following two choices. The percentage that picked each option is indicated between brackets.

(A) a sure win of $30 [78 per cent]
(B) 80% chance to win $45 [22 per cent]

The expected utility of option B is .80 × $45 = $36, which is higher than that of A ($30). Still, the overwhelming majority preferred the sure thing over the gamble.

Third, there is the "reflection effect," which suggests that the preference order in the negative domain mirrors the preference order in the positive domain. This implies that how choices are framed matters for how preferences are ordered. Framing is "the process by which a communication source constructs and defines a social or political issue for its audience" (Nelson et al. 1997: 221). A decision frame, then, refers to the "decision-maker's conception of the acts, outcomes, and contingencies [that is the conditional probabilities that relate outcomes to acts] associated with a particular choice" (Tversky and Kahneman 1981: 453). For example, when people are faced with 10 percent unemployment, they probably are ready to accept tough policy measures to fight unemployment. However, when the same fact is reformulated in positive terms, namely, that employment is at 90 percent, they probably are less inclined to accept harsh measures to increase the level of employment. In other words, framing the same fact differently reverses preferences (Quattrone and Tversky 2000[1988]).

Finally, we mention the effect of the "status quo bias": individuals have a "strong tendency to remain at the status quo, because the disadvantages of leaving it loom larger than advantages" (Kahneman et al. 2000: 163). Actually, a better way of expressing the point is to say that there is a reference point bias. This bias "subsumes the status quo bias whenever the reference point is defined as the status quo, and under those conditions it will be stabilizing and reinforce the status quo. If the reference point is preferred to the status quo, however, the reference point bias is destabilizing because it induces risky behavior to avoid the losses inherent in the status quo" (Levy 2003: 223).

The deviations from expected utility theory's predictions occur among other factors because of the combination of the above biases: loss aversion, the status quo bias, the negativity effect, and the certainty effect (see also Jones 2001; Gilovich et al. 2002; Jervis 2004; Weyland 2006, 2012). Baron (2010: 10) argues that political behavior might be even more prone to decision biases than is market behavior.

9.4. GOING BACK TO THE ROOTS: ON THE ORIGIN OF PROSPECT-THEORETICAL PREFERENCES

But why do people display these biases in decision making?[2] Why are we not what Thaler and Sunstein (2008) label *Econs*, individuals who think and choose unfailingly well and fully in line with textbook economics, but *Humans*, individuals who display biases in decision making and consequently fail to even come close to the textbook standard? An increasing amount of work

---

[2] This section draws extensively on Vis (2011b).

drawing on evolutionary biology and neuro-economics suggests that we, so to speak, cannot help ourselves, as this behavior is hardwired. McDermott et al. (2008), for example, propose that prospect-theoretical preferences have an evolutionary origin (see also Camerer 2005: 129; Rieger 2009).[3] By adapting a model from risk-sensitive optimal foraging theory, McDermott et al. show how risk-accepting behavior in the domain of losses (e.g., when facing starvation) and risk aversion in the domain of gains may be the optimal strategy for an individual who (1) endeavors to maximize his or her chances of survival over time and who (2) is subjected to an environment in which abundance and scarcity vary.

If prospect-theoretical "tendencies concerning risk propensity lie more deeply rooted in human evolutionary psychology" (McDermott et al. 2008: 336), the implications for decision making are far-reaching. First, it suggests that cognitive biases, the deviations from rationality, are hard to overcome. Second, and related, it indicates that individuals may not be very likely to learn over time or through experience to overcome these tendencies (Harbaugh et al. 2001).

Experimental evidence on primates, more specifically on capuchin monkeys, shows that behavioral biases – such as loss aversion – also extend beyond the human species (Chen et al. 2006). These monkeys prove to have clear preferences, as humans do, and their preferences change when they are facing gambles (i.e., in the presence of risk). The monkeys preferred the experimenter who showed first one apple and later with a 50–50 chance delivered two apples instead of one over the experimenter who first showed two apples and later with a 50–50 chance delivered one apple instead of two. This finding suggests that monkeys also do not like to lose (by having first two apples and later only one). Although Silberberg et al. (2008) argue that there is a problem with Chen et al.'s experimental design, the experiments of Hayden and Platt (2009) support the latter's finding that the decision patterns of humans and monkeys are surprisingly similar. This result indicates that decision-making patterns and biases may indeed extend beyond species. Individuals' tendency to make choices consistent with prospect theory's predictions may thus not only be hardwired but loss aversion as well may be an innate and evolutionary ancient feature of human preferences. It is a function of decision-making systems, which evolved before the common ancestors of capuchins and humans diverged (Chen et al. 2006: 520).

Given these findings on the evolutionary origin of prospect-theoretical preferences, it hardly comes as a surprise that the greater sensitivity to losses than to gains according to some studies shows up in our brain activity as well (Smith et al. 2002; Kuhnen and Knutson 2005; Loewenstein et al. 2008: 652–655). For example, based on experiments with two individuals with damage to the

---

[3] See Lopez and McDermott (2012) for an outline of evolutionary political science, of which the work of McDermott et al. (2008) is an example.

amygdala – a region in the brain – and matched control experiments with individuals without such damage, De Martino et al. (2010) show that the amygdala likely plays an important role in the computational process leading to loss aversion. That is to say, the amygdala is the neural structure mediating loss aversion. However, earlier findings by Tom et al. (2007) conflict with De Martino et al.'s results. Using functional magnetic resonance imaging (fMRI) to examine which brain systems represent potential losses vis-à-vis potential gains at the time when a decision is being made (so-called decision utility), Tom et al. find hardly any amygdala activity when the size of the potential loss increases. Since amygdala activation typically occurs during negative affective responses (such as fear, discomfort, or vigilance), this would suggest that the amygdala's role in loss aversion is at least not necessary. These two examples indicate that people's responses to losses and gains do seem to be traceable in brain activity. However, how this happens exactly and which neural structures are involved remains an area requiring more work. These findings indicate that people's tendency to act in line with prospect theory's predictions is very strong and probably even hardwired. If prospect theory is applicable to political actors' decision making in, for instance, welfare state reform – as we argue it is – these results suggest that political actors typically fall prey to the diversions from expected utility theory.

9.5. PROBLEMS IN PROSPECT THEORY AND EMPIRICAL ILLUSTRATIONS

There are a number of problems in prospect theory. One of the biggest is the determination of the reference point. As Levy (1997: 100) has put it, prospect theory "is a reference-dependent theory without a theory of the reference point." Note that this problem is comparable to the problem of rational choice theory, which is a preference-dependent theory without a theory of preferences. Because there is no theoretical foothold in prospect theory to determine an actor's frame, the "temptation to reason backwards, from choice to domain to frame, is strong" (see Mercer 2005: 4). This is problematic since, as Boettcher (2004: 333) notes, the "key to understanding the impact of prospect framing thus becomes the identification of the reference point."

There are various ways to determine the reference point, including status quo as reference point, aspiration as reference point, heuristics, analogies, and emotion (Mercer 2005: 4). It is plausible in the case of the welfare state to take the status quo as a reference point for establishing the actors' domain as a loss or a gain. This is because, first, welfare state reform is all about changing a situation that is characterized by institutional resilience and electoral resistance against change, and second, because the status quo bias holds for both the reformers and those affected by reforms. Detailed case studies and comparative accounts have documented the considerable and persisting support of national publics for their welfare states as they are (see Chapter 2).

A second and well-known theoretical problem concerns the lack of a generally accepted theory of framing. Instead, there are distinct approaches to framing, including the sociological approach common in, for example, communication science and the psychological approach as developed in the work of, among others, Kahneman and Tversky. In these approaches the conceptualizations and operationalizations of framing differ substantially (see Borah 2011 for a content analysis of 93 published journal articles on framing). As a result, prospect theory does not provide an answer for how to determine when political actors consider themselves to be in a gains or losses domain. This is crucially important because this establishes whether actors are risk-averse or risk-acceptant. Despite an attempt by Kanner (2005) to develop a formal dynamic theory of framing and work by Kam and Simas (2010) that shows *who* is more or less likely to be affected by different frames, this problem is far from being solved. Still, the issue of the importance of framing is increasingly taken up in welfare state studies, particularly under the influence of Schmidt's (2002) work on discourse and ideas in reform politics (see also Kuipers 2006 and Chapter 6).

In addition to these problems, there are other pending issues. For instance, can prospect theory deal with group behavior and with strategic interaction? There is no definite answer here, but – as in rational choice theory – the suggestion is that the unitary actor assumption is a legitimate tool (on the condition that its validity is empirically substantiated; Levy 1997: 102), so that prospect theory can be applied to group behavior. Experimental evidence (Bone et al. 1999) suggests that pairs of individuals violate the predictions of expected utility theory in (almost) the same manner as do individuals – that is, risk acceptance in the domain of losses, and risk adversity in the domain of gains. This indicates that the central finding of prospect theory extends to situations of collective decision making. The work of Weyland (2002), furthermore, offers an example of how a prospect theoretical approach can deal with the strategic interaction between leaders and citizens. Our linking of prospect theory to the theory of blame avoidance is another route, which we elaborate later. Still, the final verdict as regards group decision making is still pending, because Kugler et al.'s (2012) review shows that groups often behave more in line with rationality assumptions than individuals do.

This exposition of prospect theory, then, would tell us that policymakers avoid risks as long as they consider themselves in a domain of gains, that is, when they see their current situation as still acceptable or tolerable. Paraphrasing Berejekian (1997: 793), the theory yields two predictions for governments as the major decision makers in reform politics. First, governments will opt for the certainty of the status quo (their current situation is acceptable), when they view this as a gain (their position of power is safe) and are confronted with a choice between (1) the status quo (no reform) and (2) some gamble (reform) with both a *positive* expected value (e.g., electoral gain) and some smaller risk of loss (electoral punishment smaller than the expected gain). Second, governments will opt for the gamble when they view their current situation as a loss and are confronted with a choice between (1) the status quo (no reform) and (2) some gamble (reform) with both an expected value of *further loss* (further electoral loss) and some smaller prospect for improvement (an electoral reward smaller than the expected loss). Governments in a gains domain pursue absolute gains and are unwilling to engage in risky reform efforts, while governments in a losses domain pursue relative gains and are more willing to accept the risks of reform (see Berejekian 1997: 789).

Following Weyland (1996), the same reasoning could be applied to voters, interest groups, or the public at large. For reasons of clarity, we elaborate this only for voters. First, voters will prefer the certainty of the status quo when they view this as a gain (their level of welfare is acceptable) and are confronted with a choice between (1) the current situation (no reform) and (2) some gamble (reform) with both a *positive* expected value (e.g., higher welfare) and some smaller risk of loss (a loss of welfare smaller than the expected gain). Second, voters will prefer the gamble when they view the status quo as a loss (their level of welfare is unacceptable) and are confronted with a choice between (1) the current situation (no reform) and (2) some gamble (reform) with both an expected value of *further loss* (a further loss of welfare) and some smaller prospect for improvement (a welfare gain smaller than the expected loss).

Table 9.1 illustrates the corollaries of this reasoning. First, governments will undertake welfare state reforms with risky electoral repercussions ("gamble") only if they consider their current situation a loss (either cell I or II in Table 9.1). Second, if governments pursue reforms, there are two possible outcomes: (1) the implementation of a reform will be relatively easy if voters are reform friendly, that is, if they consider themselves in a losses domain (cell II); (2) the implementation of a reform will be relatively difficult if voters are reform hostile, that is, if they consider themselves in a gains domain (cell I). Third, if governments consider their current situation a gain (cells III and IV), they will not undertake risky reforms. Fourth, if governments do not favor reform, there are two possible outcomes: (1) there will be no conflict if voters also consider their current situation a gain (cell III); (2) there will be conflict if voters consider their current situation a loss (cell IV).

Following this theoretical line of argument, it is thus the change in a government's domain that influences its risk attitude and consequently its willingness to pursue an unpopular, electorally risky reform that it was unwilling to take earlier. Let us illustrate the theoretical mechanism with two examples. First, we examine the puzzling reform experience in Italy where – after decades of immobility – the 1990s saw a sudden outburst of reform activities. Second, we assess the recent reform in the German welfare state, the 4th Law on Modern Service of the Labor Market, better known as Hartz IV.

Ferrera and Gualmini (2004) have explained the unexpected outbreak of reform activities in Italy as an institutional and political learning process under pressure of the entrance criteria of the Economic and Monetary Union (EMU)

TABLE 9.1. *Voters' and government's domains, risk attitudes, and the need for blame avoidance*

		Government	
		Losses domain (status quo -/-)	Gains domain (status quo +)
Voters	Gains domain (status quo +)	(risk-averse, risk-acceptant) Conflict: Government wants reform; Voters oppose reform **I**	(risk-averse, risk-averse) No conflict: Neither the government nor the voters want reform **III**
	Losses domain (status quo -/-)	(risk-acceptant, risk-acceptant) No conflict: Both the government and the voters want reform **II**	(risk-acceptant, risk-averse) Conflict: Voters want reform; Government opposes reform **IV**

Note: The risk attitude of the voters is listed first.
Source: Vis and Van Kersbergen (2007: 160).

in Europe. We hold, conversely, that the empirical material actually allows for a better explanation based on prospect theory.

Italy's decision to join the Maastricht process toward EMU was a risky decision in light of the country's limited political reform capacity and precarious budgetary situation at the time (see Ferrera and Gualmini 2004: 66). The decision was risky because it was highly unlikely that Italy would come even close to reaching the stringent criteria set by EMU. It seemed impossible that Italy would be able to reduce its budget deficit to 3 percent of GDP with a deficit of 10.7 percent in 1992. Also, reaching a public debt of 60 percent of GDP seemed unrealistic as Italy's public debt was almost 110 percent in 1992 (Ferrera and Gualmini 2004: 14). Still, trying to implement drastic measures in order to qualify for EMU seemed the "rational" choice for Italy. The political and monetary crises of the early 1990s had already taught politicians a painful lesson. In 1992–93, financial markets had attacked Italy's currency, the lira; the currency had to be devaluated vastly; and Italy was forced to exit the European Monetary System. Ferrera and Gualmini (2004: 24) formulate the choices the Italian government faced as follows:

[A]s the 1999 deadline approached it became in fact clear that being denied entry into the new EMU club would originate high penalties on the side of international financial markets. Thus, the real alternative was no longer between adjusting for EMU or maintaining the status quo: it was an alternative between adjusting or losing ground. Actors had to choose between a potentially positive sum outcome (adjustment and entry) and a negative sum outcome (no or insufficient adjustment, non-entry and therefore high losses for virtually all actors). Choosing in favour of the first scenario was facilitated by the fact that the losses started to hit immediately: between 1995 and 1997 the exchange and interest rates of EMU candidate countries (especially the weaker ones) were closely

linked to the probabilities of admission assigned by international rating institutions....
[T]he low (and actually declining) probabilities of EMU admission due to the political
crisis and the stalling negotiations on pension reform resulted in high penalties on both
the exchange and interest rates.

According to Ferrera and Gualmini, the Italian government thus faced two
choices: (1) a negative sum outcome of limited to no reform (incurring high
losses); and (2) a potential positive sum outcome of reform (adjusting and
entering the EMU). The choice between (3) the status quo (i.e., no reform); and
(4) reform (i.e., trying to enter the EMU) was no longer an option. Confronted
with options 1 and 2, the rational choice from a vote-seeking perspective seems
to be option 2 (reform) as option 1 produces certain losses whereas option 2
has potential benefits. The corollary of this reasoning is that the Italian government opted for pursuing drastic reforms in the 1990s because it was rational
to do so.

Notwithstanding the intuitive plausibility of this argument and the explanatory power it seems to have, we argue that the choices the Italian government
faced in the 1990s were actually different from options 1 and 2 as presented
by Ferrera and Gualmini. More precisely, we hold that they underestimated the
risks involved in undertaking the radical reform measures. The actual choices
should be described as follows. Option 5 is similar to option 1 but we propose
to present it somewhat differently, namely, as no reform, meaning a certain
loss. Option 6 is similar to option 2 but again presented differently since this
option has two possible outcomes. Outcome 6A: The reforms are unsuccessful,
so that the benefits of EMU membership cannot be reaped and the government
is likely punished for its unpopular and failed measures with a substantial loss
of votes. Outcome 6B: The reforms are successful and the benefits of EMU
membership can be collected, but voters – given their attachment to the established rights of the welfare state – are still likely to punish the government for
having undertaken the unpopular reform measures. The difference between
options 5 and 6 is that the losses in option 5 are certain, whereas the losses
in option 6 are uncertain. Given the "immobility" of the Italian welfare state
and the state of the Italian economy in the 1990s, outcome 6A seemed much
more likely than outcome 6B. As is easy to see, the losses under 6A are higher
than those under 6B. In addition, it seems – especially given the potential loss
of votes under option 6 – reasonable to assume that the total (potential) losses
are higher under option 6 than under option 5. Thus, a rational actor would
not opt for the "gamble" of reform, but would simply take the loss.

So, if the choices that the Italian government actually faced are presented
properly, that is, as choices between options 5 and 6, a rational choice account
would not predict nor could it explain why the government pursued such
a radical reform agenda. The puzzling choice the government in fact made,
however, was precisely the one our prospect-theoretical account would predict. At the time of the choice, the Italian government found itself in a losses
domain, which was primarily evoked by the precarious condition of the Italian

economy and the labor market. The budget deficits and debts, the interest rates, and the long-term and youth unemployment rates were significantly above the European Union (EU) average. Decreasing productivity, accelerating labor costs, and declining competitiveness in the tertiary sector (Ferrera and Gualmini 2004: 66) were all unacceptable, especially as Italy aspired to become a member of the EMU club. So the government found itself in a losses domain, meaning that actors were risk-acceptant and therefore willing to pursue risky reform projects.

Also, a 2004 reform in the German welfare state, the 4th Law on Modern Service of the Labor Market, or Hartz IV, can be explained by drawing on insights from prospect theory. Central to this reform is the merger of the unemployment assistance scheme (*Arbeitslosenhilfe*) and the social assistance scheme (*Sozialhilfe*) into one, means-tested benefit (*Arbeitslosengeld II*, or *ALG II*). Notwithstanding some transitory arrangements, like supplements payable for up to two years after the exhaustion of ALG (ISSA 2006, no. 3326), this reform entails lower benefits for most unemployed individuals previously receiving unemployment assistance as well as the loss of eligibility of those unemployed individuals with partners who were employed (due to the stricter means-testing). Additionally, the definition of suitable work changed considerably, with ALG II claimants being in principle required to accept any legal job offer.

The Hartz IV reform qualifies as unpopular, since it was opposed by trade unions, parts of the Social Democratic Party and citizens (especially in the new *Länder*) (Fleckenstein 2008). The citizens' protests were most clearly visible in the so-called *Montagsdemonstrationen* (Monday demonstrations) in (largely) East Germany in 2004, but were also reflected in the miserable opinion polls for the social democrats and several crushing defeats of the party in the *Länder* elections (Clasen 2005; Helms 2007). Following the prospect-theoretical argument outlined earlier, this would suggest that the government implementing the reform found itself in a domain of losses, so either in cell II or, theoretically and empirically more likely, cell I of Table 9.1. The theory also suggests that the domain in the previous cabinet period (Schröder's first term in office) was one of gains. Prospect theory indicates that the shift from a domain of gains to one of losses is responsible for the changed risk attitude of the government and the consequent higher degree of unpopular and therefore risky reform pursued. Let us see to what extent these hypotheses find support in this particular case.

Both in terms of its political position and the socioeconomic situation, the first Schröder cabinet was in a relatively good position, that is, in a domain of gains (see Vis 2010: table A3 and appendix C). The social democrats had won the 1998 elections, mostly at the expense of the Christian democrats, and the election results offered a clear mandate for a Red-Green coalition. Despite some setbacks, such as losses in several *Länder* elections and the European Parliamentary election, the social democrats' and the greens' political position was reasonably good in this period in office. The same holds for the socioeconomic situation. Although the level of unemployment was high (on average about 8 percent), it was stable. As it is downward deviations that trigger risk-accepting behavior and not so much a high level of unemployment per se, we would hold that the socioeconomic situation during Schröder I was not that weak. Also the level of economic growth in the first three years of the cabinet period was well above 1 percent. In the final year, the growth rate fell to close to 0 percent.

The political position of the second Schröder cabinet was very different from the first, as was the socioeconomic situation in which the cabinet found itself (Vis 2010: table A3 and appendix C). Regarding the political position, the Red-Green coalition had a very small majority of the seats in the *Bundestag* (Parliament). It would probably not have reached a majority at all if it had not been for the war in Iraq and the flood in Eastern Germany in the run-up to the elections. Whereas the greens won in terms of votes, the substantially larger social democrats ended up with 2.4 percent less votes. The government's political position deteriorated further when it presented its "Agenda 2010," a plan for far-reaching reforms in the German welfare state. This plan had not figured in the election campaign, as a result of which the public felt misinformed. The socioeconomic situation was equally poor. In 2003, the German economy contracted 0.2 percent and the level of unemployment increased further, from less than 4 million in 2002 to 4.5 million a year later. Also the level of employment decreased to the lowest in 10 years (Clasen 2005: 74).

Was it the shift in domain from gains to losses that can help to account for the Hartz IV reform that was pursued in Schröder's second period in office? An analysis of the process leading up to the reform suggests that it was. For one, based on the "Third Way/Die Neue Mitte" paper that the British Prime Minister Tony Blair and Schröder published in 1999 (Blair and Schröder 1999), it is plausible to assume that Schröder would have preferred to implement such a reform in his first period in office. However, in this first cabinet period, the so-called modernizers in the social democratic party – headed by Schröder himself – were not able to convince the so-called traditionalists – supported by the trade unions – of the need for reform. According to observers, the lack of success for Schröder was at least partly due to the relatively weak problem pressure at the time (Clasen 2005: 72; Dyson 2005). Drawing on insights from prospect theory allows for making a clearer prediction about Schröder's failure to convince his fellow party members and the trade unions that something needed to be done. While the modernizers within the social democratic party considered the status quo no longer tenable, the traditionalists and the trade unions wanted to keep this status quo. The latter found themselves in a domain of gains (cell III in Table 9.1) and were unwilling to accept the electoral risk involved in pursuing reform. Although Schröder and the other modernizers were already in cell I, and thus acceptant of the risk involved in reform, the overriding view in the government was one of remaining at the status quo.

The situation, the domain, changed due to both the deteriorating socioeconomic situation and the so-called placement scandal (see Leibfried and Obinger

2003: 213–214; Clasen 2005; Fleckenstein 2008; Stiller 2010: chapter 6). The placement scandal concerned manipulated statistics on the number of unemployed who had been successfully reintegrated by the *Bundesanstalt für Arbeit* early 2002. The scandal made clear that the current system was not functioning well, indicating to the traditionalists within the social democratic party and the trade unions that the status quo might no longer be the "best" option available. The rising levels of unemployment added to the idea that something needed to be done. Given the radical nature of the reform, the social democrats "first had to muster the necessary courage to bear the resulting conflict; we did not dare to tackle the issue immediately" (interview with a social democratic member of Parliament, 25 January 2005, quoted in Stiller 2010: 145). In prospect theoretical terminology, they had to be willing to accept the risk involved in implementing the reform and for that a domain shift was needed. This is precisely what happened. The domain in which the government found itself changed from one of gains in Schröder's first period in office to one of losses in the second. It is the government's change in risk attitude that made it willing to face the potential electoral losses involved and to implement the reform nonetheless.

The account of the occurrence of the Hartz IV reform complements the existing explanations such as those put forward by Clasen (2005), Fleckenstein (2008), and Stiller (2010). The advantage of our prospect-theoretical explanation is that it can travel across countries and over time. Often, an account of a specific reform is tied to the peculiarities of that particular case. While such idiosyncrasies are relevant for an in-depth understanding of a reform process, our approach allows for more general – but still specific – hypotheses. The Hartz IV case illustrates that a shift in domain was responsible for the change in risk attitude of the German government and the accompanying reform (Vis 2010).

In conclusion, prospect theory gives us the necessary condition under which electorally risky welfare state reform can occur: when governments view their current situation as a loss (cells I and II of Table 9.1). This theory, then, gives us an explanation for why governments pursue risky reforms at all, that is, for the empirical fact for which institutional approaches have no account. Prospect theory thus shows us the conditions under which political actors are likely to act on their ideas and pursue the reforms that are "necessary" given the functional pressures that have been building up. Moreover, prospect theory offers an indication of the conditions under which welfare state reform is likely to be successful: either when voters are also in a domain of losses so that they seek the risk of reform (cell II), or when the government is able to overcome the reform-hostility of the voters in the domain of gains (cell I). The case of cell I poses the question of how a government deals with the resistance against reform. To identify the causal mechanisms that link the so-called basic cause for reform (a losses domain) with the effect (risky welfare state reform), we turn to the theory of blame avoidance.

9.6. THE CAUSAL MECHANISMS OF WELFARE REFORM

Drawing on prospect theory, we argued that political actors will pursue risky reform projects, that is, respond to the "objective" functional pressures for reform, only if they consider themselves to be in a losses domain. In addition, we reasoned that welfare state reform is likely to be successful if voters are also in a domain of losses or if the government is able to overcome the reform-hostility of the voters who consider themselves to be in a gains domain.

In the case of the public, one can imagine that in some contexts voters are risk-acceptant (as in cell II of Table 9.1). Weyland (1996) gives an interesting account in his study of radical economic reforms in Latin America. Asking "what gains and losses loom largest for leaders and citizens?" (190), Weyland first posits that income is the main economic concern for common people. He then argues that in Latin America, "runaway inflation is the single biggest threat that can thrust large numbers of people suddenly into a domain of losses. The speed of this deterioration prevents them from lowering their expectations and redefining their reference point for assessing gains and losses" (190). In the context of developed welfare states, it is not so much runaway inflation but physical and social security that are the main concerns of people. However, because the support for the welfare state among the public remains firm and high (see Chapter 2) and when there is no immediate threat to the continuing existence of the welfare state, it is unlikely that voters will consider their present situation as a loss. As a consequence, the condition is such that governments consider themselves to be in a domain of losses whereas voters regard their situation as a gain. This creates a large need for strategies to minimize the risk involved in reform, for instance, electoral punishment.

In the literature on party-political decision making, three kinds of motivations are distinguished: (1) credit claiming, (2) "good policy," and (3) blame avoidance (Weaver 1986: 372). In the context that we focus on, that is, situations where the government, but not the voters, is in a losses domain and therefore needs to overcome the reform-hostility of the voters in order to be successful, blame avoidance is the most relevant motivation. Governments are here most likely to search for blame avoidance strategies because this will help them to be successful, that is, attain the goal (reform) that – because they find themselves in a losses domain – they have been forced to set, while avoiding the well-known risk of blame that accompanies such hazardous reform.

Can blame avoidance strategies in this sense be politically (rather than policy) effective? We give a positive answer that is based on the negativity effect described earlier. Hood (2002: 20), for example, has observed a rising negativity bias among both voters and politicians. In addition, Pierson (2001a) has correctly argued that the benefits of reforms are widely dispersed electorally, whereas the losses tend to be concentrated among voter groups. We take this to imply that voters who are negatively affected by welfare state reforms remember such reforms much better and longer than reforms that affect them positively. Or, as Weaver (1988: 21) states, voters "are more sensitive to what has been done *to* them than what has been done *for* them" (italics in original). So, how to do things to voters and get away with it?

The theory of blame avoidance, which can be traced back to Downs's (1957) theory of electoral competition, has had a clear focus on explaining why governments have a strong incentive to refrain from pursuing policies that are unpopular among voters. It was, in fact, one of the theoretical underpinnings of the welfare state resilience thesis. Interest group theory at the same time had been informing us that "in addition to resisting to vetoing reforms, strong organized interests also reinforce the blame avoidance incentives of governments because trade unions and elderly lobbies are able to mobilize large segments of voters in elections" (Hering 2003: 4, referring to Weaver 1986: 394–395).

Indeed and interestingly, the resistance-against-change theorem was definitively one of the specific consequences of the politics of blame avoidance that Weaver (1986: 394) pointed to:

Blame avoidance … helps to explain why policies are so difficult to change, even if they fail. If policymakers and their constituents perceived costs and benefits symmetrically, they would be willing to change policies quite freely, at least as long as the new policies promised at least as high a surplus of concentrated benefits over costs as the status quo. But substantial vested interests often develop around programmes. Because costs and benefits are perceived asymmetrically, policymakers fear that new policies will not win them as much support as dismantling the old ones will lose.

However, this theory can also be used to account for how governments can get away with unpopular initiatives. For example, Armingeon and Giger (2008) show that many governing parties are not punished at the next election for having curtailed benefit entitlements (see also Giger 2011; Giger and Nelson 2011, forthcoming; Schumacher et al. 2013). Armingeon and Giger find that voters punished the governing parties only when the issue was highly salient in the election campaign. Of the 30 governments that cut entitlements by minimally 5 percent, most (16) were not punished for it by losing minimally 5 percent of the votes. Some governments (7) did lose minimally 5 percent of the votes, but not because of the cutbacks. However, some governments (7) did lose because of the enacted cutbacks. These figures suggest that blame avoidance strategies may work over 50 percent of the time. For governments wanting to pursue reform, this is good news. The problem for researchers interested in the politics of welfare state reform is that it is very difficult to identify whether a government has used a blame avoidance strategy and, if so, which one and why it was successful. So far, the best the literature has to offer is a sort of tautological reasoning in which the absence of electoral punishment is equated with the success of a blame avoidance strategy. We need to go beyond this and try to arrive at a more systematic way of identifying and assessing blame avoidance strategies.

Blame Avoidance Strategies

Which blame avoidance strategies are available and how can we identify them?[4] The latter is an intricate question because the theory of blame avoidance is a strategy-dependent theory without a theory of strategies. Consequently, there is a lack of theoretically informed means to identify blame avoidance strategies in reality. We offer a first step in solving this lacuna by linking blame avoidance theory to well-established theories and empirically corroborated hypotheses of the mainstream welfare state literature. To do so, the question of how to conceptualize what is an electorally risky welfare state reform is important. Recall that this is, in fact, a highly controversial issue among welfare state researchers and is known as the dependent variable problem (see Chapter 4). There have been at least two powerful suggestions on how to think about this. The first is Pierson's respecification of welfare state reform in various dimensions and how these might be linked to the inner regime logics. The second concerns Iversen and Wren's hypotheses on the most likely strategies that the regimes adopt to cope with what they termed the postindustrial trilemma among balanced budgets (fiscal discipline), employment growth, and earnings equality.

We adopt Pierson's (2001a) analytical clarification of the dimensions of welfare state reform and the correlate estimation of the political link with the regime type. Very helpful is his insight that welfare state change cannot be measured along a single scale. This would reduce the problem of welfare state retrenchment and reform to a false dichotomy of "less" versus "more" and "intact" versus "dismantled," which is an unwarranted theoretical simplification. Pierson proposed to look at three dimensions of welfare state change:

- Recommodification: the attempt "to restrict the alternatives to participation in the labour market, either by tightening eligibility or cutting benefits" (Pierson 2001a: 422), that is, strengthening the whip of the labor market. In our repertoire of definitions of the different types of welfare state reform, recommodification equals retrenchment (see Chapter 1). In our analysis even a moderate recommodification would count as a radical and risky reform

---

[4] In a recent book on the complex blame game that public actors play at different levels and in interaction with each other, Hood (2011) discusses three main types of blame avoidance strategies that can be divided further into subtypes. The first ones are presentational strategies, which try to turn a situation that normally generates blame into a blessing in disguise by means of reframing or spinning the story. This strategy's slogan is "spin your way out of trouble" (Hood 2011: 18). Agency strategies are the second kind of available strategies and come down to searching for a scapegoat onto which blame can be shifted. Finally, there are policy strategies in which the space for the occurrence of blame is minimized by smart selecting policy and/or procedures, that is to say, by not making "contestable judgments that create losers." Tepe and Vanhuysse (2011) identify another strategy to avoid major electoral losses: to accelerate smaller cutbacks when the socioeconomic context requires it. This would, for example, be the case when unemployment is mounting or population aging is clearly becoming a (in our terminology) functional requirement for reform. The acceleration of smaller cutbacks aims at staving off bigger, more risky reforms.

because it is a departure from customary social policy practices and well-entrenched arrangements that were installed to protect employees against the market.

- Cost containment: the attempt to keep balanced budgets through austerity policies, including deficit reduction and tax moderation. Recall that we consider cost containment to be a subcategory of retrenchment.
- Recalibration: "reforms which seek to make contemporary welfare states more consistent with contemporary goals and demands for social provision" (Pierson 2001a: 425), that is, what we label updating.

Of course, it is very difficult to distinguish between the various dimensions in practice, but a number of hypotheses that relate these dimensions to the welfare state regimes can be helpful in guiding empirical research of welfare state reform. Pierson (2001a) argued that each regime (social democratic, liberal, or conservative) is characterized by its own specific "new politics" of welfare state reform.

In the liberal regime, voters are less likely to be attached to the welfare state than in the conservative or social democratic regimes. Recommodification is here most likely the pivotal feature of welfare state reform. However, because of the residual nature of the welfare state in the liberal regime and the rise of new social risks, we would argue that recalibration is a distinct possibility too (think of U.S. president Obama's health care reform of 2010–12 as an example).

In the social democratic welfare regime, voters are highly attached to, and dependent on, the welfare state. We see Pierson's point when he argues that recommodification is not likely to be high on the political agenda of reform, but – if only because of the sheer size of the public sector – cost containment is. But this is obviously also an empirical matter and we would not exclude the possibility of radical reform in the social democratic regime.

The conservative regime is probably the most ill-adapted model of the three worlds of welfare capitalism, as a result of which recalibration and cost containment are the two dimensions of reform that are expected to dominate. Here the issues are how to stimulate job growth in the underdeveloped service sector and how to contain the exploding costs of pensions, disability, and health. However, we would argue that with the increasing prominence of activation policies also on the European continent, it remains an open issue whether the stimulation of labor market participation is a policy of workfare (implying recommodification) or of welfare (see Vis 2007, 2008).

The regime typology also allows for a specification of the expected preferences of reform goals of major political actors in postindustrial society. Iversen and Wren (1998) argued that contemporary governments face a trilemma among the goals of employment growth, fiscal discipline, and earnings equality, where only two can be achieved at the same time, at the cost of the third:

Because budgetary restraint precludes any rapid expansion of public sector employment, governments wedded to such discipline must either accept low earnings equality

TABLE 9.2. *Types of blame avoidance strategies*

		Type of compensation	
		Rhetorical	"Real"
Actors	Governments only	Political Communication Strategy (A)	Symbolic Policy Content Strategy (B)
	Governments plus other actor(s)	Domain Manipulation Strategy (D)	Coalition Logic Strategy (C)

in order to spur growth in private service employment or face low growth in overall employment. Alternatively, governments may pursue earnings equality and high employment, but they can do so only at the expense of budgetary restraint (Iversen and Wren 1998: 513).

In the social democratic welfare states, fiscal discipline is most often the victim; in the conservative ones it is employment growth that suffers most; and in the liberal welfare states earnings equality is sacrificed.

We can link these reconceptualizations of reform to the blame avoidance strategies that Weaver (1986) developed to explain the difficulty of reform but which can be adapted and extended to help explain the success of (unpopular) reform. These strategies can be differentiated based on (1) the actors involved (only the government or the government plus one or more other actors) and (2) the type of compensation ("real" or rhetorical). We propose to make an analytical distinction – appreciating that in empirical reality such strategies are most likely overlapping and intertwined – among four main types of strategies: (A) Political Communication; (B) Symbolic Policy Content; (C) Coalition Logic; and (D) Domain Manipulation, displayed clockwise in Table 9.2.

A. Political Communication Strategy
The first type of strategy focuses on political communication by specifically trying to deal with the problem of how to communicate ("sell") unpopular policies to the public (the voters). This relates to Pierson's (1994: 19ff.) so-called obfuscation strategy, which seeks to "manipulate information flows to decrease public awareness of their actions or of the negative consequences of them" (19). One example of a political communication blame avoidance strategy is *redefine the issue*, which is primarily an attempt to spread the costs of reform, and can thereby foster reform. This political communication strategy can be recognized in recommodification policies that are presented as cost containment. Cost containment, while the demand for social expenditures remains the same or increases, implies recommodification. We may assume that no government will ever present reform policies of popular social programs as explicitly aiming at reducing the level of protection from the market, that is, as explicitly

recommodifying. Instead, harsh retrenchment policies will be portrayed as necessary efficiency measures.

B. *Symbolic Policy Content Strategy*
The second type of blame avoidance strategy, symbolic policy content, uses substantive policy to try to "soften" the reaction of voters to unpopular measures, either by suggesting that harsh measures are not as harsh as they initially seem or by hiding the harsh effects. This strategy also relates to Pierson's (1994) obfuscation strategy as well as to his strategy of compensation, that is, offering side payments to those negatively affected by the reform. One example of a symbolic policy content strategy is to *throw good money after bad*, or formulating policies that try to soften the pain of reforms by offering a small compensation. This strategy is more difficult to translate directly into the terms of mainstream welfare state theory. Nevertheless, we know that in many countries various cost containment measures were introduced – varying from tightening the eligibility criteria and lowering the benefit replacement rates to the restructuring or abolishment of whole social programs (see Jordan et al. 2013) – that were subsequently followed by measures to compensate partly the disadvantageous impact on income equality and poverty. However, cross-national studies of aggregate data and of survey data on income (e.g., the Luxembourg Income Study, LIS) indicate that generally speaking both income inequality and poverty have increased (see, e.g., Huber and Stephens 2001: chapters 6 and 7). One may infer from this that most probably throwing good money after bad does not fully compensate retrenchment but is used as a political strategy for its high symbolic positive potential, particularly shortly before elections, giving rise to the more familiar phenomenon of the electoral business cycle.

Another example is *pass the buck*, which is delegation of the blame and includes "automatic government" (e.g., indexation; see Weaver 1988; or dismantling by default; Green-Pedersen et al. 2013). Retrenchment policies very often take the form of national framework laws that specify general objectives for lower level government to attain. To redefine competencies and delegate them to lower levels of government or to quasi-governmental institutions or, in a national emergency event such as in Italy in the autumn of 2011, to an "apolitical" government of experts, are also options. This strategy, including decentralization and privatization, therefore includes various shifts in governance that aim to shun direct government responsibility. Another feature of welfare schemes particularly suitable for passing the buck is found in indexation, a usually highly technical and therefore poorly visible matter. Many benefits are automatically coupled to developments in the economy, for instance, the inflation rate, the growth rate of private sector wages, the level of the minimum wage, and others. Passing the buck would imply that a blame avoiding retrenchment strategy would tinker with the indexation rather than with, for instance, the replacement rate of benefits, leading to "creeping disentitlement" (Van Kersbergen 2000). To know more about this strategy, we would need to look at how and at what level the basic (or lowest) social benefits are coupled to the (minimum) wage development in the economy. An increasing distance between benefits and wages, presented as a technical adjustment of indexation, would be an indication of "passing the buck."

C. Coalition Logic Strategy
The third type of blame avoidance strategy is labeled Coalition Logic, as blame is avoided – or at least limited – by including in the reform proposal other actors (e.g., opposition parties), lower government levels (e.g., municipalities) or higher ones (e.g., the European Union). An example of this strategy is *circling the wagons*, which aims to share as much blame as possible, such as by including the opposition in a reform package that is highly unpopular. This is an important strategy for avoiding blame in major cost containment operations, particularly in the form of a consensus among all (relevant) parties to diffuse blame (Hering 2008). This would imply that in systems with multiple veto points and veto players, such as Germany, all major reforms necessarily are the result of system-wide bargains such as a grand coalition. It would also imply that in multi-party systems the number of surplus coalitions as opposed to minimal winning coalitions increases and/or that the size of the surplus increases. The unexpected and unlikely occurrence of a spectrum-wide coalition in a highly divided and polarized system, say, the Greek government that entered office in autumn 2011, was fabricated for blame sharing purposes and to break through the political gridlock that blocked the imposed radical reforms. In fact, blame avoidance in Greece went so far that it led to th.: "postponement" of democracy by blocking a referendum on the EU/IMF reform demands and early elections.

Another example of this type of strategy is *stop me before I kill again* (or Ulysses and the Sirens), which is restricting the discretion over the choice so that it appears that the government has no autonomous room to maneuver. This strategy is frequently used when, for cost containment reasons, coalition partners agree upon certain budget norms to govern their spending behavior during their period in office or when a system-wide bargain is struck that incorporates such a budget method in law or even the constitution. At the European level, Ulysses (the member states) has delegated his power over monetary policy to an independent European Central Bank so as not to be able to react to the seductive song of the sirens (the pressure for inflationary spending). The cost of this change is that national political actors no longer have control over monetary policy, but the gain is that domestically they can withstand the unpopular refusal to spend more by invoking an external constraint. The European Central Bank emerges as the cause of tied hands and consequently blame can be shifted. Also the so-called Fiscal Compact (a stricter version of the previous Stability and Growth Pact), which all EU member states (except the Czech Republic and the United Kingdom) signed in March 2012, presents national governments with blame-shifting opportunities. These governments need to retrench in order to meet the criteria of the Fiscal Compact, such as national budgets being in balance or in surplus within one year after the Compact entered into force (which was January 2013). Moreover, it will help politicians to *find a scapegoat* – another Coalition Logic strategy for avoiding blame – thereby shifting responsibility for cost containment operations whenever they get into trouble. This can be used by all governments, because it is also possible to scapegoat intangible aspects (e.g., that the economy is to blame).

A final blame avoidance strategy that fits under the umbrella Coalition Logic strategy is Pierson's (1994) division strategy. With this strategy, reforms only affect certain groups but not others. This is, for instance, what has happened with the reforms that have led to dualization in the continental welfare states (see Chapter 8).

D. Domain Manipulation Strategy

The first three types of blame avoidance strategies are frequently discussed in the literature, even though they are seldom empirically identified (but see Fernandez 2010; Prince 2010; Sulitzeanu-Kenan 2010; Hood 2011). Here we propose a new type of strategy (cf. Vis and Van Kersbergen 2007). Drawing on our prospect-theoretical approach outlined earlier, we can identify strategies that governments can use not so much to avoid blame directly but to influence the voters' domain and thus avoid blame indirectly. They can do so by trying to make voters more risk-accepting and hence less likely to punish the government for the reform by vote switching.[5] A first example of this strategy is *damned if you do, damned if you don't*. With this strategy governments try to manipulate the domain of the voter so that the gains domain is reframed into a losses domain. It is essentially an attempt to make plausible that no matter which party or government rules, the reform will take place because the status quo is untenable. This strategy may be found in major government communication and information campaigns that explain the necessity of reform such as cost containment measures, implying that the status quo is no longer tenable and that no other options but the proposed reforms are

---

[5] The blame avoidance strategy we propose resembles Elmelund-Præstekær and Emmenegger's (2013) strategic reframing strategy. A strategic reframing strategy aims to reframe an originally unpopular reform into a "popular" one, hence turning the reform into a potential vote winner. According to Elmelund-Præstekær and Emmenegger (28), our domain-shifting blame avoidance strategies still assume that "retrenchment is [i]nstrinsically unpopular (even) if a government can survive harsh retrenchment by means of strategic framing." However, our account allows for originally unpopular reforms to possibly win the government votes, that is to say, if the government successfully reframes the voters' domain from gains into losses, so that voters also want reform (see Table 9.1). But given the existence of the negativity effect, we consider it very unlikely that when the government's framing strategy fails, "punishment in terms of lost votes is smaller than the amount of votes to be won in case of a successful framing strategy" (Elmelund-Præstekær and Emmenegger 2013: 31).

available. The intended effect is twofold: it reframes the domain of voters into losses, making the public risk-acceptant, and defines the political position of the opposition party (or parties) as fundamentally identical to the policy stance of the government. An example would be the campaign that the Danish government launched in January 2011 after it had announced the abolishment of the popular early retirement scheme (*efterløn*) to convince the public of the necessity of the reform. It consisted of page-sized advertisements that informed the public about the sorry state of Denmark's welfare state with the help of very alarming graphs and statistics that left only one conclusion: doing nothing is no option.

A second example of a Domain Manipulation Strategy is *creative accounting* and *lies, damn lies, and statistics*. With this strategy governments try to redefine the terms according to which the outcomes are measured that are feared to have negative consequences, once again to change the domain of voters from gains into losses. This strategy simply tries to hide the effects of cost containment and recommodification measures by redefining the standards of accounting. For instance, in order to stimulate a losses domain among the public, a government may publish future scenarios that are based on assumptions that are known to lead to bad results. Slightly adjusting or not incorporating estimated productivity growth, for instance, has a huge impact on the predicted costs of aging.

9.7. CONCLUSION

Welfare state reform may be necessary in the light of "objective" functional pressures, but it is not guaranteed to take place, if only because some political actors have an (electoral) interest in letting policies drift. However, in a democratic political context, political actors who are convinced that reform is necessary and are willing to act accordingly, still find it, sometimes prohibitively, difficult to implement their preferred reforms. Welfare state reforms tend to be risky in that they go against the interests or preferences of a substantial segment of the voters. As a result, such reforms not only face powerful institutional restrictions but are also likely to prompt electoral retaliation. Yet such electorally risky welfare state reform does happen. To explain why political actors pursue risky reforms, we proposed an account inspired by prospect theory. One of prospect theory's central findings is that people are risk-accepting in the domain of losses and risk-averse in the domain of gains. Consequently, political actors will abstain from reforming if they are in a gains domain, even if they are convinced that reforms are necessary. They will pursue risky reform policies if the status quo is no longer seen as tenable, that is, when they find themselves in a losses domain, even if they would rather prefer to let policies drift. The existence of a losses domain is thus a key condition for political actors to act upon "objective" functional pressures and implement risky reforms to address these.

Prospect theory furthermore predicts that reforms can be implemented relatively easily if the voters consider themselves to be in a losses domain as well, while voters will oppose reforms if they consider themselves to be in a gains domain. The former situation is, however, unlikely to arise in the context of the welfare state. This discrepancy between political actors' attitude – a willingness to pursue risky reform – and voters' attitude – opposing the reform – indicates that political actors wanting to get away electorally with the reform need to invoke one or more strategies to avoid the possible blame. Different from a large part of the literature that takes blame avoidance strategies to explain the resilience of welfare states, we proposed to view them as strategies that avoid the blame that accompanies risky welfare state reform. In addition to well-known strategies such as finding a scapegoat, we introduced two new blame avoidance strategies inspired by prospect theory: (1) damned if you do, damned if you don't, and (2) creative accounting and lies, damn, lies and statistics. The former strategy aims to manipulate the voters' domain so that they no longer find themselves in a gains domain but in a losses domain. This makes the voter risk-acceptant, like the government is, and allows the government to pursue the reform without having to suffer the electoral consequences. This is because the originally risky reform is now also the voters' preference. The second strategy also strives to change the voters' domain, but now by redefining the terms according to which the outcomes are measured, that is, hiding the effects of the reform. By bringing prospect theory and the theory of blame avoidance together, we add additional theoretical baggage to our open functional approach to welfare state reform. Prospect theory offers insights into *when* political actors respond to the "objective" functional pressures and the theory of blame avoidance provides understanding of *how* they can do this.

In the final chapter of the book, we turn to what perhaps is *the* test case for whether and how "objective" functional pressures affect political actors' ideas and actions as regards welfare state reform: the financial crisis and its economic aftermath since 2008. We examine the extent to which functional pressures have been building up further as a consequence of the crisis and study the results hereof.

10

Can and Will the Welfare State Survive the Great Recession?

10.1. WHAT HAVE WE LEARNED SO FAR? ANSWERS TO THE "BIG" QUESTIONS

In this book, we asked "big" questions about the welfare state in order to uncover, map, and explain the political opportunities and constraints of different types of welfare state reform in advanced capitalist democracies. We have one "big" question to go: can and will the welfare state survive the Great Recession (Bermeo and Pontusson 2012a) – the economic downturn that followed the financial crisis in 2008 and, in Europe, was aggravated by a series of sovereign debt crises? Before we can tackle that question properly and directly, we first shortly present the answers to the big questions we have answered so far and that can help us answer the final one.

Why did we need a welfare state in the first place and how did we get it? All welfare states have their origin in the need to respond to the socially disruptive consequences of modernization. The fast economic and social developments in the 19th century created unfettered capitalist labor markets that resulted in massive dislocation, poverty, and misery. Labor legislation arose everywhere as a counter force to the disruption caused by these labor markets. Early social insurance legislation directly addressed the social risks of the market-based industrial society but was also designed to foster the political integration of the working class and to assist national state-building. Increasingly, the whole edifice of social policies and the welfare state came to revolve around the realization that the type of social risks that emerge in capitalist market societies cannot be covered by the family and that markets are notoriously ill-equipped to deal with these risks. Hence, it was the state that had to take the responsibility for organizing social protection by pooling and redistributing social risks.

How exactly this was done and with what consequences was largely a matter of which political actors and coalitions under which societal conditions were powerful enough to impose their preferred solution to the problems associated with social risk protection. This, in a nutshell, answers the big question: *why did we get different worlds of welfare?* Certain types of cleavage structures in combination with specific electoral systems explain why in some cases and not in others the middle class became part of the pro-welfare political coalitions. The inclusion of the middle class implied a significant move away from what we now identify as the liberal, residual welfare state that almost exclusively targets the poor and assumes that the market provides insurance. Where the (agrarian) middle class coalesced with the working class's representative, social democracy, the most encompassing and redistributive version of the welfare state emerged. If the welfare state was built with the help of the cross-class Christian democrats in various coalitions, the welfare state became particularistic, not very redistributive, but not quite residual either.

Do we still have these different worlds of welfare? Yes, to an amazing extent; replication studies and newly gathered data show that at least until the mid-2000s and in spite of major adaptation, updating, retrenchment, and restructuring, there are still different types of welfare states that come with distinct sorts of problems for reform.

What do welfare states actually do? The answer to this big question is – *a lot.* Although we stressed that measuring the impact of the welfare state on social outcomes, such as poverty and inequality, is difficult to do in any precise way, our analysis also demonstrated that it covers citizens against old social risks (e.g., unemployment, sickness, and old age) and, at least to some extent, against new risks also (e.g., the problem of reconciling work and family). Welfare states also fight poverty and reduce income inequality. Regime differences are vast, however. The social democratic regime is comprehensive in its social risk coverage, egalitarian, and effective in its poverty reduction. The liberal regime is at the opposite end and the conservative regime is somewhat in the middle. Moreover, there is also substantial variation within the regimes, especially the conservative one.

Why do we need to reform the welfare state? First, because we found that no welfare state offers full coverage of social risks, prevents poverty entirely, and is capable of continuing to reduce income inequality, reform is needed. Second, we need to reform the welfare state because globalization generates major pressures to adapt, either "positively" so as to compensate domestically for the social costs of economic integration via expansionary social policies, or "negatively" so as to concede to capital demands by rolling back the welfare state, taxes, and social expenditures. Third, the postindustrialization of society has created a new social risk structure that fundamentally challenges the existing social policy arrangements financially, organizationally, and politically. In short, welfare state reform is a necessity.

Necessary as welfare state reform may be, there is no guarantee that it will happen. There are powerful institutional forces and embedded insider interests at work that defend the welfare status quo or adapt the welfare state in such a way that the insiders are defended at the cost of outsiders. We also know that, generally speaking, welfare state reform is risky business electorally, because voters simply do not like reform and are likely to punish the government for it (especially social democrat parties, Christian democratic parties, and socialist parties). So, *why do politicians and governments pursue electorally risky reforms?* They would never take such a risk unless they deemed their political situation (popularity, the socioeconomic condition of their country) as a "loss" and unless pursuing a risky reform has a (slight) chance to improve their situation. Just to be on the safe side, politicians and governments will try to design their reform package in such a way that allows them to avoid the voters' blame.

10.2. THE FINAL "BIG" QUESTION: CAN AND WILL THE WELFARE STATE SURVIVE THE GREAT RECESSION?

In the previous chapters, we have argued that welfare state reform has been continuous, sometimes radical, at other times incremental, and always difficult. We examined the variation across countries, across welfare state regimes, and over time, and mapped the "objective" pressures from without and from within that push for different types of welfare state reform. We have shown that these pressures are already formidable and that the welfare state is never safe. In this final chapter, we examine whether and to what extent perhaps the biggest "objective" functional pressure in decades, the financial crisis and its economic aftermath since 2008, is threatening to ravage the welfare state's edifice. Did the financial crisis imply a sudden increase in the functional pressures to reform? Did it open up new political opportunities for hitherto unfeasible reform by pulling politicians and governments into a (socioeconomic) domain of losses? Did policymakers react by radically cutting back social spending? Or did the adaptive capacity of the welfare state and the flexibility of its institutions prove to be such that they can endure even the economic repercussions of the financial crisis? To answer these and related questions, we examine (1) the effects of the crisis (e.g., the changes in growth rates and unemployment levels), assessing how these effects influence the domain in which governments find themselves; (2) the political responses to the crisis (i.e., the reform measures taken, or the decisions to abstain from action) and their underlying ideas as causal beliefs; and (3) the possible shift in public opinion on welfare state issues (e.g., whether the crisis make citizens more willing to accept unpopular initiatives, such as higher retirement ages).

We propose that the political opportunities of reform and the willingness of governments to act on these opportunities will be highest when three conditions are met: the functional pressures have been building up to such an extent that the political actors enter a domain of losses; ideas as causal beliefs on how to solve the crisis suggest welfare state reform; and public opinion is (more) open to reform initiatives. To assess this hypothesis, we zoom in on the selected representatives of the three welfare regimes: Germany, the United Kingdom, the United States, Sweden, Denmark, and the Netherlands. Our case selection allows us to examine how much functional pressures for reform (e.g., rising unemployment) affect public opinion and hence the political opportunities for reform, and to what extent this translates into noticeable policy responses (i.e., the policy measures to deal with the effects of the crisis). Each individual country offers, so to speak, a natural experiment where the (1) "objective" functional pressures, (2) the political opportunities for reform, and (3) the political choices as regards welfare state reform can be compared *pre-test* (i.e., before the financial crisis) and *post-test* (i.e., after it has had its impact). The economic effects of the crisis are still unfolding, and new and grave financial difficulties (the sovereign debt crisis in the eurozone) are adding to an already considerable sense of crisis. In other words, in this chapter we are dealing with a moving target, and this post-test cannot be as "clean" as we would want it to be. Still, our focus on countries from different welfare state regimes enables us to see whether regime differences are still producing different political and policy responses, or whether the functional pressures of financial markets force governments to opt for roughly similar solutions. In this sense, our analysis offers an important illustration of the analytical usefulness of our open functional approach.

10.3. DOES THE GREAT RECESSION INDUCE MAJOR WELFARE STATE REFORM?

Are the financial crisis of 2008 and its economic aftershocks spurring major reform efforts in key social policy domains in Western welfare states?[1] It is interesting to note that in most, if not all, mainstream approaches to welfare state change, financial and economic crises play a theoretical role of instigators of structural and radical reform (see, e.g., Kuipers 2006: chapter 2 for an overview). Recall the typical argument – that although tremendous pressures for reform have been accumulating in the past decades, they generally do not translate into radical reform because of the various institutional and political forces that work against it. A crisis, in the sense of an indubitable threat of immediate breakdown, is assumed to set these forces free and bring about radical reforms more or less instantaneously.

The institutionalist approach, for one, arguably has a good tool box to explain social policy continuity for normal times and what has been termed "progressive change," that is, the kind of adaptation that does not involve a brutal departure from a developmental path but has a specific direction nonetheless (Palier 2010b: 31; see Chapter 2). But an institutionalist analysis would also suggest that a crisis offers a critical juncture at which it is possible to divert from the original path of development and embark upon more

---

[1] The rest of this chapter draws on Vis, Van Kersbergen, and Hylands (2011). Many thanks to Tom Hylands for allowing us to make use of this work.

substantial reform, including harsh retrenchment and major restructuring (see Palier 2010a). Or as Bermeo and Pontusson (2012b: 1) put it: "Crises are surely periods of peril, but they also facilitate change." Similarly, a socioeconomic account would predict that socioeconomic dire straits make functional demands on the political system that are likely to translate into drastic reform at the moment they are perceived or felt as systemic or existential threats (see Schwartz 2001 and Starke 2006 for overviews). Given pressures exerted by the financial crisis and its economic aftershocks, such as rapidly rising levels of unemployment and increasing budget deficits, this perspective predicts radical retrenchment almost as an inescapable and immediate outcome. An ideational account, in turn, would suggest that ideas assume a transformative capacity under extreme conditions. A crisis causes urgent uncertainty and fosters the prompt take-up of groundbreaking and previously unacceptable ideas to transform the welfare state radically and rapidly (see, e.g., Béland and Cox 2011; Stiller 2010). Finally, Iversen and Wren's (1998) service sector trilemma approach would predict a fast transformation of regime-specific paths. In their approach, the governments of the different welfare regimes have to make tough choices about which of three generally desirable yet irreconcilable goals – balanced budgets (fiscal discipline), employment growth, and earnings equality – would have to be sacrificed. Interestingly, and contrary to Iversen and Wren's prediction, the conservative regime did not opt for a continuation of the welfare-without-work path but, like the social democratic regime, has sacrificed budgetary restraint. The liberal regime also went in a slightly different direction from what was expected, by protecting employment at the expense of budgetary restraint (see Table 10.1). All representatives of the welfare regimes were therefore facing a massive task of budget consolidation by 2009. The projected budget deficits for 2013, which Table 10.1 also displays, demonstrate that the deficits in the Netherlands, Denmark, and the United States seem to be falling – albeit from comparatively relatively high levels. In Germany, Sweden, and the United Kingdom, conversely, the projections for 2013 indicate stability compared to 2012. In the two EMU countries (Germany and Sweden), the deficit was already close to zero or in surplus in 2011 and 2012. In the United Kingdom, the deficit remains high (between 6.5 and 7 percent of GDP), which Britain can afford because it does not need to stick to the EMU rules.

The main theoretical perspectives thus converge around the anticipation that the financial crisis in the short run and its economic aftershocks in the somewhat longer run open up an opportunity if not a necessity for radical welfare state reform. Our open functional approach stresses that reform in the context of a continuously changing environment is a permanent feature of welfare state politics, unless policy drift is the outcome of conscious decisions not to adapt. We imagine that the functional pressure to reform has been building up for some time. We hypothesize that this pressure is so large that even in those countries in which radical welfare state reform (including far-reaching social budget cuts) has not been a prominent part of the political agenda, politicians

TABLE 10.1. *Budget surplus/deficit (% of GDP), 2007–2013*

	2007	2008	2009	2010	2011	2012	2013
United Kingdom	−2.8	−5.0	−10.9	−10.1	−8.3	−6.6	−6.9
United States	−2.9	−6.6	−11.9	−11.4	−10.2	−8.5	−6.8
Germany	0.2	−0.1	−3.1	−4.2	−0.8	−0.2	−0.4
Netherlands	0.2	0.5	−5.6	−5.0	−4.4	−3.8	−3.0
Denmark	4.8	3.3	−2.8	−2.7	−2.0	−4.1	−2.1
Sweden	3.6	2.2	−1.0	0.0	0.2	−0.3	−0.8

Notes: A minus indicates a deficit. Data for 2013 are projections.
Source: OECD (2012).

at some point will be pulled into a losses domain. When they find themselves in such a losses domain, they are more willing to contemplate far more radical, and electorally risky, options than they have done before, or to reconsider the social consequences of their decision to let policies drift. For example, the fear that the Euro might collapse in the wake of the Greek sovereign debt crisis and the increasing financial predicament of Ireland, Portugal, Spain, and Italy, and perhaps even France, has led to the appearance on the European political agenda of the hitherto taboo and contentious idea of a European economic government. The recognition that the lack of European economic policy coordination may have worsened the consequences of the financial crisis (Cameron 2012) may be increasing the acceptability of a transfer of competences that would greatly constrain the Member States' autonomy and their domestic capacity to defend their existing welfare arrangements.

Has the Great Recession set in motion a (radical) restructuring of the welfare state and a program of serious cutbacks in social expenditures? Is it already possible to find empirical indications for this that would support the theoretical expectations outlined here? We show that, at least until the second period of profound financial turmoil in 2011, the financial crisis and its economic aftershocks did not – at least not everywhere – lead to radical reform. This stems from a combination of three factors. First, there is the high political hurdle because of citizens' continuing – and in some countries even increasingly – positive attitude toward the welfare state. Second, in the first phases of response to the crisis, strong ideas on radical welfare state retrenchment or restructuring as a solution to the crisis were absent. If anything, expansion of social policies was considered the "good idea." Third and finally, even though the crisis was very real when it commenced in 2008, its effects on the real economy were limited at first. Only when the aftershocks of the crisis continued to be felt and the sovereign debt crisis hit the eurozone did the functional pressures become so large that they began to threaten the entire system. It is at that point that politicians and governments moved into a domain of socioeconomic losses and gradually became more willing to pursue types of reform until then considered unacceptable. Since then, governments increasingly have adhered to the "dangerous idea" of austerity (Blyth 2013) and have pursued draconian budget cuts to allow them to pay for the private debt they have taken on (e.g., through bank bailouts) and turned into public debt.

We conducted a qualitative content analysis of national public debates in print and online media, focusing on how governments dealt with the crisis aftershocks between October 2009 and August 2011.[2] The analysis shows that despite substantial cross-national differences, the early, first responses to the crisis by and large were similar everywhere. Different from their responses to the crises in the 1970s and 1980s, governments did not immediately respond with cutbacks or radical restructuring. On the contrary, the initial response of all governments was to reserve or invest resources to support or bail out banks and, somewhat later, industrial sectors. All governments acted on the same idea. With a seemingly unprecedented, but ultimately also unsuccessful, attempt at international coordination (see Cameron 2012), all countries embarked upon a fairly classical Keynesian intervention (see Armingeon 2012; Clasen et al. 2012; Pontusson and Raess 2012; Starke et al. 2013: chapter 6), first, to prevent the collapse of the banking sector, and second, to prevent a massive drop in demand for goods and services. In this first phase, the similarity in response across these very different welfare states is what is most striking. In the second phase, it became rapidly clear that in spite of the interventions, the financial crisis had started to hit the real economy and was causing an economic downturn that threatened to turn into a recession, with severe consequences for the labor market. Consequently, all countries expanded social programs or adjusted them to cushion the shock of the crisis and the expected economic malaise. Again, there was much similarity in very different countries in their responses, with most countries making an effort to prevent mass unemployment and to ensure that laid-off workers would retain their relation with the labor market (for example, through "part-time unemployment," where employees retain their contracts but work fewer paid hours than before).

However, since then we have entered a third phase in the response to the financial crisis and its economic aftershocks. The Keynesian intervention and the resulting protective measures were a costly affair and they caused already growing budget deficits and the public debt to increase even more rapidly and in many countries beyond acceptable levels. In some cases (Greece, Italy), financial markets responded furiously by demanding prohibitively high interest rates on government loans to refinance debts. It might be that the existing

---

[2] For the qualitative content analysis we used search functions on the following websites: LexisNexis, the Economist, OECD, ICPSR, and Google News. LexisNexis search sources included: Major U.S. and World Publications, News Wire Services, TV and Radio Broadcast Transcripts, and Web Publications. We used the search terms: "public opinion," "welfare state," "social policy," reform, change, amendment, initiative, development, economic, crisis, "credit crunch," Germany, US, USA, "United States," America, UK, "Great Britain," "United Kingdom," Sweden, Denmark, Italy, Netherlands.

theoretical perspectives will prove to be right in the end if the crisis and the policy responses turn out to have been revolutionizing the social and political foundations of the welfare state consensus to the extent that a more radical overhaul has become a reality. Our open functional approach, however, offers a more precise account than these perspectives can present of why this is the case. If the pessimistic (realistic?) economists are right (e.g., Stiglitz 2010) and the world economy is not recovering quickly, also precisely because governments discontinue to stimulate demand, the cumulative effects of lower tax income and social security contributions, continuing expensive financial support policies, and rising social expenditures are likely to further deteriorate the already dire budgetary condition of the welfare states, adding to the functional pressure for radical reform exerted, for example, by speculative financial markets. Such dire straits could very well pull citizens into a domain of socioeconomic losses as well, thereby lowering substantially the political hurdle for radical welfare state reform.

Summing up, while governments' responses in the first and second phases did not have the instant effect of triggering policies that harm core social programs, during the third phase we see an increasingly keen and nervous awareness of budgetary stress and commitment to cutbacks everywhere. The idea as causal belief that reforming the welfare state will help to reduce at least some of the negative effects of the crises is gaining ground. In fact, we see that radical retrenchment and restructuring have been capturing the political agenda in many nations. Ironically, governments are forced to find increasingly more drastic and far-reaching ways to cope with the gaping budget deficits that they created in an attempt to solve the ensuing monetary crisis that they did not cause. Still, the functional pressure for radical reform is not felt with equal strength everywhere, and national political systems offer different solutions to the pressures that seem similar. The governments we focus on differ in the specific ideas they have about what such reform should look like, but governments from the same regime resemble one another to some extent. In other words, even if there has been some convergence in welfare state politics and policies in the initial responses to the crises, we now see regime differences reemerging.

10.4. SIMILAR PRESSURES?

To what extent did Denmark, Germany, the Netherlands, Sweden, the United Kingdom, and the United States face similar functional pressures as a result of the financial crisis and its aftershocks? Important indicators for the state of the economy and the fate of the welfare state are the level and change in unemployment. Figure 10.1 displays the development of the harmonized unemployment rates in these six countries from the first quarter in 2008 (Q108) to the second quarter of 2011 (Q211). Overall, the level of unemployment displayed an upward trend until late 2009, early 2010. As of the second quarter of 2010 (Q210), this level started to fall a bit, but remained (very) high nonetheless. More specifically, until

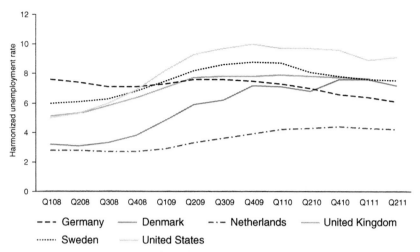

FIGURE 10.1. Development of harmonized unemployment rates, 2008–2011.
Notes: Unemployment rates adjusted for seasonal variation; entries are the 1st quarter of 2008, the 2nd quarter of 2008, et cetera. Data for Q210 for Sweden and the United Kingdom are estimates.
Source: OECD (2010a, 2011).

early 2010, the unemployment level rose substantially in Sweden, the United Kingdom, and the United States. The increase was particularly sharp from the third quarter of 2008 (Q308) onward. This was also when unemployment started to increase in Denmark, in fact almost doubling between Q308 and Q309 from 3.3 percent to 6.2 percent. In the Netherlands, unemployment levels had risen as of Q409, although less than in the other countries (except Germany). Germany is the outlier in terms of unemployment, because the level did not rise throughout the period we study. However, because Germany already had 7.6 percent unemployment, it had the poorest performance in terms of unemployment of these six countries. By Q409, this was no longer the case: the United States (10 percent) had the worst unemployment rate, trailed by Sweden (8.9 percent). Despite the differences among the countries, these figures show that unemployment was clearly a common problem and thus a pressure that had to be dealt with in all the countries examined. Precisely because of how governments addressed this pressure initially – for instance, by initiating or extending part-time unemployment schemes – made that citizens – expressed in prospect theoretical terms, see Chapter 9 – remained in their domain of gains. The rise in unemployment, and especially how this rise was felt in their purses, was not yet high enough to make citizens willing to accept radical reform measures, and they continued to express faith in the welfare state (see later).

The surge in unemployment is a symptom of interlinked problems that all countries faced. The banking sector in developed democracies had serious credibility and stability problems, with many banks requiring very large sums of capital injections. In the period we looked at (until 2011), the Swedish government spent the smallest amount among our six cases in helping banks that were in trouble, namely, €5 billion (about 1.5 percent of GDP). Compared to banks in other countries, the Swedish banks were less eager to take this money because of the heavy conditions attached, and these conditions were a result of lessons learned in the banking crisis that Sweden had faced in the early 1990s (see, e.g., Englund 1999). In terms of numbers, the Danish government was next in line, with two rounds of capital injections to solve the capital deficiency in the banking sector, totaling around €18 billion (about 8 percent of GDP). In addition, the government intervened after the collapse of two of Denmark's (albeit relatively small) banks, covering the losses. The situation was similar in the Netherlands, where the government spent about €20 billion to take over a bank and another €20 billion on capital injections (about 7 percent of GDP) to assist banks and to prevent them from collapsing. The German figures were substantially higher: in December 2008, the German parliament approved capital injections of €480 billion (about 20 percent of GDP). The American response resembled that of Germany in terms of the absolute level of spending, with capital injections amounting to $700 (€519) billion (about 5 percent of GDP). The United Kingdom topped this figure, with £850 (€960) billion of expenditures (about 60 percent of GDP). Although the exact figures vary across the six cases, the trend indicates that the banking sector in each country required massive government assistance to survive the crisis. The problems in the banking sector affected governments' and politicians' situation, especially because of the (very) high costs involved in the bailouts and capital injections. Yet, again, it is unlikely that in this period citizens were en masse finding themselves in a domain of losses.

Unemployment also rose because of falling exports, caused by universally lower consumer confidence. Figure 10.2 shows exports in goods in billions of US dollars in our six countries from the final quarter of 2008 to the final quarter of 2010. Exports fell everywhere between Q408 and Q109. The highest reduction took place in Sweden (−15.9 percent), trailed by the United Kingdom (−15 percent), the United States (−14.3 percent) and, at some distance, the Netherlands (−12.9 percent), Germany (−10.7 percent), and Denmark (−8.7 percent). In most countries, exports picked up after the first quarter of 2009, but not in Germany (another 2 percent reduction) and the United States (−1.3 percent). Between the second and fourth quarters of 2009, all countries saw their exports increase again, despite an occasional drop (such as the 7.5 percent reduction in exports in Denmark between Q409 and Q210).

The increase in unemployment, the expenditures to uphold the banking sector, and the reduction in exports are some of the factors that put government budgets under pressure. Table 10.1, which displays the budget surpluses or deficits in the six countries between 2007 and 2010, demonstrates that in 2007 and 2008, Denmark, Sweden, Germany, and the Netherlands were still running

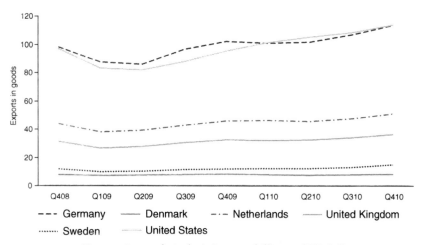

FIGURE 10.2. Exports in goods (value), in 2005 billions of US dollars, 2008–2010.
Source: OECD (2010a, 2011).

budget surpluses – albeit only small ones in the latter two cases. As of 2009, these countries also faced budget deficits, although in Sweden the deficit was only 0.7 percent of GDP. In the United Kingdom and the United States, which had budget deficits already in 2007 and 2008, the effects of the financial crisis boosted the deficit substantially: in the United Kingdom from 5 percent in 2008 to over 11 percent in 2009; in the United States from around 3 percent in 2008 to 10 percent in 2010. Although the level of the budget deficit decreased somewhat between 2009 and 2010 in most countries (the United Kingdom, the United States, the Netherlands, and Sweden – in the latter even to 0 percent, i.e., a balanced budget) and remained stable in another (Denmark), it is clear that the sharply rising and in some cases very high budget deficits were a problem everywhere.

Overall, the data on unemployment, the banking sector, exports, and budget deficits show that our six countries largely were dealing with similar problems. Did these similar problems evoke similar initial responses?

10.5. SIMILAR RESPONSES?

Which measures have the American, British, Danish, Dutch, German, and Swedish governments taken to cope with the adverse effects of the crisis? As indicated, since we are dealing with a moving target, many proposals are still being developed, are under debate, and are sometimes withdrawn or expanded. To get at least some idea of what has been going on, we have been collecting data on government responses from various sources (see footnote 2). Table 10.2 summarizes the measures taken in the first and second phases (late 2008 until

TABLE 10.2. *Summary of crisis measures taken in phases I and II*

	US	NL	UK	DE	DK	SW
Keynesian measures						
Investing in jobs	٧	٧	٧	٧	٧	٧
Investing in infrastructure				٧		
Tax measures				٧		٧
Tax relief				٧	٧	
Monetary policy						
Lowering interest rate	٧	٧	٧	٧	٧	٧
Money creation			٧			
Buying government bonds			٧			
Circumventing bankruptcy						
Guarantees on problem bank assets	٧					
Financial support to banks or companies	٧	٧	٧	٧	٧	٧
Takeover of banks		٧			٧	
Liquidity fund for banks					٧	
Reestablishing trust in banking sector						
Guarantees on savings (or increasing its level)		٧		٧	٧	٧
Guarantees for interbank lending		٧				
Increase of supervision		٧				

Notes: A "٧" in the table indicates that one or more measures were taken that fall under a specific category (such as investing in jobs). To assess whether a particular measure was taken, we conducted a qualitative content analysis of written and (online) media sources (see footnote 2). Tax measures are, for instance, increases in the Value Added Tax (VAT).

US = United States; NL = the Netherlands; UK = United Kingdom; DE = Germany; DK = Denmark; SW= Sweden.

early 2010) of governments' responses to the financial crisis and its economic aftershocks. This summary indicates the absence of the idea that radical welfare state reform can address the effects of the crisis. It is rather the expansion of policies that seems the "good idea" on which governments act. We subsume their measures under four categories: (1) Keynesian measures (investment in jobs, investment in infrastructure, tax measures such as an increase in Value Added Tax (VAT), and tax relief), (2) monetary policy (lowering interest rates, money creation, buying government bonds), (3) circumventing bankruptcy (creation of "bad" banks, guarantees on problem assets, financial support to banks or companies, takeover of banks, liquidity fund for banks), and (4) reestablishing trust in the banking sector (guarantees on savings, guarantees of interbank lending, an increase of supervision).

If we look at the indicators under the heading of "circumventing bankruptcy" and "reestablishing trust" in Table 10.2, we observe similar responses. Germany is a special case because in this country a Keynesian type of response seems to have been most systematically formulated.

TABLE 10.3. *Labor market–related measures in phase II*

	US	NL	UK	DE	DK	SW
Labor demand measures						
Job subsidies, recruitment incentives, public job creation			√			√
Reductions in nonwage labor costs					√	√
Short-time working schemes		√		√	√	
Measures to help the unemployed find work						
Activation requirements			√	√		
Job search assistance and matching	√	√	√	√		√
Job finding and business startup incentives			√			
Work experience programs	√		√			√
Training programs	√	√	√	√	√	√

Notes: US = United States; NL = the Netherlands; UK = United Kingdom; DE = Germany; DK = Denmark; SW= Sweden.

Activation requirements mean that the unemployed are required to participate in activation activities, such as a training program.

Sources: Clegg (2010, Table 1 [Compiled from Glassner and Galgoczi (2009); EEO (European Employment Observatory) (2009); European Monitoring Centre on Change http://www.eurofound.europa.eu/emcc/index.htm], Mandl and Salvatore (2009: 12–3), OECD (2009: 3, Table 1).

Our content analysis reveals that in the second response phase the labor market is the area to which most attention has been directed and where policymaking initiatives have been most frequent (and most frequently discussed). Still, the need for more general welfare state reform and major restructuring in the fields of health, education, housing, and pensions continued to be a hot issue. Specifically, our analysis indicates that next to the direct financial predicament, rising unemployment (or the expectation that more jobs will be lost) was by far the greatest worry of all governments. If anywhere, it is thus likely that labor market-related policies were being adjusted in the wake of the financial crisis. Table 10.3 summarizes data on this.

In the United States, for example, unemployment compensation was extended and incentives were created for businesses to hire unemployed workers as part of the American Recovery and Reinvestment Act (February 2009) of $787 billion (€ 546 billion, approximately 5 percent of GDP) (US Recovery Act 2009). Table 10.3 indicates that most countries, although not in all specific fields and to the same extent, formulated new or updated existing measures in the area of both active and passive labor market policies. Our data also indicate that in none of the countries were cuts made in core functions, at least not until 2011. If we examine the details of the measures taken, the United Kingdom stands out. Although it had the lowest score on supportive labor market policies of all the 15 EU countries before the crisis, the government was very reluctant to improve these policies, even temporarily (Clegg 2010). The main measures taken in Britain fall under the heading of active labor market policies. As of January 2009, there was extra support for jobseekers who had been unemployed for more than six months, additional funding for the public employment office (Jobcentre Plus), a bonus of up to £2,500 (€3,000) for employers to hire and train an unemployed person, new training places, work-focused volunteering options, and help to establish a business. The total costs of these measures amounted to approximately £0.5 billion (€553 million). Furthermore, the government was committed to another £1.3 billion (€1.4 billion, about 0.1 percent of GDP) so that those individuals who became unemployed could receive their benefit more quickly (EEO 2009: 15–16). In a comparative perspective, these measures were not that substantial. Overall, the approach to tackling the crisis was characterized mostly by tax cuts in an attempt to boost economic activity (Clegg 2010). Conversely, nothing was done to address those who were becoming unemployed – a feature in which the United Kingdom differs substantially from the rest of Western Europe. Partial unemployment was perhaps the most important of these. In Germany, there was already a partial unemployment scheme in place – in the form of structurally lower working time – which was extended from 6 to 18 months ("stimulus package 1") and was extended further after that. Also the contribution from the government was increased (Clegg 2010).

Our analysis of national public debates in print and online media reveals that after mid-2010, all countries entered a third phase in the response to the financial crisis and its aftershocks. A broad political consensus emerged, an idea as causal belief that substantial cuts needed to be made in the long term to balance the budget. Still, for quite a long period of time, political actors avoided discussing exactly how, where, and when such cuts had to be made. We propose that this was because citizens continued to support the welfare state, which made proposing radical reform electorally hazardous. For instance, the main political parties in the United Kingdom were not specific with numbers on planned cuts during the 2010 election campaign. Moreover, the country was far from the truly dire straits that the EU has been in since then. Still, after the elections the new coalition government (conservatives and liberal democrats) adopted a plan for £30 billion in spending cuts (about €34 billion, about 1.8 percent of GDP) in its June 2010 budget. Proposed measures included an increase in the VAT tax by 2.5 percent (to 20) and a spending reduction of 25 percent over the next four years for all civil service departments, except health and overseas aid. Over the next five years, welfare spending was to be cut by £11 billion (about €13 billion, 0.8 percent of GDP). Child benefits would be frozen, the family tax credit would be reduced, housing benefits would be capped, medicals for disability benefits would be limited, and the increase of eligibility for the state pension from 65 to 66 would be accelerated (European Institute 2010). Total spending cuts by 2014–15 were expected to amount to £81 billion (€90.7 billion, 5.6 percent of GDP) (UK HM Treasury 2010). These cuts, among other things, were likely to hit welfare and public service pensions further (as well as environmental levies). Additionally, the government said it would "radically change the welfare system" (UK HM Treasury 2010: 28) by replacing the current system of means-tested working age benefits with a new Universal Credit that would enable work always to pay. Simultaneously, the government wished to reduce fraud and error through a new approach and implemented a so-called Work Programme for the long-term unemployed. In its 2011 budget, the government planned a total consolidation of £126 billion (about €144 billion, 8.7 percent of GDP) a year by 2015–16, four times more than proposed in the 2010 budget. This amount was to be arrived at through total reductions in spending of £95 billion (about €108 billion, 6.6 percent of GDP) and a net increase in taxes of £30 billion (€34 billion, 2.1 percent of GDP) (UK HM Treasury 2011: 10). This was a retrenchment larger than anything since World War II (Hay 2010; Taylor-Gooby 2011), which put the United Kingdom on a different and leaner spending trajectory than before (Taylor-Gooby and Stoker 2011). Proposed measures included an increase in 2018 in the eligibility age for the state pension, cuts in child benefits, a cap on household benefits based on income levels, a progressive increase in employee contributions, and a freeze in public sector pay. Furthermore, the changes reflected a restructuring of social security, shifting responsibilities to individuals and third parties. The coalition also proposed some measures to stimulate the economy: reducing corporate taxes and cutting taxes for entrepreneurs starting businesses. Investments were to be made in infrastructure and transport projects too. Apprenticeship places as well as work experience places were to be funded so as to stimulate the labor market. Housing policies offering support for first-time buyers and a scheme to support mortgages were extended. Finally, the bank levy, an annual tax on the value of all of the debts of banks, was continued to discourage banks from relying on risky forms of borrowing.

The German center-right government in 2011 also appeared to be committed to meeting tough deficit targets, altering the stance it took in November 2009. At that time, the government decided to inject a stimulus package worth up to €22 billion into the economy by 2010. Prime Minister Merkel declared that spending cuts were out of the question because the government's aim was to keep the economy stable and save jobs. In July 2010, however, the German government agreed on significant cutbacks in a savings plan (*Sparprogramm*), amounting to approximately €80 billion between 2011 and 2014 (about 3 percent of GDP). The package was a mixture of cancellation of existing subsidies, higher taxation, a major reform of the army, public administration reforms, reform of the financial sector, and several – taken on their own – relatively minor benefit cuts and entitlement restrictions (Bundesregierung 2010). Moreover, the 2011 budget stated that unemployment benefits were to be discontinued, old age pension schemes (a unification legacy) were no longer to be reimbursed, and maternal and paternal leave allowances were to be deducted from unemployment benefits. The policy statements of the German government of April

2011 concerned consolidation packages to balance the budget, reflecting the increasing attention for cuts in spending and fiscal discipline. For example, the age of pension eligibility was increased from age 65 to 67, effective as of 2012. There was also a plan to cut back on unemployment benefits so that Germans under 50 would receive only 60 percent of their last salary before taxes for up to a year. At the same time, the savings package reserved €12 billion to invest in education, research, and development (Bundesregierung 2011; Bundesfinanzministerium 2011).

In the Netherlands, the exact cutbacks and their timing dominated the electoral campaign in the spring of 2010, and they were a crucial part of the negotiations during the formation of the center-right coalition government. Cutbacks were projected to be around €18 billion (about 3 percent of GDP), to be raised in case of lower-than-expected growth rates. The aim of the government was to restore a balanced budget by 2015. Proposed measures concerned modest to considerable retrenchments across various sectors, including health, pensions (a gradual increase of the retirement age), childcare, disability, and social assistance.

The Danes faced spending cuts of, for them, a draconian size (€3.2 billion, almost 1.5 percent of GDP). Proposed measures of the conservative government involved the further reduction of the unemployment benefit from four to two years, 20,000 fewer jobs in the public sector, a 5 percent reduction of child benefits, and an increase in the retirement age. At the same time, the government called for further initiatives targeted at the unemployed, including increased traineeship opportunities. To support firms, additional funding for the market for venture capital was to be made available along with a reduction in the corporate tax rate. Furthermore, the government initiated public investments in green transport policy. The new center-left government, which came to power in the fall of 2011, aimed to rebalance the budget by 2020. Yet it also promised to limit inequality and poverty. The main reforms focused on taxes and the labor market. The government wished to increase labor supply and proposed reforms in a range of areas, including activation, social assistance, flexjobs, disability pensions, and education to achieve this. It planned to introduce a large-scale tax reform that would be budget neutral and would significantly lower taxes on labor. It also promised to "kick start" the Danish economy by extra investments in infrastructure, social housing, and subsidies for energy-saving renovation in private housing.[3]

Sweden, with a center-right government, is the only one of our six countries where severe cutbacks in public spending were not envisioned. Sweden benefited from the strict fiscal rules it had already implemented in the 1990s (European Institute 2010). In the Swedish budget bill for 2010, presented in September 2009, the government announced further investments in infrastructure aimed

---

[3] http://www.stm.dk/publikationer/Et_Danmark_der_staar_sammen_11/Regeringsgrundlag_okt_2011.pdf (Accessed December 2011).

at fighting unemployment. Also, the in-work tax credit was expanded as well as support for the short-term unemployed. Pensions were to decrease by 3 percent via the introduction of a three-year moving average, but the income tax for pensioners was reduced. Also, tax exemptions for capital gains and dividends on business-related shares were proposed. Finally, the government announced further investments in health care. In October 2010, the 2011 budget bill was presented. Plans for introducing a general income insurance covering unemployment (a social security reform) were announced. The standard deduction regarding housing sublets was to be increased and was to stimulate housing supply. To fight unemployment, supporting mechanisms were temporarily augmented. Income taxes for pensioners were further reduced and the age of pension of eligibility was increased (Swedish Budget Bill 2010, 2011).

In the United States, the Obama administration succeeded in reforming health care – although this cannot be seen as a reaction to the financial crisis – in 2010. Moreover, credit was made available for small businesses, and tax cuts were introduced. The 2010, 2011, and 2012 budget issues make clear that the attention now has shifted toward budget consolidation (US Budget 2010, 2011, 2012). At least partly as a consequence of the crisis, the United States reached its official maximum debt limit of $14,300 billion (€10,000 billion) in early August 2011. After tiring negotiations, in which the Democrats were pitted against the Republicans, the House of Representatives and the Senate accepted the proposed bill. This bill increased the debt ceiling by $900 billion (€624 billion) and proposed cuts in expenditures of $917 billion (€636 billion). Moreover, it installed a committee to investigate a long-term solution for the debt problem, including even more cutbacks.

10.6. CONTINUING SUPPORT FOR THE WELFARE STATE

We have highlighted some of the financial, economic, and social policy responses to the financial crisis of 2008 and its economic aftershocks in six key advanced welfare states. With our focus on functional pressures, we stressed that the crisis clearly intensified the pressure to reform the welfare state. However, this pressure has not been translated immediately into drastic welfare state reform, as mainstream approaches to welfare state reform would have it. The governments' responses seem to fail to confirm their expectations, because political actors were expected to take the opportunity the crisis offered to implement substantial reforms, but they did not. The fact that governments first jumped to the rescue of the financial sector and then introduced measures to stimulate demand, at the cost of a balanced budget (see Table 10.1), does fit our open functional approach. The governments we focus on here almost all lean right or center-right politically. However, if we expand our focus to other developed democracies, we see that the protective and demand stimulating initial response has occurred regardless of the political leaning of the ruling parties. This is in line with our observation that governments have not yet (entirely) found themselves in a domain of losses. Moreover, during the crisis and its aftershocks, the causal idea still dominated that the welfare state was a crucial institution protecting people from ill fortunes beyond their control. We hypothesize that it was an important precondition for the initial similarity in policy responses that the crisis did not undermine public support for the welfare state's core institutions and the role the institutions play in mitigating the domestic impact of the whims of the global financial markets.

As elaborated in Chapters 2 and 9, one of the major defensive mechanisms of the welfare state against radical reforms and drastic cutbacks concerns public opinion supportive of the status quo. It is important to note that the current crisis differs substantially from the crises of the 1970s and, especially, the 1980s. At those times, the idea was that the "big" (welfare) state was one of the primary *causes* of the crisis, crowding out money for investments and thereby inhibiting economic and employment growth. In sharp contrast, public opinion data now show that the public by and large does not blame the welfare state for the current crisis. In fact, currently the welfare state is viewed as a *solution* to at least some of the problems caused by the financial sector and the economic aftershocks.

There are two mechanisms that can bolster support for the welfare state in the wake of the financial crisis. If public opinion is supportive of the welfare state, this increases welfare-friendly policies. But social policies in place also increase their own support once needed most, as in the current crisis. Together, these two mechanisms work against the dramatic scaling back of the welfare state. To see whether the current crisis has been undermining public support for the welfare state, we would have to await the results of public opinion research. A study of welfare state attitudes in Denmark, France, and the United Kingdom shows that support for the welfare state remains high, especially for traditional social protection (i.e., covering "old risks") (Diamond and Lodge 2013). Also, the data from our content analysis (see footnote 2) seem to indicate that there is indeed continuing support for the welfare state in spite of the mounting financial constraints that limit the extent to which governments can meet such demands. In fact, we find indications that voters cherish the welfare state even more because of the crisis, because it shields people from losing their jobs or protects their income in case of unemployment (see Margalit 2013).

Between the liberal regime countries, the United States and the United Kingdom, there is some degree of divergence in public outlook. While a late 2009 Ipsos-MORI poll in the Britain showed that voters there were not ready for spending cuts, Gallup polls indicate that a slight majority of Americans accept the need for temporary government expansion, but that a very large majority want it wound back either immediately or as soon as the crisis is resolved (Ipsos MORI 2009; Gallup 2009a, 2009b).

From our analysis and the literature, we can draw some tentative general conclusions. First, it seems that the crisis and its aftershocks are increasing rather than decreasing public support for welfare provision (see Blekesaune and Quadagno 2003). In fact, recent research shows that the Great Recession has a big positive impact on public preferences, even in the least likely case: as U.S. citizens faced the increased risk of unemployment, they also became considerably more pro-welfare (Margalit 2013). This fits other work showing that popular demand for social protection is a combined function of the risk exposure and income of individuals (Rehm 2011; Rehm et al. 2012). Second, social policy remains a salient issue that the public has relatively clear and coherent views on, as a result of which public opinion continues to influence government policymaking and action (see Burstein 1998). For example, in Scandinavian elections, social policy always ranks among the top salient issues (Oscarsson and Holmberg 2008: 54; Karlsen and Aardal 2011: 134). Third, governments are responding with increased support for the welfare state where possible (see Brooks and Manza 2006b). Quite clearly, a pro-welfare state rhetoric is still dominating in most countries, in spite of frequently expressed worries about the need to balance the budget. We infer that in the near future many political systems are likely to experience an increased political tension between the popular demand to uphold welfare arrangements and the financial and economic (functional) demands to balance the budget. It is likely that activation and maximization of labor market participation (including, for instance, an extension of the pension age) are elements of the solution promoted in the wake of the crisis. Contrary to Brooks and Manza (2007), we expect domain-specific trade-offs to occur where specific domains receive extra support at the expense of less-salient domains, in spite of the fact that increases in aggregate welfare state effort or in welfare state generosity are limited because of budgetary constraints.

If we look at the Ipsos-MORI polls of 2009, for instance, we observe that the UK public was willing to accept government spending cuts but refused to accept cuts on health care. A Financial Times/Harris Poll (2010) supports this result. Only 8 percent of Britons thought that health care should bear the biggest part of the spending cut burden. Interestingly, the same poll shows that a little over 50 percent of Britons considered it acceptable that unemployment benefits were cut the most. In this respect, the United Kingdom differed radically from the United States where only 22 percent considered this the best policy to cut, which is about the same level as in Germany. Another interesting finding is that around 70 percent of the respondents in the United States, Britain, and Germany agreed with the statement that "the large budget deficits and the spending cuts that have happened or been proposed call for a reexamination of Europe's welfare states." Unfortunately, the poll did not provide any information about what this reexamination should look like.

It may be that the public holds contradictory views: the expensive welfare state is heartily supported, but so are cuts in government spending (see Schumacher et al. 2013). Nevertheless, we conclude that the welfare state is still cherished as a major protection against the impact of financial and economic shocks. The continued public support for the welfare state is proving to be quite robust, especially now that expensive social policy is not blamed for the financial crisis, as was the case with the 1980s crisis. The welfare state, then, is typically included in the political solutions for the crisis. The data on public opinion and on policy developments in the United Kingdom, the United States, Germany, the Netherlands, Denmark, and Sweden reveal the public's continued support for and trust in the welfare state.

10.7. CONCLUSION

Welfare states face common problems, including rising unemployment, reduced credibility of the banking sector, falling exports, and rising budget deficits. This partly explains the remarkable commonality in governments' reactions across the board. However, the immediate response to help the financial sector and to protect demand has been an immensely costly affair and ushered in a third phase in the response to the Great Recession. Labor market policy and banking reform have clearly received the most attention in the first phase, but measures have also been taken or are being considered in other policy areas, such as pensions and housing, announcing the arrival of a more austere period to restore balanced budgets. The theme that runs throughout is that spending has been, albeit temporarily, increased in key areas, as governments tried to support those who were adversely affected by the Great Recession. However, a broadly shared political conviction (idea as causal belief) has developed that the costly initial response is not sustainable in the long run because it has caused deficit spending to rise dramatically.

The third phase is characterized by an emerging political agreement, inculcated by the responses of financial markets, that deficit spending has reached its limits. Consequently, the politics of reform increasingly has come to revolve around the question of who pays what, when, and how, or in other words, who will carry the heavy burden of financial and economic recovery. The crucial political issues are to determine whether a swift return to a balanced budget is a *conditio sine qua non* for economic recovery, and if so, whether drastic retrenchment or a substantial increase in taxes is the key. Governments in some of our countries (especially the United Kingdom, Germany, Denmark, and the Netherlands; see Vis et al. 2013) have already agreed on significant public spending cuts that may or may not add up to drastic reforms and induce new distributional conflicts. Such decisions might spark public resistance as occurred in Greece or Spain, because the crisis has also bolstered public support for the welfare state. Public opinion remains an important factor in determining the timing, extent, and pace of social spending cuts. In addition, the well-known resilience mechanisms of long- and well-established social programs will be automatically triggered by such measures, making outcomes uncertain.

Our conclusion is twofold. On the one hand, and in line with our open functional approach and prospect-theoretical account, we found that so far there has not been a major onslaught against the welfare state in the immediate wake of the financial crisis. On the other hand, and again in line with our expectations, we observe that increasingly drastic spending cuts are envisaged and already carried through. Still, for a variety of political and institutional reasons, a considerable gap will probably remain between the intentions and achievements of retrenching governments. The functional pressures that impel radical reform have gained further strength, yes, but the welfare state is simply not that easily toppled. This, however, does not imply that there has been no welfare state reform or change. In fact, as we stressed throughout the book, reform is a continuous feature of the politics and policies of the welfare state. During the last 20 years or so, welfare states have continually adjusted to new economic and social demands, and governments have pursued, albeit with considerable variation, apparently well-adapted and innovative social policies. But under increasing functional stress, especially in the wake of large budget deficits and pressures from financial markets, it is not evident that core social programs can be protected through reform; they may become victims of the pending distributional battles or of further policy drift. Welfare states have been remarkably flexible and capable in their adjustment to their permanently changing environments. Their core social arrangements remain highly popular so that any attempt at a radical overhaul continues to meet public resistance. Yet, severe budgetary problems, the unpredictable but threatening responses of financial markets, and the real economic consequences of the financial crisis not only press for further reform but possibly undermine the political capacity to implement those reforms needed to guarantee the continued protection of people against social risks that the welfare state has so far offered.

References

Abrahamson, Peter (1999). "The Welfare Modelling Business," *Social Policy & Administration*, 33(4): 394–415.

Adelantado, José, and Calderón, Eduardo, C. (2006). "Globalization and the Welfare State: The Same Strategies for Similar Problems?" *Journal of European Social Policy*, 16(4): 374–86.

Adema, Willem (2000). "Revisiting Real Social Spending across Countries: A Brief Note," *OECD Economic Studies*, 30(1): 191–97.

Adema, Willem, and Ladaique, Maxime (2009). "How Expensive Is the Welfare State? Gross and Net Indicators in the OECD Social Expenditure Database (SOCX)," *OECD Social, Employment and Migration Working Papers*, No. 92. Paris: OECD. http://www.oecd-ilibrary.org/docserver/download/fulltext/5ks712h5cg7l.pdf?expi res=1287748439andid=0000andaccname=guestandchecksum=2C5A8369C614B 561A10DB53F80AB24B8 (accessed October 2010).

Adserà, Alcia, and Boix, Carles (2002). "Trade, Democracy and the Size of the Public Sector: The Political Underpinnings of Openness," *International Organization*, 56(2): 229–62.

Adviescommissie Arbeidsongeschiktheid (2001). *Werk Maken van Arbeidsgeschiktheid* [Making Work of the Ability to Work]. The Netherlands: The Hague. http://www. ohcbv.nl/hulppagina/documenten/rapportdonner2.pdf (accessed July 2011).

Afonso, Alexandre (2013). *Social Concertation in Times of Austerity. European Integration and the Politics of Labour Market Reforms in Austria and Switzerland.* Amsterdam: Amsterdam University Press.

Akalis, Scott A. (2008). "A New Spin on Losses Looming Larger than Gains: Asymmetric Implicit Associations from Slot Machine Experience," *Journal of Behavioral Decision Making*, 21(4): 378–98.

Albæk, Erik, Eliason, Leslie C., Nørgaard, Asbjorn S., and Schwartz, Herman M. (eds.) (2008). *Crisis, Miracles, and Beyond: Negotiated Adaptation of the Danish Welfare State.* Aarhus: Aarhus University Press.

Alber, Jens (1981). "Government Responses to the Challenge of Unemployment: The Development of Unemployment Insurance in Western Europe." In Flora and Heidenheimer (eds.) (1981a), pp. 151–83.

(1982). *Vom Armenhaus zum Wohlfahrtsstaat. Analysen zur Entwicklung der Sozialversicherung in Westeuropa*. Frankfurt and New York: Campus.

(1988). "Is There a Crisis of the Welfare State? Cross-National Evidence from Europe, North America, and Japan," *European Sociological Review*, 4(3): 181–207.

Allan, James P., and Scruggs, Lyle A. (2004). "Political Partisanship and Welfare State Reform in Advanced Industrial Democracies," *American Journal of Political Science*, 48(3): 496–512.

Amable, Bruno, and Palombarini, Stefano (2009). "A Neorealist Approach to Institutional Change and the Diversity of Capitalism," *Socio-Economic Review*, 7(1): 123–43.

Andreß, Hans-Jürgen, and Lohmann, Henning (2008). *The Working Poor in Europe*. Cheltenham/Northampton: Edward Elgar.

Armingeon, Klaus (2003). "OECD and National Welfare State Development." In Armingeon and Beyeler (eds.), pp. 226–41.

(2012). "The Politics of Fiscal Responses to the Economic Crisis, 2008–2009," *Governance: An International Journal of Policy, Administration, and Institutions*, 25(4): 543–65.

(2013). 'Breaking with the Past? Why the Global Financial Crisis Led to Austerity Policies But Not to Modernization of the Welfare State'. In Pierson, Christopher, Castles, Francis G., and Naumann, Ingela K. (eds.), *The Welfare State Reader* (3rd edition). Cambridge: Polity Press.

Armingeon, Klaus, and Beyeler, Michelle (eds.) (2003). *The OECD and European Welfare States*. Cheltenham and Northampton: Edward Elgar.

Armingeon, Klaus, and Bonoli, Giuliano (eds.) (2006). *The Politics of Post-Industrial Welfare States: Adapting Post-War Social Policies to New Social Risks*. London and New York: Routledge.

Armingeon, Klaus, and Giger, Nathalie (2008). "Conditional Punishment: A Comparative Analysis of the Electoral Consequences of Welfare State Retrenchment in OECD Nations, 1980–2003," *West European Politics*, 31(3): 558–80.

Arndt, Christoph (2013). *The Electoral Consequences of Third Way Welfare State Reforms. Social Democracy's Transformation and Its Political Costs*. Amsterdam: Amsterdam University Press.

Arts, Wil A., and Gelissen, John (2010). "Models of the Welfare State." In Castles et al. (eds.), pp. 586–83.

Aspalter, Christian (2011). "The Development of Ideal-Typical Welfare Regime Theory," *International Social Work*, 54(6): 735–50.

(2013). "Real-typical and Ideal-typical Methods in Comparative Social Policy." In Greve, Bent (ed.), *The Routledge Handbook of the Welfare State*. New York: Routledge, pp. 293–306.

Atkinson, Anthony B., Marlier, Eric, Montaigne, Fabienne, and Reinstadler, Anne (2010). "Income Poverty and Income Inequality." In Atkinson, Anthony B. and Marlier, Eric (eds.), *Income and Living Conditions in Europe*. Brussels: Eurostat. http://epp.eurostat.ec.europa.eu/cache/ITY_OFFPUB/KS-31-10-555/EN/KS-31-10-555-EN.PDF (accessed June 2011), pp. 101–31.

Balassa, Bela (1966). "Tariff Reductions and Trade in Manufacturers among the Industrial Countries," *American Economic Review*, 56(3): 466–73.

Baldwin, Peter (1990). *The Politics of Social Solidarity: Class Bases of the European Welfare State, 1875–1975*. Cambridge: Cambridge University Press.

Banting, Keith G. (1995). "The Welfare State as Statecraft: Territorial Politics and Canadian Social Policy." In Leibfried, Stephan and Pierson, Paul (eds.), *European*

Social Policy: Between Fragmentation and Integration. Washington, DC: Brookings Institution, pp. 269–300.

Baron, Jonathan (2010). "Cognitive Biases in Moral Judgments that Affect Political Behavior," *Synthese,* **172**(1): 7–35.

Barr, Nicholas (2004). *The Economics of the Welfare State.* Oxford: Oxford University Press (4th edition).

Barry, Brian (1990). "The Welfare State versus the Relief of Poverty." *Ethics,* **100**(3): 503–29.

Bauer, Michael W., and Knill, Christoph (2012). "Understanding Policy Dismantling: An Analytical Framework." In Bauer et al. (eds.), pp. 30–51.

Bauer, Michael W., Jordan, Andrew, Green-Pedersen, Christopher, and Héretier, Adrienne (eds.) (2012). *Dismantling Public Policy. Preferences, Strategies, and Effects.* Oxford: Oxford University Press.

Baumol, William J. (1967). "Macroeconomics of Unbalanced Growth: The Anatomy of Urban Crisis." *American Economic Review,* **57**(3): 415–26.

Bazant, Ursula, and Schubert, Klaus (2009). "European Welfare Systems: Diversity beyond Existing Categories." In Schubert, Klaus, Hegelich, Simon, and Bazant, Ursula (eds.), *The Handbook of European Welfare Systems.* Oxford: Routledge, pp. 513–34.

Becher, Michael (2010). "Constraining Ministerial Power: The Impact of Veto Players on Labor Market Reforms in Industrial Democracies, 1973–2000," *Comparative Political Studies,* **43**(1): 33–60.

Beck, Hermann (1995). *The Origins of the Authoritarian Welfare State in Prussia: Conservatives, Bureaucracy, and the Social Question, 1815–70.* Ann Arbor: University of Michigan Press.

Becker, Jos (2005). *De Steun voor de Verzorgingsstaat in de Publieke Opinie, 1970–2002: Een Analyse van Trends in Meningen* [The Support for the Welfare State in Public Opinion: An Analysis of Trends in Opinions]. The Hague: Social and Cultural Planning Office of the Netherlands.

Becker, Uwe (1988). "From Social Scientific Functionalism to Open Functional Logic," *Theory and Society,* **17**(6): 865–83.

(2009). *Open Varieties of Capitalism. Continuity, Change and Performances.* Houndmills: Palgrave Macmillan.

(ed.) (2011). *The Changing Political Economic of Small West European Countries.* Amsterdam: Amsterdam University Press.

Béland, Daniel (2005). "Ideas and Social Policy: An Institutionalist Perspective," *Social Policy & Administration,* **39**(1): 1–18.

(2007). "The Social Exclusion Discourse: Ideas and Policy Change," *Policy & Politics,* **35**(1): 123–39.

(2011). "Ideas and Politics." In Béland and Cox (eds.), pp. 3–20.

Béland, Daniel, and Cox, Robert H. (eds.) (2011). *Ideas and Politics in Social Science Research,* Oxford: Oxford University Press.

Bell, Daniel (1979). *The Cultural Contradictions of Capitalism.* London: Heinemann.

Berejekian, Jeffrey (1997). "The Gains Debate: Framing State Choice," *American Political Science Review,* **91**(4): 789–805.

Bermeo, Nancy, and Pontusson, Jonas (eds.) (2012a). *Coping with Crisis. Government Reactions to the Great Recession.* New York: Russell Sage Foundation.

(2012b). "Coping with Crisis: An Introduction." In Bermeo and Pontusson (2012a), pp. 1–31.

Beyeler, Michelle (2003). "Introduction: A Comparative Study of the OECD and European Welfare States." In Armingeon and Beyeler (eds.), pp. 1–12.

Bhagwati, Jagdish (1995). *Protectionism*. Cambridge, MA: MIT Press.

Birch, Anthony H. (1984). "Overload, Ungovernability and Delegimation: The Theories and the British Case," *British Journal of Political Science*, 14(2): 135–60.

Blair, Tony, and Schröder, Gerhard (1999). *Europe: The Third Way/Die Neue Mitte*. http://www.fcpp.org/publication.php/349 (accessed June 2011).

Blais, André, Kim, Jiyoon, and Foucault, Martial (2010). "Public Spending, Public Deficits and Government Coalitions," *Political Studies*, 58(5): 829–46.

Blekesaune, Morten, and Quadagno, Jill (2003). "Public Attitudes toward Welfare State Policies: A Comparative Analysis of 24 Nations," *European Sociological Review*, 19(5): 415–27.

Block, Fred (1990). *Postindustrial Possibilities. A Critique of Economic Discourse*. Berkeley, CA: University of California Press.

Blomberg, Helena, and Kroll, Christian (1999). "Who Wants to Preserve the 'Scandinavian Services State'? Attitudes to Welfare Services among Citizens and Local Government Elites in Finland, 1992–6." In Svallfors and Taylor-Gooby (eds.), pp. 52–86.

Blossfeld, Hans-Peter (2009). "Educational Assortative Marriage in Comparative Perspective," *Annual Review of Sociology*, 35: 513–30.

Blyth, Mark (2001). "The Transformation of the Swedish Model: Economic Ideas, Distributional Conflict, and Institutional Change," *World Politics*, 54(1): 1–26.

(2002). *Great Transformations: Economic Ideas and Institutional Change in the Twentieth Century*. Cambridge: Cambridge University Press.

(2013). *Austerity: The History of a Dangerous Idea*. New York: Oxford University Press.

Boeri, Tito, Börsch-Supan, Axel, and Tabellini, Guido (2001). "Would You Like to Shrink the Welfare State? A Survey of European Citizens," *Economic Policy*, 16(32): 9–50.

Boettcher III, William A. (2004). "The Prospects for Prospects Theory: An Empirical Evaluation of International Relations Applications of Framing and Loss Aversion," *Political Psychology*, 25(3): 331–62.

Bone, John, Hey, John, and Suckling, John (1999). "Are Groups More (or Less) Consistent than Individuals?" *Journal of Risk and Uncertainty*, 18(1): 63–81.

Bonoli, Giuliano (2000). *The Politics of Pension Reform*. Cambridge: Cambridge University Press.

(2001). "Political Institutions, Veto Points, and the Process of Welfare State Adaptation." In Pierson (ed.) (2001b), *The New Politics of the Welfare State*. Oxford: Oxford University Press, pp. 238–64.

(2005). "The Politics of New Social Policies: Providing Coverage against New Social Risks in Mature Welfare States," *Policy & Politics*, 33(3): 431–49.

(2006). "New Social Risks and the Politics of Post-Industrial Social Policies." In Armingeon and Bonoli (eds.), pp. 3–26.

(2007). "Time Matters: Postindustrialization, New Social Risks, and Welfare State Adaptation in Advanced Industrial Democracies," *Comparative Political Studies*, 40(5): 495–520.

(2008). "The Political Economy of Activation: Explaining Cross-National Variation in Active Labour Market Policy," *Working Paper De l'IDHEAP* 1–21.

http://www.idheap.ch/idheap.nsf/view/83E413A8FB594809C1257458002D8EA D/$File/working%20paper%202008-1.pdf (accessed July 2011).

(2012). "Blame Avoidance and Credit Claiming Revisited." In Bonoli and Natali (eds.) (2012b), pp. 93–110.

Bonoli, Giuliano, and Häusermann, Silja (2009). "Who Wants What from the Welfare State? Socio-Structural Cleavages in Distributional Politics: Evidence from Swiss Referendum Votes," *European Societies*, 11(2): 211–32.

Bonoli, Giuliano, and Natali, David (2012a). "Multidimensional Transformations in the Early 21st Century Welfare States." In Bonoli and Natali (eds.) (2012b), pp. 287–306.

(eds.) (2012b). *The Politics of the New Welfare State*. Oxford: Oxford University Press.

Bonoli, Giuliano, and Palier, Bruno (2007). "When Past Reforms Open New Opportunities: Comparing Old-age Insurance Reforms in Bismarckian Welfare States," *Social Policy & Administration*, 41(6): 555–73.

Borah, Porismita (2011). "Conceptual Issues in Framing Theory: A Systematic Examination of a Decade's Literature," *Journal of Communication*, 61(2): 246–63.

Borrás, Susana, and Jacobsson, Kerstin (2004). "The Open Method of Co-Ordination and New Governance Patterns in the EU," *Journal of European Public Policy*, 11(2): 185–208.

Bowles, Samuel, and Gintis, Herbert (1982). "The Crisis of Liberal Democratic Capitalism: The Case of the US," *Politics & Society*, 11(1): 51–93.

Brady, David (2003). "The Politics of Poverty: Left Political Institutions, the Welfare State, and Poverty," *Social Forces*, 82(2): 557–88.

(2005). "The Welfare State and Relative Poverty in Rich Western Democracies, 1967– 1997," *Social Forces*, 83(4): 1329–64.

Brady, David, Beckfield, Jason, and Seeleib-Kaiser, Martin (2005). "Economic Globalization and the Welfare State in Affluent Democracies, 1975–2001," *American Sociological Review*, 70(6): 921–48.

Brittan, Samuel (1975). "The Economic Contradictions of Democracy," *British Journal of Political Science*, 5(2): 129–59.

Brooks, Clem, and Manza, Jeff (2006a). "Why Do Welfare States Persist?" *Journal of Politics*, 68(4): 816–27.

(2006b). "Social Policy Responsiveness in Developed Democracies," *American Sociological Review*, 71(3): 474–94.

(2007). *Why Welfare States Persist: The Importance of Public Opinion in Democracies*. Chicago: University of Chicago Press.

Brülhart, Marius, Murphy, Anthony, and Strobl, Eric (2004). *Intra-Industry Trade and Job Turnover*. Mimeo: University of Lausanne/ University College Dublin/CORE, University of Louvain.

Bueno de Mesquita, Bruce, McDermott, Rose, and Cope, Emily (2001). "The Expected Prospect for Peace in Northern Ireland," *International Interactions*, 27(2): 129–67.

Bundesfinanzministerium (2011). http://www.bundesfinanzminesterium.de (accessed May 2011).

Bundesregierung (2010). "Sparprogramm." http://www.bundesregierung.de/Webs/Breg/ DE/Sparprogramm/sparprogramm.html (accessed August 2010).

(2011). http://www.bundesregiering.de (accessed May 2011).

Burgoon, Brian (2001). "Globalization and Welfare Compensation: Disentangling the Ties that Bind," *International Organization*, 55(3): 509–51.

(2006). "Globalization Is What Parties Make of It: Welfare and Protectionism in Party Platforms," *GARNET Working Paper*, No. 03/06. http://www.garnet-eu.org/fileadmin/documents/working_papers/0306.pdf (accessed October 2010).

(2009). "Social Nation and Social Europe. Support for National and Supranational Welfare Compensation in Europe," *European Union Politics*, 10(4): 427–55.

Burstein, Paul (1998). "Bringing the Public Back In: Should Sociologists Consider the Impact of Public Opinion on Public Policy?" *Social Forces*, 77(1): 27–62.

(2003). "The Impact of Public Opinion on Public Policy: A Review and an Agenda," *Political Research Quarterly*, 56(1): 29–40.

Busemeyer, Marius R. (2009). "From Myth to Reality: Globalisation and Public Spending in OECD Countries Revisited," *European Journal of Political Research*, 48(4): 455–82.

Bussemaker, Jet, and Van Kersbergen, Kees (1994). "Gender and the Welfare State: Some Theoretical Reflections." In Sainsbury, Diane (ed.), *Gendering Welfare States*. London: Sage, pp. 8–25.

Cabral, Manuel, and Silva, Joana (2007). "Intra-Industry Trade Expansion and Employment Reallocation between Sectors and Occupations," *Review of World Economies*, 142(3): 496–520.

Camerer, Colin (2005). "Three Cheers – Psychological, Theoretical, Empirical – for Loss Aversion," *Journal of Marketing Research*, 42(2): 129–33.

Cameron, David R. (1978). "The Expansion of the Public Economy: A Comparative Analysis," *American Political Science Review*, 72(4): 1243–61.

(2012). "European Fiscal Responses to the Great Recession." In Bermeo and Pontusson (eds.) (2012a), pp. 91–129.

Campbell, John L. (2002). "Ideas, Politics, and Public Policy," *Annual Review of Sociology*, 28: 21–38.

Cantillon, Bea (2010). *The Social Contract Revisited. Crisis and the Welfare State: The Need for a New Distributional Agenda*. Oxford: Foundation for Law, Justice and Society.

(2011). "The Paradox of the Social Investment State: Growth, Employment and Poverty in the Lisbon Era," *Journal of European Social Policy*, 21(5): 432–49.

Carstensen, Martin B. (2010). "The Nature of Ideas, and Why Political Scientists Should Care: Analyzing the Danish Jobcentre Reform from an Ideational Perspective," *Political Studies*, 58(5): 847–65.

Casey, Bernard H., and Gold, Michael (2005). "Peer Review of Labour Market Programmes in the European Union: What Can Countries Really Learn from One Another?" *Journal of European Public Policy*, 12(1): 23–43.

Castles, Francis G. (ed.) (1993). *Families of Nations: Patterns of Public Policy in Western Democracies*. Aldershot: Dartmouth.

(2004). *The Future of the Welfare State: Crisis Myths and Crisis Realities*. Oxford: Oxford University Press.

(2010). "Black Swans and Elephants on the Move: The Impact of Emergencies on the Welfare State," *Journal of European Social Policy*, 20(2): 91–101.

Castles, Francis G., Leibfried, Stephan, Lewis, Jane, Obinger, Herbert, and Pierson, Christopher (eds.) (2010). *The Oxford Handbook of the Welfare State*. Oxford: Oxford University Press.

Castles, Francis G., and Mitchell, Deborah (1993). "Worlds of Welfare and Families of Nations." In Castles, et al. (eds.), pp. 93–128.

CBS (2010). "Meer zelfstandigen geven er de brui aan" [More self-employed stop their business]. http://www.cbs.nl/nl-NL/menu/themas/arbeid-sociale-zekerheid/publi-caties/artikelen/archief/2010/2010-3029-wm.htm (accessed May 2010).

(2012). *Welvaart in Nederland. Inkomen, Vermogen en Bestedingen van Huishoudens en Personen* [Prosperity in the Netherlands. Income, Capital and Expenditures of Households and Individuals]. Den Haag/Heerlen: CBS.

Chan, Chak Kwan, Ngok, King Lun, and Philips, David (2008). *Social Policy in China. Development and Well-Being*. Bristol: Policy Press.

Chen, Keith M., Lakshminarayanan, Venkat, and Santos, Laurie R. (2006). "How Basic Are Behavioral Biases? Evidence from Capuchin Monkey Trading Behavior," *Journal of Political Economy*, 114(3): 517–37.

Chinn, Menzie D., and Ito, Hiro (2008). "Global Current Account Imbalances: American Fiscal Policy versus East Asian Savings," *Review of International Economics*, 16(3): 479–98.

Christian, Jennifer L. (2008). "When Does Public Opinion Matter?" *Journal of Sociology and Social Welfare*, 35(1): 133–56.

Christopher, Karen (2002). "Welfare State Regimes and Mothers' Poverty," *Social Politics* 9(1): 60–86.

Clasen, Jochen (2005). *Reforming European Welfare States: Germany and the United Kingdom Compared*. Oxford: Oxford University Press.

(2007). *Reforming European Welfare States. Germany and the United Kingdom Compared*. Oxford: Oxford University Press.

Clasen, Jochen, and Clegg, Daniel (2003). "Unemployment Protection and Labour Market Reform in France and Great Britain in the 1990s: Solidarity Versus Activation?" *Journal of Social Policy*, 32(3): 361–81.

(eds.) (2011a). *Regulating the Risk of Unemployment: National Adaptations to Post-Industrial Labour Markets in Europe*. Oxford: Oxford University Press.

(2011b). "The Transformation of Unemployment Protection in Europe." In Clasen and Clegg (eds.), pp. 333–45.

Clasen, Jochen, and Siegel, Nico A. (eds.) (2007). *Investigating Welfare State Change: The "Dependent Variable Problem" in Comparative Analysis*. Cheltenham: Edward Elgar.

Clasen, Jochen, Clegg, Daniel, and Kvist, Jon (2012). "European Labour Market in (the) Crisis." *ETUI (European Trade Union Institute) Working Paper*, no. 2012.12. http://www.etui.org/Publications2/Working-Papers/European-labour-market-policies-in-the-crisis (accessed January 2013).

Clayton, Richard, and Pontusson, Jonas (1998). "Welfare-State Retrenchment Revisited: Entitlement Cuts, Public Sector Restructuring, and Inegalitarian Trends in Advanced Capitalist Societies," *World Politics*, 51(1): 67–98.

Clegg, Daniel (2010). "Labour Market Policy and the Crisis: Britain in Comparative Perspective," *Journal of Poverty and Social Justice*, 18(1): 5–17.

Cook, Linda J. (2010). "Eastern Europe and Russia." In Castles et al. (eds.), pp. 671–86.

Cox, Robert H. (2001). "The Social Construction of an Imperative: Why Welfare Reform Happened in Denmark and the Netherlands but not in Germany," *World Politics*, 53(3): 463–98.

Crettaz, Eric (2011). *Fighting Working Poverty in Post-industrial Economies. Causes, Trade-offs and Policy Solutions*. Cheltenham/Northampton: Edward Elgar.

Crozier, Michel, Huntington, Samuel P., and Watanuki, Jöji (1975). *The Crisis of Democracy: Report on the Governability of Democracies to the Trilateral Commission*. New York: New York University Press.

Cutright, Phillips (1965). "Political Structure, Economic Development, and National Social Security Programmes," *American Journal of Sociology*, 70(5): 537–91.

Daly, Mary (2000). "A Fine Balance: Women's Labor Market Participation in International Comparison." In Scharpf and Schmidt (eds.), Vol. II, pp. 467–510.

Däubler, Thomas (2008). "Veto Players and Welfare State Change: What Delays Social Entitlement Bills?" *Journal of Social Policy*, 37(4): 683–706.

Davidsson, Johan B., and Emmenegger, Patrick (2012). "Insider-Outsider Dynamics and the Reform of Job Security Legislation." In Bonoli and Natali (eds.), pp. 206–29.

D'Addio, Anna Christina, and Mira d'Ercole, Marco (2005). "Trends and Determinants of Fertility Rates in OECD Countries: The Role of Policies." *OECD Social, Employment and Migration Working Papers*, No. 27. Paris: OECD.

Deane, Phyllis (2000). *The First Industrial Revolution*. Cambridge: Cambridge University Press (2nd edition).

De Beer, Paul, Hoogenboom, Marcel, Kok, Lucy, and Schils, Trudie (2009). *Wie Zorgt voor Zekerheid?* [Who Arranges Security?] Den Haag: SDU.

De la Porte, Caroline, and Pochet, Philippe (2004). "The European Employment Strategy: Existing Research and Remaining Questions," *Journal of European Social Policy*, 14(1): 71–8.

De Martino, Benedetto, Camerer, Colin F., and Adolphs, Ralph (2010). "Amygdala Damage Eliminates Monetary Loss Aversion," *Proceedings of the National Academy of Sciences of the United States of America*, 107(8): 3788–92.

Demerath III, N. J. (1966). "Synecdoche and Structural-Functionalism," *Social Forces*, 44(3): 390–401.

Den Ridder, Josje, and Dekker, Paul (2010). *Het tweede kwartaalbericht uit het Continu Onderzoek Burgerspectieven van 2010* [The second quarterly message from the Continuous Research into Citizens of 2010]. The Hague: Social and Cultural Planning Office of the Netherlands. http://www.scp.nl/dsresource?objectid=2579 4andtype=org (accessed March 2011).

Diamond, Patrick, and Lodge, Guy (2013). "European Welfare States after the Crisis Changing Public Attitudes," *Policy Network Paper*. www.policy-network.net (accessed March 2013).

Dion, Michelle L., and Birchfield, Vicki (2010). "Economic Development, Income Inequality, and Preferences for Redistribution," *International Studies Quarterly*, 54(2): 315–34.

Dollar, David (1992). "Outward-Oriented Developing Economies Really Do Grow More Rapidly: Evidence from 95 LDC's, 1976–1985," *Economic Development and Cultural Change*, 40(3): 523–44.

Down, Ian (2007). "Trade Openness, Country Size and Economic Volatility: The Compensation Hypothesis Revisited," *Business and Politics*, 9(2): 1–20.

Downs, Anthony (1957). *An Economic Theory of Democracy*. New York: Harper and Row.

Dreher, Axel (2006). "Does Globalization Affect Growth? Evidence from a New Index of Globalization," *Applied Economics*, 38(10): 1091–110.

Dreher, Axel, Sturm, Jan-Egbert, and Ursprung, Heinrich W. (2008a). "The Impact of Globalization on the Composition of Government Expenditures: Evidence from Panel Data," *Public Choice*, 134(3–4): 263–92.

Dreher, Axel, Gaston, Noel, and Martens, Pim (2008). *Measuring Globalization – Gauging Its Consequences*. New York: Springer.

Dyson, Kenneth (2005). "Binding Hands as a Strategy for Economic Reform: Government by Commission," *German Politics*, 14(2): 224–47.

Ebbinghaus, Bernhard (2000). "Any Way Out of 'Exit from Work'? Reversing the Entrenched Path-ways of Early Retirement." In Scharpf and Schmidt (eds.), Vol. II, pp. 511–53.

(2010a). "Reforming Bismarckian Corporatism: The Changing Role of Social Partnership in Continental Europe." In Palier (ed.) (2010a), pp. 255–78.

(2010b). "Unions and Employers." In Castles et al. (eds.) (2010), pp. 196–10.

Economist, The (2000). *Anti-Capitalist Protests: Angry and Effective*. September 23, 97–103.

Edwards, Sebastian (1998). "Openness, Productivity and Growth: What Do We Really Know?" *Economic Journal*, 108(447): 383–98.

EEO (European Employment Observatory) (2009). "Background Paper on Measures to Deal with the Economic Crisis." http://www.eu-employment-observatory.net/resources/reports/EEOBackgroundPaper-EconomicCrisisMeasures11April2009.pdf (accessed February 2010).

Eger, Maureen A. (2010). "Even in Sweden: The Effect of Immigration on Support for Welfare State Spending," *European Sociological Review* 26(2): 203–17.

Eichhorst, Werner, Konle-Seidl, Regina, Koslowski, Alison, and Marx, Paul (2011). "Quantity over Quality? A European Comparison of the Changing Nature of Transitions between Non-Employment and Employment." In Clasen and Clegg (eds.) (2011a), pp. 281–96.

Eichhorst, Werner, and Marx, Paul (2011). "Reforming German Labour Market Institutions: A Dual Path to Flexibility," *Journal of European Social Policy*, 21(1): 73–87.

Ellison, Nick (2006). *The Transformation of Welfare States?* London: Routledge.

Elmelund-Præstekær, Christian, and Emmenegger, Patrick (2013). "Strategic Re-framing as a Vote Winner: Why Vote-seeking Governments Pursue Unpopular Reforms," *Scandinavian Political Studies*, 36(1): 23–42.

Emmenegger, Patrick, Häusermann, Silja, Palier, Bruno, and Seeleib-Kaiser, Martin (eds.) (2012). *The Age of Dualization. The Changing Face of Inequality in Deindustrializing Countries*. Oxford: Oxford University Press.

Engeli, Isabelle, and Häusermann, Silja (2009). "Government Strategies for Successful Reforms in Controversial Policy Fields." *EUI Working Paper Red Number Series*, MWP 2009/01.

Englund, Peter (1999). "The Swedish Banking Crisis: Roots and Consequences," *Oxford Review of Economic Policy*, 15(3): 80–97.

Esping-Andersen, Gøsta (1985a). *Politics against Markets. The Social Democratic Road to Power*. Princeton, NJ: Princeton University Press.

(1985b). "Power and Distributional Regimes," *Politics & Society*, 14(2): 223–56.

(1990). *The Three Worlds of Welfare Capitalism*. Cambridge: Polity Press.

(1996a). "After the Golden Age? Welfare State Dilemmas in a Global Economy." In Esping-Andersen, Gøsta (ed.), *Welfare States in Transition: National Adaptations in Global Economies.* London: Sage, pp. 1–31.

(1996b). "Welfare States without Work: The Impasse of Labour Shedding and Familialism in Continental European Social Policy." In Esping-Andersen, Gøsta (ed.), *Welfare States in Transition: National Adaptations in Global Economies.* London: Sage, pp. 66–87.

(1999). *Social Foundations of Postindustrial Economies.* Oxford: Oxford University Press.

(2000). "Multi-dimensional Decommodification: A Reply to Graham Room," *Policy & Politics*, 28(3): 353–59.

(ed.) (2002). *Why We Need a New Welfare State.* Oxford: Oxford University Press.

(2005). "Putting the Horse in Front of the Cart: Towards a Social Model for Mid-Century Europe." *WRR-Lecture*, December 8. The Hague: WRR.

(2007). "Sociological Explanations of Changing Income Distributions," *American Behavioral Scientist*, 50(5): 639–58.

(2009). *The Incomplete Revolution: Adapting to Women's New Roles.* Cambridge: Polity Press.

Esping-Andersen, Gøsta, and Myles, John (2009). "Economic Inequality and the Welfare State." In Salverda, Wiemer, Nolan, Brian, and Smeeding, Timothy M. (eds.) *The Oxford Handbook of Economic Inequality.* Oxford: Oxford University Press, pp. 639–64.

European Commission (2004). *The Social Situation in the European Union 2004.* Luxembourg: European Commission.

European Institute (2010). EU Austerity: A Country-by-Country Table. http://www.europeaninstitute.org/June-2010/eu-austerity-a-country-by-country-table/html (accessed August 2010).

European Values Survey (1999/2000). *European Values Survey, 3rd Wave.* http://www.europeanvaluesstudy.eu/evs/data-and-downloads/ (accessed December 2010).

European Values Survey (2008). *European Values Survey, 4th Wave.* http://www.europeanvaluesstudy.eu/evs/data-and-downloads/ (accessed December 2010).

Eurostat (2011). In Work at-Risk-of-Poverty Rate. http://epp.eurostat.ec.europa.eu/tgm/table.do?tab=tableandinit=1andplugin=1andlanguage=enandpcode=tsdsc320 (accessed June 2011).

Falleti, Tulia G., and Lynch, Julia F. (2009). "Context and Causal Mechanisms in Political Analysis," *Comparative Political Studies*, 42(9): 1143–66.

Fernandez, Juan J. (2010). "Economic Crises, High Public Pension Spending and Blame-avoidance Strategies Pension Policy Retrenchments in 14 Social-insurance Countries, 1981–2005," *MPIfG Discussion Paper* 10/ 9. http://www.mpifg.de/pu/mpifg_dp/dp10-9.pdf (accessed January 2013).

Ferragina, Emanuele and Seeleib-Kaiser, Martin (2011). "Welfare Regime Debate: Past, Present, Futures?" *Policy & Politics*, 39(4): 583–611.

Ferragina, Emanuele and Seeleib-Kaiser, Martin, and Mark Tomlinson (2012). "Unemployment Protection and Family Policy at the Turn of the 21st Century: A Dynamic Approach to Welfare Regime Theory," *Social Policy & Administration*, doi: 10.1111/j.1467–9515.2012.00855.x.

Ferreira, Fransisco H., and Ravallion, Martin (2009). "Poverty and Inequality: The Global Context." In Salverda, Wiemer, Nolan, Brian, and Smeeding, Timothy M.

(eds.), *The Oxford Handbook of Economic Inequality*. Oxford: Oxford University Press, pp. 599–636.

Ferrera, Maurizio (1996). "The 'Southern Model' of Welfare in Social Europe," *Journal of European Social Policy*, 6(1): 17–37.

(1997). "The Uncertain Future of the Italian Welfare State," *West European Politics*, 21(1): 231–41.

(2003). "European Integration and National Social Citizenship: Changing Boundaries, New Structuring?" *Comparative Political Studies*, 36(6): 611–52.

(2005). "Welfare States and Social Safety Nets in Southern Europe: An Introduction." In Ferrera, Maurizio (ed.), *Welfare State Reform in Southern Europe: Fighting Poverty and Social Exclusion in Italy, Spain, Portugal and Greece*. London: Routledge, pp. 1–23.

(2008). "The European Welfare State: Golden Achievements, Silver Prospects," *West European Politics*, 31(1): 82–107.

Ferrera, Maurizio, and Gualmini, Elisabetta (2004). *Rescued by Europe? Social and Labour Market Reforms in Italy from Maastricht to Berlusconi*. Amsterdam: Amsterdam University Press.

Financial Times/Harris Poll (2010). "Spending Cuts Are Preferred to Higher Taxes to Reduce Deficits in the U.S., Great Britain, France, Italy, Spain and Germany." http://www.harrisinteractive.com/NewsRoom/HarrisPolls/FinancialTimes/tabid/449/ct/ReadCustom%20Deafult/mid/1512/Artcleld/438/Default.aspx (accessed August 2010).

Fleckenstein, Timo (2008). "Restructuring Welfare for the Unemployed: The Hartz Legislation in Germany," *Journal of European Social Policy*, 18(2): 177–88.

Fleckenstein, Timo, and Lee, Soohyun Christine (2012). "The Politics of Postindustrial Social Policy: Family Policy Reforms in Britain, Germany, South Korea, and Sweden," *Comparative Political Studies*, doi: 10.1177/0010414012451564.

Flora, Peter (1985). "History and Current Problems of the Welfare State." In Eisenstadt, Shmuel N., and Ahimer, Ora (eds.), *The Welfare State and Its Aftermath*. Totowa (NJ): Barnes and Noble Books, pp. 11–30.

(ed.) (1986–87). *Growth to Limits*, vols. 1, 2, 4. Berlin: De Gruyter.

(1999). "Introduction and Interpretation." In Flora, Peter (with Stein Kuhnle and Derek Unwin) (eds.), *State Formation, Nation-Building, and Mass Politics in Europe: The Theory of Stein Rokkan*. Oxford: Oxford University Press.

Flora, Peter, and Heidenheimer, Arnold J. (eds.) (1981a). *The Development of Welfare States in Europe and America*. New Brunswick, NJ: Transaction Books.

Flora, Peter, and Alber, Jens (1981b). "Modernization, Democratization, and the Development of Welfare States." In Flora and Heidenheimer (eds.) (1981a), pp. 37–80.

Frankel, Jeffrey A., and Romer, David (1999). "Does Trade Cause Growth?" *American Economic Review*, 89(3): 379–99.

Franzese, Robert J., and Hays, Jude (2006). "Strategic Interaction among EU Governments in Active Labor Market Policy-Making," *European Union Politics*, 7(2): 167–89.

Fraser, Nancy (1994). "After the Family Wage: Gender Equity and the Welfare State," *Political Theory*, 22(4): 591–618.

Fu, Xuanning, and Heaton, Tim B. (2008). "Racial and Educational Homogamy: 1980 to 2000," *Sociological Perspectives*, 51(4): 735–58.

Gallup (2009a). "Americans OK with Short-Term Government Growth." http://www.gallup.com/poll/117523/Americans-Short-Term-Government-Growth.aspx (accessed April 2010).

(2009b). "Big Govt. Still Viewed as Greater Threat than Big Business." http://www.gallup.com/poll/117739/Big-Gov-Viewed-Greater-Threat-Big-Business.aspx (accessed April 2010).

Garrett, Geoffrey (1998). *Partisan Politics in the Global Economy*. New York: Cambridge University Press.

Garrett, Geoffrey, and Mitchell, Deborah (2001). "Globalization, Government Spending and Taxation in the OECD," *European Journal of Political Research*, 39(2): 145–77.

Gaston, Noel, and Rajaguru, Gulasekaran (2008). "The Rise (and Fall) of Labour Market Programmes: Domestic vs. Global Factors," *Oxford Economic Papers*, 60(4): 619–48.

Genschel, Philipp (2004). "Globalization and the Welfare State: A Retrospective," *Journal of European Public Policy*, 11(4): 613–36.

Gerring, John (2005). "Causation. A Unified Framework for the Social Sciences," *Journal of Theoretical Politics*, 17(2): 163–98.

(2010). "Causal Mechanisms: Yet, But … ," *Comparative Political Studies*, 43(11): 1499–526.

Gesthuizen, Maurice, and Scheepers, Peer (2010). "Labour Market and Welfare State Influences Economic Vulnerability among Low-Educated Europeans: Resource, Composition, Labour Market and Welfare State Influences," *Acta Sociologica*, 53(3): 247–67.

Giger, Nathalie (2011). *The Risk of Social Policy? The Electoral Consequences of Welfare State Retrenchment and Social Policy Performance in OECD Countries*. London: Routledge.

Giger, Nathalie, and Nelson, Moira (2011). "The Electoral Consequences of Welfare State Retrenchment: Blame Avoidance or Credit Claiming in the Era of Permanent Austerity?" *European Journal of Political Research*, 50(1): 1–23.

Giger, Nathalie (forthcoming). "The Welfare State or the Economy? Preferences, Constituencies, and Strategies for Retrenchment," *European Sociological Review*, doi: 10.1093/esr/jcs082.

Gilardi, Fabrizio (2010). "Who Learns from What in Policy Diffusion Processes?" *American Journal of Political Science*, 54(3): 650–66.

Gilovich, Thomas, Griffin, Dale, and Kahneman, Daniel (eds.) (2002). *Heuristics and Biases: The Psychology of Intuitive Judgment*. New York: Cambridge University Press.

Ginsburg, Norman (1979). *Class, Capital and Social Policy*. London: Macmillan.

Glassner, Vera, and Galgoczi, Béla (2009). *Plant-level Responses to the Economic Crisis in Europe*, European Trade Union Institute for Research, Education and Health and Safety (ETUI-REHS) Working Paper, No. 1/2009. ETUI: Brussels.

Glatzer, Miguel, and Rueschemeyer, Dietrich (eds.) (2005). *Globalization and the Future of the Welfare State*. Pittsburgh: University of Pittsburgh Press.

Glennerster, Howard (2010). "The Sustainability of Western Welfare States." In Castles et al. (eds.), pp. 689–702.

Goerres, Achim (2009). *The Political Participation of Older People in Europe: The Greying of Our Democracies*. Houndmills: Palgrave Macmillan.

Goerres, Achim, and Tepe, Markus (2010). "Age-Based Self-Interest, Intergenerational Solidarity and the Welfare State: A Comparative Analysis of Older People's Attitudes towards Public Childcare in 12 OECD Countries," *European Journal of Political Research*, 49(6): 818–51.

Goldstein, Judith, and Keohane, Robert O. (1993). "Ideas and Foreign Policy: An Analytical Framework." In Goldstein and Keohane (eds.), *Ideas and Foreign Policy: Beliefs, Institution, and Political Change*. Ithaca, NY: Cornell University Press, pp. 3–30.

Goodin, Robert E., Heady, Bruce, Muffels, Ruud, and Dirven, Henk-Jan (1999). *The Real Worlds of Welfare Capitalism*. Cambridge: Cambridge University Press.

Gough, Ian (1979). *The Political Economy of the Welfare State*. London: Macmillan.

Goul Andersen, Jørgen (1997). "The Scandinavian Welfare Model in Crisis? Achievements and Problems of the Danish Welfare State in an Age of Unemployment and Low Growth," *Scandinavian Political Studies*, 20(1): 1–31.

(1999). "Changing Labour Markets, New Social Divisions and Welfare State Support: Denmark in the 1990s." In Svallfors and Taylor-Gooby (eds.), pp. 13–33.

Green-Pedersen, Christoffer, (2001). "Welfare-State Retrenchment in Denmark and the Netherlands, 1982–1998. The Role of Party Competition and Party Consensus," *Comparative Political Studies*, 34(9): 963–85.

(2002). *The Politics of Justification: Party Competition and Welfare-State Retrenchment in Denmark and the Netherlands from 1982 to 1998*. Amsterdam: Amsterdam University Press.

(2004). "The Dependent Variable Problem within the Study of Welfare-State Retrenchment. Defining the Problem and Looking for Solutions," *Journal of Comparative Policy Analysis*, 6(1): 3–14.

Green-Pedersen, Christoffer, and Haverland, Markus (2002). "The New Politics and Scholarship of the Welfare State," *Journal of European Social Policy*, 12(1): 43–51.

Green-Pedersen, Christoffer, Juul Christiansen, Flemming, Euchner, Eva-Maria, Jensen, Carsten, and Turnpenny, John (2012). "Dismantling by Default? The Indexation of Social Benefits in Four Countries." In Bauer et al. (eds.), pp. 129–51.

Grey, Sandra (2002). "Does Size Matter? Critical Mass and New Zealand's Women MPs," *Parliamentary Affairs*, 55(1): 19–29.

(2006). "Numbers and Beyond: The Relevance of Critical Mass in Gender Research," *Politics & Gender*, 2(4): 492–502.

Grubel, Herbert G., and Lloyd, Peter J. (1975). *Intra-Industry Trade: The Theory and Measurement of International Trade in Differentiated Products*. London: Macmillan.

Gusmano, Michael K., Schlesinger, Mark, and Thomas, Tracey (2002). "Policy Feedback and Public Opinion: The Role of Employer Responsibility in Social Policy," *Journal of Health Politics, Policy and Law*, 27(5): 731–72.

Habermas, Jürgen (1976). *Legitimation Crisis*. London: Heinemann.

(1985). "Die Krise des Wohlfahrtsstaates und die Erschöpfung utopischer Energien." In Habermas, Jürgen, *Die neue Unübersichtlichkeit*. Frankfurt a.M.: Suhrkamp.

Hacker, Jacob S. (2004). "Privatizing Risk without Privatizing the Welfare State: The Hidden Politics of Social Policy Retrenchment in the United States," *American Political Science Review*, 98(2): 243–60.

Hacker, Jacob S., and Pierson, Paul (2010). *Winner-Take-All Politics. How Washington Made the Rich Richer – and Turned Its Back on the Middle Class*. New York: Simon and Schuster.

Haerem, Thorvald, Kuvaas, Bård, Bakken, Bjørn T., Karlsen, Tone (2011). "Do Military Decision Makers Behave as Predicted by Prospect Theory?" *Journal of Behavioral Decision Making*, 24(5): 482–97.

Haggard, Stephan, and Kaufman, Robert R. (2008). *Development, Democracy, and Welfare States. Latin America, East Asia, and Eastern Europe*. Princeton, NJ: Princeton University Press.

Hainmueller, Jens, and Hiscox, Michael J. (2006). "Learning to Love Globalization: Education and Individual Attitudes toward International Trade," *International Organization*, 60(2): 469–98.

Hall, Peter A. (1993). "Policy Paradigms, Social Learning, and the State. The Case of Economic Policymaking in Britain," *Comparative Politics*, 25(3): 275–96.

Hall, Peter A., and Soskice, David (2001) (eds.). *Varieties of Capitalism: The Institutional Foundations of Comparative Advantage*. Oxford: Oxford University Press.

Harbaugh, William T., Krause, Kate, and Vesterlund, Lise (2001). "Are Adults Better Behaved than Children? Age, Experience, and the Endowment Effect," *Economic Letters*, 70(2): 175–81.

Harrison, Ann (1996). "Openness and Growth: A Time-Series, Cross-Country Analysis for Developing Countries," *Journal of Development Economics*, 48(2): 419–47.

Häusermann, Silja (2010). *The Politics of Welfare State Reform in Continental Europe: Modernization in Hard Times*. Cambridge: Cambridge University Press.

Häusermann, Silja, and Schwander, Hanna (2012). "Varieties of Dualization? Labor Market Segmentation and Insider-Outsider Divides across Regimes." In Emmenegger et al. (eds.), pp. 27–51.

Häusermann, Silja, Picot, Georg, and Geering, Dominik (2013). "Rethinking Party Politics and the Welfare State: Recent Advances in the Literature," *British Journal of Political Science*, 43(1): 221–40.

Hay, Colin (2002). *Political Analysis. A Critical Introduction*. Houndmills: Palgrave.
  (2010). "Things Can Only Get Worse … The Political and Economic Significance of 2010," *British Politics*, 5(4): 391–401.
  (2011). "Ideas and the Construction of Interests." In Béland and Cox (eds.), pp. 65–82.

Hay, James Roy (1978). *The Development of the British Welfare State: 1880–1975*. London: Edward Arnold.

Hayden, Benjamin Y., and Platt, Michael L. (2009). "Gambling for Gatorade: Risk-sensitive Decision Making for Fluid Rewards in Humans," *Animal Cognition*, 12(1): 201–07.

Heclo, Hugh (1974). *Modern Social Politics in Britain and Sweden: From Poor Relief to Income Maintenance*. New Haven, CT: Yale University Press.

Helms, Ludger (2007). "The German Federal Election, September 2005," *Electoral Studies*, 26(1): 223–27.

Hemerijck, Anton (2013). *Changing Welfare States*. Oxford: Oxford University Press.

Hemerijck, Anton, Dräbing, Verena, Vis, Barbara, Nelson, Moira, and Soentken, Menno (2013). "European Welfare States in Motion," *NEUJOBS Working Paper*, D5.2/March 2013. http://www.neujobs.eu/sites/default/files/NEUJOBS_WP_D5%202_revision_FINAL_0.pdf (accessed March 2013).

Hemerijck, Anton, and Eichhorst, Werner (2010). "Whatever Happened to the Bismarckian Welfare State? From Labor Shedding to Employment-Friendly Reforms." In Palier (ed.) (2010a), pp. 301–32.

Hemerijck, Anton, Knapen, Ben, and van Doorne, Elle (eds.) (2009). *Aftershocks. Economic Crisis and Institutional Choice.* Amsterdam: Amsterdam University Press.

Hemerijck, Anton, Manow, Philip, and Van Kersbergen, Kees (2000). "Welfare without Work? Divergent Experiences of Reform in Germany and the Netherlands." In Kuhnle (ed.), pp. 106–27.

Hemerijck, Anton, and Schludi, Martin (2000). "Sequences of Policy Failures and Effective Policy Responses." In Scharpf and Schmidt (eds.), Vol. I, pp. 125–228.

Hennock, Ernest P. (2007). *The Origin of the Welfare State in England and Germany, 1850–1914: Social Policies Compared.* Cambridge: Cambridge University Press.

Hering, Martin (2003). "The Politics of Institutional Path-departure: A Revised Analytical Framework for the Reform of Welfare States," *Working Paper No. 65, Mannheimer Zentrum für Europäische Sozialforschung.*

(2008). "Welfare State Restructuring without Grand Coalitions: The Role of Informal Cooperation in Blame Avoidance," *German Politics,* 17(2): 165–83.

Heston, Alan, Summers, Robert, and Aten, Bettina (2011). *Penn World Table Version 7.0,* Center for International Comparisons of Production, Income and Prices at the University of Pennsylvania, May 2011. http://pwt.econ.upenn.edu/php_site/pwt_index.php (accessed August 2011).

Hewitt, Christopher (1977). "The Effect of Political Democracy and Social Democracy on Equality in Industrial Societies: A Cross-National Comparison," *American Sociological Review,* 42(3): 450–65.

Hicks, Alexander (1999). *Social Democracy and Welfare Capitalism.* Ithaca, NY: Cornell University Press.

Hicks, Alexander, and Swank, Duane (1984). "On the Political Economy of Welfare Expansion: A Comparative Analysis of 18 Advanced Capitalist Democracies 1960–1971," *Comparative Political Studies,* 17(1): 81–119.

Hill, Michael (2006). *Social Policy in the Modern World: A Comparative Text.* Malden, MA, Blackwell.

Hobsbawn, Eric (1962). *The Age of Revolution 1989–1848.* New York: Mentor.

(1979). *Industry and Empire.* Harmondsworth: Penguin.

Hood, Christoffer (2002). "The Risk Game and the Blame Game," *Government and Opposition,* 37(1): 15–37.

(2011). *The Blame Game: Spin, Bureaucracy, and Self-Preservation in Government.* Princeton, NJ: Princeton University Press.

Howard, Christopher (1997). *The Hidden Welfare State. Tax Expenditure and Social Policy in the United States.* Princeton, NJ: Princeton University Press.

Huber, Evelyne, and Bogliaccini, Juan (2010). "Latin America." In Castles et al. (eds.), pp. 644–55.

Huber, Evelyne, and Stephens, John D. (2001) *Development and Crisis of the Welfare State: Parties and Policies in Global Markets.* Chicago: University of Chicago Press.

(2012). *Democracy and the Left: Social Policy and Inequality in Latin America.* Chicago: University of Chicago Press.

Hudson, John, and Kühner, Stefan (2012). "Analyzing the Productive and Protective Dimensions of Welfare: Looking Beyond the OECD," *Social Policy & Administration* 46(1): 35–60.

Huo, Jingjing, Nelson, Moira, and Stephens, John D. (2008). "Decommodification and Activation in Social Democratic Policy: Resolving the Paradox," *Journal of European Social Policy*, 18(1): 5–20.

Immergut, Ellen M. (2010). "Political Institutions." In Castles et al. (eds.), pp. 227–40.

Ipsos MORI (2009). "Voters Not Ready for Spending Cuts." http://www.ipsos-mori. com/researchpublications/researcharchive/poll.aspx?oItemId=2473 (accessed April 2010).

Irwin, Douglas A., Katz, Lawrence F., and Lawrence, Robert Z. (2008), "Trade and Wages, Reconsidered Comments and Discussion," *Brookings Papers on Economic Activity*, 38(1): 138–54.

ISSA (2006). Social Security Worldwide/ISSA Development and Trends Database. International Social Security Association. http://www-ssw.issa.int/sswlp2/engl/page1.htm (accessed June 2009).

ISSP (International Social Survey Programme) (1996). *Role of Government III*. http://www.issp.org/page.php?pageId=4 (accessed July 2011).

(2006). *Role of Government IV*. http://www.issp.org/page.php?pageId=4 (accessed July 2011).

Iversen, Torben (2005). *Capitalism, Democracy, and Welfare*. Cambridge: Cambridge University Press.

(2010). "Democracy and Capitalism." In Castles et al. (eds.), pp. 183–95.

Iversen, Torben, and Soskice, David (2006). "Electoral Institutions, Parties, and the Politics of Coalitions: Why Some Democracies Distribute More than Others," *American Political Science Review*, 100(2): 165–81.

Iversen, Torben, and Cusack, Thomas R. (2000). "The Causes of Welfare State Expansion: Deindustrialization or Globalization?" *World Politics*, 52(3): 313–49.

Iversen, Torben, and Wren, Ann (1998). "Equality, Employment, and Budgetary Restraint: The Trilemma of the Service Sector Economy," *World Politics*, 50(3): 507–46.

Jackman, Robert W. (1975). *Politics and Social Equality: A Comparative Analysis*. New York: Wiley.

Jacobs, Alan M. (2009). "How Do Ideas Matter? Mental Models and Attention in German Pension Politics," *Comparative Political Studies*, 42(2): 252–79.

(2011). *Governing for the Long Term: Democracy and the Politics of Investment*. New York: Cambridge University Press.

Jaeger, Mads Meier (2009). "United but Divided: Welfare Regimes and the Level and Variance in Public Support for Redistribution," *European Sociological Review*, 25(6): 723–37.

(2012). "Do We All (Dis)like the Same Welfare State? Configurations of Public Support for the Welfare State in Comparative Perspective." In Kvist, Jon, Fritzell, Johan, Hvinden, Bjørn, and Kangas, Olli (eds.), *Changing Social Equality. The Nordic Welfare Model in the 21st Century*. Bristol: Policy Press, pp. 45–87.

Jahn, Detlef (2006). "Globalization as 'Galton's Problem': The Missing Link in the Analysis of Diffusion Patterns in Welfare State Development," *International Organization*, 60(2): 401–31.

Jakobsen, Tor Georg (2010). "Public versus Private: The Conditional Effect of State Policy and Institutional Trust on Mass Opinion," *European Sociological Review*, 26(3): 307–18.

Jensen, Carsten (2010). "Issue Competition and Right-Wing Government Social Spending," *European Journal of Political Research*, 49(1): 282–99.

(2011a). "Catching up by Transition: Globalization as a Generator of Convergence in Social Spending," *Journal of European Public Policy*, 18(1): 106–21.

(2011b). "Determinants of Welfare Service Provision after the Golden Age," *International Journal of Social Welfare*, 20(2): 125–34.

Jervis, Robert (2004). "The Implications of Prospect Theory for Human Nature and Values," *Political Psychology*, 25(2): 163–76.

Jochem, Sven (2007). "Pension Reform: Beyond Path Dependency?" In Clasen and Siegel (eds.), pp. 261–80.

Jones, Bryan D. (2001). *Politics and the Architecture of Choice: Bounded Rationality and Governance*. Chicago: University of Chicago Press.

Jones, Catherine (1993). "The Pacific Challenge: Confucian Welfare States." In Jones, Catherine (ed.), *New Perspectives on the Welfare State in Europe*. London: Routledge, pp. 198–217.

Jordan, Andrew, Bauer, Michael W., and Green-Pedersen, Christoffer (2013). "Policy Dismantling," *Journal of European Public Policy*, doi:10.1080/13501763.2013.7 71092.

Kahl, Sigrun (2009). "Social Doctrines and Poor Relief: A Different Causal Pathway." In Van Kersbergen and Manow (eds.), pp. 267–95.

Kahneman, Daniel (2011). *Thinking, Fast and Slow*. London: Penguin Books.

Kahneman, Daniel, and Tversky, Amos (1979). "Prospect Theory: An Analysis of Decision under Risk," *Econometrica*, 47(2): 263–92.

(eds.) (2000). *Choices, Values, and Frames*. Cambridge: Cambridge University Press.

Kahneman, Daniel, Knetsch, Jack L., and Thaler, Richard H. (2000). "Anomalies: The Endowment Effect, Loss Aversion, and Status Quo Bias." In Kahneman and Tversky (eds.), pp. 159–70.

Kalyvas, Stathis N. (1996). *The Rise of Christian Democracy in Europe*. Ithaca, NY: Cornell University Press.

Kalyvas, Stathis N., and Van Kersbergen, Kees (2010). "Christian Democracy," *Annual Review of Political Science*, 13: 183–209.

Kam, Cindy D., and Simas, Elizabeth M. (2010). "Risk Orientations and Policy Frames," *Journal of Politics*, 72(2): 381–96.

Kam, Yu Wai (2012). "The Contributions of the Health Decommodification Typologies to the Study of the East Asian Welfare Regime," *Social Policy & Administration*, 46(1): 108–28.

Kammer, Andreas, Niehues, Judith, and Peichl, Andreas (2012). "Welfare Regimes and Welfare State Outcomes in Europe," *Journal of European Social Policy*, 22(5): 455–71.

Kangas, Olli E., Niemelä, Mikko, and Varjonen, Sampo (2013). "When and Why Do Ideas Matter? The Influence of Framing on Opinion Formation and Policy Change," *European Political Science Review*, doi:10.1017/S1755773912000306.

Kanner, Michael D. (2005). "A Prospect Dynamic Model of Decision-Making," *Journal of Theoretical Politics*, 17(3): 311–38.

Karlsen, Rune, and Aardal, Bernt (2011). "Kamp om dagsorden og sakseierskap. [Battle over the Agenda and Issue Ownership]" In Aardal, Bernt (ed.), *Det politiske landskap. En studie av stortingsvalget i 2009* [The Political Landscape. A Study of the Parliamentary Election in 2009]. Oslo: Cappelen-Damm.

Katzenstein, Peter J. (1985). *Small States in World Markets: Industrial Policy in Europe.* Ithaca, NY: Cornell University Press.

Kasza, Gregory J. (2002). "The Illusion of 'Welfare Regimes,'" *Journal of Social Policy,* 31(2): 271–87.

Keman, Hans, Van Kersbergen, Kees, and Vis, Barbara (2006). "Political Parties and New Social Risks: The Double Backlash against Social Democracy and Christian Democracy." In Armingeon and Bonoli (eds.), pp. 27–51.

Kenworthy, Lane (1999). "Do Social Welfare Policies Reduce Poverty? A Cross-National Assessment," *Social Forces,* 77(3): 1119–40.

(2004). *Egalitarian Capitalism.* New York: Russell Sage.

(2008). *Jobs with Equality.* Oxford: Oxford University Press.

(2009). "The Effect of Public Opinion on Social Policy Generosity," *Socio-Economic Review,* 7(4): 727–74.

Kerr, Clark, Dunlop, John T., Harbison, Frederick H., and Myers, Charles A. (1960). *Industrialism and Industrial Man: The Problems of Labor and Management in Economic Growth.* Cambridge, MA: Harvard University Press.

Kim, So Young (2007). "Openness, External Risk and Volatility: Implications for the Compensation Hypothesis," *International Organization,* 61(1): 181–216.

King, Anthony (1975). "Overload: Problems of Governing in the 1970s," *Political Studies,* 23(2/3): 284–96.

(1983). "The Political Consequences of the Welfare State." In Spiro, Shimon E., and Yuchtman-Yaar, Ephraim (eds.), *Evaluating the Welfare State.* New York: Academic Press, pp. 7–25.

King, Gary, Keohane, Robert O., and Verba, Sidney (1994). *Designing Social Inquiry. Scientific Inference in Qualitative Research.* Princeton, NJ: Princeton University Press.

Kitschelt, Herbert (2001). "Partisan Competition and Welfare State Retrenchment: When Do Politicians Choose Unpopular Policies?" In Pierson (ed.) (2001b), pp. 265–302.

Kitschelt, Herbert, Marks, Gary, Lange, Peter, and Stephens, John D. (eds.) (1999). *Continuity and Change in Contemporary Capitalism.* Cambridge: Cambridge University Press.

Kittel, Bernhard, and Winner, Hannes (2005). "How Reliable Is Pooled Analysis in Political Economy? The Globalization-Welfare State Nexus Revisited," *European Journal of Political Research,* 44(2): 269–93.

Klitgaard, Michael Baggesen, and Elmelund-Praestekær, Christian (2013). "Partisan Effects on Welfare State Retrenchment: Empirical Evidence from a Measurement of Government Intentions," *Social Policy & Administration,* 47(1): 50–71.

Koole, Karin, and Vis, Barbara (2012). "Working Mothers and the State: Under Which Conditions do Governments Spend Much on Maternal Employment Supporting Policies?" *COMPASSS Working Paper,* No. 2012–71.

Korpi, Walter (1983). *The Democratic Class Struggle: Swedish Politics in a Comparative Perspective.* London: Routledge and Kegan Paul.

(2006). "Power Resources and Employer-Centered Approaches in Explanations of Welfare State and Varieties of Capitalism: Protagonists, Consenters, and Antagonists," *World Politics,* 58(2): 167–206.

Korpi, Walter, and Palme, Joachim (1998). "The Paradox of Redistribution and Strategies of Equality: Welfare State Institutions, Inequality, and Poverty in Western Countries," *American Sociological Review,* 63(5): 661–87.

Korpi, Walter (2003). "New Politics and Class Politics in the Context of Austerity and Globalization: Welfare State Regress in 18 Countries, 1975–95," *American Political Science Review*, 97(3): 425–46.

(2007). *The Social Citizenship Indicator Program (SCIP)*, Swedish Institute for Social Research, Stockholm University. https://dspace.it.su.se/dspace/handle/10102/7 (accessed March 2011).

Koster, Ferry (2009). "Risk Management in a Globalizing World: An Empirical Analysis of Individual Preferences in 26 European Countries," *International Social Security Review*, 62(3): 79–98.

Krugman, Paul R. (1992). "Does New Trade Theory Require a New Trade Policy?" *The World Economy*, 15(4): 423–41.

(1995). "Growing World Trade: Causes and Consequences," *Brookings Papers on Economic Activity*, 26(1): 327–62.

(2008). "Trade and Wages, Reconsidered," *Brookings Papers on Economic Activity*, 38(1): 103–54.

Kruis, Geerten, and Blommesteijn, Marieke (2010). *The Netherlands. In-Work Poverty and Labour Market Segmentation: A Study of National Policies*. Brussels: European Commission, DG Employment, Social Affairs and Equal Opportunities.

Keubler, Daniel (2007). "Understanding the Recent Expansion of Swiss Family Policy: An Idea-Centred Approach," *Journal of Social Policy*, 36(2): 217–37.

Kelly, Jamie Terence (2012). *Framing Democracy: A Behavioral Approach to Democratic Theory*. Princeton, NJ: Princeton University Press.

Kremer, Monique (2007). *How Welfare States Care. Culture, Gender and Parenting in Europe*. Amsterdam: Amsterdam University Press.

Kugler, Tamar, Kausel, Edgar E., and Kocher, Martin G. (2012). "Are Groups More Rational than Individuals? A Review of Interactive Decision Making in Groups," *CESifo Working Paper No. 3701*.

Kuhnen, Camelia M., and Knutson, Brian (2005). "The Neural Basis of Financial Risk Taking," *Neuron*, 47(5): 763–70.

Kuhnle, Stein (ed.) (2000). *The Survival of the European Welfare State*. London: Routledge.

(2003). "Productive Welfare in Korea: Moving Towards a European Welfare State Type?" In Mishra, Ramesh, Kuhnle, Stein, Gilbert, Neil, and Chung, Kyungbae (eds.), *Modernizing the Korean Welfare State: Towards the Productive Welfare Model*. New Brunswick, NJ: Transaction Publishers, pp. 47–64.

Kuhnle, Stein, and Sander, Anne (2010). "The Emergence of the Welfare State." In Castles et al. (eds.), pp. 61–80.

Kuipers, Sanneke L. (2006). *The Crisis Imperative: Crisis Rhetoric and Welfare State Reform in Belgium and the Netherlands in the Early 1990s*. Amsterdam: Amsterdam University Press.

Lambert, Priscilla A. (2008). "The Comparative Political Economy of Parental Leave and Child Care: Evidence from Twenty OECD Countries," *Social Politics*, 15(3): 315–44.

Larsen, Christian Albrekt (2008a). "The Institutional Logic of Welfare Attitudes," *Comparative Political Studies*, 41(2): 145–68.

(2008b). "The Political Logic of Labour Market Reforms and Popular Images of Target Groups," *Journal of European Social Policy*, 18(1): 50–63.

Larsen, Christian Albrekt, and Andersen, J. Goul (2009). "How New Economic Ideas Changed the Danish Welfare State: The Case of Neoliberal Ideas and Highly Organized Social Democratic Interests," *Governance*, 22(2): 239–61.

Lau, Richard R. (1985). "Two Explanations for Negativity Effects in Political Behavior," *American Journal of Political Science*, 29(1): 119–38.

Lee, Honggue (2004). "Regime Selection as an Alternative to the Grubel-Lloyd Index." Paper presented at the Econometric Society 2004 Far East Meeting, Econometric Society.

Leibfried, Stephan (1992). "Towards a European Welfare State? On Integrating Poverty Regimes into the European Community." In Ferge, Zsuzsa, and Kolberg, Jon Eivind (eds.), *Social Policy in a Changing Europe*. Frankfurt a.M.: Campus, pp. 245–79.

Leibfried, Stephan, and Pierson, Paul (1995). "Semisovereign Welfare States: Social Policy in a Multitiered Europe." In Leibfried, Stephan, and Pierson, Paul (eds.), *European Social Policy. Between Fragmentation and Integration*. Washington, DC: Brookings Institution, pp. 43–77.

Leibfried, Stephan, and Obinger, Herbert (2003). "The State of the Welfare State: German Social Policy between Macroeconomic Retrenchment and Microeconomic Recalibration." *West European Politics*, 26(4): 199–218.

Levine, Ross, and Renelt, David (1992). "A Sensitivity Analysis of Cross-Country Growth Regressions," *American Economic Review*, 82(4): 942–63.

Levine Frader, Laura (2008). *Breadwinners and Citizens: Gender in the Making of the French Social Model*. Durham: Duke University Press.

Levy, Jack S. (1997). "Prospect Theory, Rational Choice, and International Relations," *International Studies Quarterly*, 41(1): 87–112.

(2003) "Applications of Prospect Theory to Political Science," *Synthese*, 135(2): 215–41.

Levy, Jonah D. (1999). "Vice into Virtue? Progressive Politics and Welfare Reform in Continental Europe," *Politics & Society*, 27(2): 239–74.

Lewis, Jane (2001). "The Decline of the Male Breadwinner Model: Implications for Work and Care," *Social Politics*, 8(2): 152–69.

Lieberman, Robert C. (2002). "Ideas, Institutions, and Political Order: Explaining Political Change," *American Political Science Review*, 96(4): 697–712.

Lindbom, Anders (2007). "Obfuscating Retrenchment: Swedish Welfare Policy in the 1990s." *Journal of Public Policy*, 27(2): 129–50.

Lindvall, Johannes (2010). "Power Sharing and Reform Capacity," *Journal of Theoretical Politics*, 22(3): 359–76.

Lindvall, Johannes, and Rueda, David (2012). "Insider-Outsider Politics: Party Strategies and Political Behavior in Sweden." In Emmenegger et al. (eds.), pp. 277–303.

Loewenstein, George, Rick, Scott, and Cohen, Jonathan D. (2008). "Neuroeconomics," *Annual Review of Psychology*, 59: 647–72.

Lopez, Anthony C., and McDermott, Rose (2012). "Adaptation, Heritability, and the Emergence of Evolutionary Political Science," *Political Psychology*, 33(3): 343–62.

Lupu, Noam, and Pontusson, Jonas (2011). "The Structure of Inequality and the Politics of Redistribution," *American Political Science Review*, 105(2): 316–36.

Lynch, Julia (2006). *Age in the Welfare State: The Origins of Social Spending on Pensioners, Workers, and Children*. Cambridge: Cambridge University Press.

Lynch, Julia, and Myrskylä, Mikko (2009). "Always the Third Rail? Pension Income and Policy Preferences in European Democracies," *Comparative Political Studies*, 42(8): 1068–97.

Mahoney, James, and Thelen, Katleen (eds.) (2010). *Explaining Institutional Change: Ambiguity, Agency, and Power*. Cambridge: Cambridge University Press.

Mandl, Irene, and Salvatore, Lidia (2009). "Tackling the Recession: Employment-Related Public Initiatives in the EU Member States and Norway." Dublin: European Foundation for the Improvement of Living and Working Conditions. http://www.eurofound.europa.eu/docs/erm/tn0907020s/tn0907020s.pdf (accessed February 2010).

Manow, Philip (2004). "The Good, the Bad, and the Ugly": Esping-Andersen's Regime Typology and the Religious Roots of the Western Welfare State. Mimeo: Cologne. http://www.hks.harvard.edu/inequality/Summer/Summer04/papers/Manow.pdf (accessed June 2011).

(2005). "Germany: Co-operative Federalism and the Overgrazing of the Fiscal Commons." In Herbert Obinger, Herbert, Leibfried, Stephan, and Castles, Francis G. (eds.), *Federalism and the Welfare State: New World and European Experiences*, pp. 222–63. Cambridge: Cambridge University Press.

Manow, Philip, and Van Kersbergen, Kees (2009). "Religion and the Western Welfare State: The Theoretical Context." In Van Kersbergen and Manow (eds.), pp. 1–38.

Manow, Philip, Van Kersbergen, Kees, and Schumacher, Gijs (2013). "De-industrialization and the Expansion of the Welfare State: A Reassessment." In Wren (ed.), pp. 227–47.

Manza, Jeff, and Cook, Fay L. (2002). "A Democratic Polity? Three Views of Policy Responsiveness in the United States," *American Politics Research*, 30(6): 630–67.

Margalit, Yotam (2013). "Explaining Social Policy Preferences: Evidence from the Great Recession." *American Political Science Review*, 107(1): 80–103.

Marier, Patrik (2008). "Empowering Epistemic Communities: Specialised Politicians, Policy Experts and Policy Reform," *West European Politics*, 31(3): 513–33.

Marshall, Thomas H. (1964). *Class, Citizenship and Social Development*. Garden City, NY: Doubleday.

Marvel, Howard P., and Ray, Edward J. (1987). "Intraindustry Trade: Sources and Effects on Protection," *Journal of Political Economy*, 95(6): 1278–91.

Marx, Ive, and Nolan, Brian (2012). "In-Work Poverty," *Gini Discussion Paper 51*, July 2012. Amsterdam: AIAS.

Maselli, Ilaria (2012). "The Evolving Supply and Demand of Skills in the Labour Market," *Intereconomics*, 47(1): 22–30.

Matthews, J. Scott, and Erickson, Lynda (2008). "Welfare State Structures and the Structure of Welfare State Support: Attitudes towards Social Spending in Canada, 1993–2000," *European Journal of Political Research*, 47(4): 411–35.

Mau, Steffen, and Veghte Benjamin (eds.) (2007). *Social Justice, Legitimacy, and the Welfare State*. London: Ashgate.

Mayda, Anna Maria, and Rodrik, Dani (2005). "Why Are Some People (and Countries) More Protectionist than Others?" *European Economic Review*, 49(6): 1393–430.

McDermott, Rose (2004). "Prospect Theory in Political Science: Gains and Losses from the First Decade," *Political Psychology*, 25(2): 289–312.

McDermott, Rose, Fowler, James H., and Smirnov, Oleg (2008). "On the Evolutionary Origin of Prospect Theory Preferences," *Journal of Politics*, 70(2): 335–50.

Mehlkop, Guido, and Neumannn, Robert (2012). "Explaining Preferences for Redistribution: A Unified Framework to Account for Institutional Approaches and Economic Self-Interest for the Case of Monetary Transfers for Families and Children," *European Journal of Political Research*. doi: 10.1111/j.1475-6765.2011.02002.x.

Mehta, Jal (2011). "The Varied Roles of Ideas in Politics: From 'Whether' to 'How.'" In Béland and Cox (eds.), pp. 23–46.

Meinhard, Stephanie, and Potrafke, Niklas (2012). "The Globalization-Welfare State Nexus Reconsidered," *Review of International Economics*, 20(2): 271–87.

Meltzer, Allan H., and Richard, Scott F. (1981). "A Rational Theory of the Size of Government," *Journal of Political Economy*, 89(5): 914–27.

Mercer, Jonathan (2005). "Prospect Theory and Political Science," *Annual Review of Political Science*, 8: 1–21.

Merton, Robert K. (1996). *Social Theory and Social Structure*. New York: Free Press.

Milward, Alan S. (1992). *The European Rescue of the Nation State*. London: Routledge.

Mishra, Ramesh (1984). *The Welfare State in Crisis. Social Thought and Social Change*. Brighton: Wheatsheaf.

Mommsen, Wolfgang J., and Mock, Wolfgang (1981). *The Emergence of the Welfare State in Britain and Germany, 1850–1950*. London: Croom Helm/German Historical Institute in London.

Moran, Michael (1988). "Crises of the Welfare State," *British Journal of Political Science*, 18(3): 397–414.

Morgan, Kimberly (2006). *Working Mothers and the Welfare State. Religion and Politics of Work-Family Policies in Western Europe and the United States*. Stanford, CA: Stanford University Press.

  (2013). "Path Shifting of the Welfare State: Electoral Competition and the Expansion of Work-Family Policies in Western Europe," *World Politics*, 65(1): 73–115.

Mudde, Cas (2009 [2007]). *Populist Radical Right Parties in Europe*. Cambridge: Cambridge University Press.

Myles, John, and Quadagno, Jill (2002). "Political Theories and the Welfare State," *Social Service Review*, 76(1): 34–57.

Myrskylä, Mikko, Kohler, Hans-Peter, and Billari, Francesco C. (2009). "Advances in Development Reverse Fertility Declines," *Nature*, 460 (August): 741–43.

Naumann, Ingela (2012). "Childcare Politics in the 'New' Welfare State: Class, Religion, and Gender in the Shaping of Political Agendas." In Bonoli and Natali (eds.) (2012b), pp. 158–81.

Nelson, Thomas E., Oxley, Zoe M., and Clawson, Rosalee A. (1997). "Towards a Psychology of Framing Effects," *Political Behavior*, 19(3): 221–46.

Neugart, Michael (2008). "The Choice of Insurance in the Labor Market," *Public Choice*, 134(3/4): 445–62.

Newell, James (2000). *Parties and Democracy in Italy*. Aldershot: Ashgate.

Nolan, Brian, and Marx, Ive (2009). "Inequality, Poverty and Exclusion." In Salverda, Wiemer, Nolan, Brian, and Smeeding, Timothy M. (eds.), *The Oxford Handbook of Economic Inequality*. Oxford: Oxford University Press, pp. 315–41.

Norman, Emma R., and Delfin, Rafael (2012). "Wizards under Uncertainty: Cognitive Biases, Threat Assessment, and Misjudgments in Policy Making," *Politics & Policy*, 40(3): 369–402.

Obinger, Herbert, and Wagschal, Uwe (2010). "Social Expenditure and Revenues." In Castles et al. (eds.), pp. 333–52.

Obinger, Herbert, and Wagschal, Uwe, Schmitt, Carina, and Starke, Peter (2013). "Policy Diffusion and Policy Transfer in Comparative Welfare State Research," *Social Policy & Administration* 47(1): 111–29.

O'Connor, James R. (1973). *The Fiscal Crisis of the State*. New York: St. Martin's Press.

OECD (1981). *The Welfare State in Crisis*. Paris: OECD.

(1985). *Social Expenditures 1960–1990. Problems of Growth and Control.* Paris: OECD.

(1999). *Employment Outlook.* Paris: OECD.

(2002). *Labour Force Statistics.* Paris: OECD.

(2004a). *Employment Outlook.* Paris: OECD.

(2004b). *Economic Outlook.* Paris: OECD.

(2007a). *Society at a Glance.* www.oecd.org/els/social/indicators (accessed 22 July 2009).

(2007b). *OECD Population Pyramids in 2000 and 2050.* Paris: OECD. http://www.oecd.org/dataoecd/52/31/38123085.xls (accessed April 2010).

(2008). *Growing Unequal? Income Distribution and Poverty in OECD Countries,* Paris: OECD.

(2009). *Addressing the Labour Market Challenges of the Economic Downturn: A Summary of Country Responses to the OECD-EC Wuestionnaire.* Paris: OECD. http://www.oecd.org/dataoecd/15/29/43732441.pdf (accessed February 2010).

(2010a). *Main Economic Indicators.* http://lysander.sourceoecd.org/vl=5371915/cl=38/nw=1/rpsv/ij/oecdstats/16081234/v195n1/s1/p1 (accessed August 2010).

(2010b). *OECD Family Database.* http://www.oecd.org/document/4/0,3343,en_2649_34819_37836996_1_1_1_1,00.html (accessed October 2010).

(2011). *Main Economic Indicators.* http://www.oecd-ilibrary.org/economics/data/main-economic-indicators_mei-data-en (accessed August 2011).

(2012). *Key Tables from the OECD: 20. Government Deficit/Surplus as a Percentage of GDP.* http://www.oecd-ilibrary.org/economics/government-deficit_gov-dfct-table-en (accessed March 2013).

Offe, Klaus (1984) (Keane, John, ed.). *Contradictions of the Welfare State.* London: Hutchinson.

Okun, Arthur (1975). *Equality and Efficiency: The Big Tradeoff.* Washington, DC: Brookings Institution.

Olson, Kevin (2006). *Reflexive Democracy. Political Equality and the Welfare State.* Cambridge. MA: MIT Press.

Oscarsson, Henrik, and Holmberg, Sören (2008). *Regeringsskifte: väljarna och valet 2006* [Change of Government: Voters and the Election of 2006]. Stockholm: Norstedts Juridik.

Paetzold, Jorg (2012). "The Convergence of Welfare State Indicators in Europe: Evidence from Panel Data," *Working Papers in Economics and Finance*, No. 201204, University of Salzburg.

Palier, Bruno (ed.) (2010a). *A Long Goodbye to Bismarck? The Politics of Welfare Reform in Continental Europe.* Amsterdam: Amsterdam University Press.

(2010b). "Ordering Change: Understanding the 'Bismarckian' Welfare Reform Trajectory." In Palier (ed.), pp. 19–44.

(2010c). "The Long Conservative Corporatist Road to Welfare Reforms." In Palier (ed.) (2010a), pp. 333–87.

(2012). "Turning Vice into Vice: How Bismarckian Welfare States Have Gone from Unsustainability to Dualization." In Bonoli and Natali (eds.) (2012b), pp. 233–55.

Panitch, Leo (1986). *Working Class Politics in Crisis.* London: Verso.

Peng, Ito, and Wong, Joseph (2010). "East Asia." In Castles et al. (eds.), pp. 656–70.

Perla Jr., Héctor (2011). "Explaining Public Support for the Use of Military Force: The Impact of Reference Point Framing and Prospective Decision Making," *International Organization,* 65(1): 139–67.

Peters, B. Guy, Pierre, Jon, and King, Desmond S. (2005). "The Politics of Path Dependency: Political Conflict in Historical Institutionalism," *Journal of Politics*, 67(4): 1275–300.

Petersen, Michael Bang, Slothuus, Rune, Stubager, Rune, and Togeby, Lise (2011). "Deservingness versus Values in Public Opinion on Welfare: The Automaticity of the Deservingness Heuristic," *European Journal of Political Research*, 50(1): 24–52.

Pfau-Effinger, Birgit (2003). "Socio-Historical Paths of the Male Breadwinner Model. An Explanation of Cross-National Differences." *British Journal of Sociology*, 55(3): 377–99.

Pierson, Christopher (1991). *Beyond the Welfare State? The New Political Economy of Welfare*. Cambridge: Polity Press.

Pierson, Paul (1994). *Dismantling the Welfare State. Reagan, Thatcher, and the Politics of Retrenchment*. Cambridge: Cambridge University Press.

(1996). "The New Politics of the Welfare State," *World Politics*, 48(2): 143–79.

(1998). "Irresistible Forces, Immovable Objects: Welfare States Confront Permanent Austerity," *Journal of European Public Policy*, 5(4): 539–60.

(2000). "Increasing Returns, Path Dependence, and the Study of Politics," *American Political Science Review*, 94(2): 251–67.

(2001a). "Coping with Permanent Austerity: Welfare State Restructuring in Affluent Democracies." In Pierson (ed.), *The New Politics of the Welfare State*. Oxford: Oxford University Press, pp. 410–56.

(ed.) (2001b). *The New Politics of the Welfare State*. Oxford: Oxford University Press.

(2001c). "Post-Industrial Pressures on the Mature Welfare States." In Pierson (ed.), *The New Politics of the Welfare State*. Oxford: Oxford University Press, pp. 80–104.

(2004). *Politics in Time: History, Institutions, and Social Analysis*. Princeton, NJ: Princeton University Press.

(2011). The Welfare State over the Very Long Run, *ZeS-Working Paper*, No. 02/2011. http://en.zes.uni-bremen.de/ccm/research/publikationen/the-welfare-state-over-the-very-long-run.en;jsessionid=022CEBD89BB5F4697D87CE4A85350A4F (accessed July 2011).

Pierson, Paul, and Leibfried, Stephan (1995). "Multitiered Institutions and the Making of Social Policy." In Leibfried, Stephan, and Pierson, Paul (eds.). *European Social Policy. Between Fragmentation and Integration*. Washington, DC: Brookings Institution, pp. 1–40.

Plantenga, Janneke (2002). "Combining Work and Care in the Polder Model: An Assessment of the Dutch Part-Time Strategy," *Critical Social Policy*, 22(1): 53–71.

Plümper, Thomas, Troeger, Vera E., and Manow, Philip (2005). "Panel Data Analysis in Comparative Politics: Linking Method to Theory," *European Journal of Political Research*, 44(2): 327–54.

Polanyi, Karl (1944 [1957]). *The Great Transformation: The Political and Economic Origins of Our Time*. Boston, MA: Beacon Press.

Pontusson, Jonas, and Raess, Damian (2012). "How (and Why) Is This Time Different? The Politics of Economic Crisis in Western Europe and the United States," *Annual Review of Political Science*, 15: 13–33.

Powell, Martin, and Barrientos, Armanda (2011). "An Audit of the Welfare Modelling Business," *Social Policy & Administration*, 45(1): 69–84.

Prince, Michael J. (2010). "Avoiding Blame, Doing Good, and Claiming Credit: Reforming Canadian Income Security," *Canadian Public Administration*, 53(3): 293–322.

Pryor, Frederick L. (1968). *Public Expenditure in Communist and Capitalist Countries*. London: Allen and Unwin.

Przeworski, Adam, and Sprague, John (1986). *Paper Stones: A History of Electoral Socialism*. Chicago: University of Chicago Press.

Quattrone, George A., and Tversky, Amos (2000 [1988]). "Contrasting Rational and Psychological Analyses of Political Choice." In Kahneman and Tversky (eds.), pp. 451–72.

Quinn, Dennis P., and Toyoda, A. Maria (2007). "Ideology and Voter Preferences as Determinants of Financial Globalization," *American Journal of Political Science*, 51(2): 344–63.

Raven, Judith, Achterberg, Peter, Van der Veen, Romke, and Yerkes, Mara (2011). "An Institutional Embeddedness of Welfare Opinions? The Link between Public Opinion and Social Policy in the Netherlands (1970–2004)," *Journal of Social Policy*, 40(2): 369–86.

Ray, Rebecca, Gornick, Janet C., and Schmitt, John (2010). "Who Cares? Assessing Generosity and Gender Equality in Parental Leave Policy Designs in 21 Countries," *Journal of European Social Policy*, 20(3): 196–216.

Rehm, Philipp (2009). "Risks and Redistribution: An Individual-Level Analysis," *Comparative Political Studies*, 42(7): 855–81.

 (2011). "Social Policy by Popular Demand." *World Politics*, 63(2): 271–99.

Rehm, Philipp, Hacker Jacob S., and Schlesinger, Mark (2012). "Insecure Alliances: Risk, Inequality, and Support for the Welfare State," *American Political Science Review*, 106(2): 386–406.

Rein, Martin, and Turner, John (2001). "Public-Private Interactions: Mandatory Pensions in Australia, the Netherlands and Switzerland," *Review of Population and Social Policy*, 10: 107–53.

Ricardo, David (2004 [1817]). *The Principles of Political Economy and Taxation*. London: J. M. Dent.

Rice, Deborah (2013). "Beyond Welfare Regimes: From Empirical Typology to Conceptual Ideal Types." *Social Policy & Administration*, 47(1): 93–110.

Rieger, Marc O. (2009). "Evolutionary Stability of Prospect Theory Preferences," *Working Papers Institute of Mathematical Economics, No. 422*. http://www.imw. uni-bielefeld.de/papers/files/imw-wp-422.pdf (accessed June 2011).

Rieger, Elmar, and Leibfried, Stephan (2003). *Limits to Globalization*. Cambridge: Polity Press.

Rimlinger, Gaston V. (1968). "Social Change and Social Security in Germany," *Journal of Human Resources*, 3(4): 409–21.

 (1971). *Welfare Policy and Industrialization in Europe, America, and Russia*. New York: Wiley.

Ringen, Stein (1987 [2006]). *The Possibility of Politics. A Study in the Political Economy of the Welfare State*. New Brunswick, NJ: Transaction.

Rodríguez, Francisco, and Rodrik, Dani (2000). "Trade Policy and Economic Growth: A Skeptic's Guide to the Cross-National Evidence." NBER Working Paper.

Rodrik, Dani (1997). *Has Globalization Gone Too Far?* Washington, DC: Institute for International Economics.

(1998). "Why Do More Open Economies Have Bigger Governments?" *Journal of Political Economy*, 106(5): 997–1032.

(1999). *The New Global Economy and Developing Countries: Making Openness Work*. ODC Policy Essay, No. 24. Baltimore, MD: Johns Hopkins University Press.

Rokkan, Stein (1975). "Dimensions of State Formation and Nation Building: A Possible Paradigm for Research on Variations within Europe." In Tilly, Charles (ed.), *The Formation of National States in Western Europe*. Princeton, NJ: Princeton University Press, pp. 575–91.

Ross, Fiona (1997). "Cutting Public Expenditures in Advanced Industrial Democracies: The Importance of Avoiding Blame," *Governance: An International Journal of Policy and Administration*, 10(2): 175–200.

(2000). "Beyond Left and Right: The New Partisan Politics of Welfare," *Governance: An International Journal of Policy and Administration*, 13(2): 155–83.

Rothgang, Heinz, Obinger, Herbert, and Leibfried, Stephan (2006). "The State and Its Welfare State: How Do Welfare State Changes Affect the Make-up of the Nation State?" *Social Policy & Administration*, 40(3): 250–66.

Rothstein, Bo, Samani, Marcus, and Teorell, Jan (2010). "Quality of Government, Political Power and the Welfare State." *QoG Working Paper Series*, No. 2010:6.

Rueda, David (2006). "Social Democracy and Active Labour-Market Policies: Insiders, Outsiders and the Politics of Employment Promotion," *British Journal of Political Science*, 36(3): 385–406.

(2007). *Social Democracy Inside Out: Partisanship and Labor Market Policy in Industrialized Democracies*. Oxford: Oxford University Press.

Sachs, Jeffrey D., and Warner, Andrew (1995). "Economic Reform and the Process of Global Integration," *Brookings Papers on Economic Activity*, 1, 1–118.

Sattler, Thomas, and Walter, Stephanie (2009). "Globalization and Government Short-Term Room to Maneuver in Economic Policy: An Empirical Analysis of Reactions to Currency Crises," *World Political Science Review*, 5(1): 1–30.

Saunders, Peter (2010). "Inequality and Poverty," in Castles et al., pp. 526–38.

Scarbrough, Elinor (2000). "West European Welfare States: The Old Politics of Retrenchment," *West European Politics*, 38(2): 225–59.

Scharpf, Fritz W. (1991 [1987]). *Crisis and Choice in European Social Democracy*. Ithaca, NY: Cornell University Press.

Scharpf, Fritz W., and Schmidt, Vivien A. (eds.) (2000). *Welfare and Work in the Open Economy. Vol. I: From Vulnerability to Competitiveness, Vol. II: Diverse Responses to Common Challenges*. Oxford: Oxford University Press.

Scherer, F. M. (2010). The Dynamics of Capitalism, *Harvard Kennedy School Faculty Research Working Paper Series*, January 2010, RWP10–001. http://web.hks.harvard.edu/publications/workingpapers/citation.aspx?PubId=6988 (accessed July 2011).

Scheve, Kenneth F., and Slaughter, Matthew J. (2001). "What Determines Individual Trade-Policy Preferences?" *Journal of International Economics*, 54(2): 267–92.

Schmidt, Manfred G. (1983). "The Welfare State and the Economy in Periods of Economic Crisis," *European Journal of Political Research*, 11(1): 1–26.

(1993). "Gendered Labour Force Participation." In Castles, Francis G. (ed.), *Families of Nations: Patterns of Public Policy in Western Democracies.* Aldershot: Ashgate/Dartmouth, pp. 179–237.

(2010). "Parties," in Castles et al., pp. 211–26.

Schmidt, Vivien A. (2002). "Does Discourse Matter in the Politics of Welfare State Adjustment?" *Comparative Political Studies*, 35(2): 168–93.

(2008). "Discursive Institutionalism: The Explanatory Power of Ideas and Discourse," *Annual Review of Political Science*, 11: 303–26.

(2011). "Give Peace a Chance: Reconciling the Four (not Three) New Institutionalisms." In Béland and Cox, pp. 47–64.

Schmitt, Carina, and Starke, Peter (2011). "Explaining Convergence of OECD Welfare States: A Conditional Approach," *Journal of European Social Policy*, 21(2): 120–35.

Schubert, Klaus, Hegelich, Simon, and Bazant, Ursula (2009). "European Welfare Systems: Current State of Research and Some Theoretical Considerations." In Schubert, Klaus, Hegelich, Simon, and Bazant, Ursula (eds.), *The Handbook of European Welfare Systems*. London: Routledge, pp. 3–28.

Schumacher, Gijs (2012). "*Modernize or Die*"? *Social Democrats, Welfare State Retrenchment and the Choice between Office and Policy*, PhD Dissertation, VU University Amsterdam.

Schumacher, Gijs, Vis, Barbara, and Van Kersbergen, Kees (2013). "Political Parties' Welfare Image, Electoral Punishment and Welfare State Retrenchment," *Comparative European Politics*, 11(1): 1–21.

Schumpeter, Joseph A. (1976 [1942]). *Capitalism, Socialism and Democracy*. New York: Harper Perennial.

Schwartz, Christine R. (2010). "Earnings Inequality and the Changing Association between Spouses's Earnings," *American Journal of Sociology*, 115(5): 1524–57.

Schwartz, Herman (2001). "Round Up the Usual Suspects! Globalization, Domestic Politics, and Welfare State Change." In Pierson (ed.) (2001b), pp. 17–44.

SCP (Social and Cultural Planning Office of the Netherlands.) (2001). *De Sociale Staat van Nederland 2001* (The Social State of the Netherlands). The Hague: SCP. http://www.scp.nl/Publicaties/Alle_publicaties/Publicaties_2001/De_sociale_staat_van_Nederland (accessed August 2010).

Scruggs, Lyle A. (2004). Welfare State Entitlement Data Set: A Comparative Institutional Analysis of Eighteen Welfare States, version 1.1. http://sp.uconn.edu/~scruggs/wp.htm (accessed March 2011).

Scruggs, Lyle A., and Allan, James P. (2006). "The Material Consequences of Welfare States: Benefit Generosity and Absolute Poverty in 16 OECD Countries," *Comparative Political Studies*, 39(7): 880–904.

(2008). "Social Stratification and Welfare Regimes for the Twenty-First Century. Revisiting the Three Worlds of Welfare Capitalism." *World Politics*, 60(4): 642–64.

Scruggs, Lyle, and Lange, Peter (2001). "Unemployment and Union Density." In Bermeo, Nancy (ed.), *Unemployment in the New Europe*. Cambridge: Cambridge University Press, pp. 145–72.

Seeleib-Kaiser, Martin, van Dyk, Silke, and Roggenkamp, Martin (2008). *Party Politics and Social Welfare: Comparing Christian and Social Democracy in Austria, Germany and the Netherlands*. Cheltenham: Edward Elgar.

Segura-Ubiergo, Alex (2007). *The Political Economy of the Welfare State in Latin America. Globalization, Democracy, and Development*. New York: Cambridge University Press.

Sharp, Elaine B. (1999). *The Sometime Connection: Public Opinion and Social Policy*. Albany: State University of New York Press.

Sihvo, Tuire, and Uusitalo, Hannu (1995). "Economic Crises and Support for the Welfare State in Finland 1975–1993," *Acta Sociologica*, 38(3): 251–62.

Silberberg, Alan, Roma, Peter A., Huntsberry, Mary E., Warren-Boulton, Frederick R., Sakagami, Takayuki, Ruggiero, Angela M., and Suomi, Stephen J. (2008), "On Loss Aversion in Capuchin Monkeys," *Journal of Experimental Analysis of Behavior*, 89(2): 145–55.

Slothuus, Rune (2007). "Framing Deservingness to Win Support for Welfare State Retrenchment," *Scandinavian Political Studies*, 30(3): 323–44.

Smeeding, Timothy M. (2005). "Public Policy, Economic Inequality, and Poverty: The United States in Comparative Perspective," *Social Science Quarterly*, 68(s1): 955–83.

Smith, Adam (2003 [1776]). *An Inquiry into the Nature and Causes of the Wealth of Nations*. New York: Bantam Dell.

Smith, Kip, Dickhaut, John, McCabe, Kevin, and Pardo, José V. (2002), "Neuronal Substrates for Choice under Ambiguity, Risk, Gains, and Losses," *Management Science*, 48(6): 711–18.

Smits, Jeroen, Ultee, Wout, and Lammers, Jan (1998). "Educational Homogamy in 65 Countries: An Explanation of Differences in Openness Using Country-Level Explanatory Variables," *American Sociological Review*, 63(2): 264–85.

Sniderman, Paul M., Petersen, Michael Bang, Slothuus, Rune, and Stubager, Rune (2013). *Crosswinds: A Study of a Clash of Liberal Democratic and Islamic Values*, unpublished manuscript, University of Aarhus.

Soede, Arjan J., Vrooman, J. Cok, Ferraresi, Pier Marco, and Segre, Giovanna (2004). *Unequal Welfare States; Distributive Consequences of Population Ageing in Six European Countries*. The Hague: Social and Cultural Planning Office.

Soskice, David, and Iversen, Torben (2006). "Electoral Institutions and the Politics of Coalitions: Why Some Democracies Redistribute More Than Others," *American Political Science Review*, 100(2): 165–81.

Starke, Peter (2006). "The Politics of Welfare State Retrenchment: A Literature Review," *Social Policy & Administration*, 40(1): 104–20.

(2008). *Radical Welfare State Retrenchment. A Comparative Analysis*. Houndmills, Basingstoke: Palgrave MacMillan.

Starke, Peter, Kaasch, Alexandra, and van Hooren, Franca (2013). *The Welfare State as Crisis Manager: Explaining the Diversity of Policy Responses to Economic Crisis*. Houndmills, Basingstoke: Palgrave Macmillan.

Statistisches Bundesamst Deutschland (2010). Detailed Results on the Gross Domestic Product in the 2nd Quarter of 2010, Press release no. 293/24 August 2010. http://www.destatis.de/jetspeed/portal/cms/Sites/destatis/Internet/EN/press/pr/2010/08/PE10__293__811,templateId=renderPrint.psml (accessed August 2010).

Stephens, John D. (1979). *The Transition from Capitalism to Socialism*. London: Macmillan.

Stiglitz, Joseph E. (2010). *Free Fall. America, Free Markets, and the Sinking of the World Economy*. New York: W.W. Norton.

(2012). *The Price of Inequality: How Today's Divided Society Endangers Our Future.* New York: W.W. Norton.

Stiller, Sabina (2010). *Ideational Leadership in German Welfare State Reform: How Politicians and Policy Ideas Transform Resilient Institutions.* Amsterdam: Amsterdam University Press.

Stinchcombe, Arthur L. (1968). *Constructing Social Theories.* New York: Harcourt, Brace and World.

Stjernø, Steinar (2004). *Solidarity in Europe: The History of an Idea.* Cambridge: Cambridge University Press.

Streeck, Wolfgang (1995). "From Market Making to State Building? Reflections on the Political Economy of European Social Policy." In Leibfried, Stephan, and Pierson, Paul (eds.), *European Social Policy. Between Fragmentation and Integration.* Washington, DC: Brookings Institution.

(1996). "Neo-Voluntarism: A New European Social Policy Regime?" In Marks, Gary, Scharpf, Fritz W., Schimtter, Philippe C., and Streeck, Wolfgang (eds.). *Governance in the European Union.* London: Sage.

(2012). "How to Study Contemporary Capitalism?" *European Journal of Sociology,* 53(1): 1–28.

Streeck, Wolfgang, and Thelen, Kathleen (2005). *Beyond Continuity: Institutional Change in Advanced Political Economies.* Oxford: Oxford University Press.

Sulitzeanu-Kenan, Raanan (2010). Reflection in the Shadow of Blame: When Do Politicians Appoint Commissions of Inquiry? *British Journal of Political Science,* 40(3): 613–34.

Svallfors, Stefan (1995). "The End of Class Politics? Structural Cleavages and Attitudes to Swedish Welfare Policies," *Acta Sociologica,* 38(1): 53–74.

(2003). "Welfare Regimes and Western Opinions: A Comparison of Eight Western Countries," *Social Indicators Research,* 64(3): 495–520.

(2010). "Public Attitudes," in Castles et al., pp. 241–51.

(2011). "A Bedrock of Support? Trends in Welfare State Attitudes in Sweden, 1981–2010," *Social Policy & Administration,* 45(7): 806–25.

(2012). *Contested Welfare States: Welfare Attitudes in Europe and Beyond.* Stanford, CA: Stanford University Press.

Svallfors, Stefan, and Taylor-Gooby, Peter (eds.) (1999). *The End of the Welfare State? Responses to State Retrenchment.* New York: Routledge.

Swank, Duane (2001). "Political Institutions and Welfare State Restructuring: The Impact of Institutions on Social Policy Change in Developed Democracies." In Pierson (ed.) (2001b), pp. 197–237.

(2002). *Global Capital, Political Institutions, and Policy Change in Developed Welfare States.* Cambridge: Cambridge University Press.

(2010). "Globalization." In Castles et al., pp. 318–30.

Swedish Budget Bill (2010). "Budget Bill 2010." http://www.sweden.gov.se/sb/d/12234/a/132192 (accessed August 2011).

(2011). "Budget Bill 2011." http://www.sweden.gov.se/sb/d/12699/a/153832 (accessed August 2011).

Taliaferro, Jeffrey W. (2004). "Power Politics and the Balance of Risk: Hypotheses on Great Power Intervention in the Periphery," *Political Psychology,* 25(2): 177–211.

Taylor-Gooby, Peter (2002). "The Silver Age of the Welfare State: Perspectives on Resilience," *Journal of Social Policy,* 31(4): 597–621.

(2005). *Ideas and Welfare State Reform in Western Europe*. Houndsmills, Basingstoke, Hampshire: Palgrave Macmillan.

(2011). "Root and Branch Restructuring to Achieve Major Cuts: The Social Policy Programme of the 2010 UK," *Social Policy & Administration*. Early View (doi: 10.1111/j.1467-9515.2011.00797.x).

Taylor-Gooby, Peter, and Stoker, Gerry (2011). "The Coalition Programme: A New Vision for Britain or Politics as Usual?" *Political Quarterly*, 82(1): 4-15.

Tepe, Markus, and Vanhuysse, Pieter (2010). "Who Cuts Back and When? The Politics of Delays in Social Expenditure Cutbacks, 1980–2005," *West European Politics*, 33(6): 1214–40.

(2012). "Accelerating Smaller Cutbacks to Delay Larger Ones? The Politics of Timing and Alarm Bells in OECD Pension Generosity Retrenchment." In Vanhuysse, Pieter, and Goerres, Achim (eds.). *Ageing Populations in Post-industrial Democracies: Comparative Studies of Policies and Politics*. London: Routledge, pp. 127–44.

Thaler, Richard H., and Sunstein, Cass R. (2008). *Nudge: Improving Decisions about Health, Wealth and Happiness*. London: Penguin Books.

Therborn, Göran (1986). *Why Some People Are More Unemployed than Others*. London: Verso.

Thomas, Sue (1994). *How Women Legislate*. New York: Oxford University Press.

Titmuss, Richard M. (1968 [fourth impression 1973]). *Commitment to Welfare*. London: Allen and Unwin.

(1974). *Social Policy: An Introduction*. London: Allen and Unwin.

Tom, Sabrina M., Fox, Craig R., Trepel, Christopher, and Poldrack, Russell A. (2007). "The Neural Basis of Loss Aversion in Decision-making under Risk," *Science*, 315(2811): 515-18.

Tsebelis, George (1995). "Decision-making in Political Systems: Veto Players in Presidentialism, Parliamentarism, Multicameralism and Multipartyism," *British Journal of Political Science*, 25(3): 289-25.

(2002). *Veto Players*. Princeton, NJ: Princeton University Press.

Tversky, Amos, and Kahneman, Daniel (1981). "The Framing of Decision and the Psychology of Choice," *Science* 211(January): 453–58.

(2000). "Advances in Prospect Theory: Cumulative Representation of Uncertainty." In Kahneman and Tversky (eds.), pp. 44–65.

UK HM Treasury (2010). "2010 HM Treasury Budget." http://www.hm-treasury.gov.uk/d/junebudget_complete.pdf (accessed May 2010).

(2011). "2011 HM Treasury Budget." http://cdn.hm-treasury.gov.uk/2011budget_complete.pdf (accessed May 2011).

US Budget (2010). "US Budget 2010." http://www.gpoaccess.gov/usbudget/fy10/index.html (accessed May 2010).

(2011). "US Budget 2011." http://www.gpoaccess.gov/usbudget/fy11/index.html (accessed May 2011).

(2012). "US Budget 2012." http://www.gpoaccess.gov/usbudget/fy12/index.html (accessed August 2011).

US Recovery Act (2009). "The American Recovery and Reinvestment Act 2009." http://www.gpo.gov/fdsys/pkg/PLAW-111publ5/content-detail.html (accessed May 2011).

Vail, Mark (2010). *Recasting Welfare Capitalism: Economic Adjustment in Contemporary France and Germany*. Philadelphia, PA: Temple University Press.

Vandenbroucke, Frank, and Vleminckx, Koen (2011). "Disappointing Poverty Trends: Is the Social Investment State to Blame? An Exercise in Soul-Searching for Policy-Makers." *CSB Working Paper*, No. 11/01.

Van der Veen, Robert Jan, and Van der Brug, Wouter (2013). "Three Worlds of Social Insurance: On the Validity of Esping-Andersen's Welfare Regime Dimensions," *British Journal of Political Science*, 43(2): 323–43.

Van Gestel, Nicolette, De Beer, Paul, and Van der Meer, Marc (2009). *Het Hervormingsmoeras van de Verzorgingsstaat: Veranderingen in de Organisatie van de Sociale Zekerheid* (The Reform Swamp of the Welfare State: Changes in the Organization of Social Security). Amsterdam: Amsterdam University Press.

Van Kersbergen, Kees (1995). *Social Capitalism: A Study of Christian Democracy and the Welfare State*. London: Routledge.

(1999). "Contemporary Christian Democracy and the Demise of the Politics of Mediation." In Kitschelt, Herbert, Lange, Peter, Marks, Gary, and Stephens, John D. (eds.), *Continuity and Change in Contemporary Capitalism*. Cambridge: Cambridge University Press, pp. 346–70.

(2000). "The Declining Resistance of National Welfare States to Change?" In Kuhnle, pp. 19–36.

(2002). "The Politics of Welfare State Reform," *Swiss Political Science Review*, 8(2): 1–19.

(2006). "The Politics of Solidarity and the Changing Boundaries of the Welfare State," *European Political Science* 5(4): 377–94.

(2012). "An Institutionalist Explanation of Welfare State Reform in Continental Europe?" *Journal of European Social Policy*, 22(1): 92–4.

Van Kersbergen, Kees, and Becker, Uwe (1988). "The Netherlands: A Passive Social Democratic Welfare State in a Christian Democratic Ruled Society," *Journal of Social Policy*, 17(4): 477–99.

Van Kersbergen, Kees, and Kremer, Monique (2008). "Conservatism and the European Welfare State." In Van Oorschot, Wim, Opielka, Michael, and Pfau-Effinger, Birgit (eds,). *Culture and the Welfare State: Values and Social Policy in Comparative Perspective*. Cheltenham: Edward Elgar, pp. 71–88.

Van Kersbergen, Kees, and Manow, Philip (eds.) (2009). *Religion, Class Coalitions, and Welfare States*. Cambridge: Cambridge University Press.

(2011). "The Welfare State." In Caramani, Daniele (ed.), *Comparative Politics* (2nd edition). Oxford: Oxford University Press, pp. 189–407.

Van Kersbergen, Kees, and Van Waarden, Frans (2004). ""Governance" as a Bridge between Disciplines: Cross-Disciplinary Inspiration Regarding Shifts in Governance and Problems of Governability, Accountability and Legitimacy," *European Journal of Political Research*, 43(2): 143–71.

Van Lancker, Wim, and Ghysels, Joris (2011). "The Unequal Benefits of Activation: An Analysis of the Social Distribution of Family Policy among Families with Young Children," *Journal of European Social Policy*, 21(5): 472–85.

Van Oorschot, Wim (2000). "Who Should Get What, and Why? On Deservingness Criteria and the Conditionality of Solidarity among the Public," *Policy & Politics*, 28(1), 33–48.

Van Oorschot, Wim, and Meuleman, Bart (2011). "Welfarism and the Multidimensionality of Welfare State Legitimacy: Evidence from the Netherlands, 2006," *International Journal of Social Welfare*, 21(1): 79–93.

Van Vliet, Olaf, and Caminada, Koen (2012). "Unemployment Replacement Rates Dataset among 34 Welfare States 1971–2009: An Update, Extension and Modification of the Scruggs' Welfare State Entitlements Data Set," *NEUJOBS Special Report No. 2*, Leiden University.

Vis, Barbara (2005). *Trade Openness, Welfare Effort and Varieties of Welfare Capitalism.* Working Papers Political Science VU University Amsterdam, No. 2005/01 (2005).

(2007). "States of Welfare or States of Workfare? Welfare State Restructuring in 16 Capitalist Democracies, 1985–2002," *Policy & Politics*, 35(1): 105–22.

(2008). "The Direction and Scope of Social Policy Change: Regime Specific or Radical Shift Towards Workfare?" *Journal of Comparative Policy Analysis*, 10(2): 151–69.

(2009a). "The Importance of Socio-Economic and Political Losses and Gains in Welfare State Reform," *Journal of European Social Policy*, 19(5): 395–407.

(2009b). "Governments and Unpopular Social Policy Reform: Biting the Bullet or Steering Clear?" *European Journal of Political Research*, 48(1): 31–57.

(2010). *Politics of Risk-Taking: Welfare State Reform in Advanced Democracies.* Amsterdam: Amsterdam University Press.

(2011a). "Under Which Conditions Does Spending on Active Labor Market Policies Increase? A FsQCA Analysis of 53 Governments between 1985 and 2003," *European Political Science Review*, 3(2): 229–52.

(2011b). "Prospect Theory and Political Decision-making," *Political Studies Review*, 9(3): 334–43.

Vis, Barbara, and Van Kersbergen, Kees (2007). "Why and How Do Political Actors Pursue Risky Reforms?" *Journal of Theoretical Politics*, 19(2): 153–72.

Vis, Barbara, Van Kersbergen, Kees, and Becker, Uwe (2008). "The Politics of Welfare State Reform in the Netherlands: Explaining a Never-Ending Puzzle," *Acta Politica*, 43(2–3): 333–56.

Vis, Barbara, Van Kersbergen, Kees, and Hemerijck, Anton (2013). "The Triple Crisis and Welfare State Reform: Is Retrenchment Really the Only Game Left in Town?" Mimeo.

Visser, Jelle, and Hemerijck, Anton (1997). *A Dutch Miracle: Job Growth, Welfare Reform, and Corporatism in the Netherlands.* Amsterdam: Amsterdam University Press.

Vrooman, J. Cok (2009). *Rules of Relief. Institutions of Social Security, and Their Impact.* The Hague: The Netherlands Institute for Social Research/SCP.

(2012). "Regimes and Cultures of Social Security: Comparing Institutional Models through Nonlinear PCA," *International Journal of Comparative Sociology* 53(5–6): 444–77.

Walker, Alan, and Wong, Chack-kie (eds.) (2005). *East Asian Welfare Regimes in Transition. From Confucianism to Globalisation*, Bristol: Policy Press.

Walter, Stephanie (2010). "Globalization and the Welfare State: Testing the Microfoundations of the Compensation Hypothesis," *International Studies Quarterly*, 54(2): 403–26.

Weaver, Kent R. (1986). "The Politics of Blame Avoidance," *Journal of Public Policy*, 6(4): 371–98.

(1988). *Automatic Government: The Politics of Indexation.* Washington, DC: Brookings Institution.

Weishaupt, Timo J. (2011). *From the Manpower Revolution to the Activation Paradigm: Explaining Institutional Continuity and Change in an Integrating Europe.* Amsterdam: Amsterdam University Press.

Wenzelburger, Georg (2011). "Political Strategies and Fiscal Retrenchment: Evidence from Four Countries." *West European Politics*, 34(6): 1151–84.

Weyland, Kurt (1996). "Risk Taking in Latin American Economic Restructuring: Lessons from Prospect Theory," *International Studies Quarterly*, 40(2): 185–07.

  (1998). "The Political Fate of Market Reform in Latin America, Africa, and Eastern Europe," *International Studies Quarterly*, 42(4): 645–673.

  (2002). *The Politics of Market Reform in Fragile Democracies: Argentina, Brazil, Peru, and Venezuela*. Princeton, NJ: Princeton University Press.

  (2006). *Bounded Rationality and Policy Diffusion: Social Sector Reform in Latin America*. Princeton, NJ: Princeton University Press.

  (2012). "Diffusion Waves in European Democratization: The Impact of Organizational Development," *Comparative Politics*, 45(1): 25–45.

Wilensky, Harold L. (1975). *The Welfare State and Equality: Structural and Ideological Roots of Public Expenditures*. Berkeley: University of California Press.

Wilensky, Harold L., and Lebeaux, Charles N. (1965 [1958]). *Industrial Society and Social Welfare. The Impact of Industrialization on the Supply and Organization of Social welfare Services in the United States*. New York: Free Press.

Wilkinson, Richard, and Pickett, Kate (2009). *The Spirit Level. Why Equality Is Better for Everyone*. London: Penguin.

Wilson, Rick K. (2011). "The Contribution of Behavioral Economics to Political Science," *Annual Review of Political Science*, 14: 201–23.

Wincott, Daniel (2011). "Ideas, Policy Change, and the Welfare State." In Béland and Cox, pp. 143–66.

Wolfe, Alan (1979). *The Limits of Legitimacy*, London: Macmillan.

Wolfinger, Nicholas, H. (2003). "Family Structure Homogamy: The Effects of Parental Divorce on Partner Selection and Marital Stability," *Social Science Research*, 32(1): 80–97.

Wren, Anne (ed.) (2013). *The Political Economy of the Service Transition*. Oxford: Oxford University Press.

WWR (Wetenschappelijke Raad voor het Regeringsbeleid) [Scientific Council for Government Policy] (1990), *Een Werkend Perspectief: Arbeidsparticipatie in de Jaren "90* [A Working Perspective: Labor Participation in the Nineties]. "s-Gravenhage: SDU Uitgeverij.http://www.wrr.nl/english/dsc?c=getobjectands=objand!ses sionid=14uZxzYXp1K78HdWziQW2wD5FEo9vlsUlCp3MoaKBFh@OqKEXX lWdpD8XH5Wf8xGandobjectid=2503and!dsname=defaultandisapidir=/gvisapi/ (accessed August 2010).

Yeates, Nicola, Haux, Tina, Jawad, Rana, and Kilkey, Majella (eds.) (2011). *In Defence of Welfare: The Impacts of the Spending Review*. The Social Policy Association. http://www.social-policy.org.uk/downloads/idow.pdf (accessed February 2011).

Zhong, Songfa, Chew, Soo H., Set, Eric, Zhang, Junsen, Xue, Hong, Sham, Pak C., Ebstein, Richard P., and Israel, Salomon (2009). "The Heritability of Attitude toward Economic Risk," *Twin Research and Human Genetics*, 12(1): 103–07.

Zohlnhöfer, Reimut (2007). "The Politics of Budget Consolidation in Britain and Germany: The Impact of Blame Avoidance Opportunities," *West European Politics*, 30(5): 1120–38.

Zutavern, Jan, and Kohli, Martin (2010). "Needs and Risks in the Welfare State." In Castles et al. (eds.), pp. 169–82.

Index

CPSIA information can be obtained at www.ICGtesting.com
Printed in the USA
LVOW07s0707241214

420169LV00002B/13/P